Art of Pi

Stefan Hollos and J. Richard Hollos

Art of Pi

by Stefan Hollos and J. Richard Hollos

Paper ISBN 978-1-887187-31-2

Ebook ISBN 978-1-887187-21-3

Abrazol Publishing

an imprint of Exstrom Laboratories LLC

662 Nelson Park Drive, Longmont, CO 80503-7674 U.S.A.

About the Cover

The cover incorporates art from this book.

Contents

PREFACE

This book is about creating art based on the properties of the number pi. The symbol mathematicians use to represent pi is π. What is π you ask? π is an irrational number that shows up in many areas of mathematics. It probably first entered human consciousness when someone tried to calculate either the area of a circle or the length of its circumference. Indeed you can define π as being equal to the ratio of the circumference to the diameter of a circle. This is true for any circle no matter how small or large. In terms of area, the ratio of the area of a circle with radius equal to 1, to the area of a square with sides of length 1, is equal to π. We could also simply say that π is the area of a circle with radius equal to 1.

The definition of π in terms of areas brings up another property of π that may be of interest to artists. In addition to being irrational, π is also transcendental. Mathematically, this means that there is no polynomial with rational coefficients that has π as one of its roots. In terms of areas it means that it is impossible to draw a square with the same area as a given circle in a finite number of steps using only a straight edge and compass.

People have been engaged in calculating the value of π since antiquity. In modern times it has almost become

1

something of a sport to see who can calculate more digits of π. The value of π is now known to trillions of digits. Still there seems to be no discernible pattern to the digits. Indeed the digits appear to be random under statistical tests.

What we have discovered however, and what this book is about, is the fact that rational approximations to π do encode many intricate patterns that can be turned into interesting drawings. We have collected 357 of these drawings together in this book. This is an art book meant to stimulate your creativity and imagination. There is no mathematics required. We have included two appendices that contain a very short explanation of some of the mathematics behind π and how the images are created, indexed by name. More detailed information on how to create the images can be found in our book:

Pattern Generation for Computational Art

May you find these images stimulating and inspiring, as we have found them.

Stefan Hollos and Richard Hollos
Exstrom Laboratories LLC
Longmont, Colorado

2

GALLERY

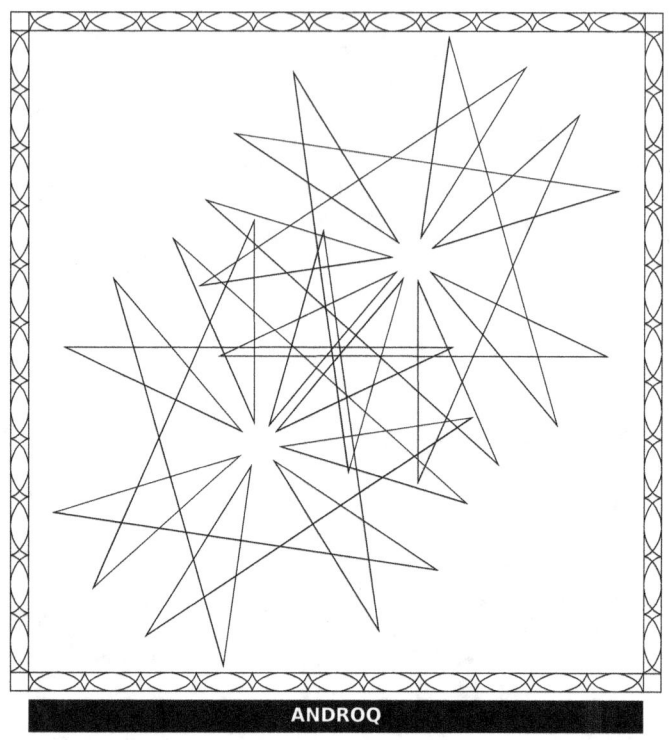

ANDROQ

There is geometry in the humming of the strings, there is music in the spacing of the spheres.
Pythagoras

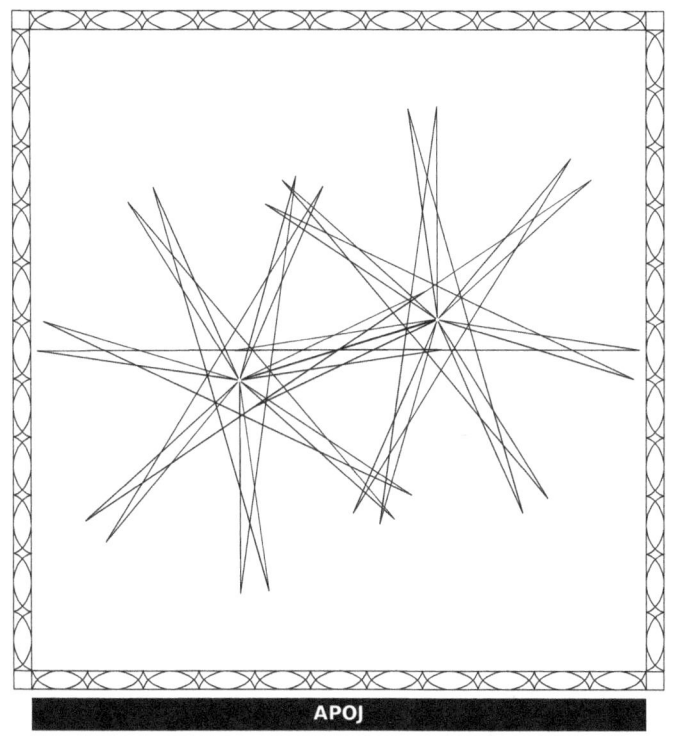

APOJ

All good science is art. And all good art is science.
John Fowles

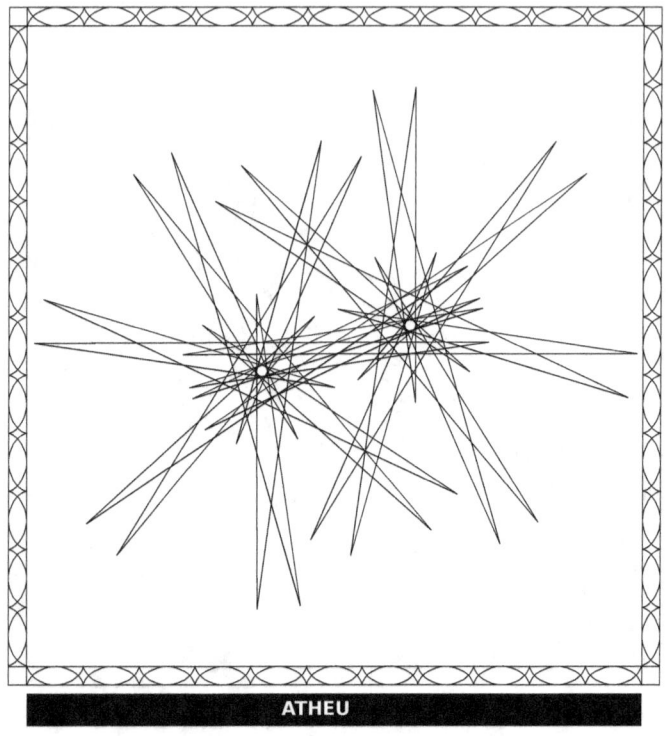

ATHEU

For me the greatest beauty always lies in the greatest clarity.
Gotthold Ephraim Lessing

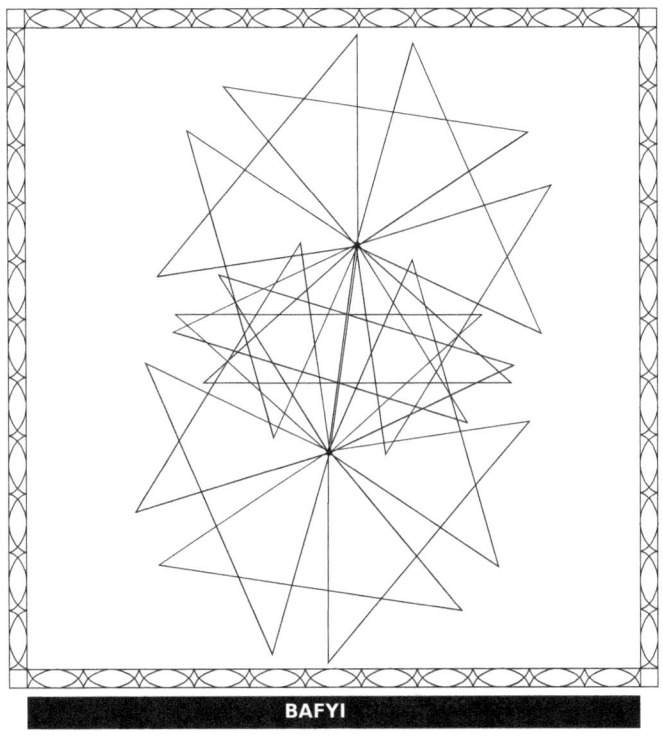

BAFYI

Be there as the witnessing presence of your inner state. You don't have to do anything. With the awareness comes transformation and freedom.
Eckhart Tolle

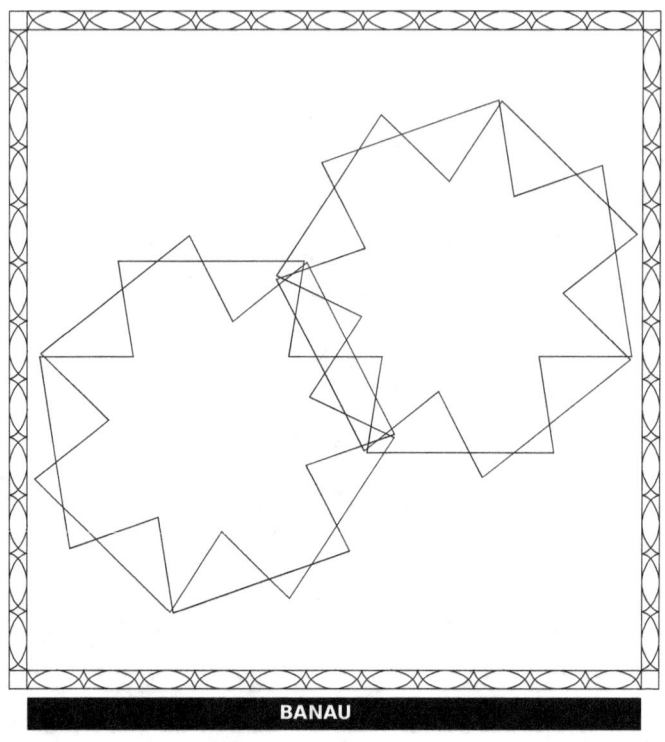

BANAU

Be who you are and say what you feel, because those who mind don't matter and those who matter don't mind.
Dr. Seuss

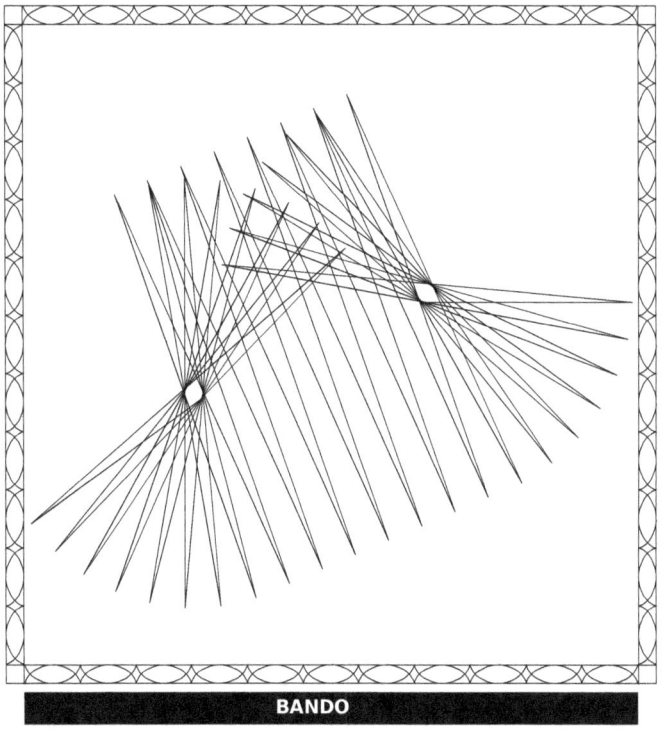

BANDO

Wisdom tends to grow in proportion to one's awareness of one's ignorance.
Anthony de Mello

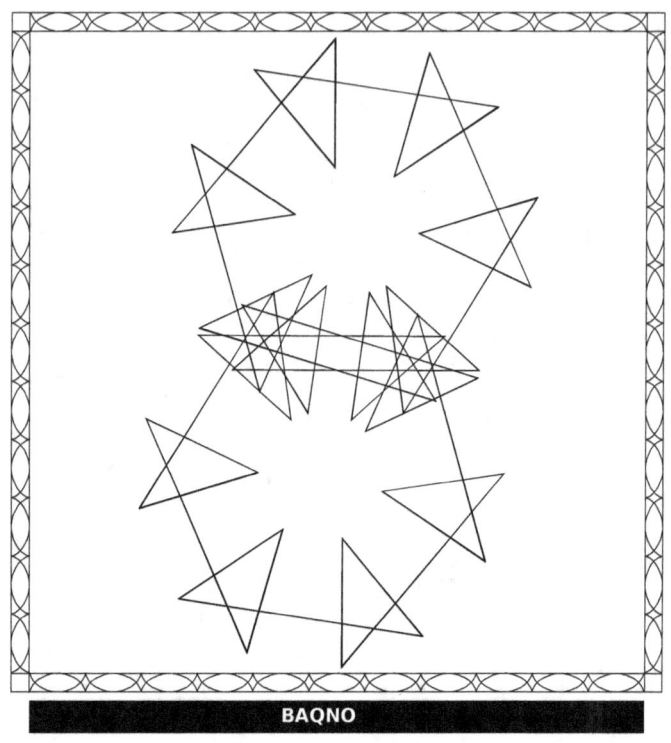

BAQNO

Being an artist is more of a mindset, a way of seeing things; it is no longer so much about producing something.
Ai Weiwei

10

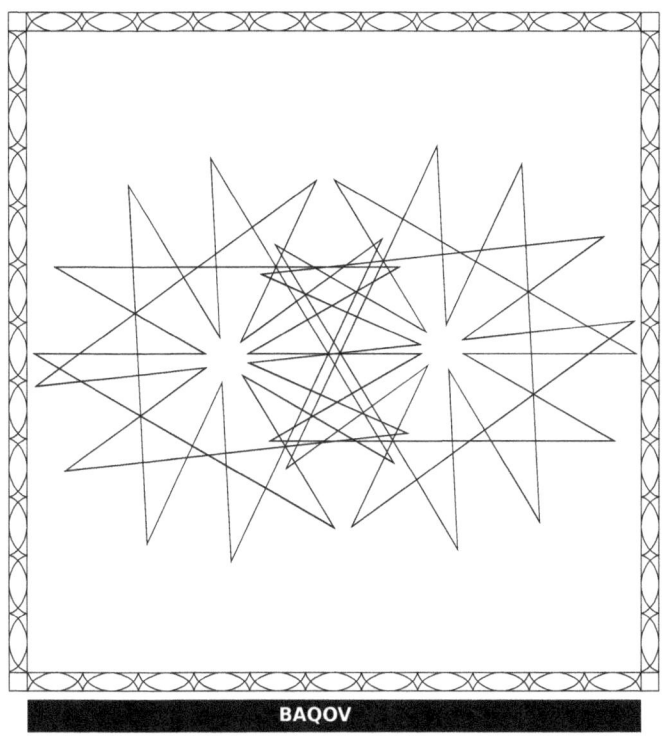

BAQOV

In the beginner's mind there are many possibilities, in the expert's there are few.

Shunryu Suzuki

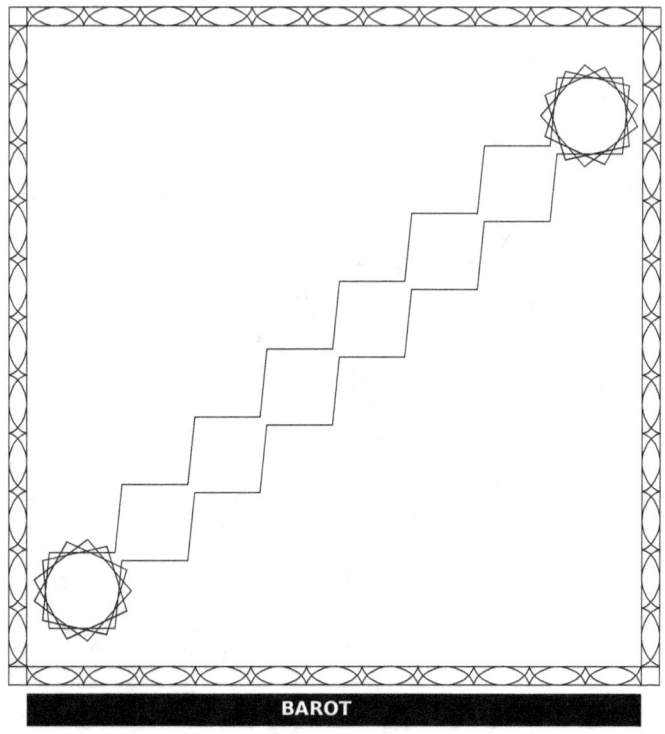

BAROT

The modernist thirst for originality makes the mediocre artist believe that the secret of originality consists simply in being different.
Nicols Gmez Dvila

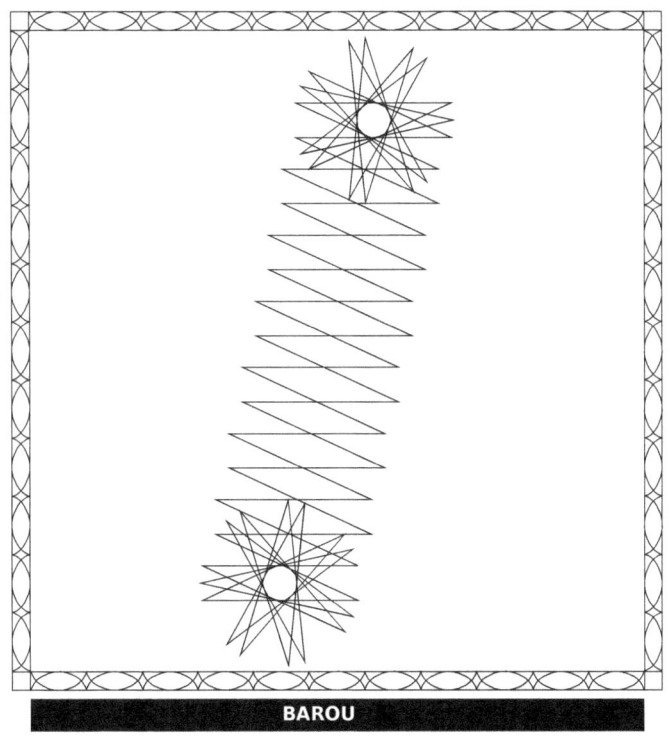

BAROU

Unless one is happy, one cannot bestow happiness on others.
Ramana Maharshi

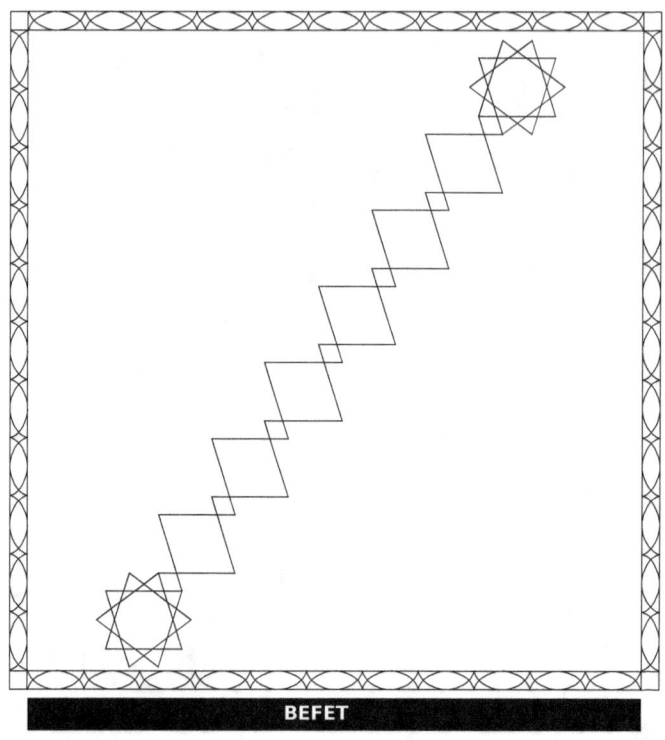

BEFET

There is no such thing as an empty space or an empty time. There is always something to see, something to hear. In fact, try as we may to make a silence, we cannot.
John Cage

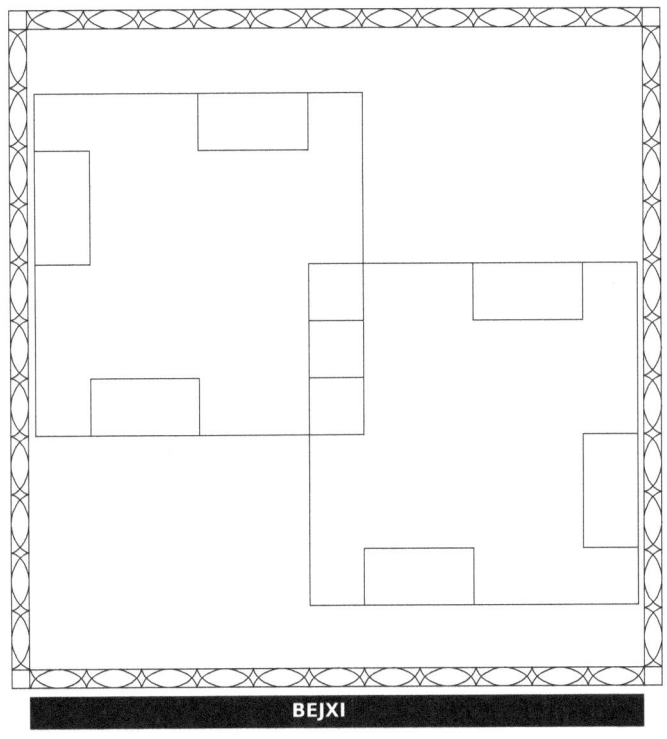

BEJXI

Don't waste yourself in rejection, nor bark against the bad, but chant the beauty of the good.

Ralph Waldo Emerson

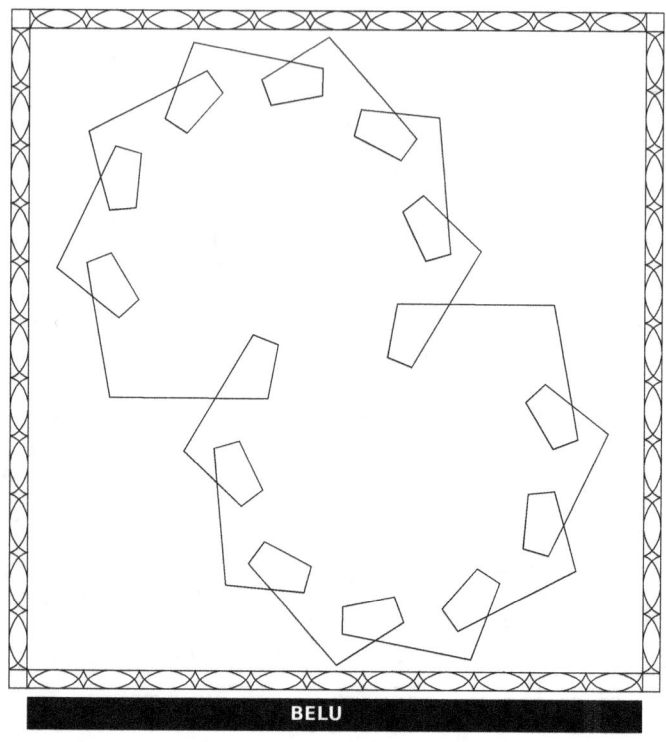

BELU

The most incredible thing about miracles is that they happen.
G. K. Chesterton

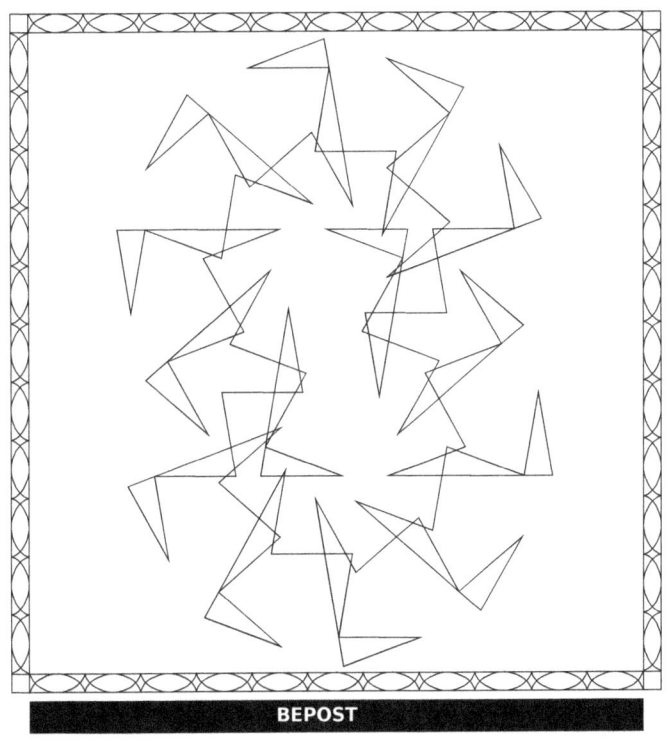

BEPOST

Thought forms in the soul the same way clouds form in the air.
Joseph Joubert

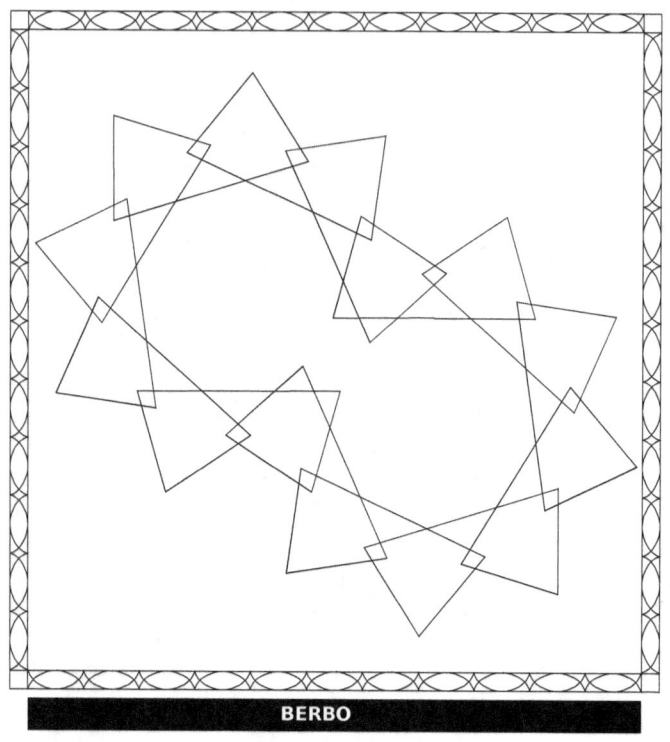

BERBO

Vision is the art of seeing what is invisible to others.
Jonathan Swift

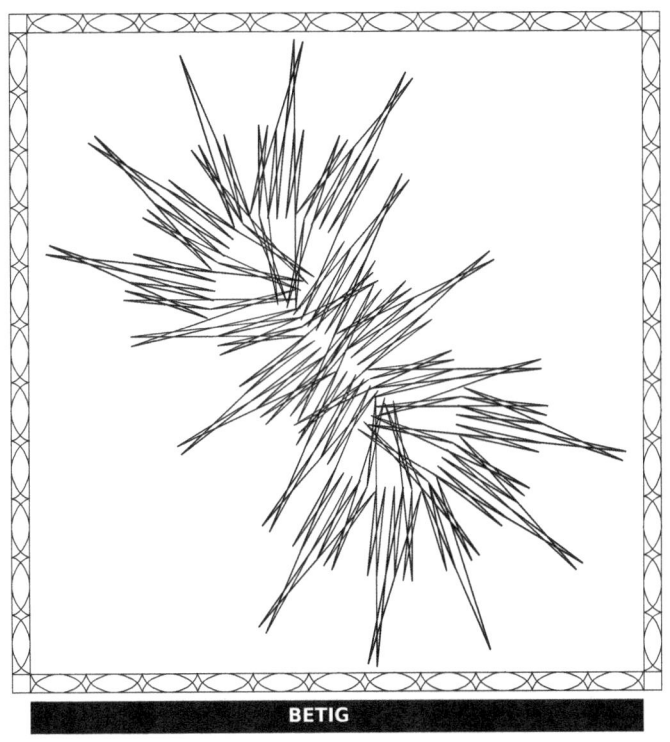

BETIG

I am so used to plunging into the unknown that any other surroundings and form of existence strike me as exotic and unsuitable for human beings.
Werner Herzog

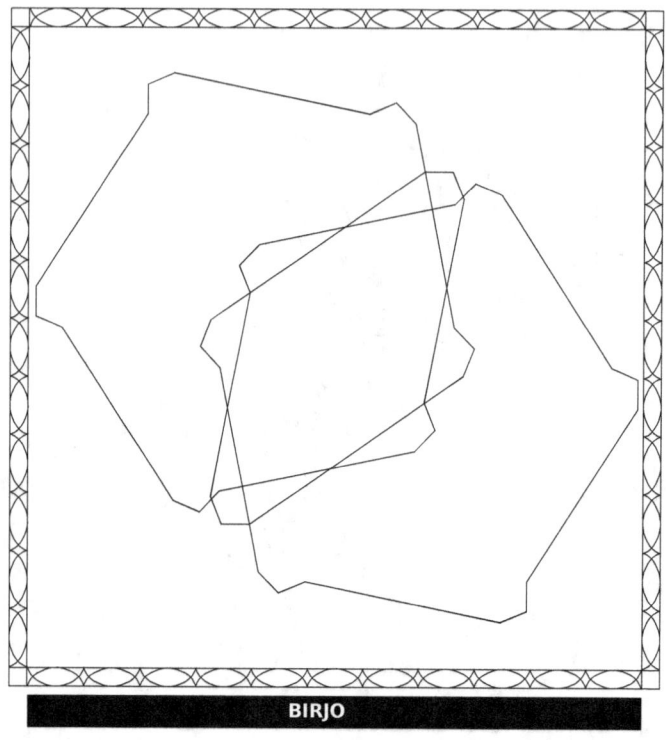

BIRJO

It is a truth very certain that, when it is not in our power to determine what is true, we ought to follow what is most probable.
Rene Descartes

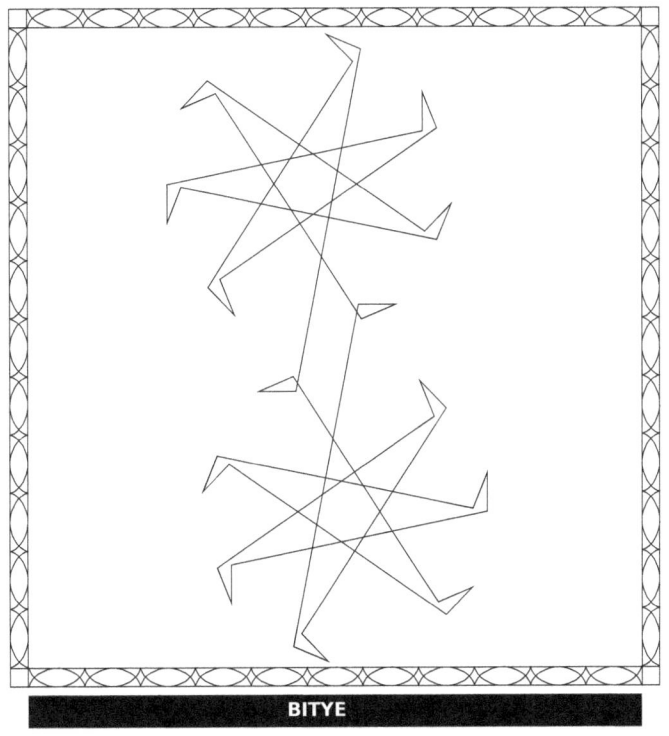

BITYE

True originality consists not in a new manner but in a new vision.

Edith Wharton

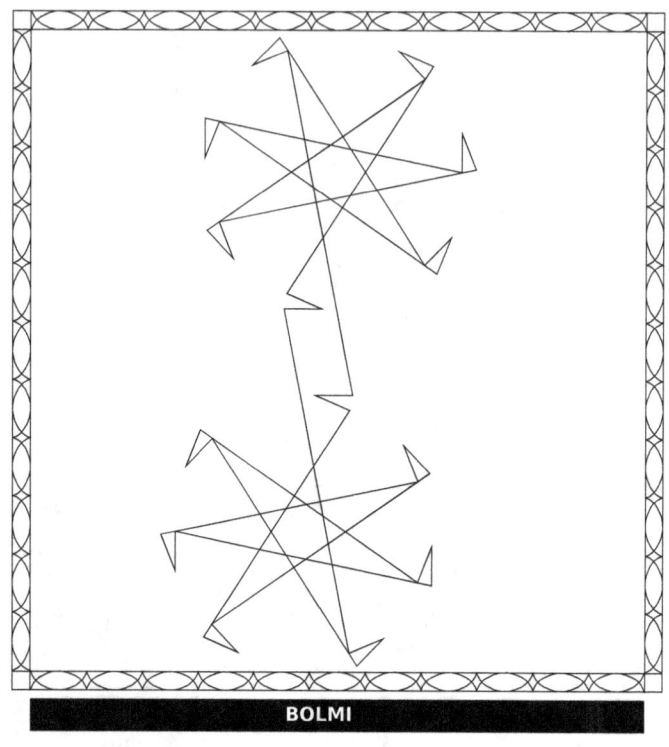

BOLMI

I'm an artist who is always looking for what is possible. I'm always looking to extend the boundaries.
Ai Weiwei

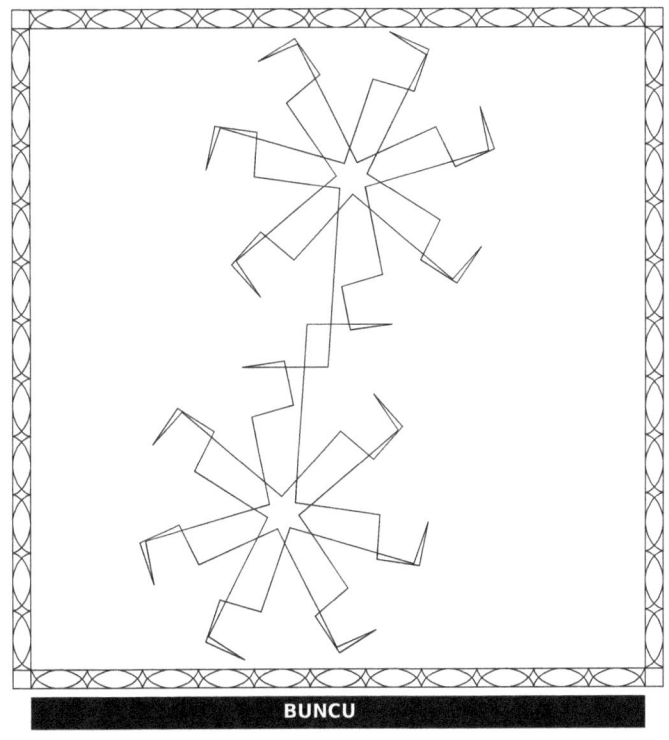

BUNCU

My hope is that the description of God's love in my life
will give you the freedom and the courage to discover . . .
God's love in yours.

Henri Nouwen

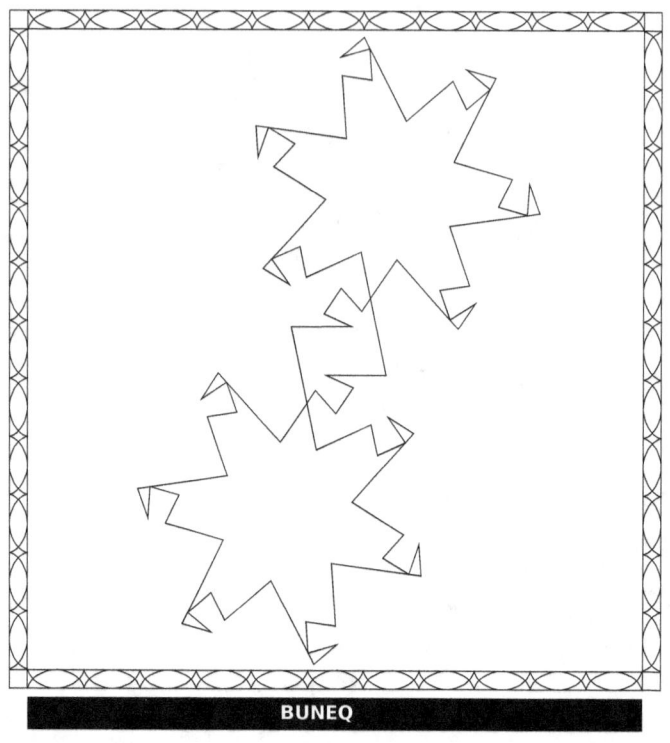

BUNEQ

One ruins the mind with too much writing. One rusts it by not writing at all.
Joseph Joubert

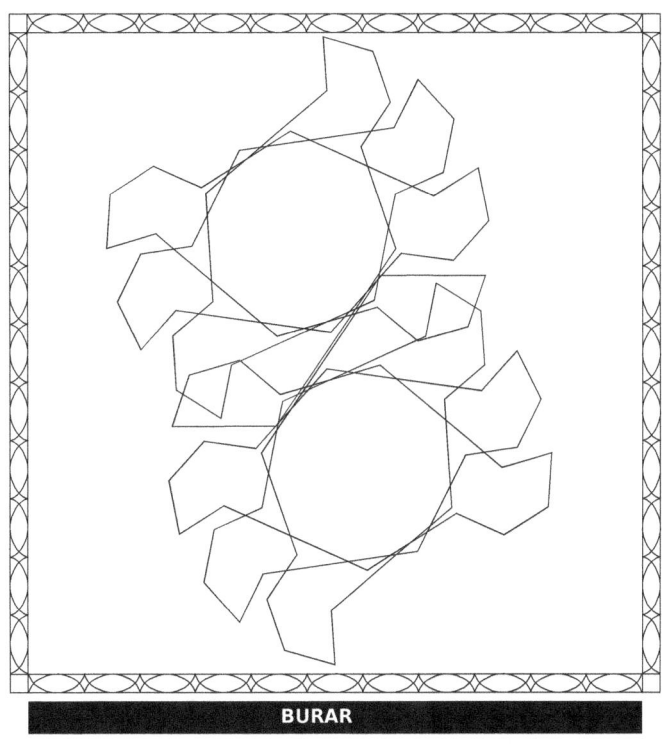

BURAR

Amusement to an observing mind is study.
Benjamin Disraeli

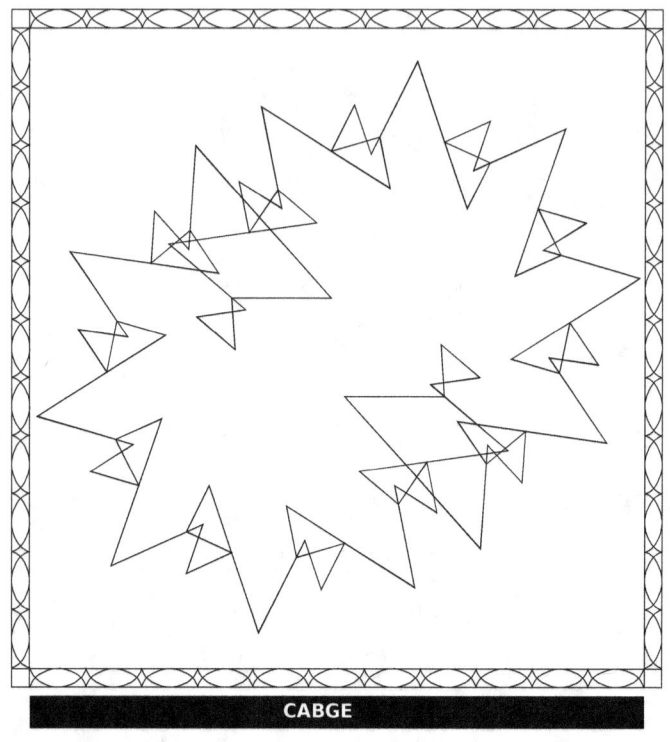

CABGE

Truth exists for the wise, beauty for the feeling heart.
Friedrich Schiller

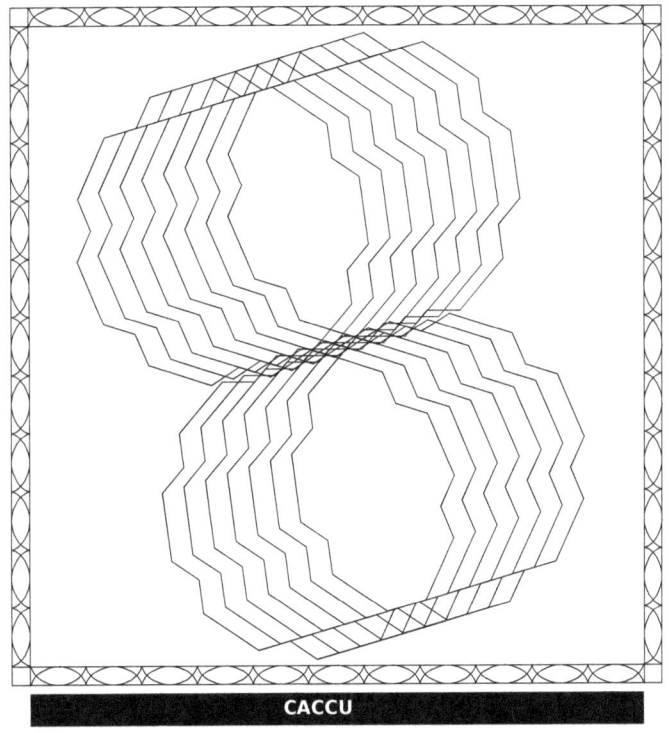

CACCU

They who have decided to dedicate their lives to spiritual perfection will never be dissatisfied or unhappy, because all that they want is in their power.

Blaise Pascal

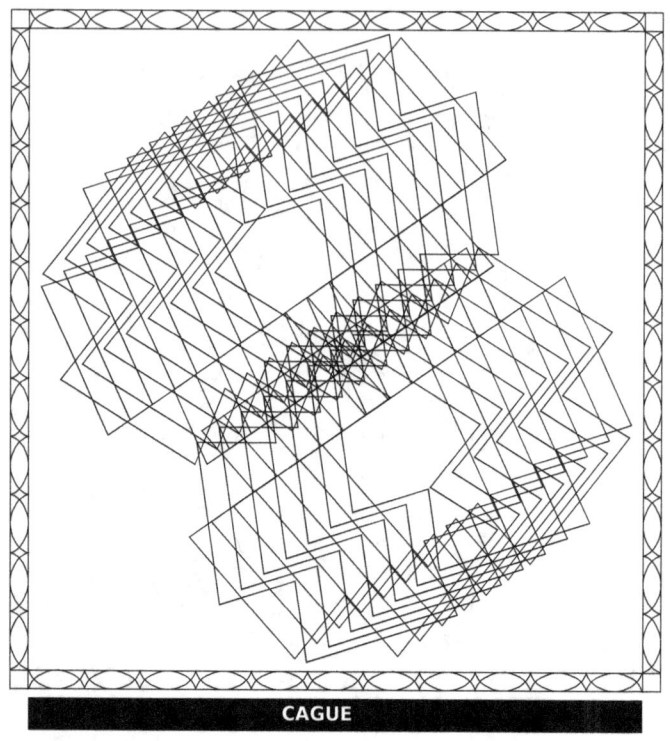

CAGUE

By reality and perfection I mean the same thing.
Baruch Spinoza

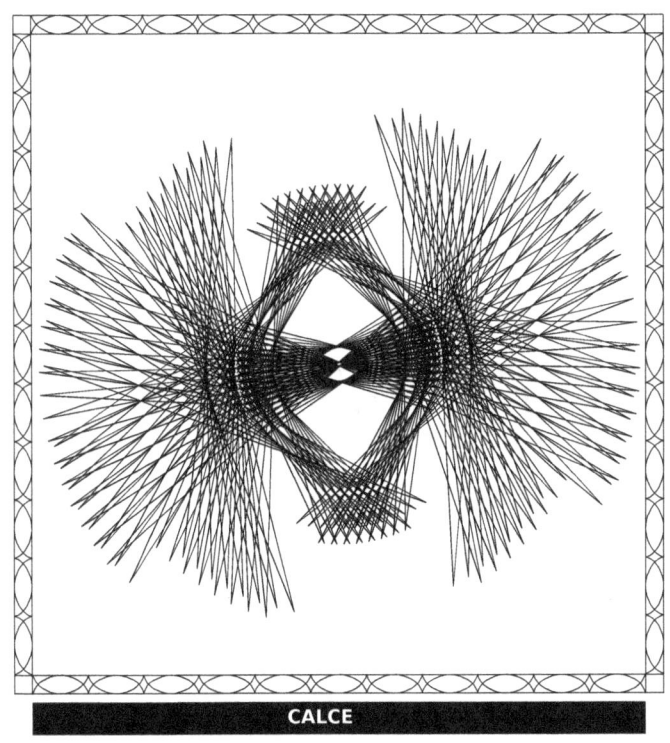

CALCE

Value judgments are destructive to our proper business, which is curiosity and awareness.
John Cage

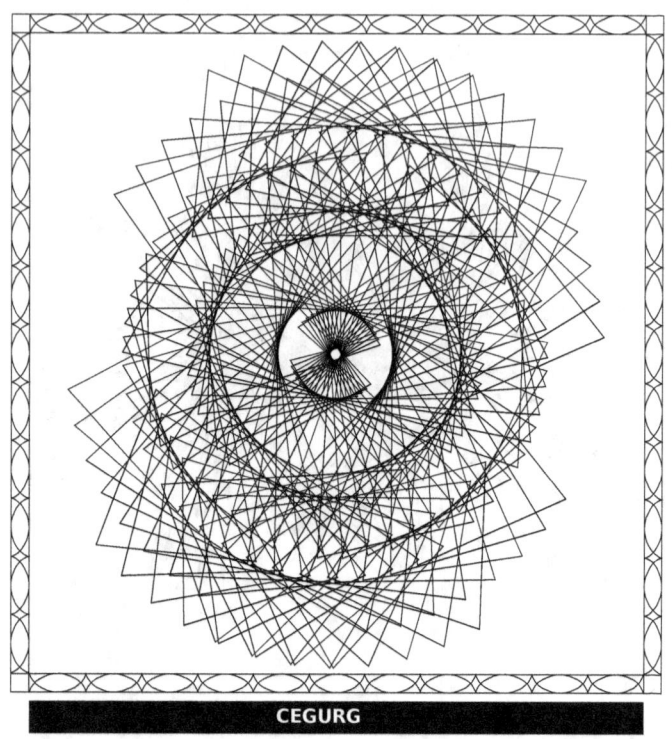

CEGURG

The art of letters will come to an end before A.D. 2000. I shall survive as a curiosity.
Ezra Pound

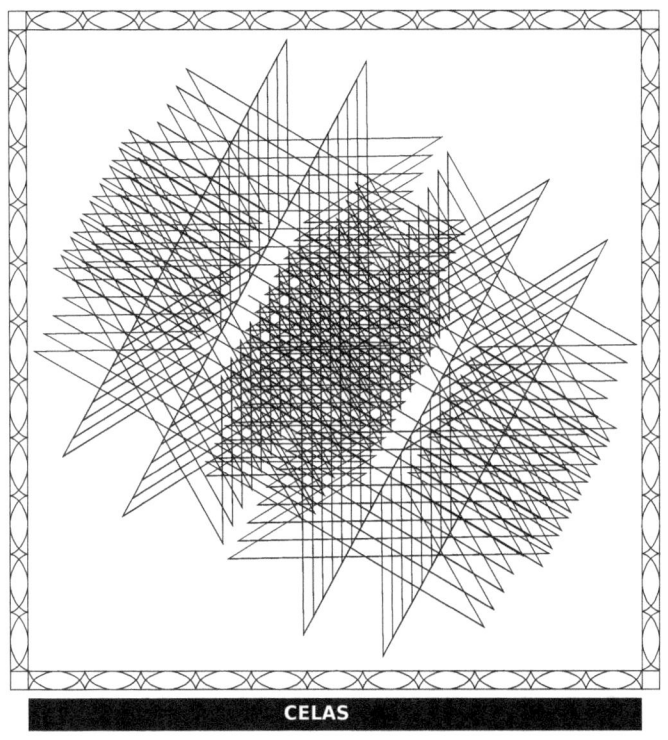

CELAS

Truth is stranger than fiction, but it is because fiction is obliged to stick to possibilities, truth isn't.

Mark Twain

31

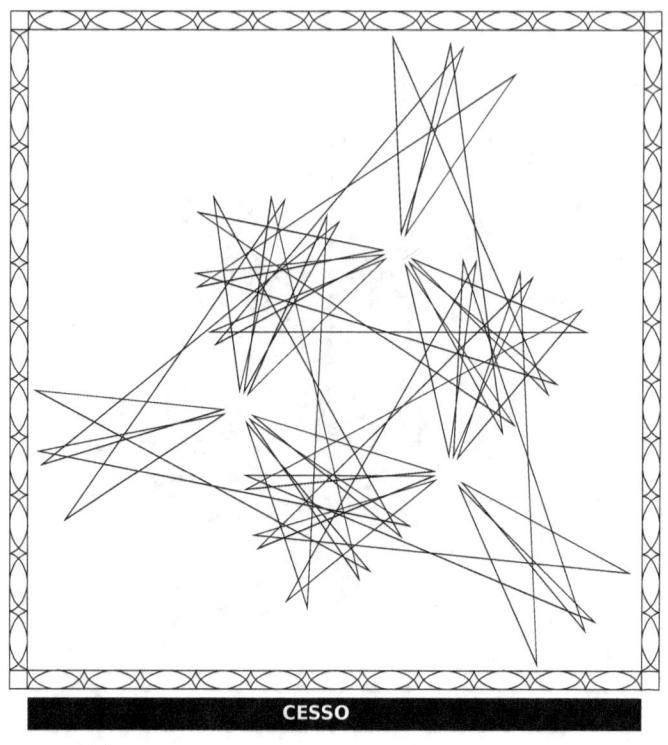

CESSO

Tough and funny and a little bit kind: that is as near to perfection as a human being can be.
Mignon McLaughlin

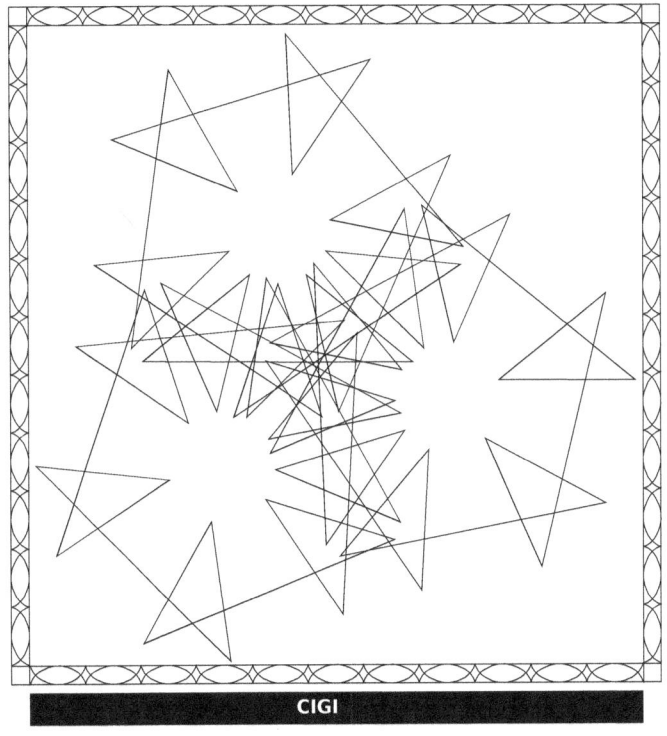

CIGI

The eyes see only what the mind is prepared to comprehend.
Henri Bergson

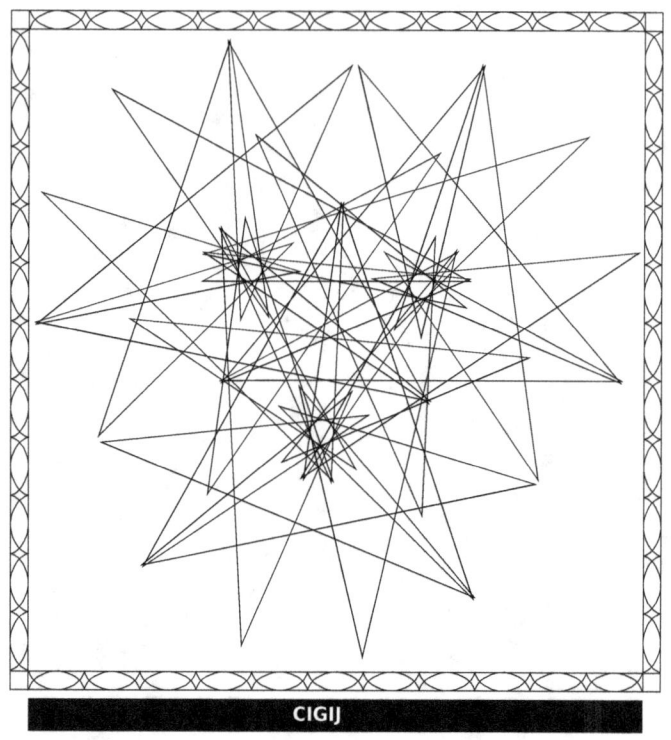

CIGIJ

The most merciful thing in the world, I think, is the inability of the human mind to correlate all its contents.
H. P. Lovecraft

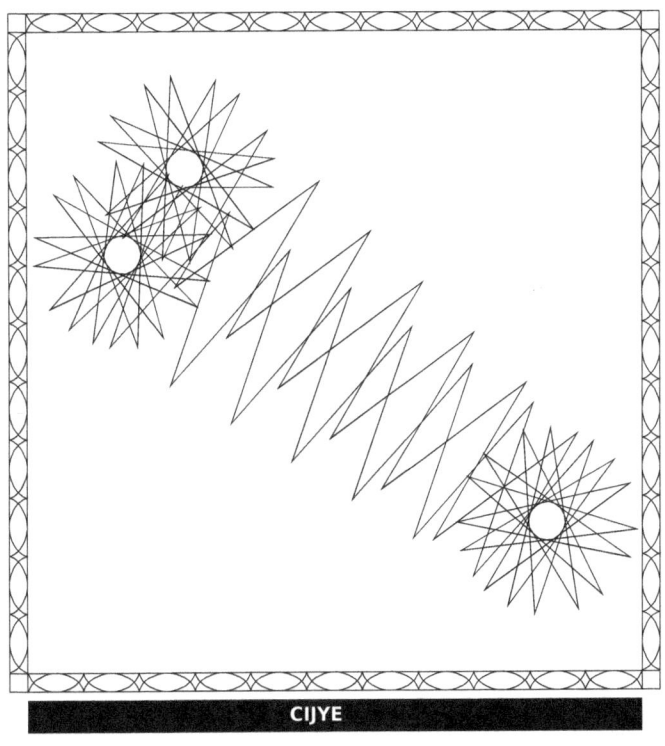

CIJYE

All art is autobiographical; the pearl is the oyster's auto-
biography.
Federico Fellini

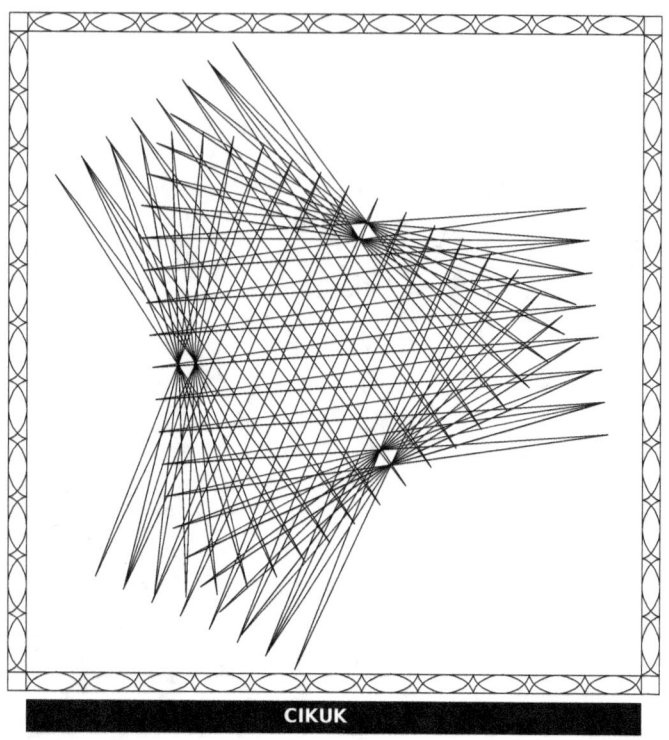

CIKUK

Come, drink the mystic wine of Night, Brimming with silence and the stars; While earth, bathed in this holy light, Is seen without its scars.
Louis Untermeyer

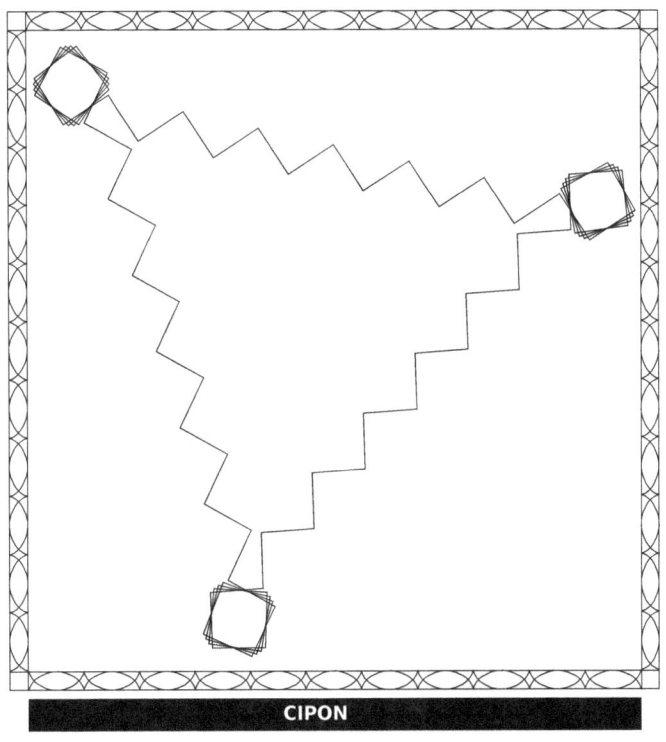

CIPON

The quality of a man's mind can generally be judged by the size of his wastepaper basket.

Jose Bergamin

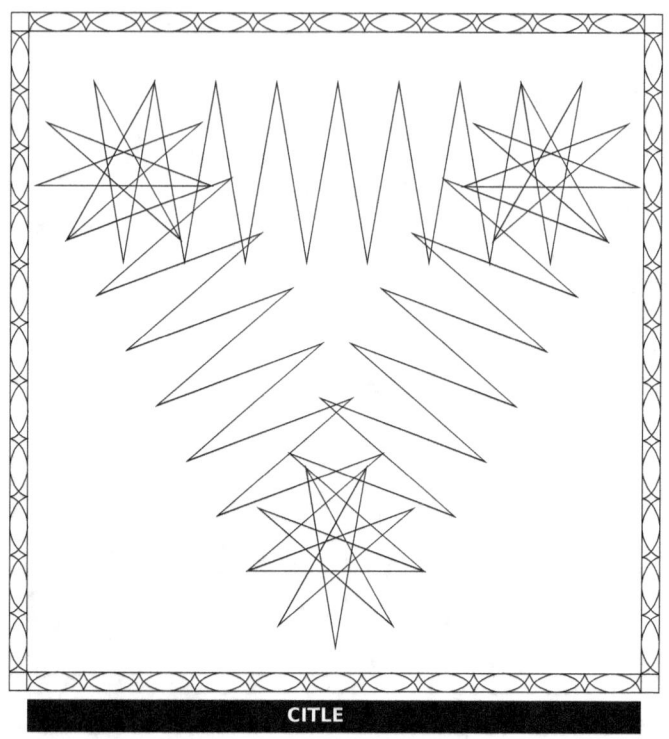

CITLE

Any loss of identity prompts people to seek reassurance and rediscovery of themselves by testing, and even by violence. Today, the electric revolution, the wired planet, and the information environment involve everybody in everybody to the point of individual extinction.
Marshall McLuhan

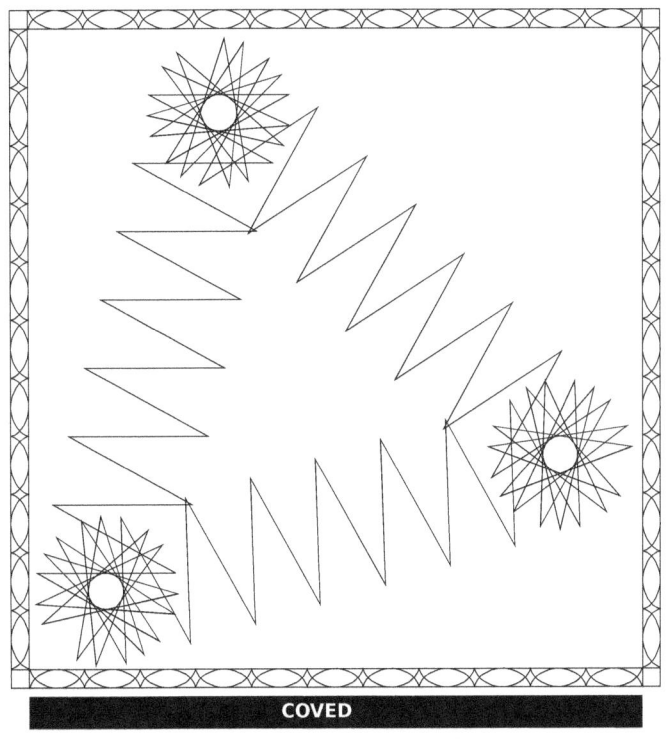

COVED

Learning to cherish others is the best solution to our daily problems, and it is the source of all our future happiness and good fortune.
Kelsang Gyatso

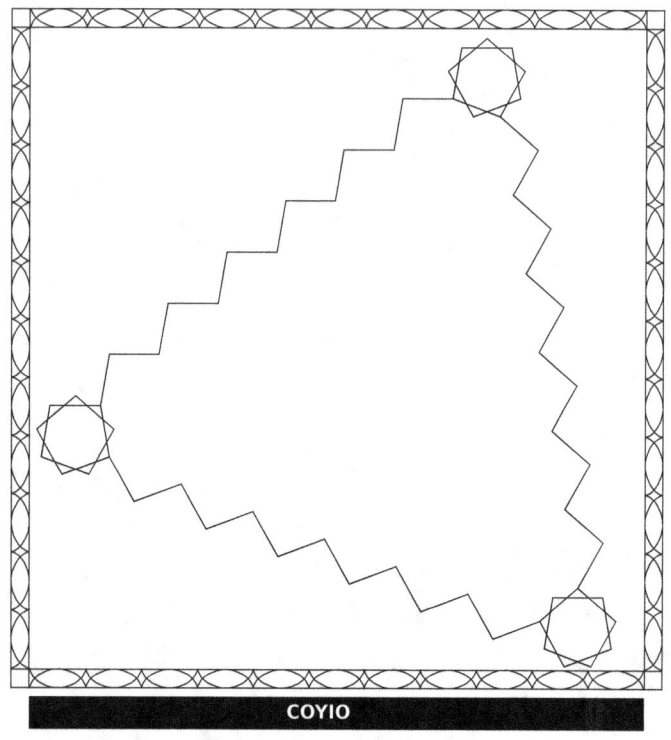

COYIO

The role of the artist is to create an anti-environment as a means of perception and adjustment.
Marshall McLuhan

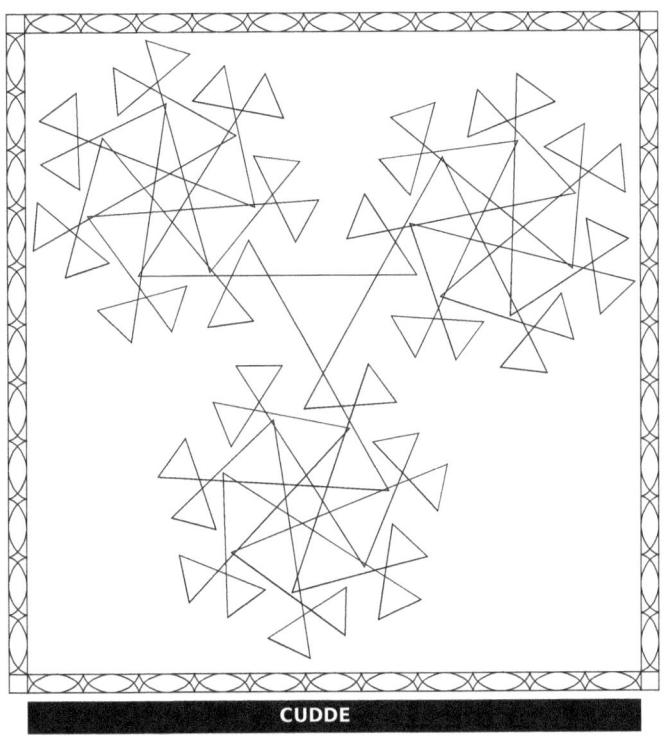

CUDDE

Learning is not a gift, it's a privilege.
Ruth Simmons

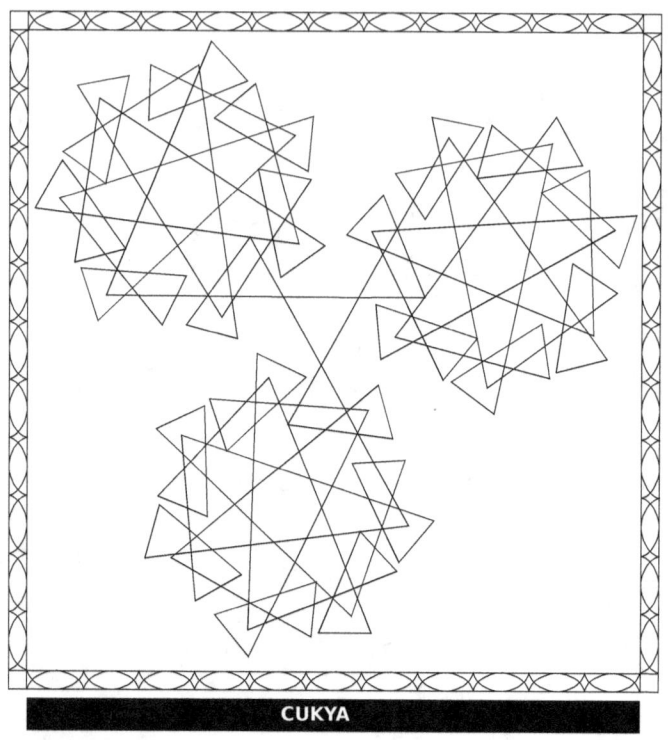

CUKYA

The role of art is to make a world which can be inhabited.
William Saroyan

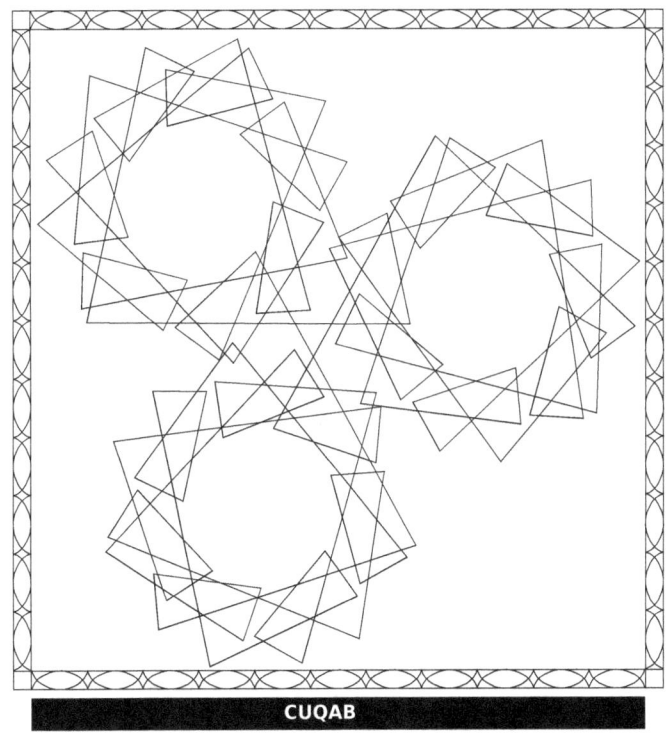

CUQAB

When you study natural science and the miracles of creation, if you don't turn into a mystic you are not a natural scientist.

Albert Hofmann

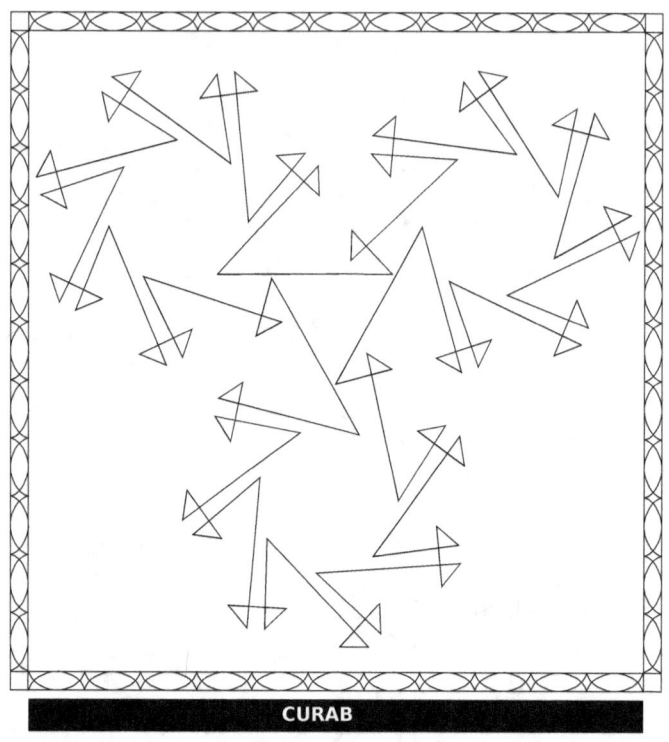

CURAB

Enlightenment is like everyday consciousness but two inches above the ground.
D. T. Suzuki

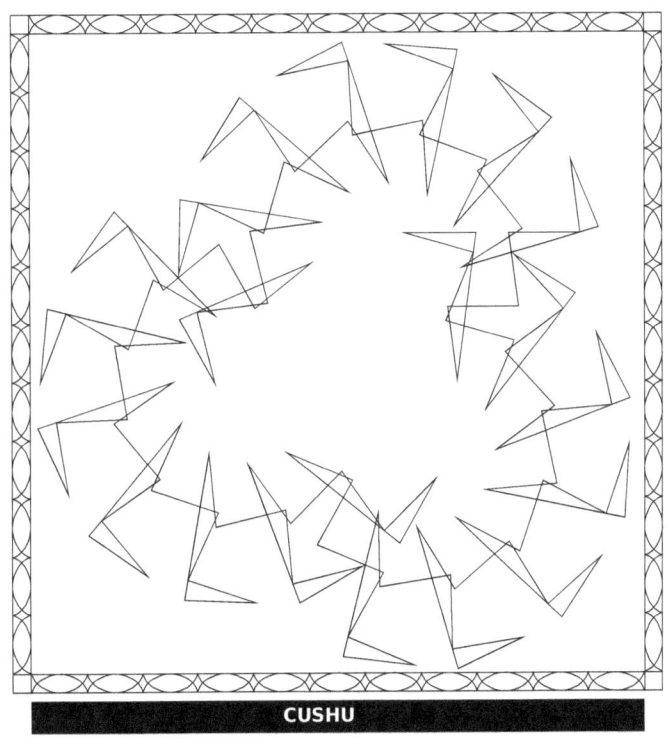

CUSHU

That side of our existence whose direction is towards the infinite seeks not wealth, but freedom and joy.
Rabindranath Tagore

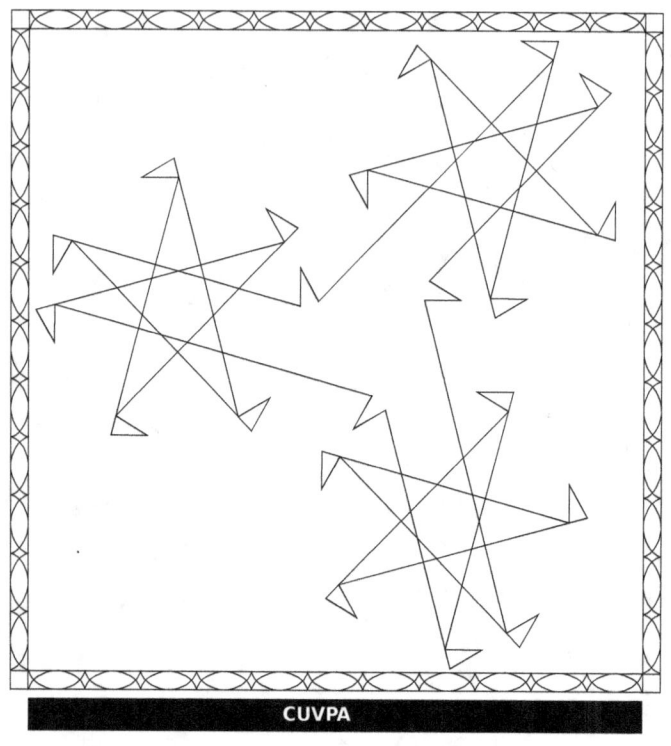

CUVPA

Proverbs are always platitudes until you have personally
experienced the truth of them.
Aldous Huxley

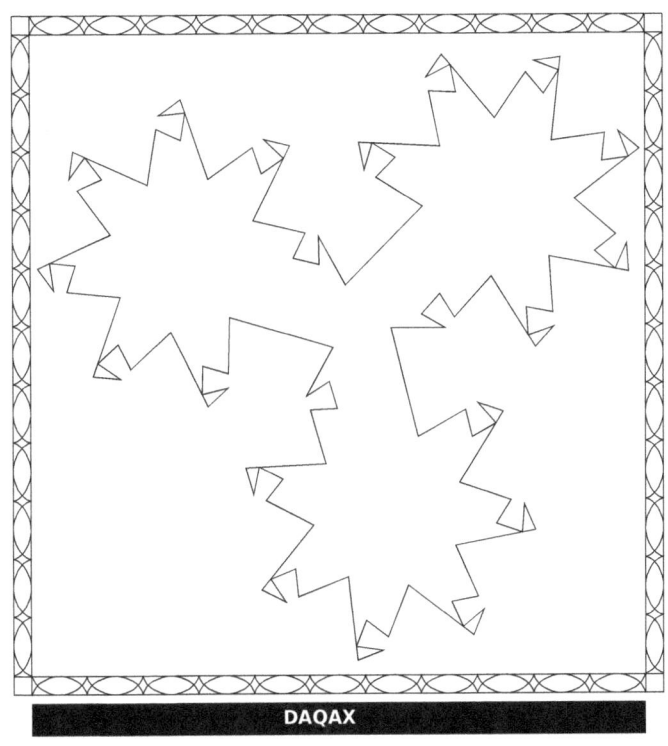

DAQAX

The art of letting go is simply about personal empowerment. Realizing what you're in charge of, realizing what you control, and more importantly, what you don't control.
Steve Maraboli

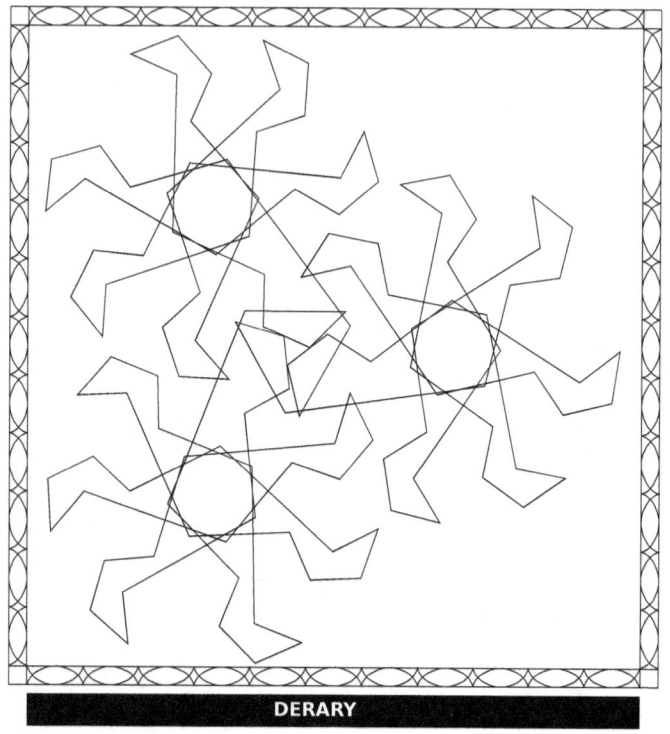

DERARY

Movement is the translation of life, and if art depicts life, movement should come into art, since we are only aware of living because it moves.
Arshile Gorky

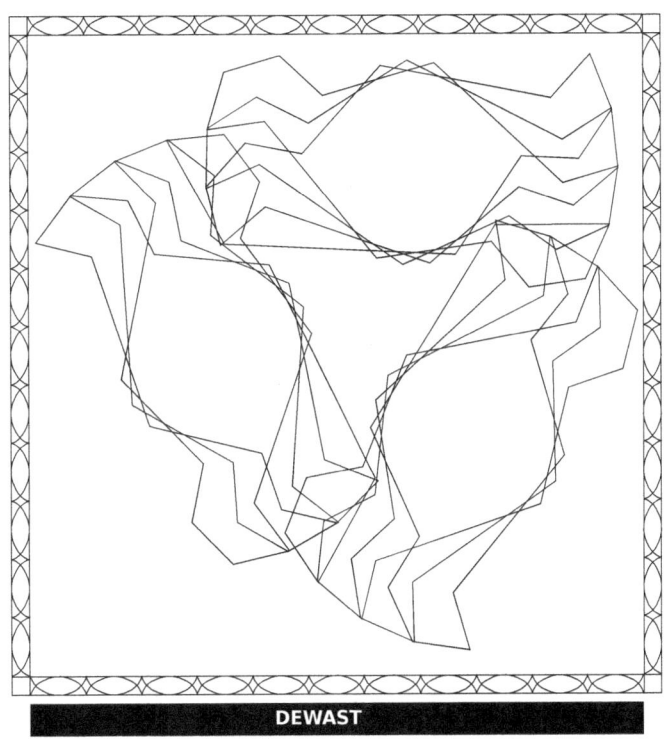

DEWAST

I do not want art for a few, any more than education for a few, or freedom for a few.
William Morris

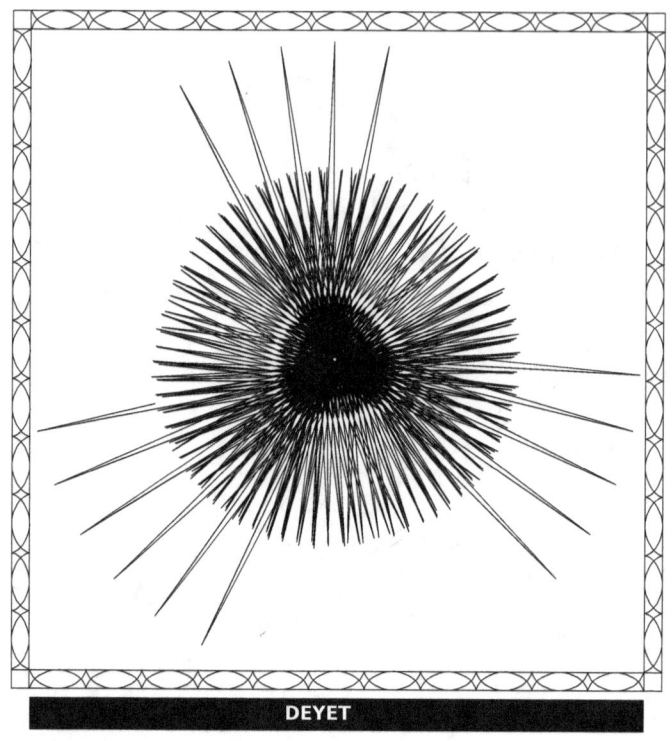

DEYET

You can never plan the future by the past.
Edmund Burke

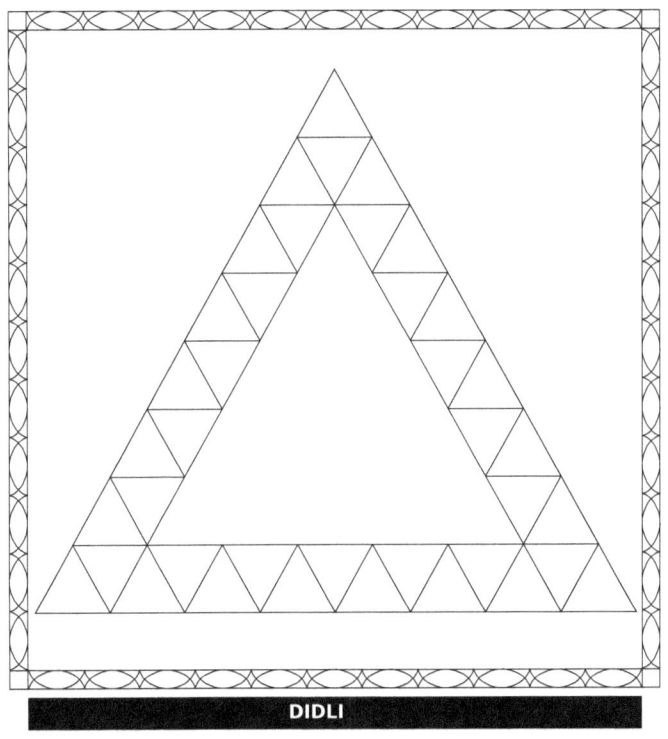

DIDLI

Life is the art of drawing without an eraser.
John W. Gardner

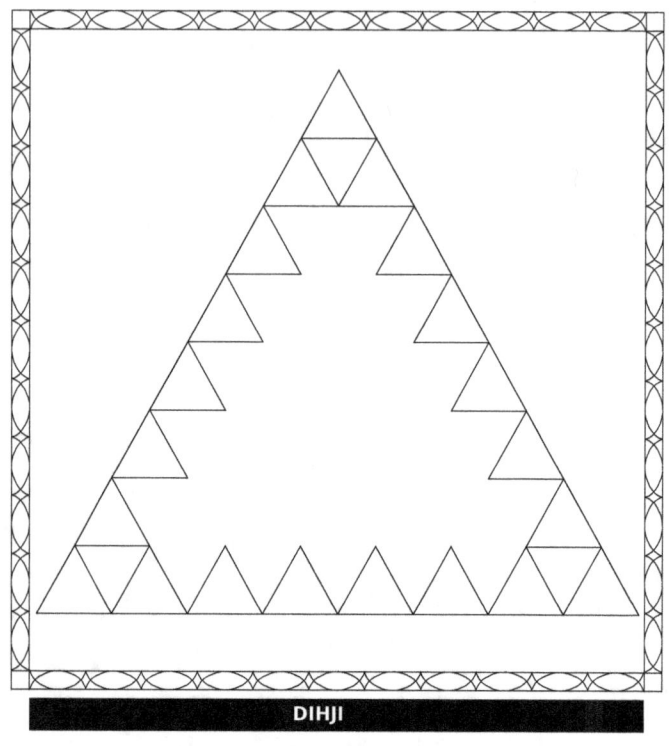

DIHJI

Those who suppress freedom always do so in the name of law and order.

Anonymous

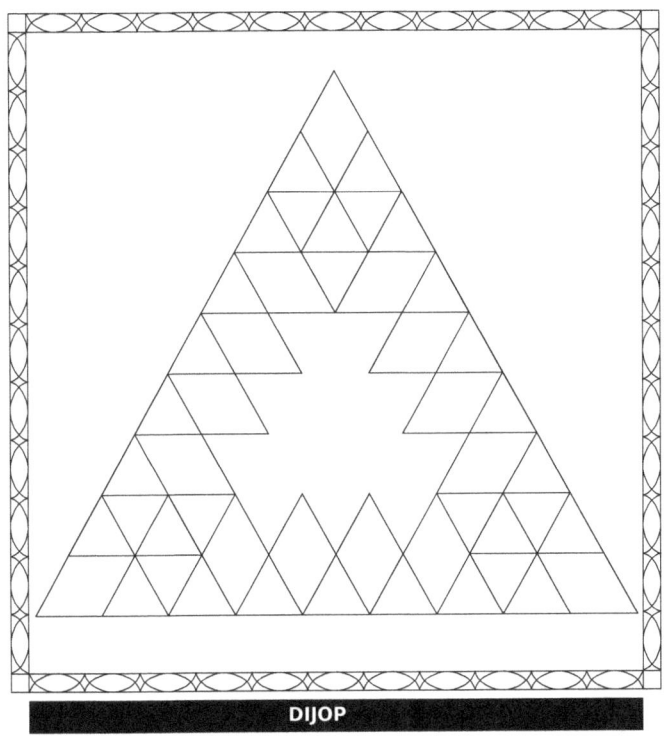

DIJOP

The first and the simplest emotion which we discover in the human mind is curiosity.

Edmund Burke

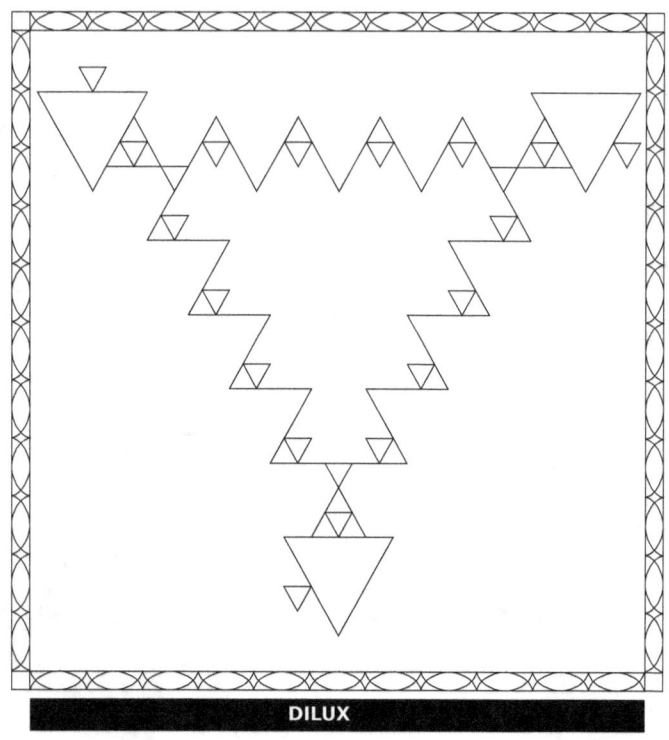

DILUX

The happiness that is genuinely satisfying is accompanied by the fullest exercise of our faculties, and the fullest realisation of the world in which we live.
Bertrand Russell

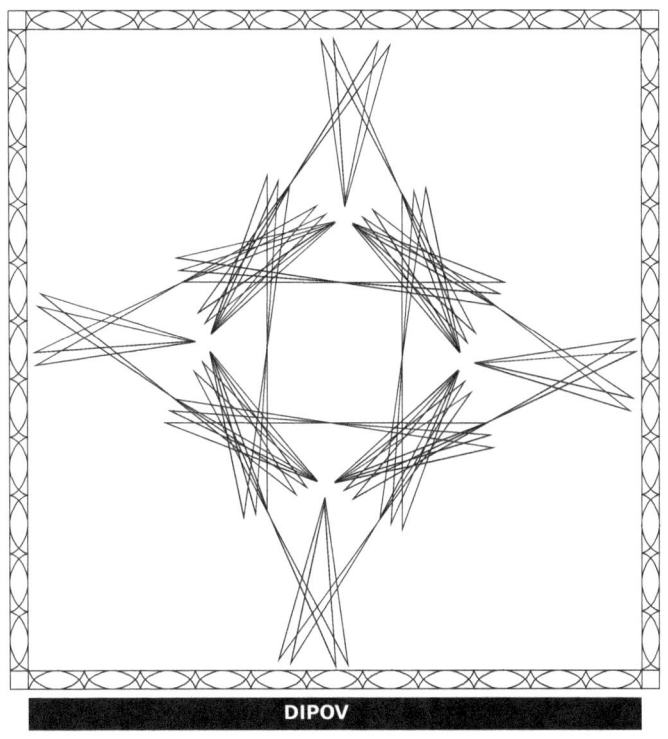

DIPOV

The exact measure of the progress of civilization is the degree in which the intelligence of the common mind has prevailed over wealth and brute force.
George Bancroft

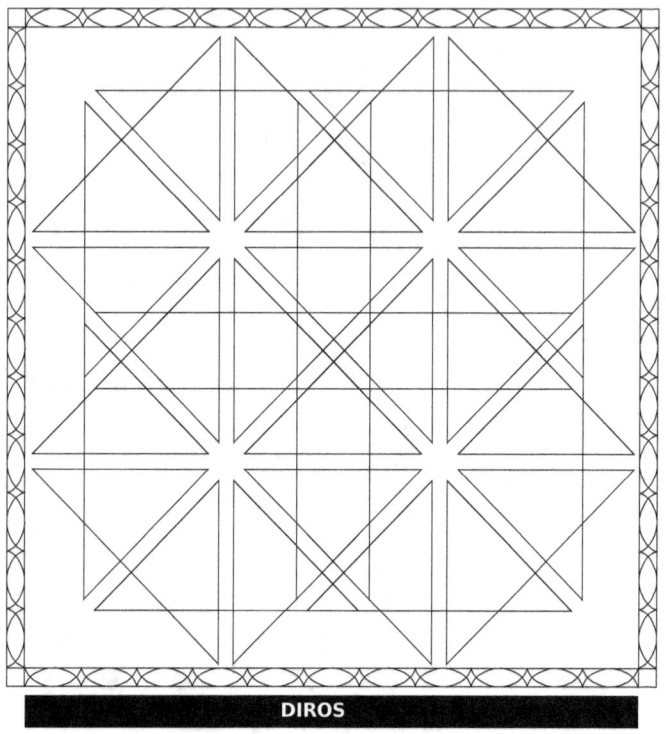

DIROS

The music that really turns me on is either running toward God or away from God. Both recognize the pivot, that God is at the center of the jaunt.

Bono

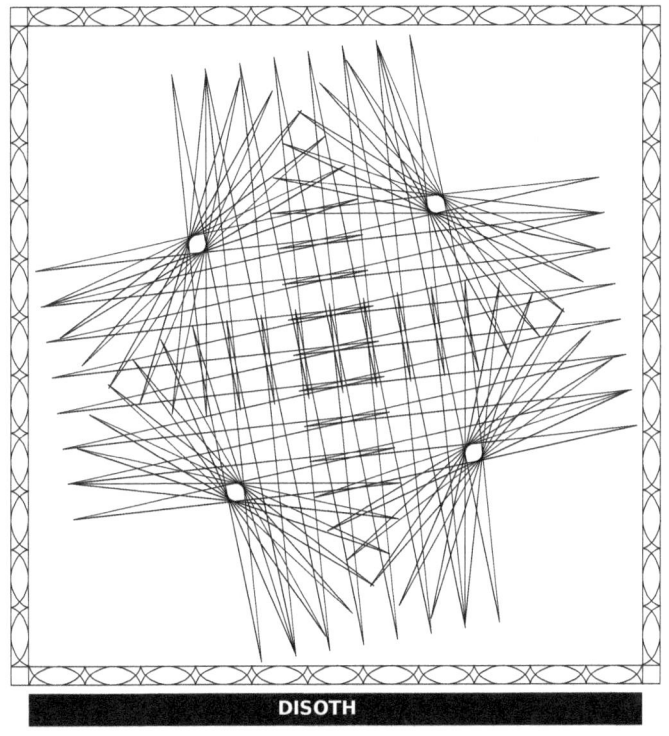

DISOTH

The awareness that we are all human beings together has become lost in war and through politics.
Albert Schweitzer

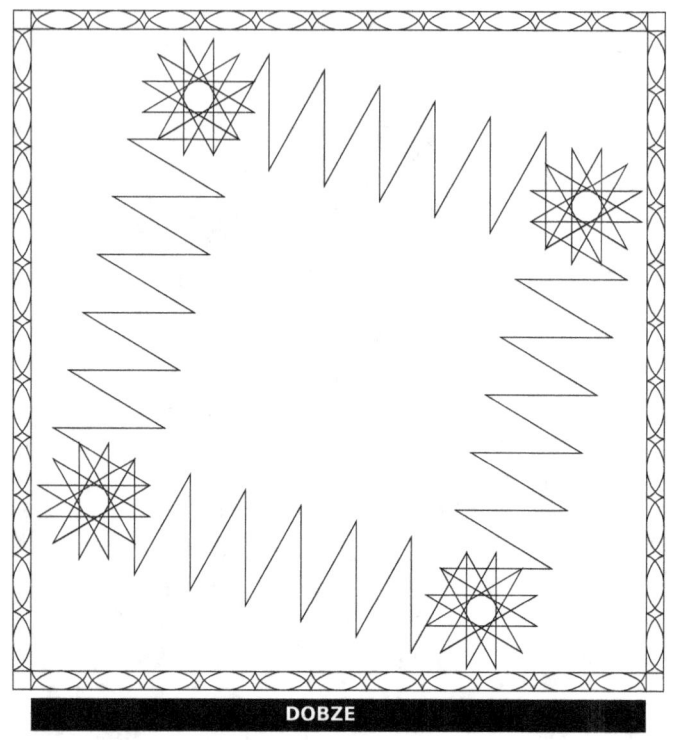

DOBZE

An artist is a man of action, whether he creates a personality, invents an expedient, or finds the issue of a complicated situation.

Joseph Conrad

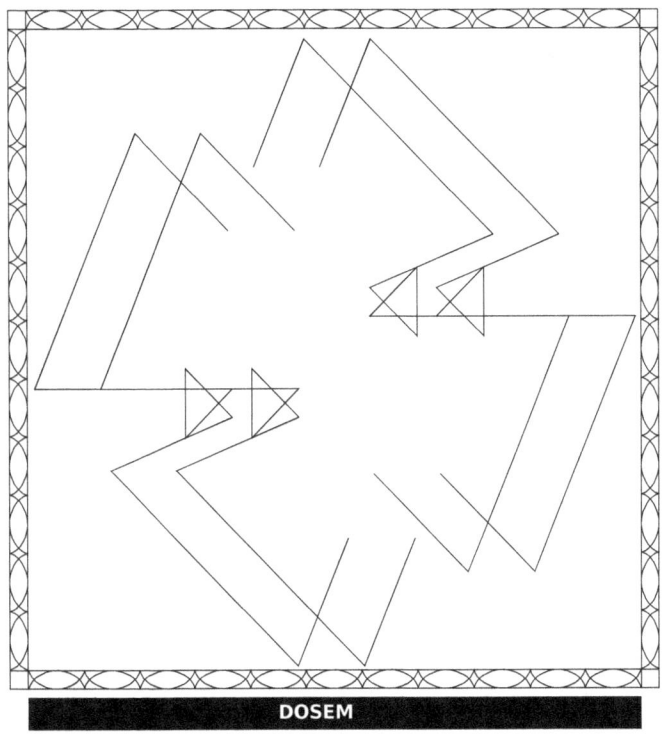

DOSEM

The activity of art is ... as important as the activity of language itself, and as universal.
Leo Tolstoy

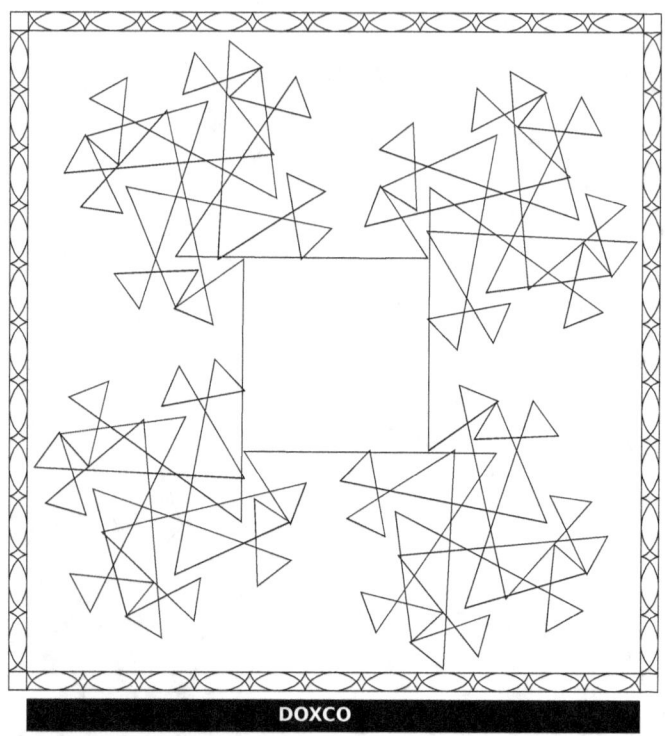

DOXCO

In exploring the shared language and poetic sensibilities of all animals, I am working toward rediscovering the common ground that once existed when people lived in harmony with animals. The images depict a world that is without beginning or end, here or there, past or present. I hope that the overall effect is an experience of wonder and contemplation, serenity and hope.

Gregory Colbert

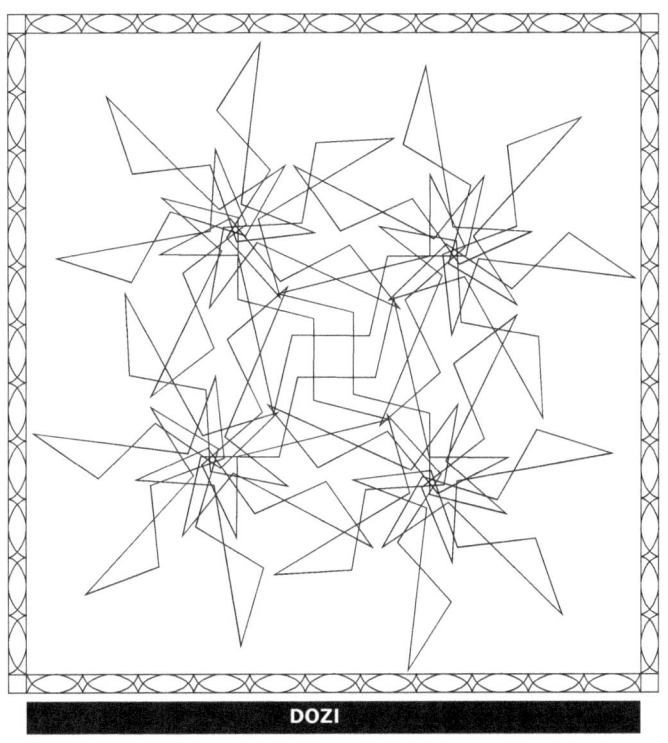

DOZI

Our soul's perfection is our life's purpose; any other purpose, keeping death in mind, has no substance.
Leo Tolstoy

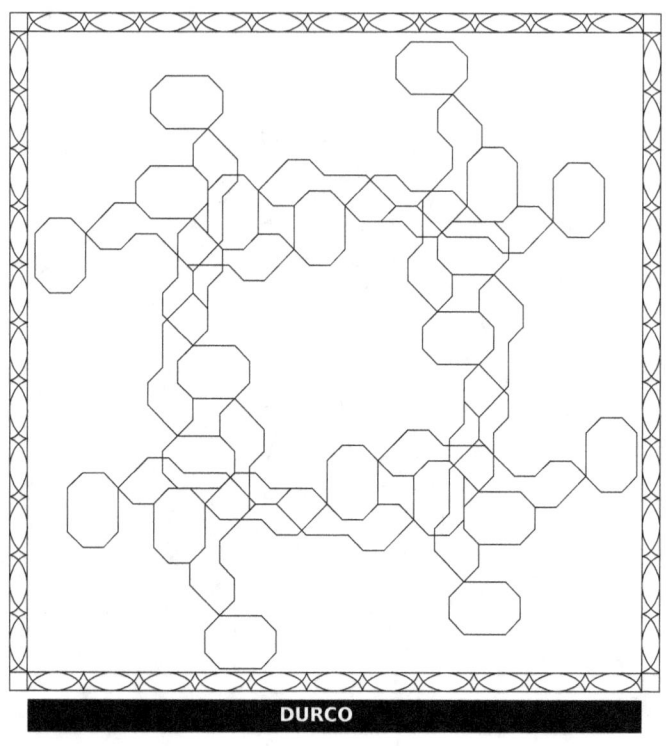

DURCO

If you shut your door to all errors truth will be shut out.
Rabindranath Tagore

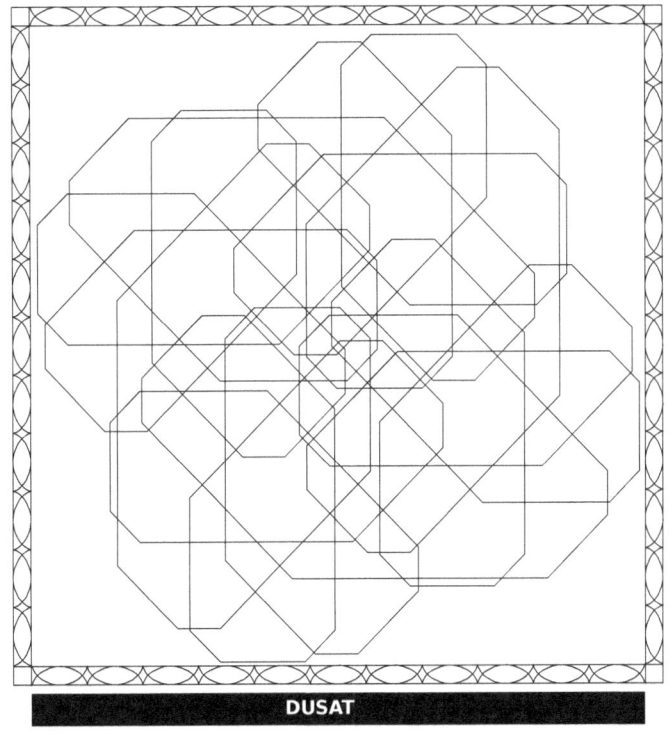

DUSAT

There is no pulse so sure of the state of a nation as its characteristic art product which has nothing to do with its material life.

Gertrude Stein

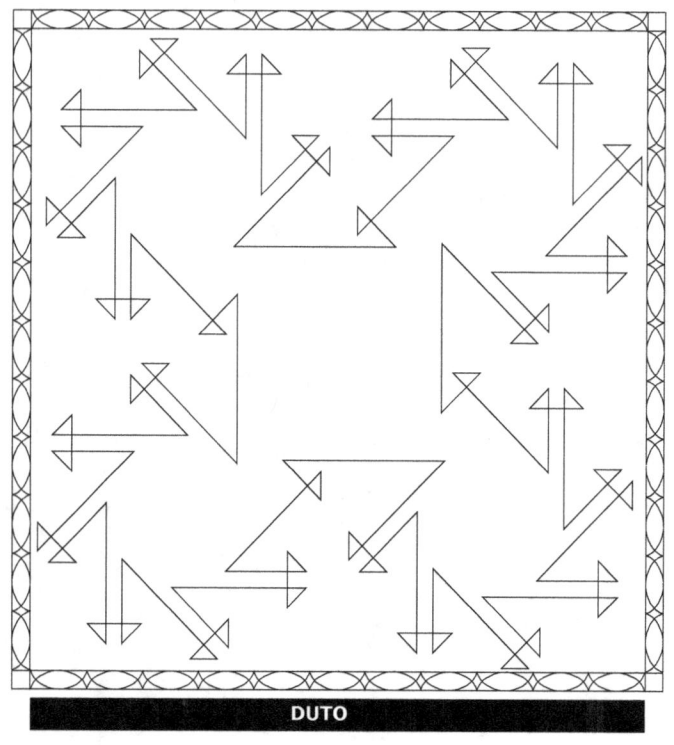

DUTO

The truth every man and woman seeks is in themselves.
Barry Long

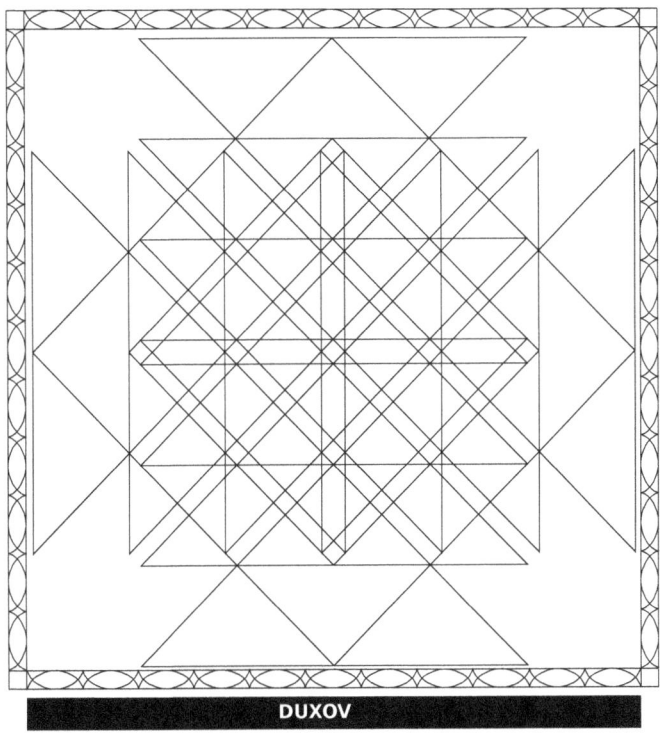

DUXOV

What is necessary to change a person is to change his awareness of himself.
Abraham Maslow

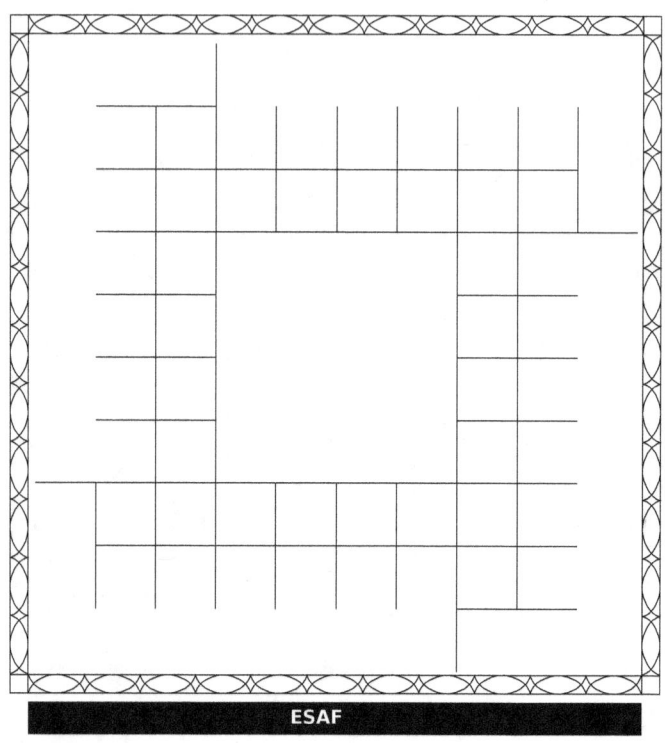

ESAF

Chase after the truth like all hell and you'll free yourself,
even though you never touch its coat tails.
Clarence Darrow

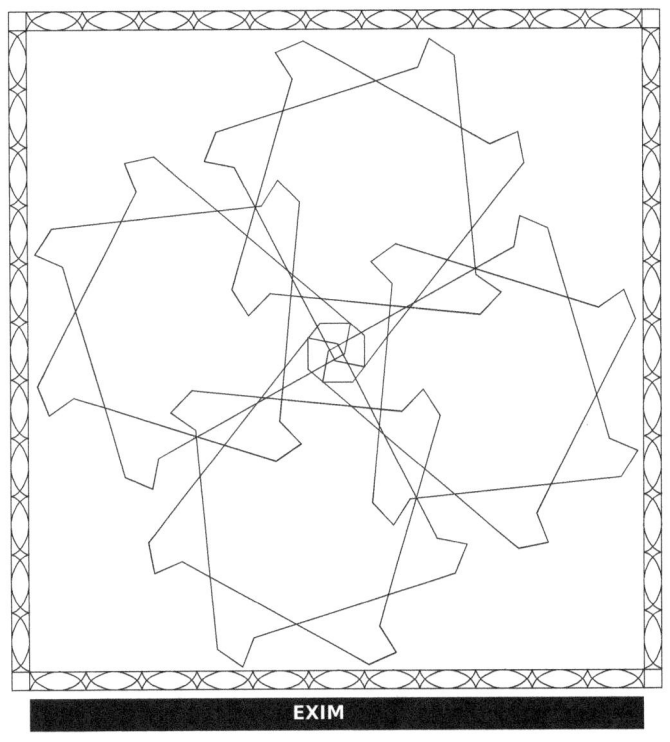

EXIM

The final purpose of art is to intensify, even, if necessary, to exacerbate, the moral consciousness of people.

Norman Mailer

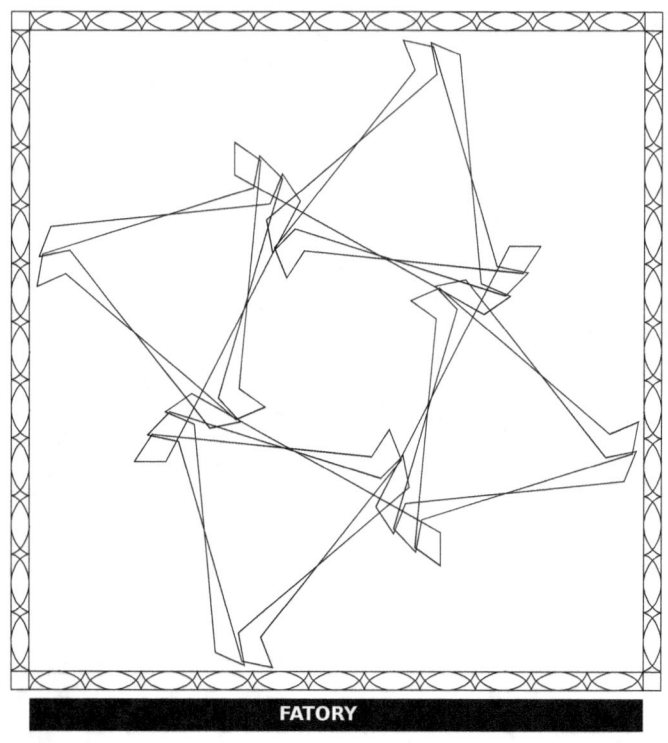

FATORY

An insult is like a drink; it affects one only if accepted. And pride is too heavy baggage for my journey; I have none.
Robert A. Heinlein

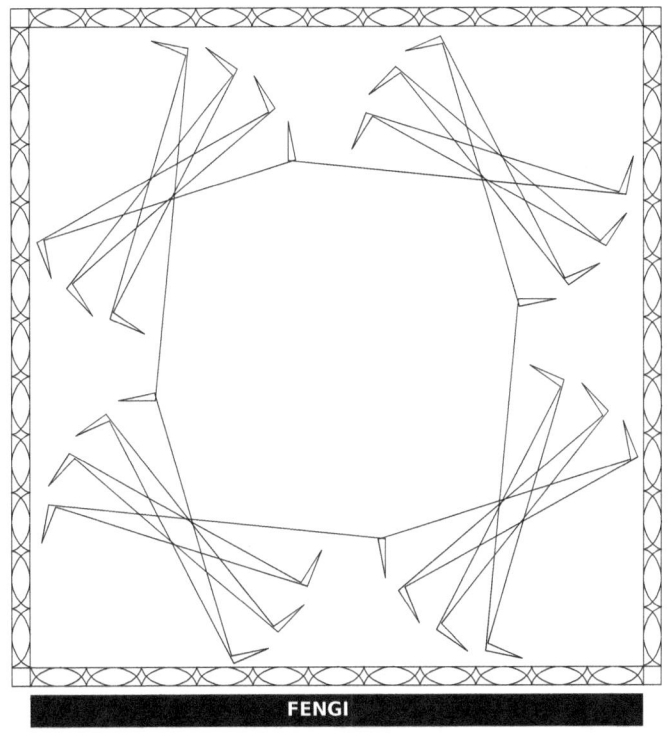

FENGI

A good mind possesses a kingdom.
English proverb

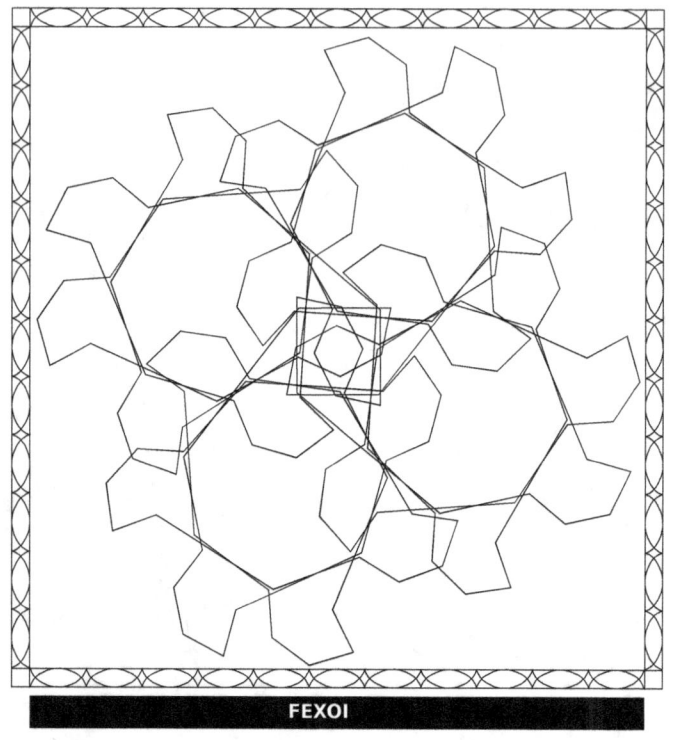

FEXOI

Life is a mystery to be lived, not a problem to be solved.
Soren Kierkegaard

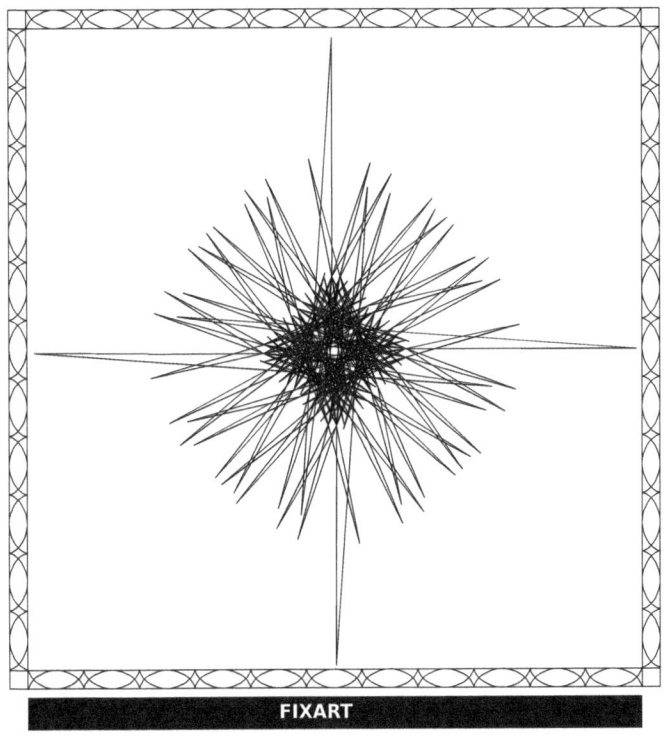

FIXART

Through play, we renew contact with childhood - My art is childlike.
Karel Appel

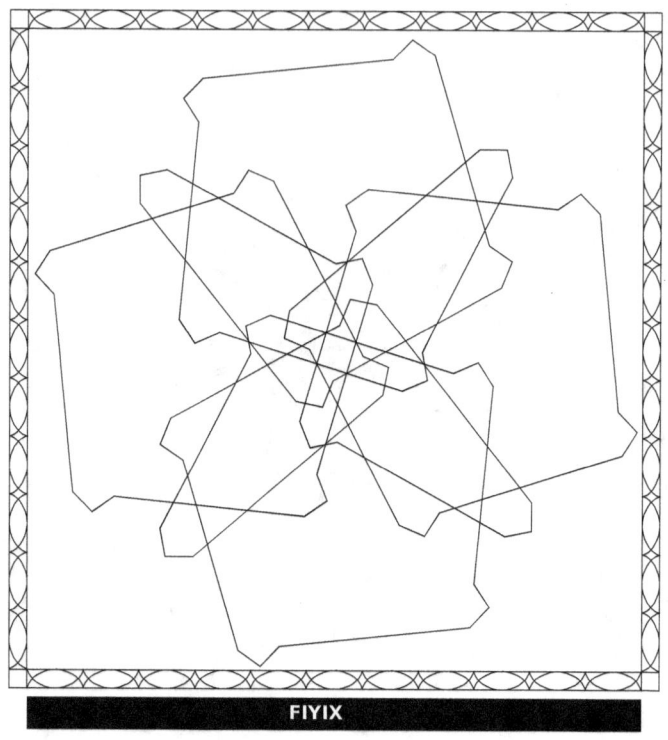

FIYIX

The seeking for truth is better than its loveless possession.
John Lancaster Spalding

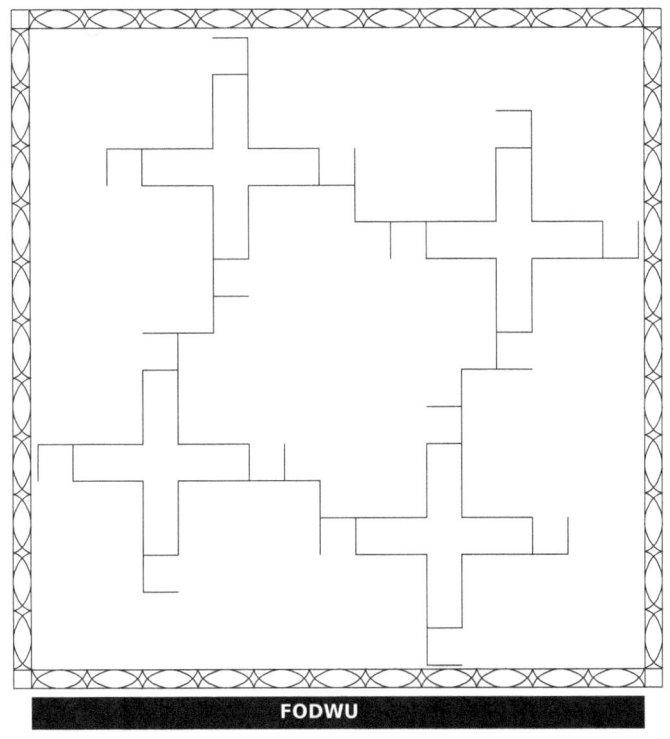

FODWU

At the root of our civilization, there is the freedom of each person of thought, of belief, of opinion, of work, of leisure. *Charles de Gaulle*

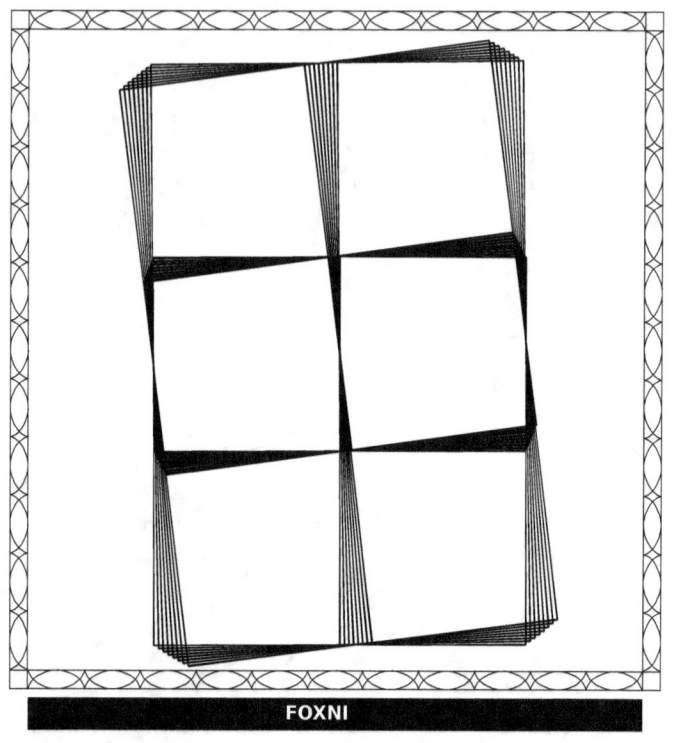

FOXNI

The worst form of inequality is to try to make unequal things equal.
Aristotle

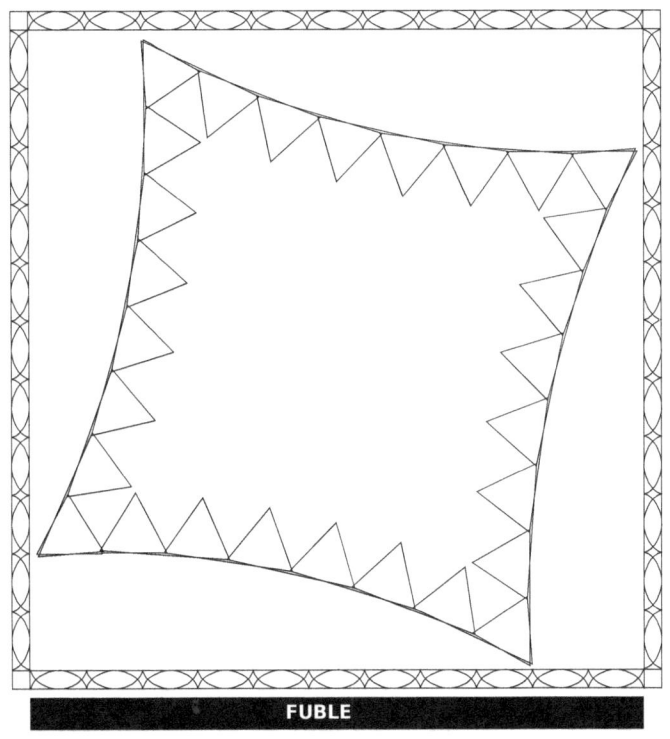

FUBLE

We are returned to mystery and the power of cooperating with life - rather than, as so often now, working against it.
Elsa Gidlow

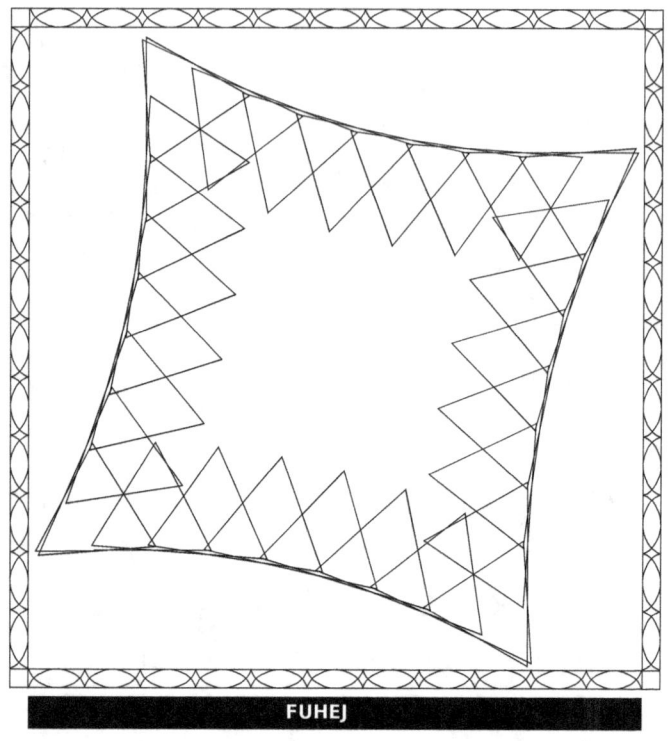

FUHEJ

Great music is a psychical storm, agitating to fathomless depths the mystery of the past within us.
Paul Elmer More

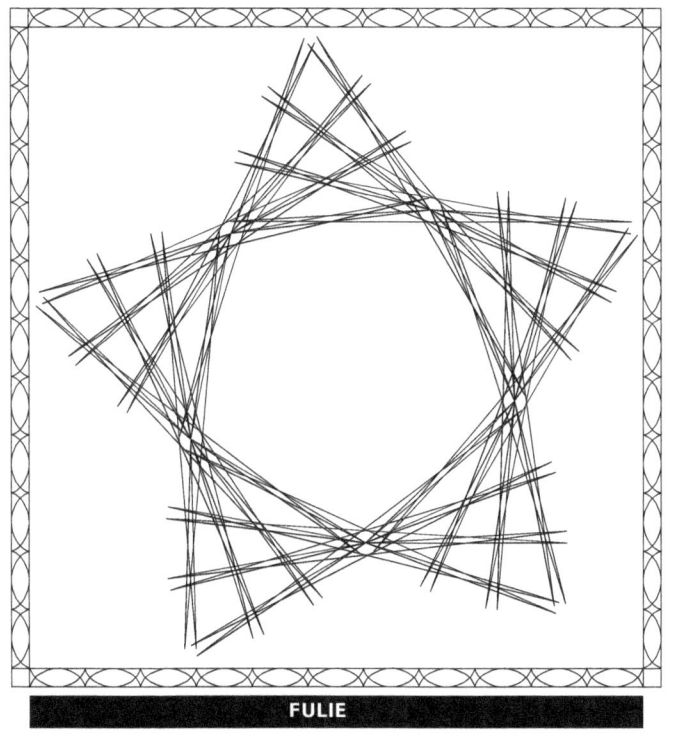

FULIE

The world would be a sad place without mysteries.
David Gemmell

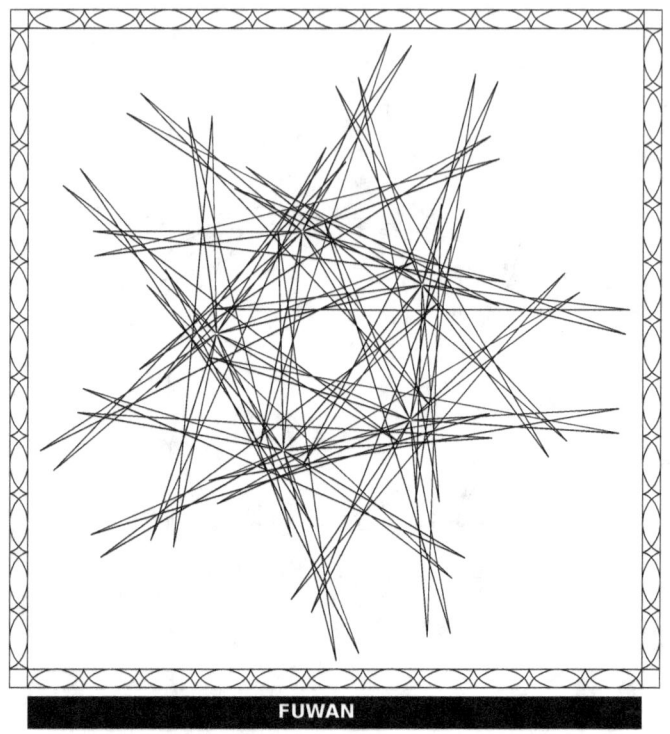

FUWAN

Poetry lifts the veil from the hidden beauty of the world,
and makes familiar objects be as if they were not familiar.
Percy Bysshe Shelley

78

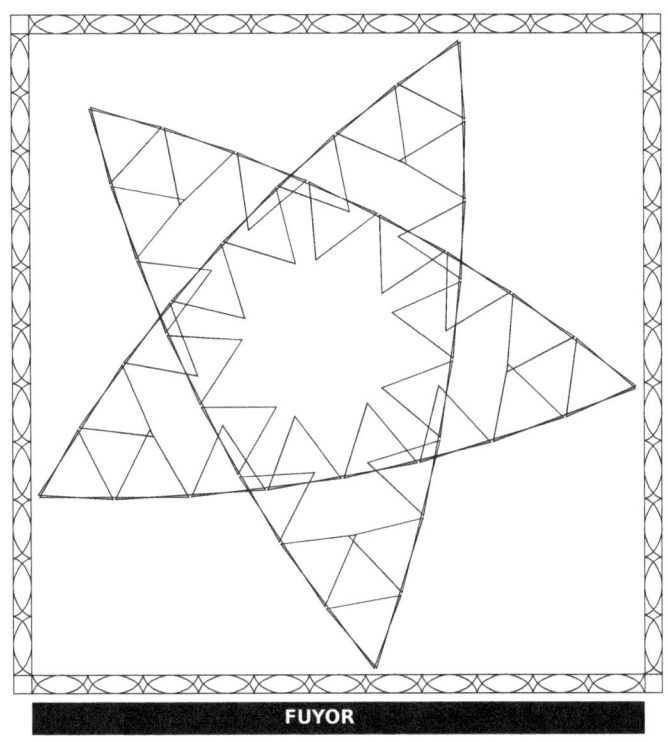

FUYOR

To claim power over what you do not understand is not wise, nor is the end of it likely to be good.

Ursula K. Le Guin

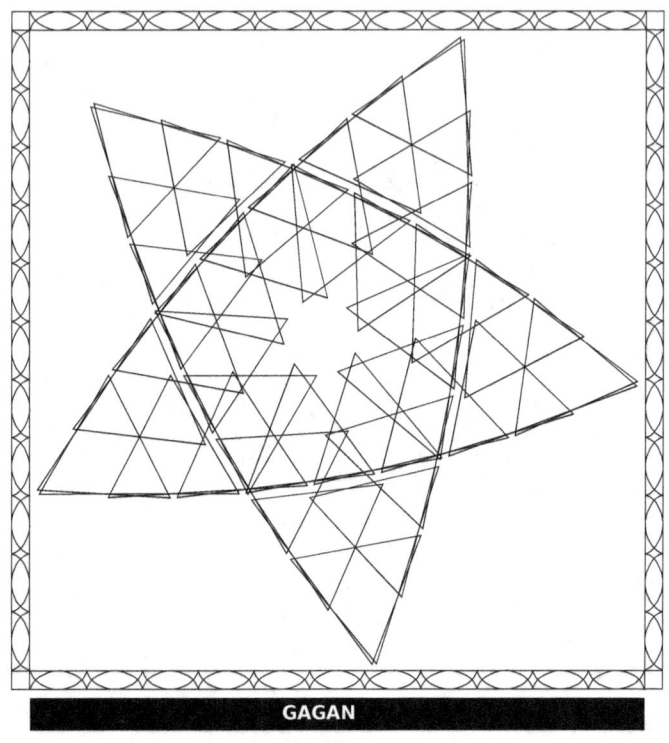

GAGAN

True artists enrich their art, not themselves.
Philippe Petit, Creativity: The Perfect Crime

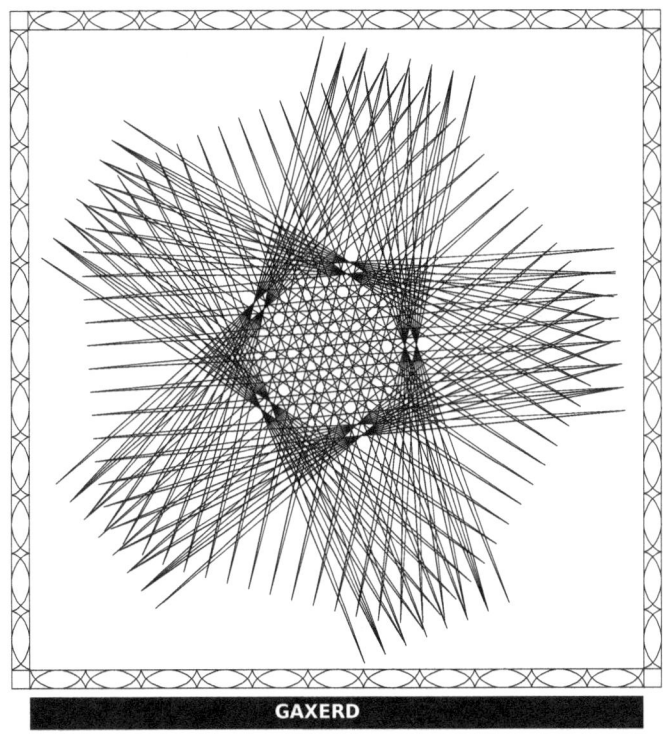

GAXERD

Poetry comes nearer to vital truth than history.
Ralph Waldo Emerson

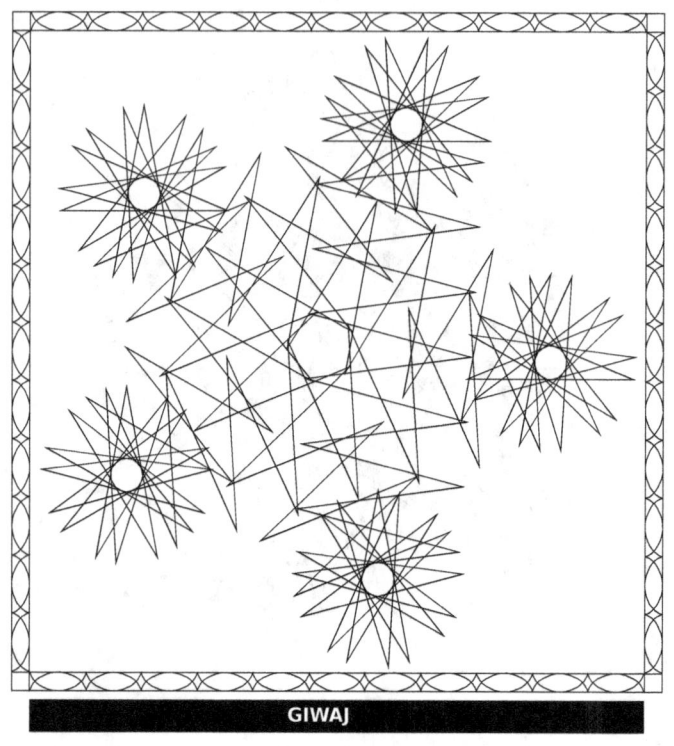

GIWAJ

Seek freedom and become captive of your desires. Seek
discipline and find your liberty.
Frank Herbert

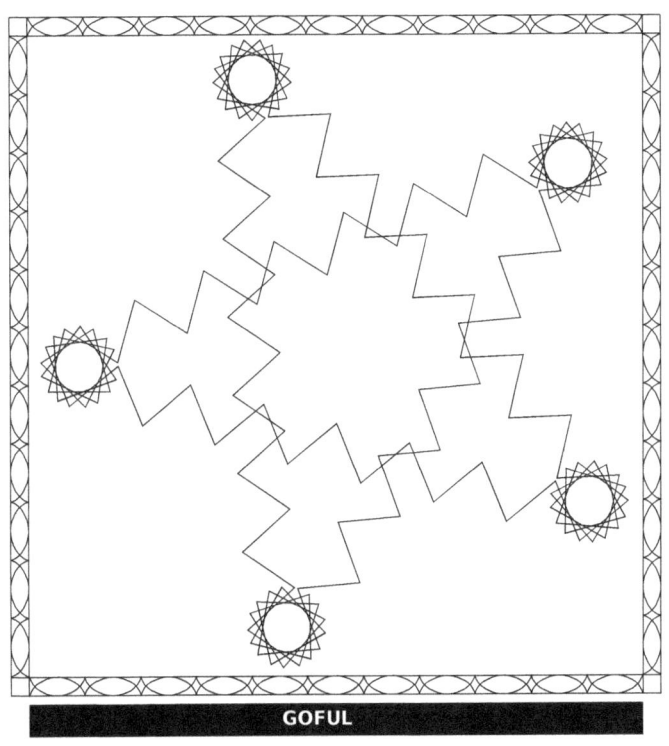

GOFUL

Do not kill your ego and do not let your ego to kill you.
Control your ego and rule over it.
Elia M. Ramollah

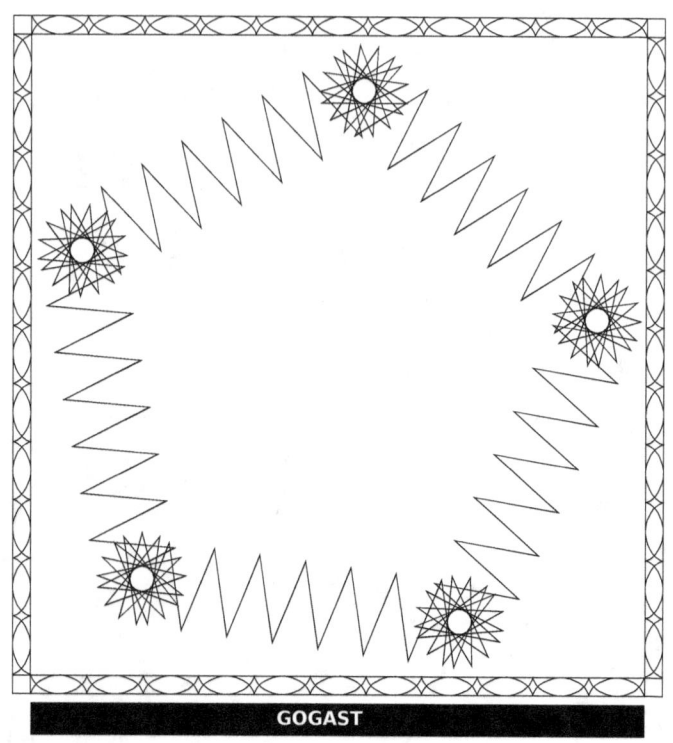

GOGAST

As free as you allow others to be, such freedom you create for yourself.
Bryant McGill

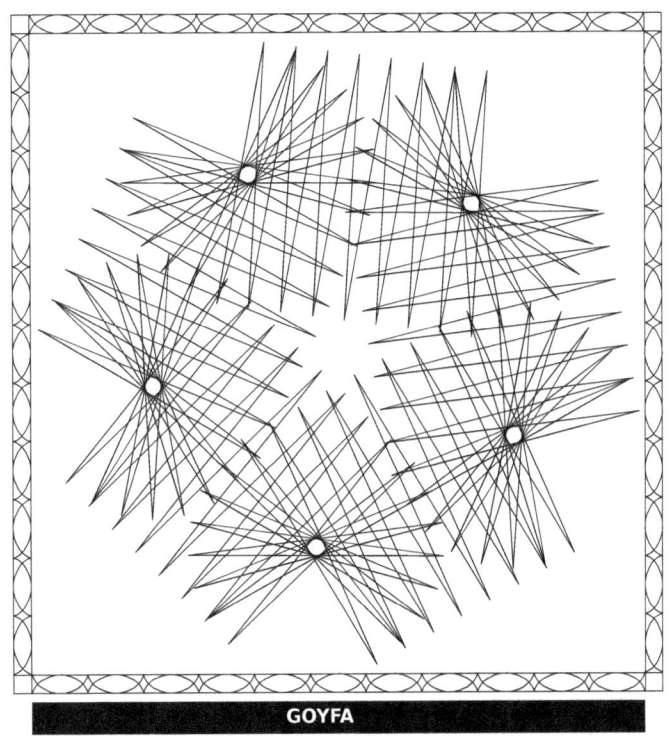

GOYFA

The pure religious consciousness lies in a region which is forever beyond all proof or disproof.
Walter Terence Stace

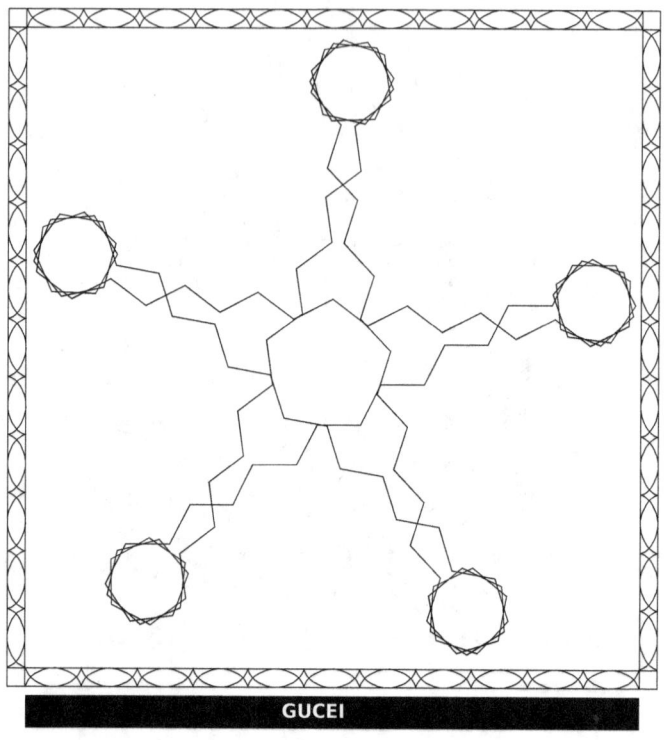

GUCEI

No two people on earth are alike, and it's got to be that
way in music or it isn't music.
Billie Holiday

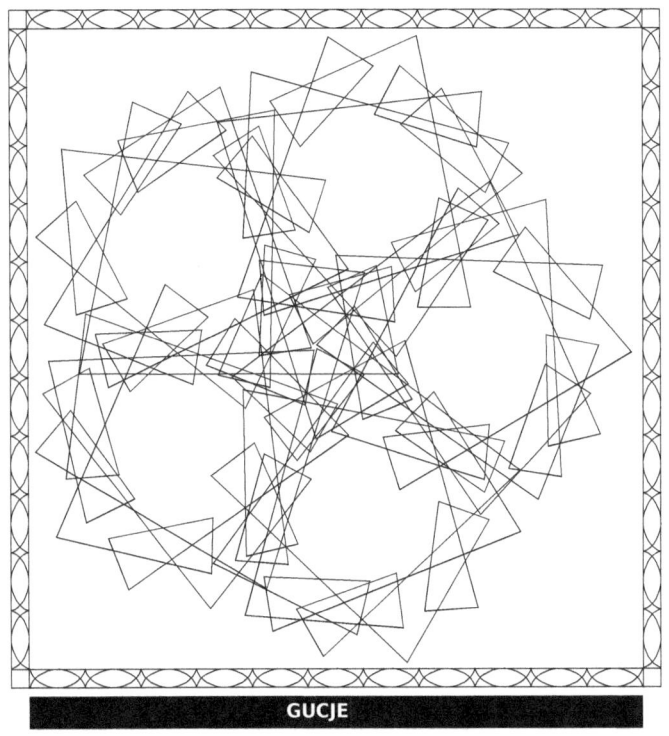

GUCJE

My own mystic bent leads me to believe that musical variations, collage, reiteration and process, or evolution, are beautiful. Life is worth living and beauty is worth making.
Beth Anderson

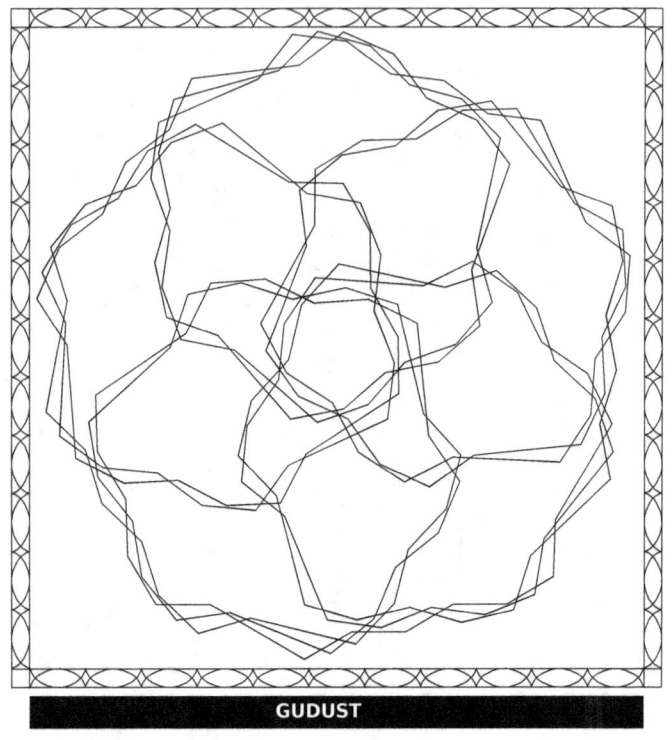

GUDUST

Solitude is happiness for one who is content, who has heard the Dhamma and clearly sees. Non-affliction is happiness in the world - harmlessness towards all living beings.
Udana

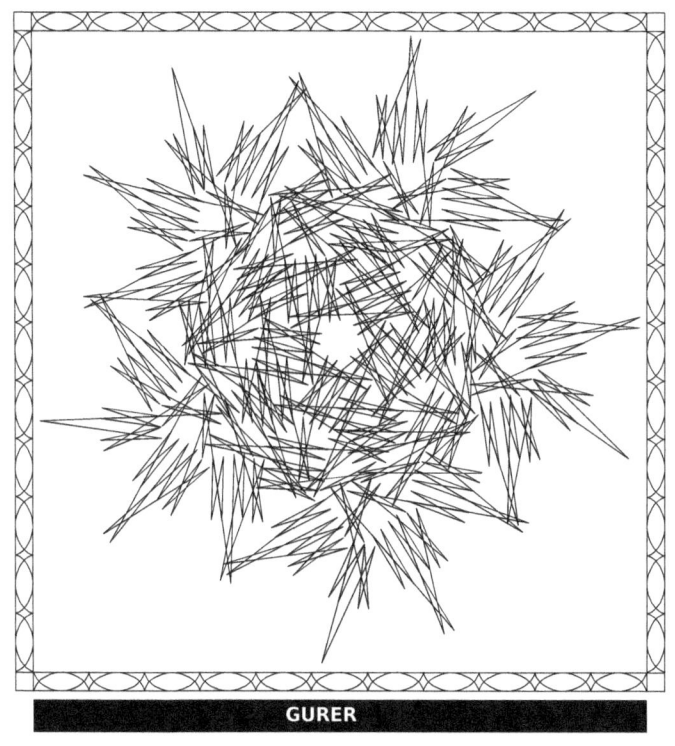

GURER

Every artist has a Dorian Gray slaving away in the attic.
John Banville

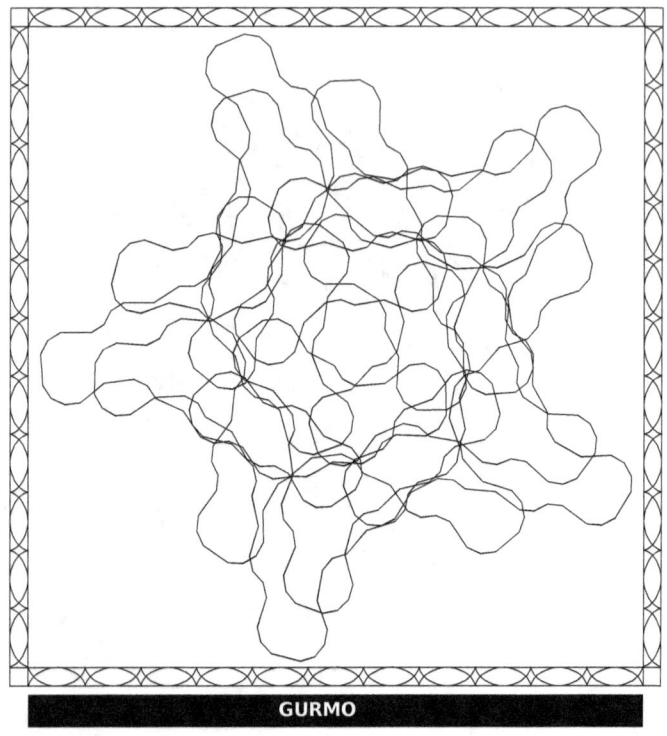

GURMO

But the cruellest thing you can do to an artist is tell them their work is flawless when it isn't.

Ben Croshaw

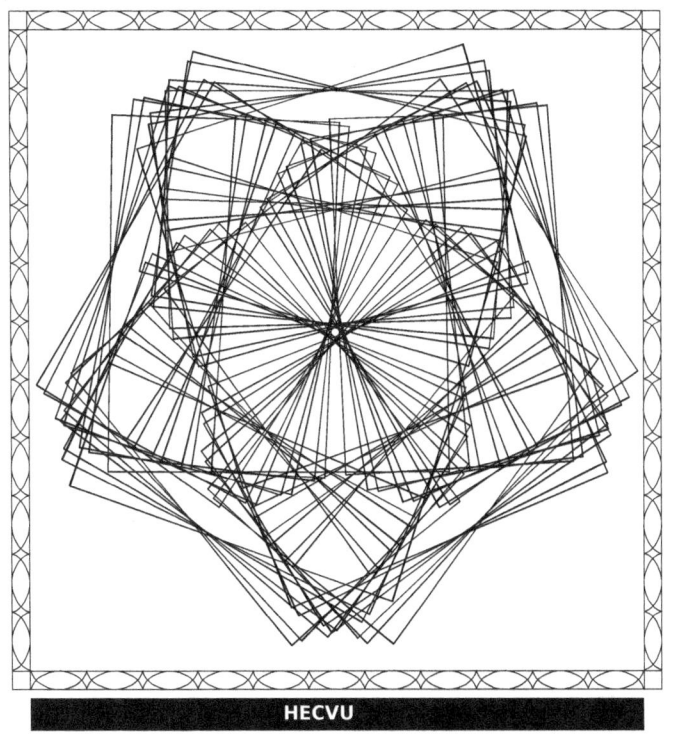

HECVU

Perfection itself is imperfection.
Vladimir Horowitz

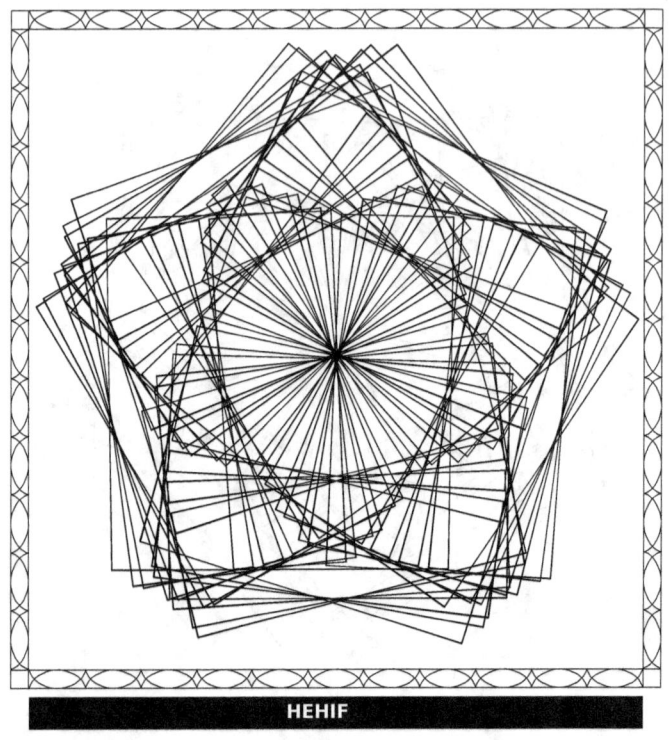

HEHIF

The truth of the matter is that you always know the right thing to do. The hard part is doing it.
Norman Schwarzkopf, Jr.

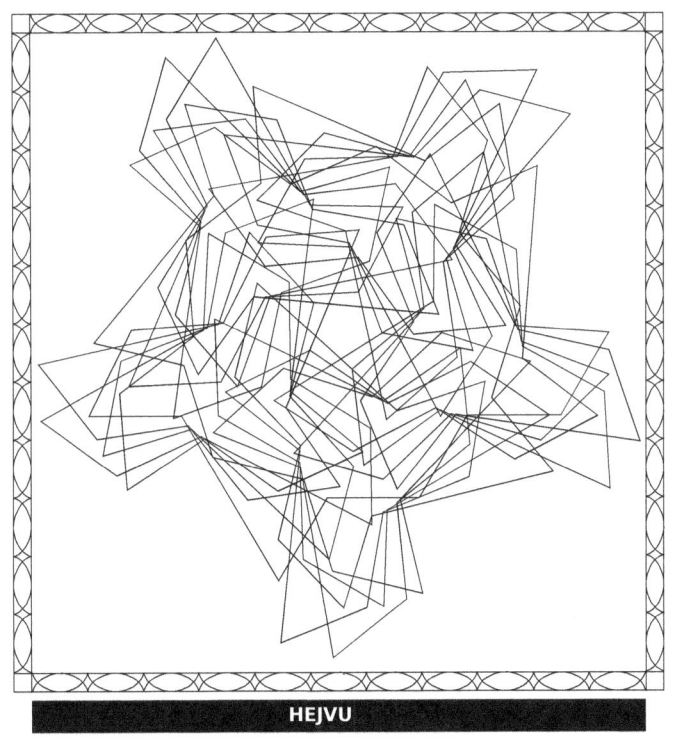

HEJVU

The great awareness comes slowly, piece by piece. The
path of spiritual growth is a path of lifelong learning. The
experience of spiritual power is basically a joyful one.
M. Scott Peck

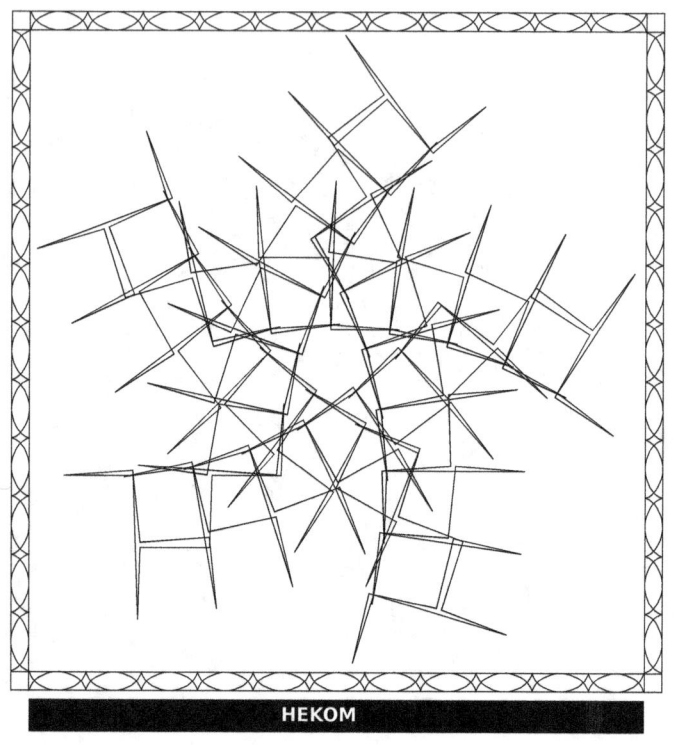

HEKOM

My art is rooted in a single reflection: why am I not as others are? ... my art gives meaning to my life.
Edvard Munch

94

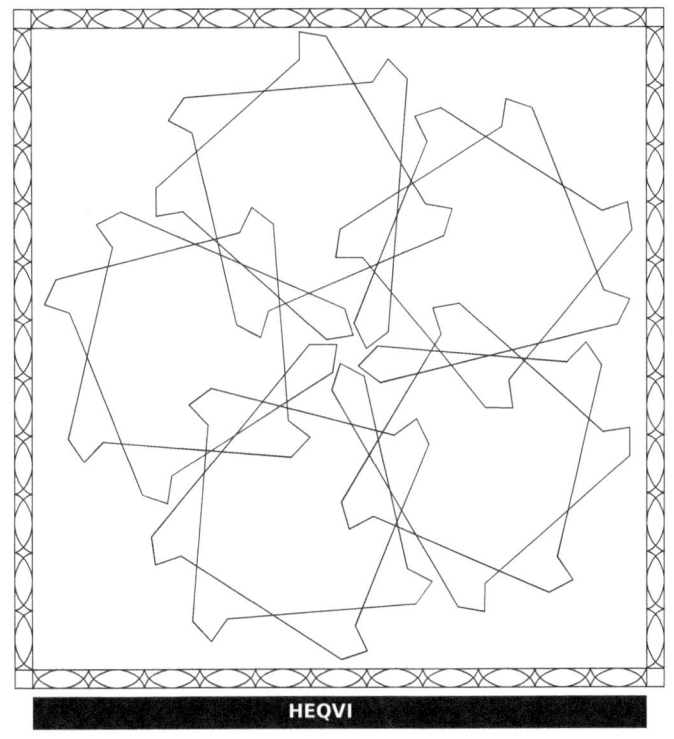

HEQVI

Life is short, art long, opportunity fleeting, experiment uncertain, and judgment difficult.
Hippocrates

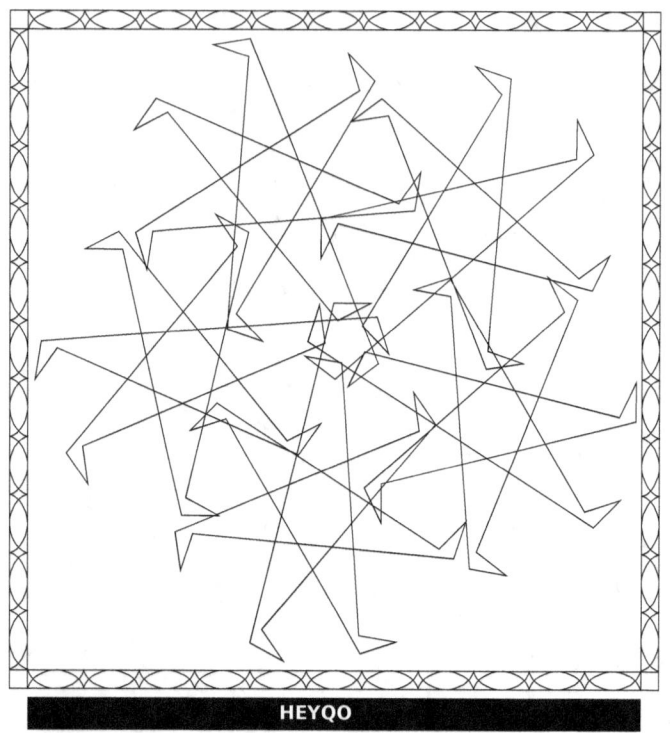

HEYQO

Spiritual pride is the worst of all pride, if it is not the worst snare of the devil. The heart is peculiarly deceitful on just this one thing.
Ichabod Spencer

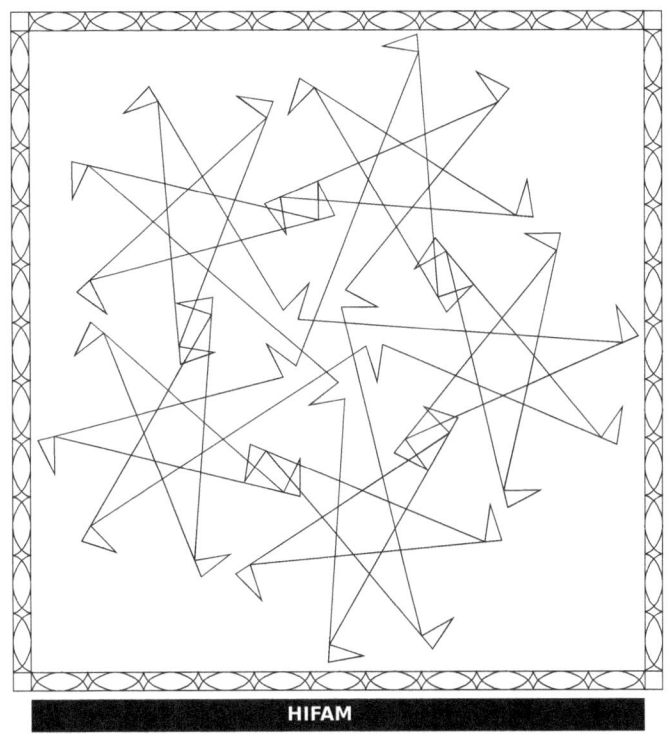

HIFAM

We are faced with the paradoxical fact that education has become one of the chief obstacles to intelligence and freedom of thought.
Bertrand Russell

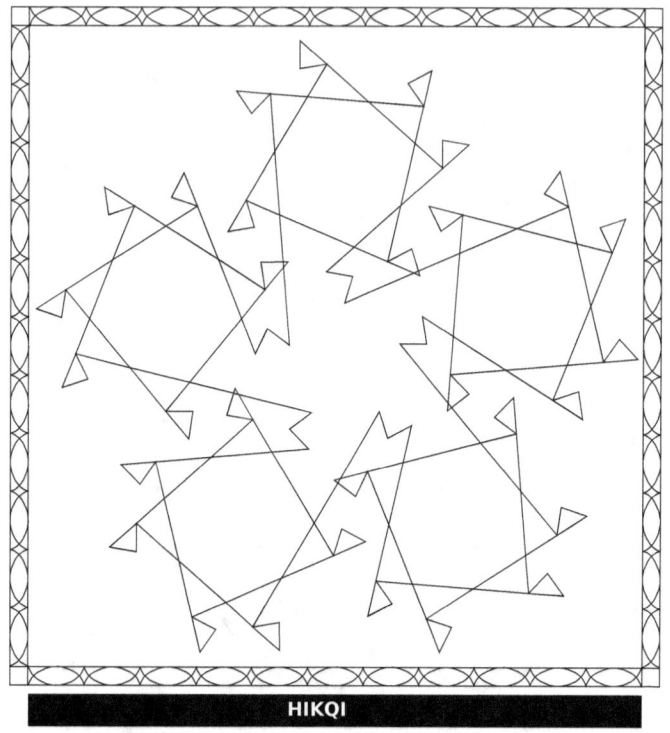

HIKQI

Besides the noble art of getting things done, there is the
noble art of leaving things undone. The wisdom of life
consists in the elimination of non-essentials.
Lin Yutang

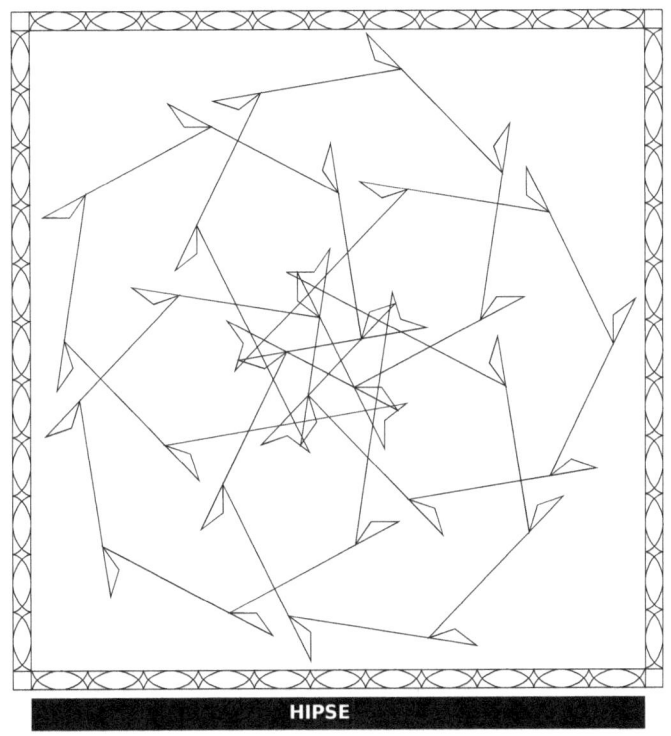

HIPSE

Moments of perfection are indescribable but a few things can be said about them. At such times we are suddenly very happy and we wonder why life ever seemed troublesome. In an instant we can see the road ahead free from all difficulties, and we think that we will never lose it again. All this and a great deal more in barely a moment, and then it is gone. But all such moments are stored in the mind. They are called sensibility or awareness of perfection in the mind.

Agnes Martin, On the Perfection Underlying Life

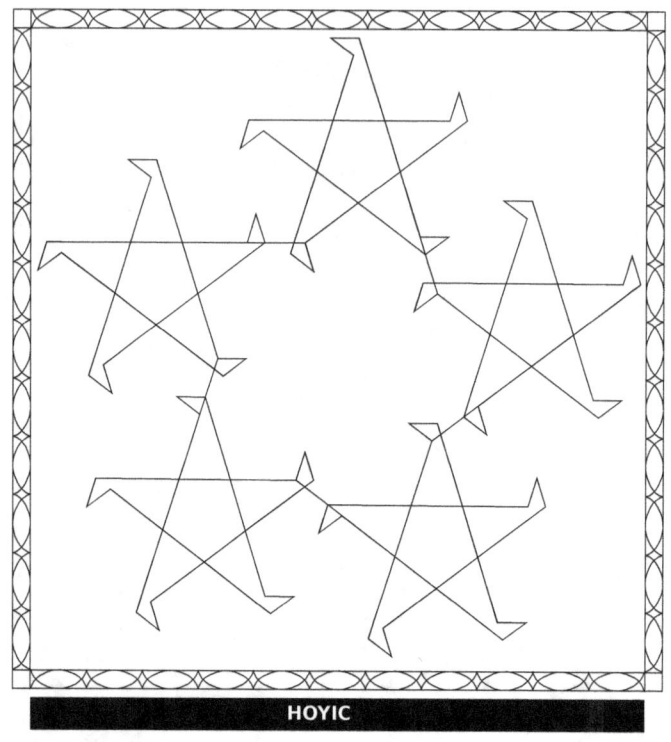

HOYIC

A committee is the only known form of life with a hundred bellies and no brain.
Robert A. Heinlein

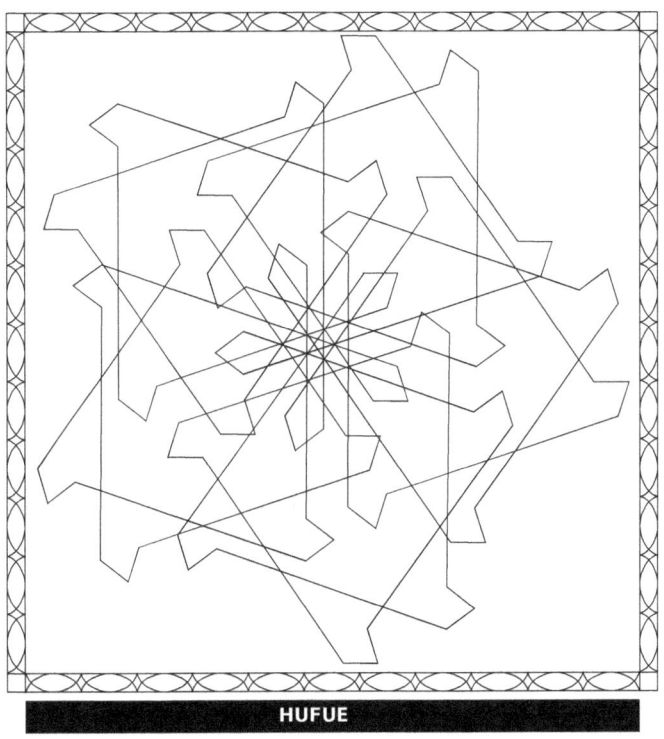

HUFUE

It is the mark of an educated mind to be able to entertain
a thought without accepting it.
Aristotle

101

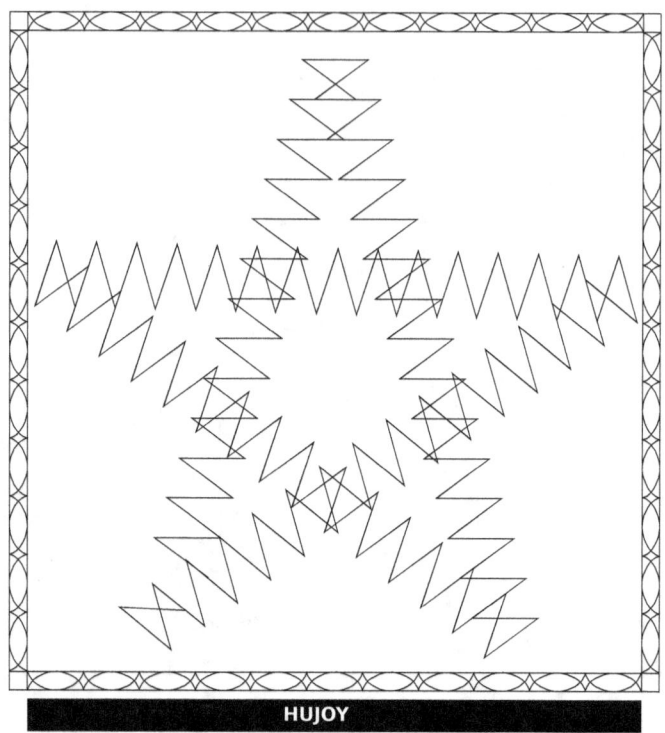

HUJOY

Many a writer has spent his life putting his favorite words in all the places they belong; but how many, like E. E. Cummings, have spent their lives putting their favorite words in all the places they don't belong, thus discovering many effects that no one had even realized were possible?
Randall Jarrell

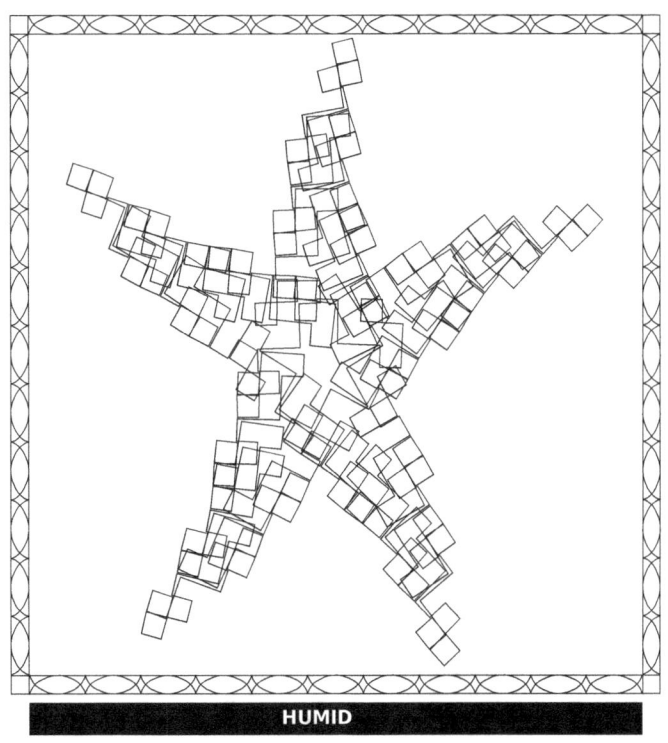

HUMID

You are a miracle, and everything you touch could be a miracle.
Thich Nhat Hanh

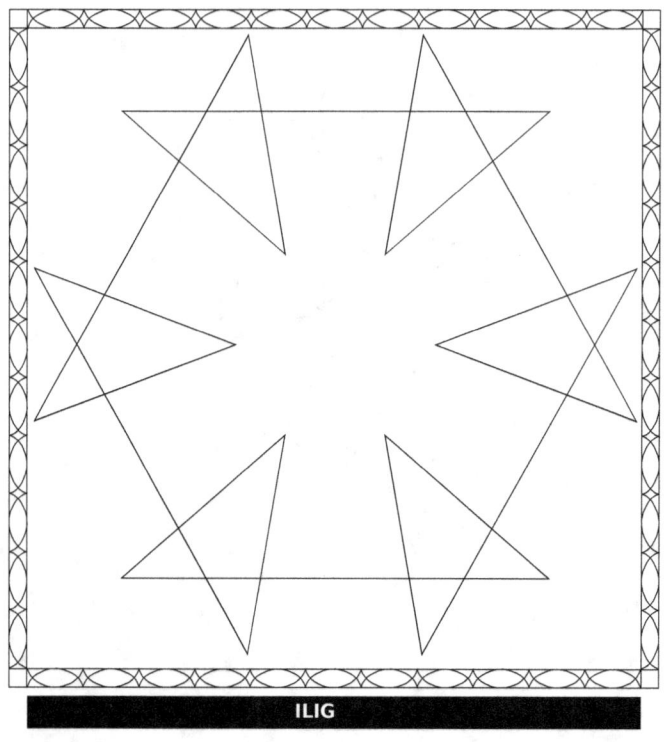

ILIG

Let thy mind rule thy tongue!
Pythagoras

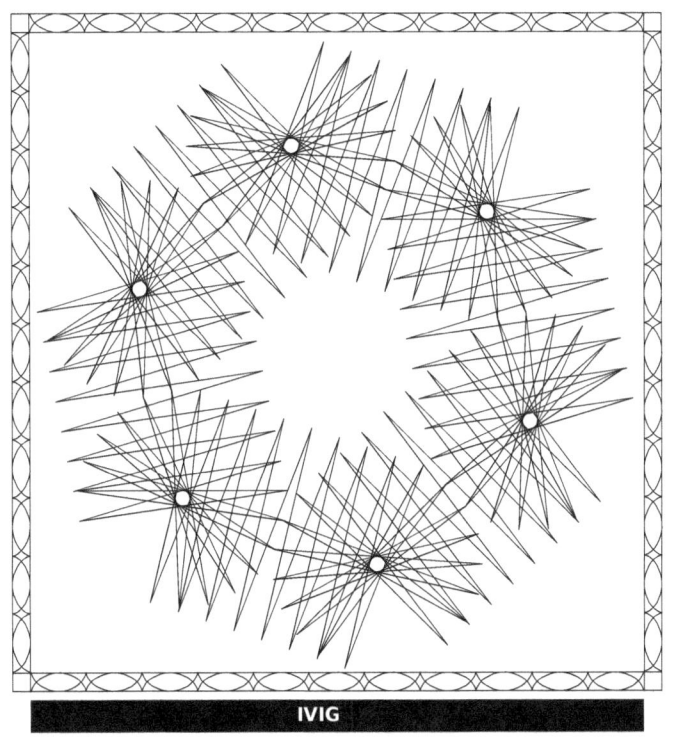

IVIG

... it will refuse to bloom if I treat it simply as a routine exercise, instead of feeling it as an adventure.
Philippe Petit, Creativity: The Perfect Crime

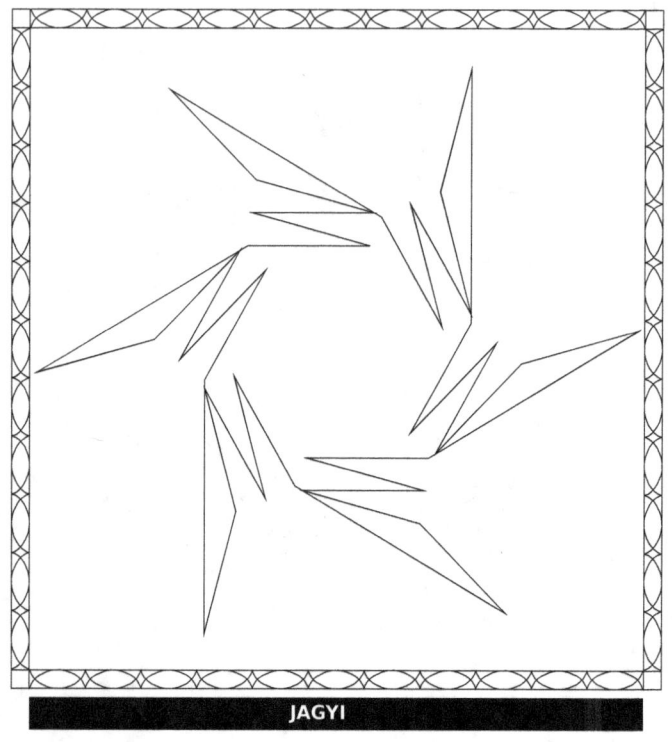

JAGYI

Listening, not imitation, may be the sincerest form of flattery.

Joyce Brothers

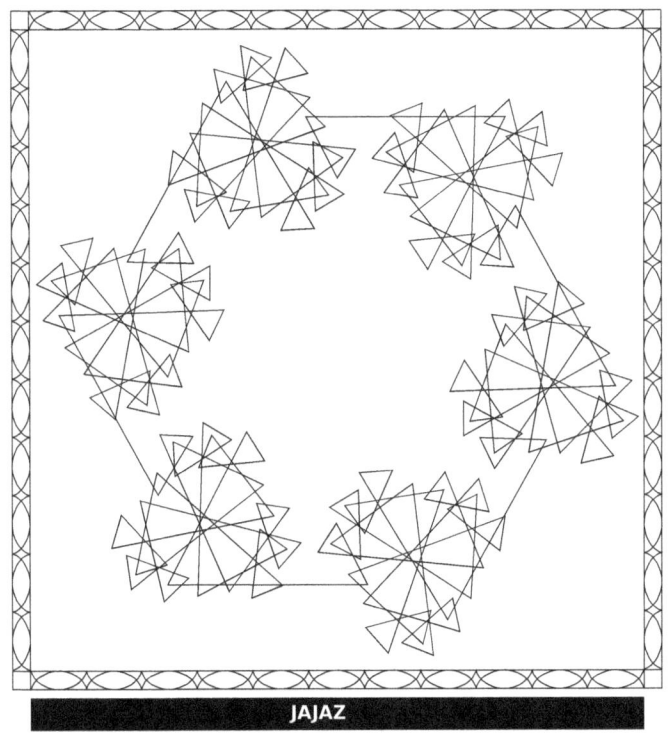

JAJAZ

I am a graphic artist heart and soul, though I find the term artist rather embarrassing.

M. C. Escher

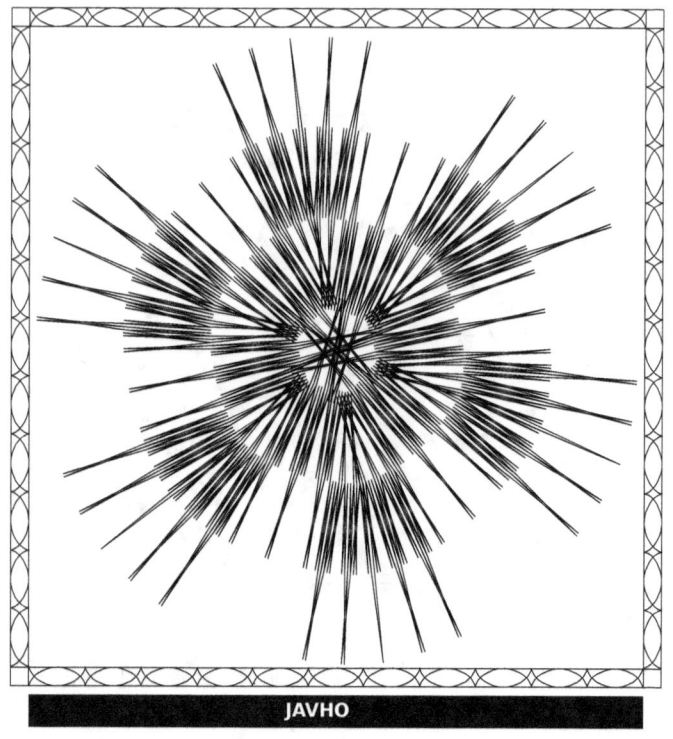

JAVHO

A fine thing: suddenly to forget about one's history, one's past, to stop feeling that one's present happiness is endangered by what one used to be.
Peter Handke

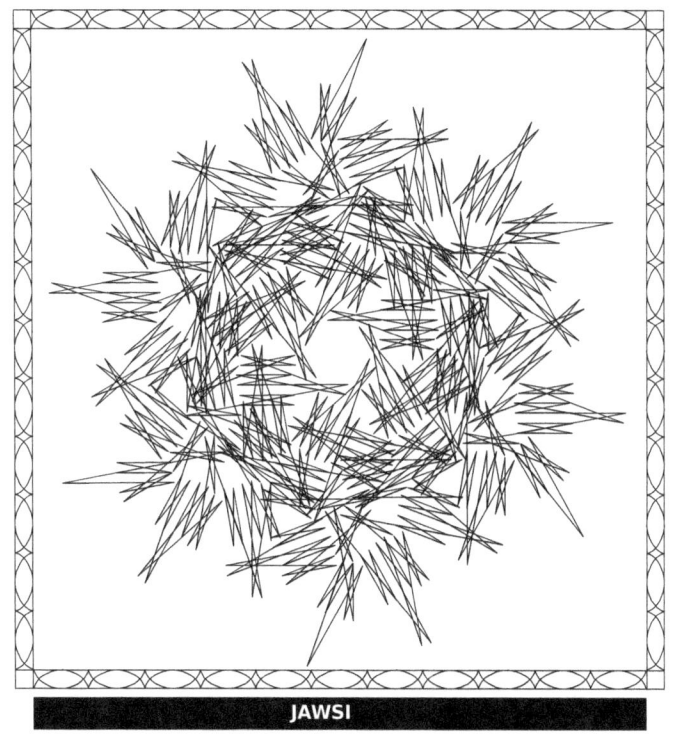

JAWSI

And certainly we should take care not to make the intellect our god; it has, of course, powerful muscles, but no personality. It cannot lead, it can only serve; and it is not fastidious in its choice of a leader.

Albert Einstein

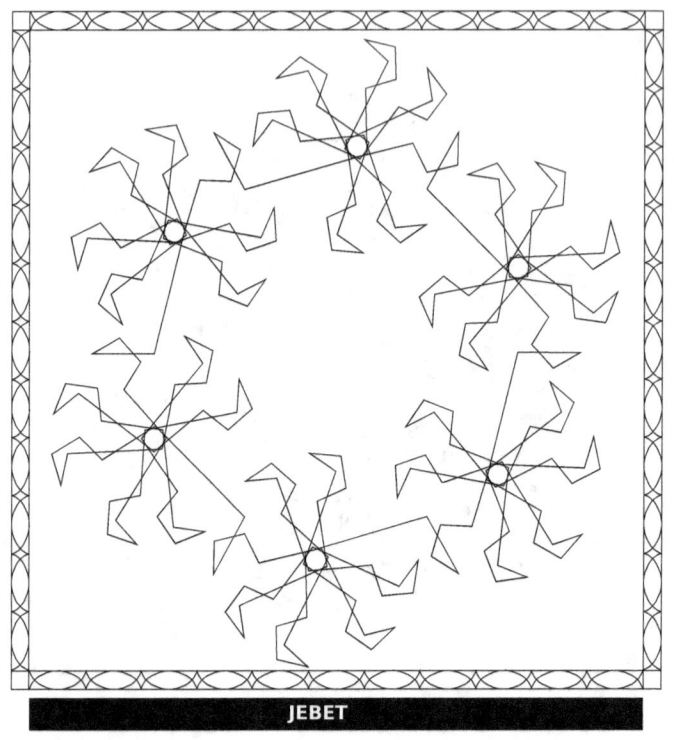

JEBET

My responsibility as an artist is to turn up at the page or the piano or the microphone. The rest is up to God.
Nick Cave

JEKAX

If my mind can conceive it; and my heart can believe it -
then I can achieve it.
Muhammad Ali

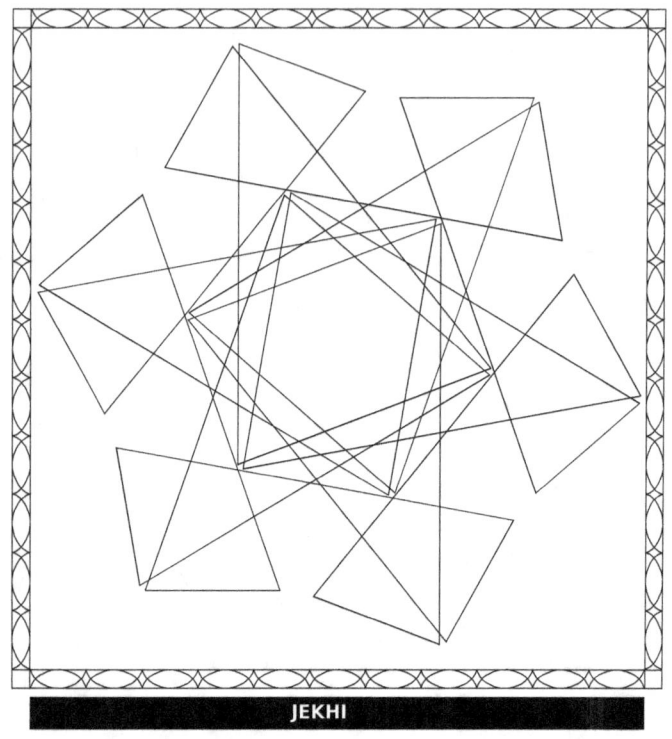

JEKHI

One should never be so formal that one loses life, but one should never be so informal that one becomes without form of any kind.

Margrethe II of Denmark

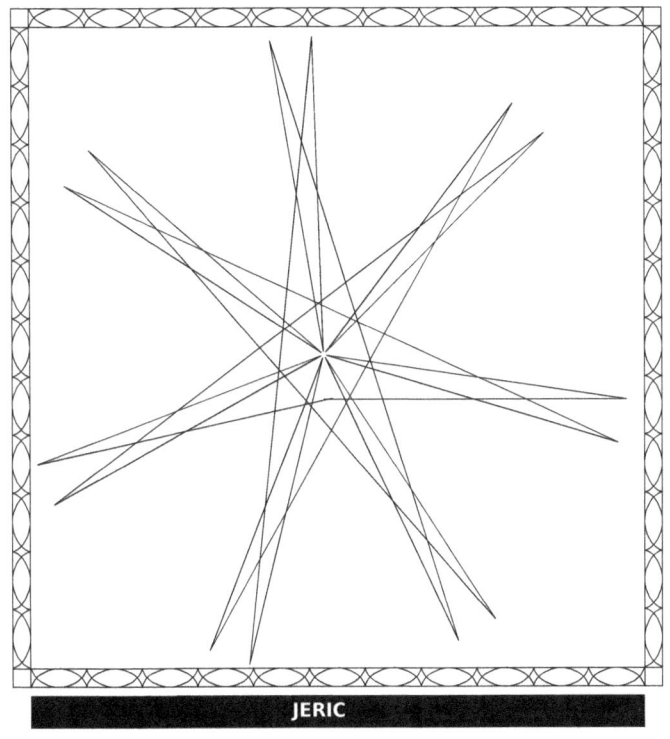

JERIC

We can't form our children on our own concepts; we must take them and love them as God gives them to us.
Johann Wolfgang von Goethe

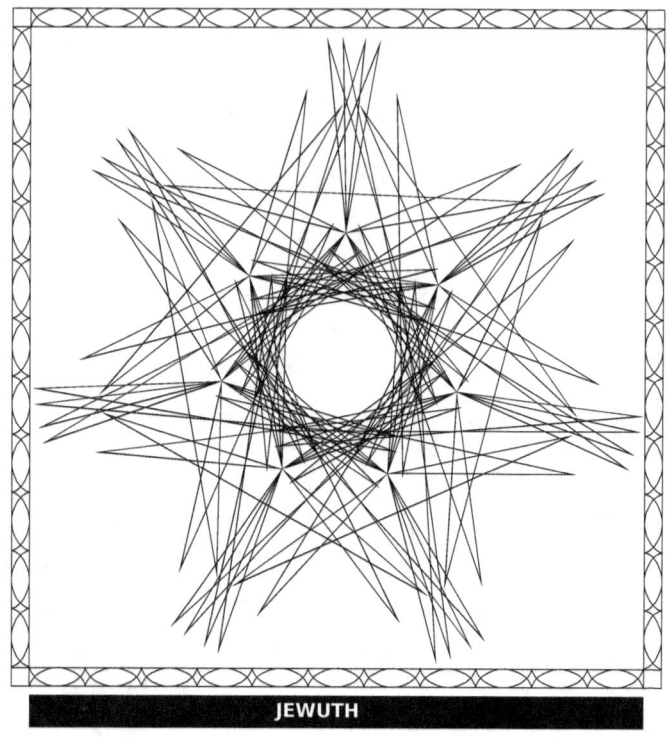

JEWUTH

Joy is the simplest form of gratitude.
Karl Barth

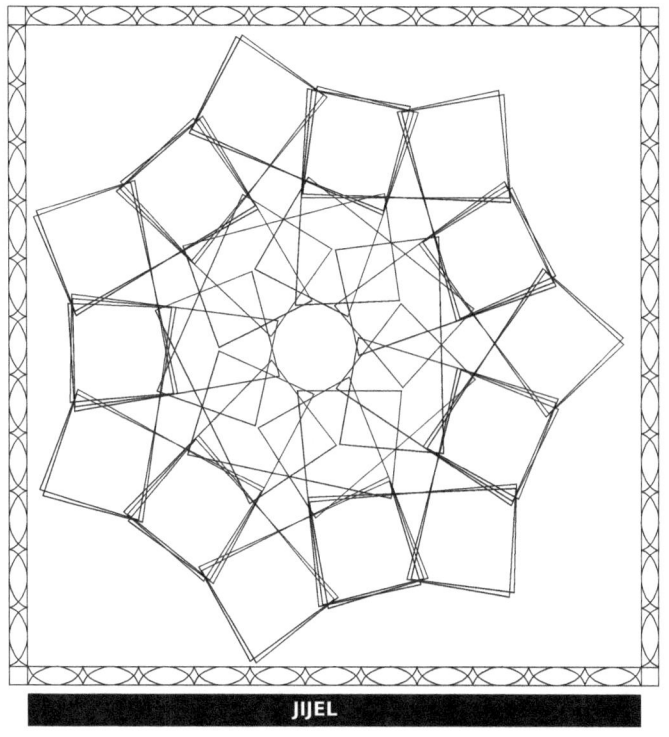

JIJEL

How can great minds be produced in a country where the test of a great mind is agreeing in the opinions of small minds?
John Stuart Mill

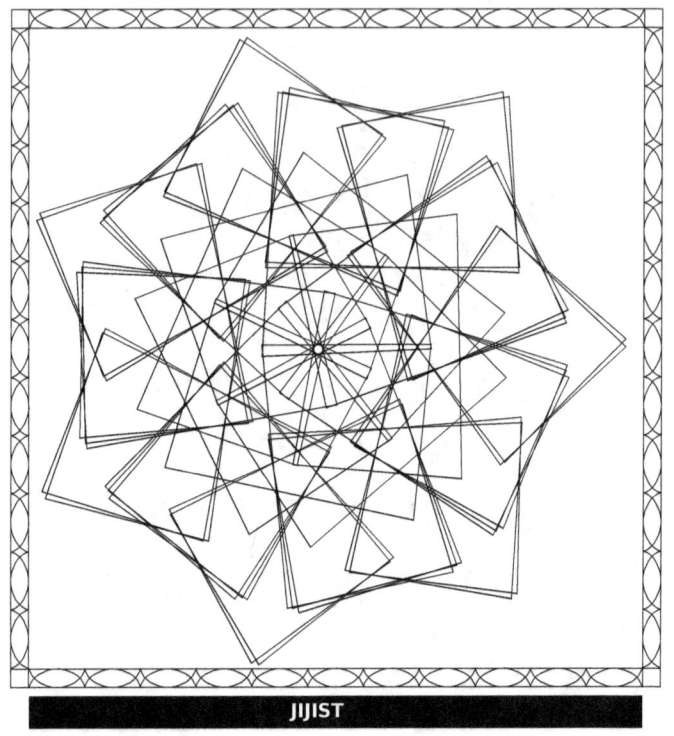

JIJIST

It is the great mystery of life itself which is at the bottom
of all the mysterious language we are obliged to employ
concerning it.
Peter Mere Latham

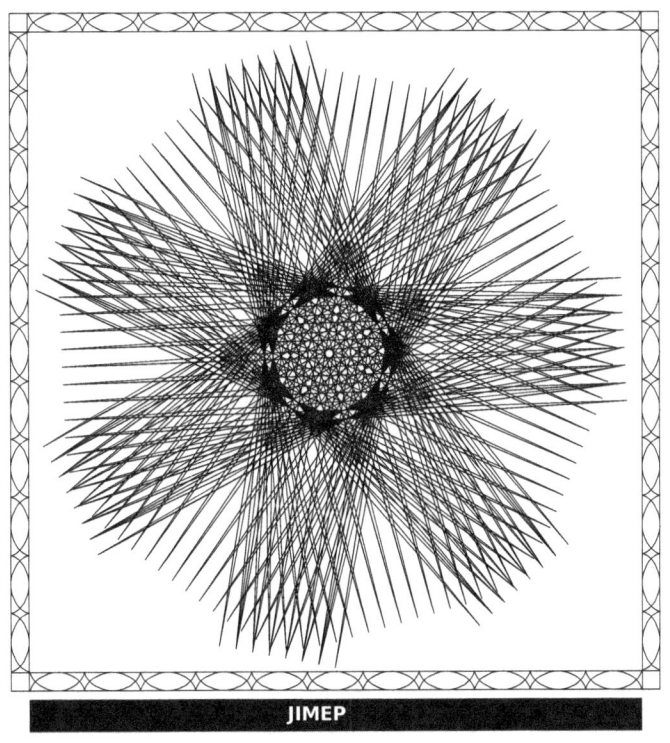

JIMEP

Jesus Christ was an extremist for love, truth and goodness.
Martin Luther King, Jr.

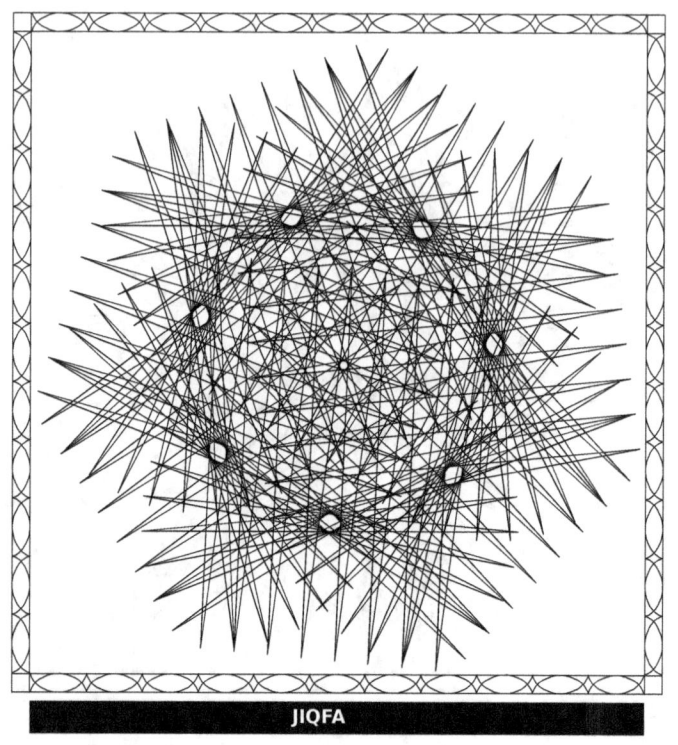

JIQFA

Time is precious, but truth is more precious than time.
Benjamin Disraeli

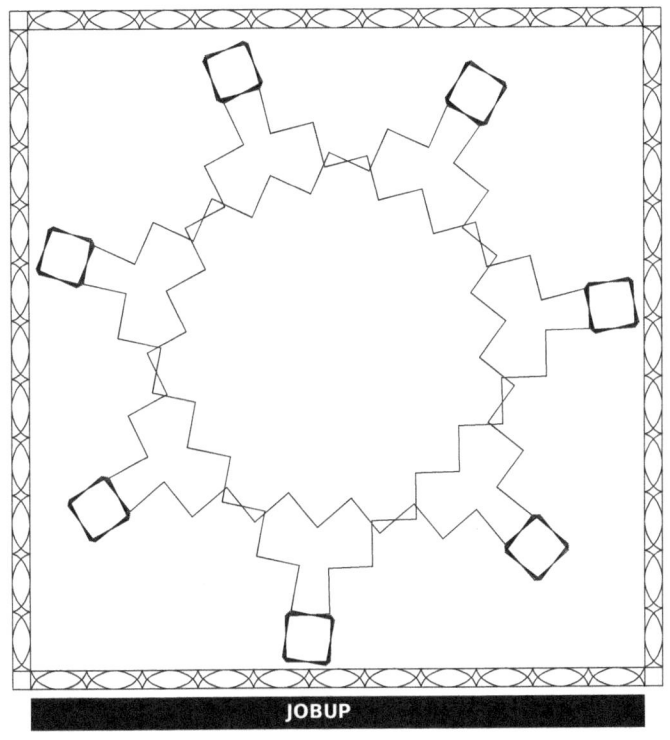

JOBUP

True enjoyment comes from activity of the mind and exercise of the body; the two are ever united.
Wilhelm von Humboldt

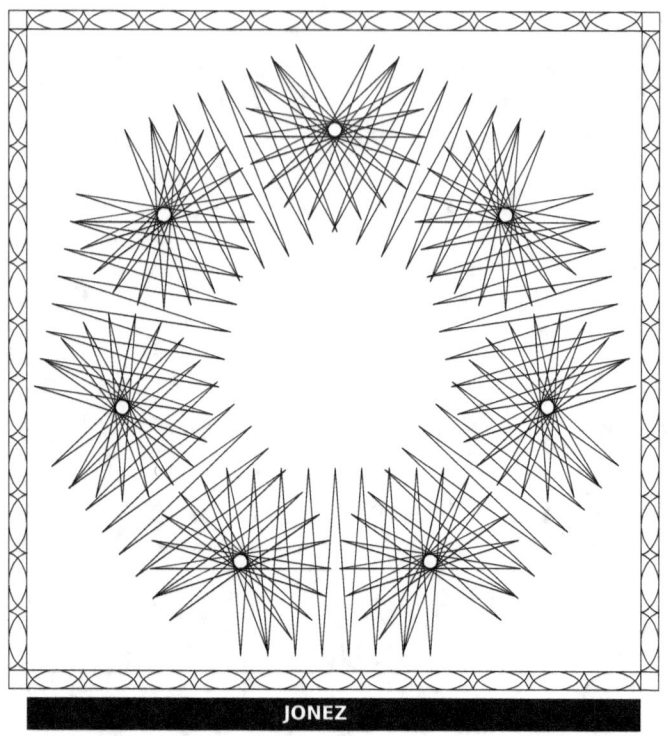

JONEZ

Beauty is no quality in things themselves: It exists merely in the mind which contemplates them; and each mind perceives a different beauty.

David Hume

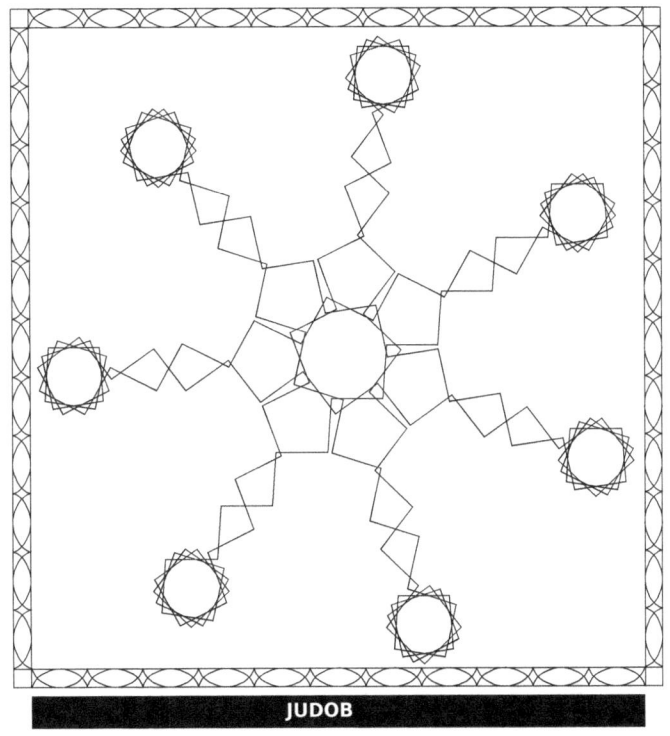

JUDOB

The essentials of human happiness are simple, so simple that sophisticated people cannot bring themselves to admit what it is they really lack.

Bertrand Russell

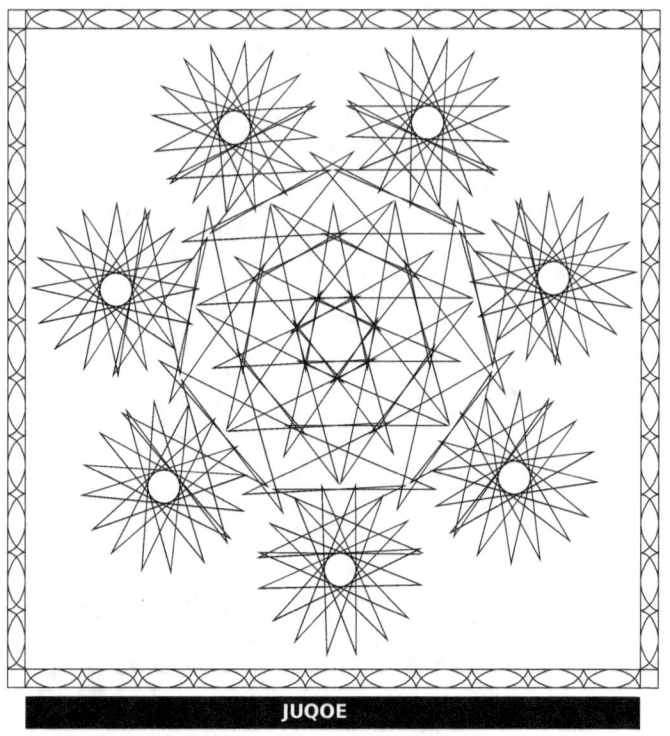

JUQOE

Truth and freedom are inextricably connected. We must speak the truth because otherwise we shall lose our freedom.
Geert Wilders

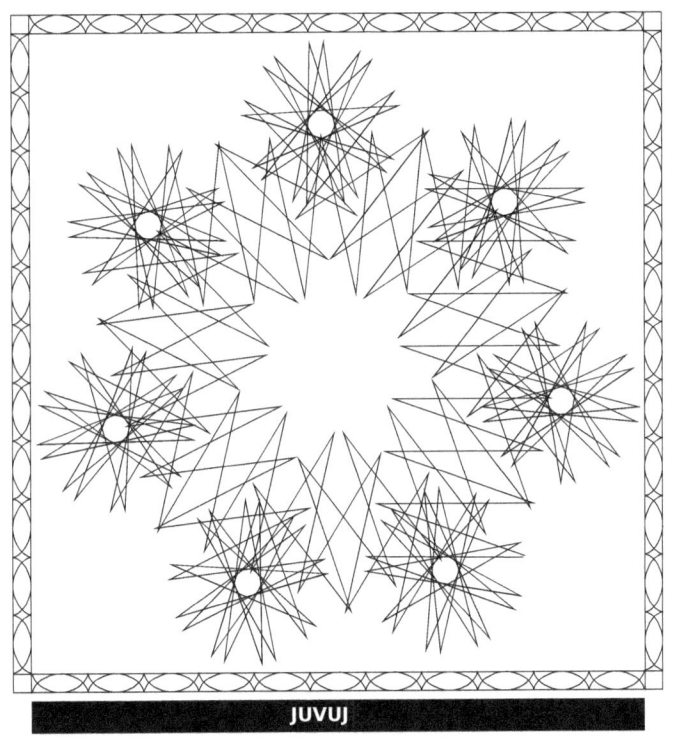

JUVUJ

People who like quotations love meaningless generaliza-
tions.
Graham Greene

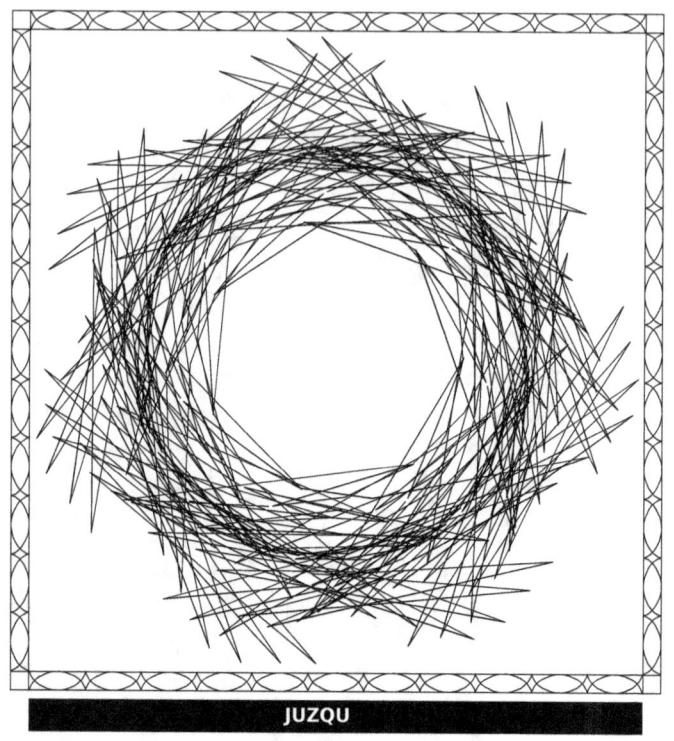

JUZQU

The conscious mind may be compared to a fountain playing in the sun and falling back into the great subterranean pool of subconscious from which it rises.
Sigmund Freud

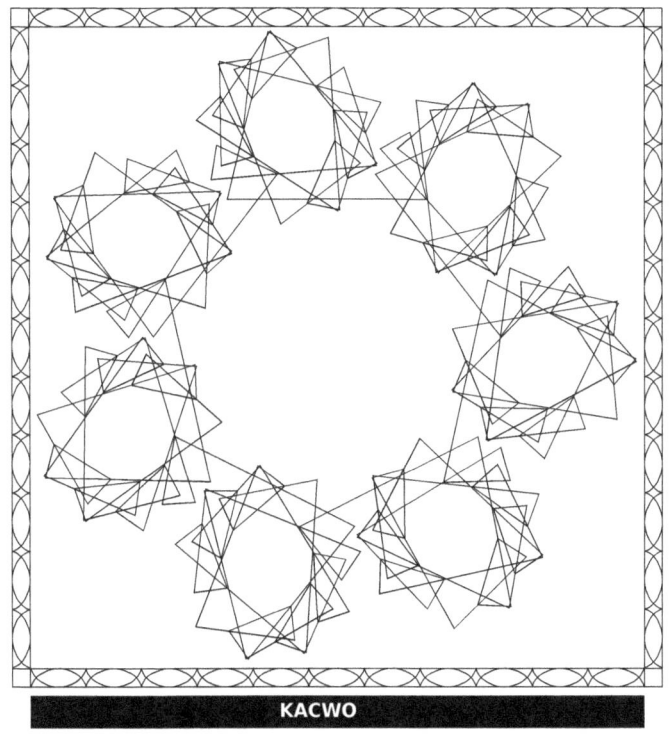

KACWO

This is deathless, the liberation of the mind through lack of clinging.
Gautama Buddha

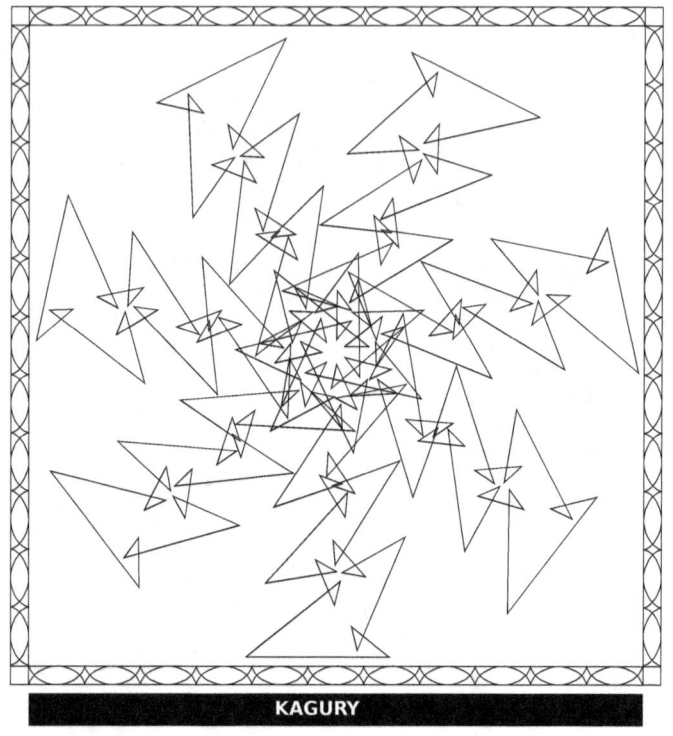

KAGURY

To read is to let someone else work for you - the most delicate form of exploitation.
Emil Cioran

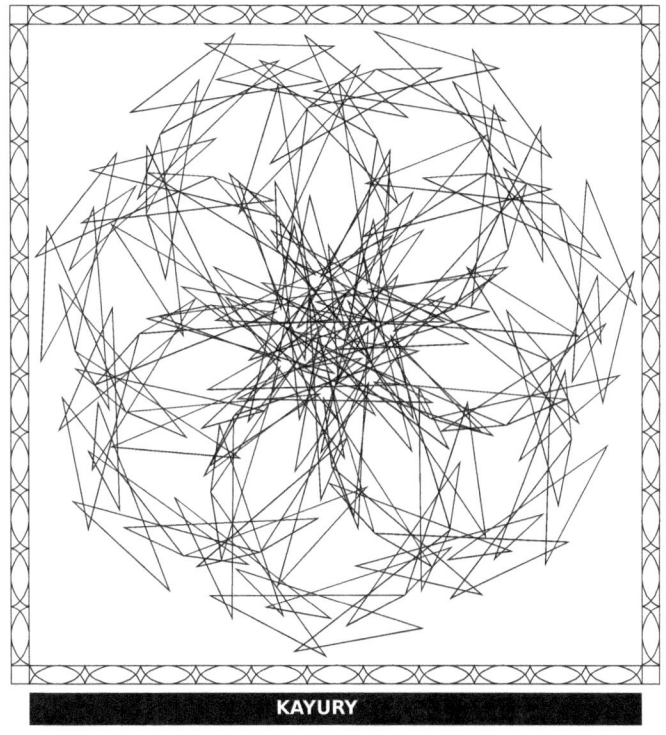

KAYURY

My music is best understood by children and animals.
Igor Stravinsky

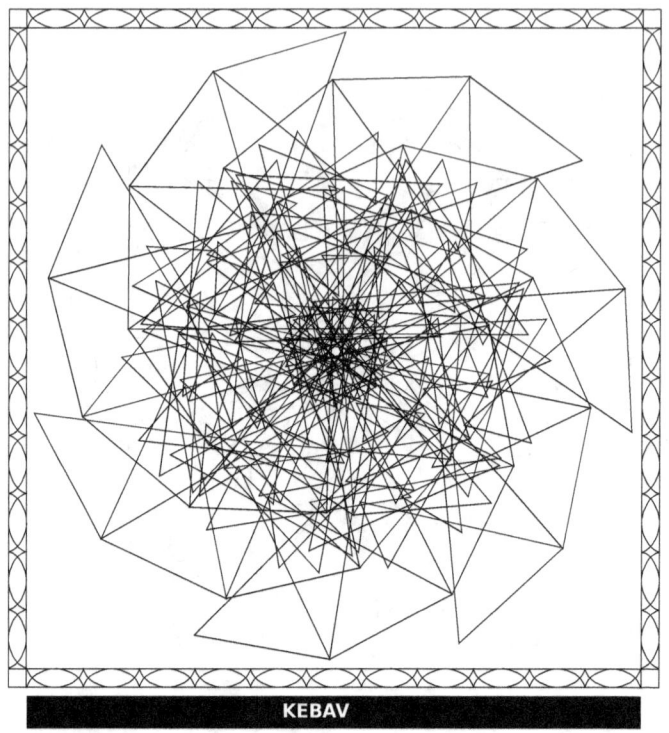

KEBAV

There is something perfect to be found in the imperfect:
the law keeps balance through the juxtaposition of beauty,
which gains perfection through nurtured imperfection.
Dejan Stojanovic

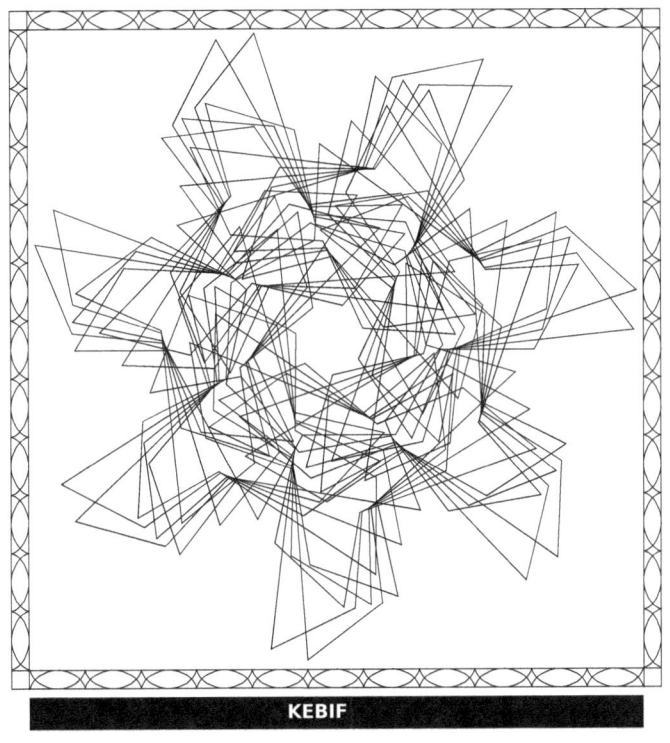

KEBIF

The divorce of poetry and music was first reflected by the printed page.
Marshall McLuhan

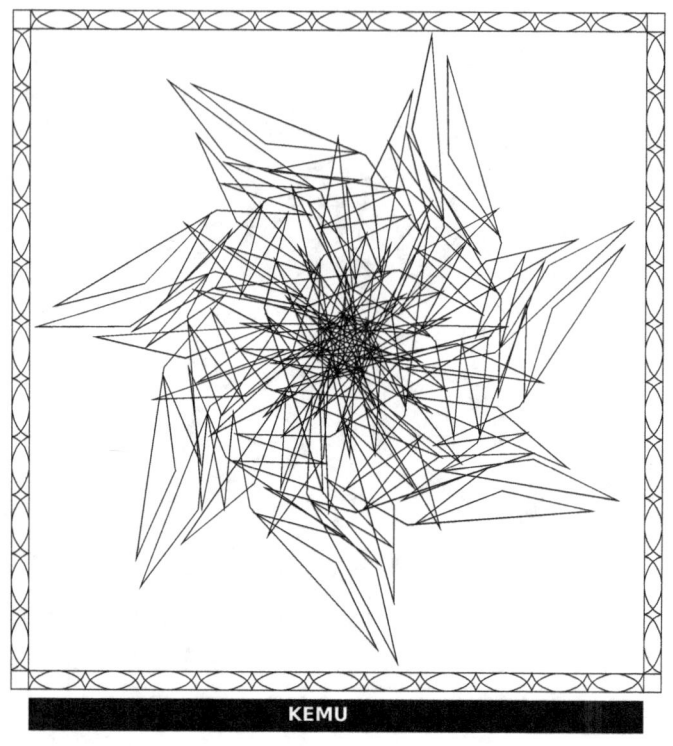

KEMU

Poetry, we might say, is concerned with the truth of what is, not with what is truth.
Herbert Read

130

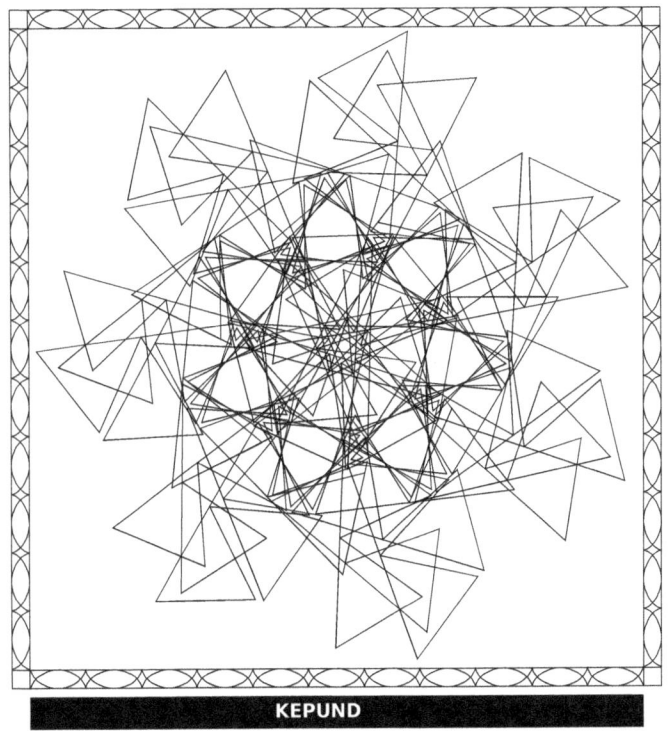

KEPUND

An artist will betray himself by some sort of sincerity.
G. K. Chesterton

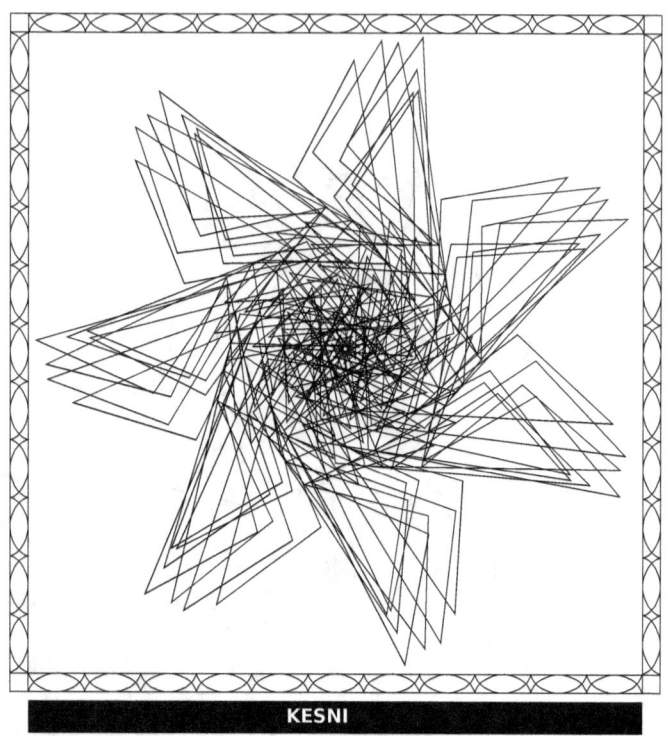

KESNI

The romantics were prompted to seek exotic subjects and to travel to far off places. They failed to realize that, though the transcendental must involve the strange and unfamiliar, not everything strange or unfamiliar is transcendental.

Mark Rothko

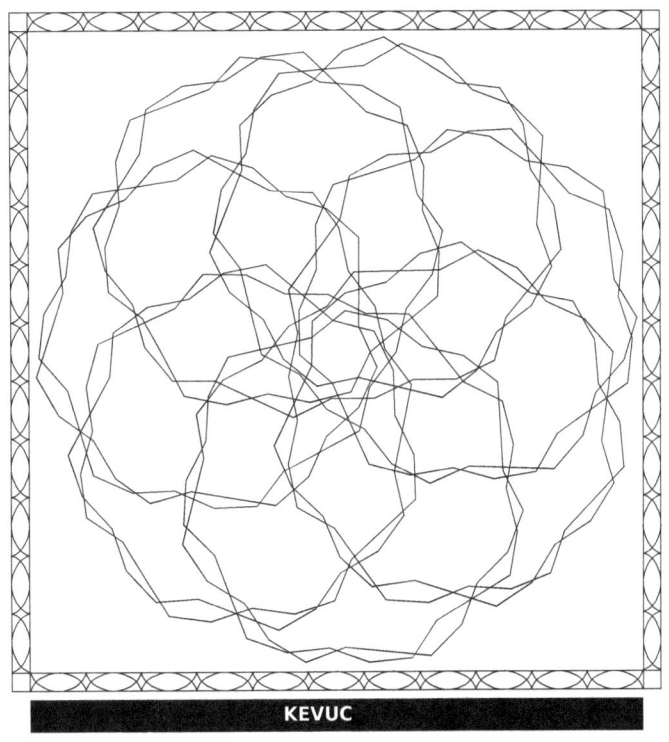

KEVUC

People who lack the clarity, courage, or determination to follow their own dreams will often find ways to discourage yours. Live your truth and don't EVER stop!
Steve Maraboli

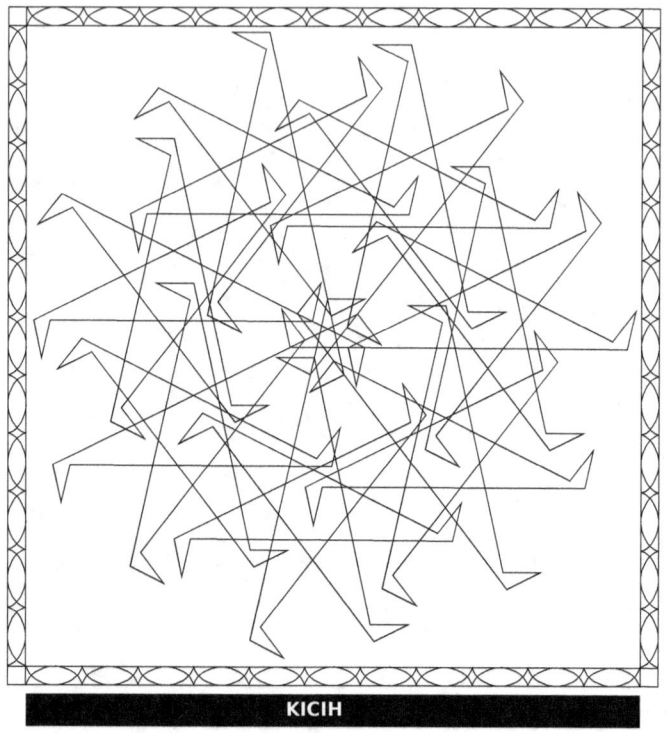

KICIH

Amending your own mind is very, very satisfying ... amending other people's minds is a fruitless, unsatisfying effort.
Richard Bergland

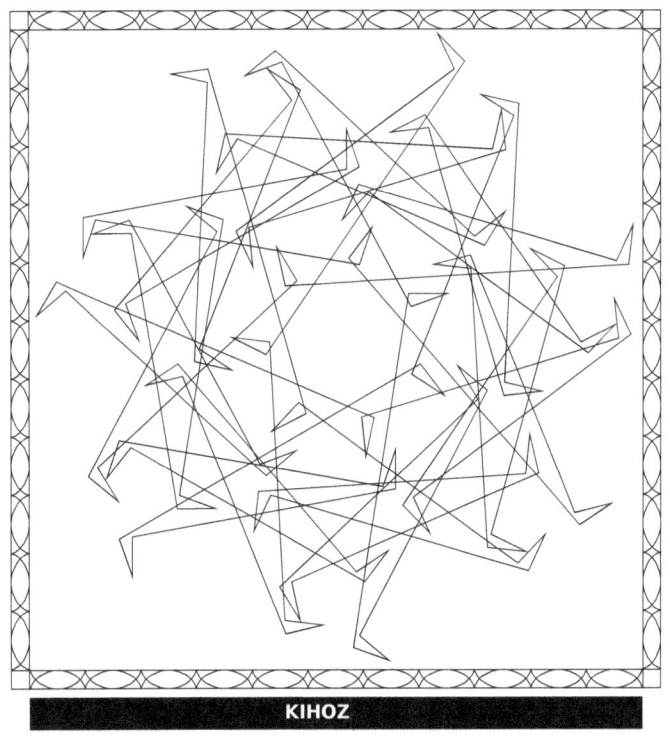

KIHOZ

A great truth is a truth whose opposite is also a truth.
Thomas Mann

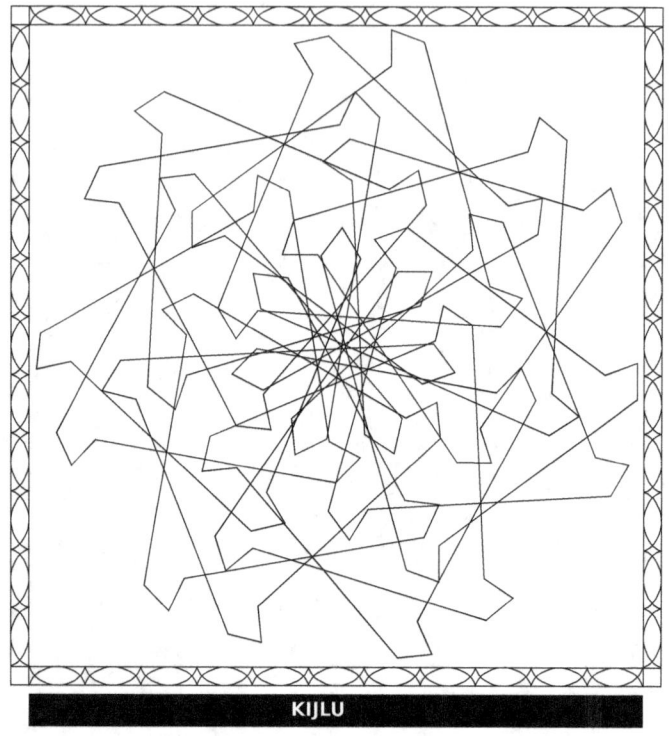

KIJLU

To love truth for truth's sake is the principal part of human perfection in this world, and the seed-plot of all other virtues.

John Locke

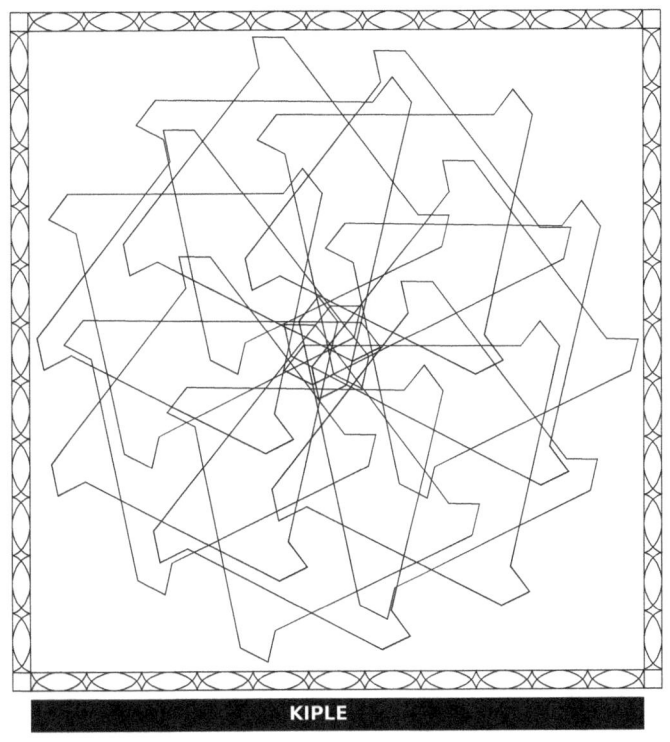

KIPLE

When a person expends the least amount of motion on one action, that is grace.
Anton Chekhov

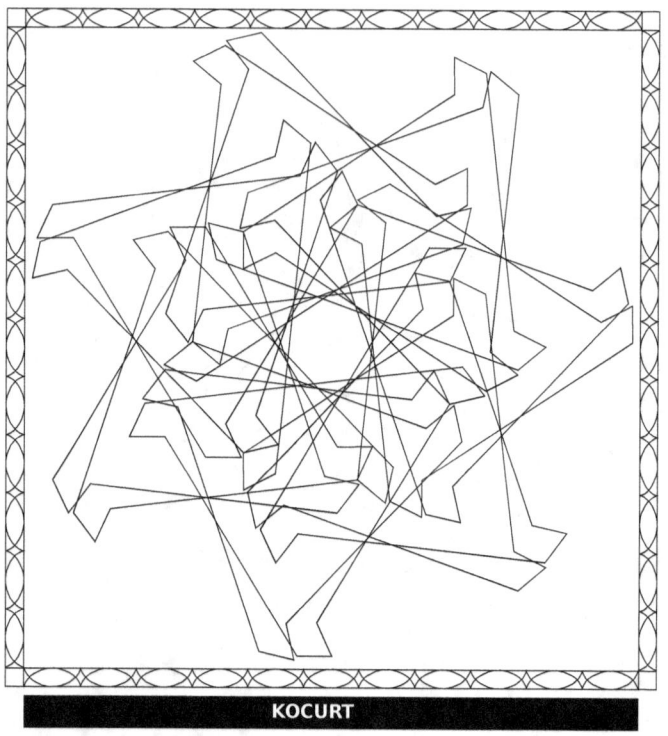

KOCURT

Let every man be occupied, and occupied in the highest employment of which his nature is capable, and die with the consciousness that he has done his best.
Sydney Smith

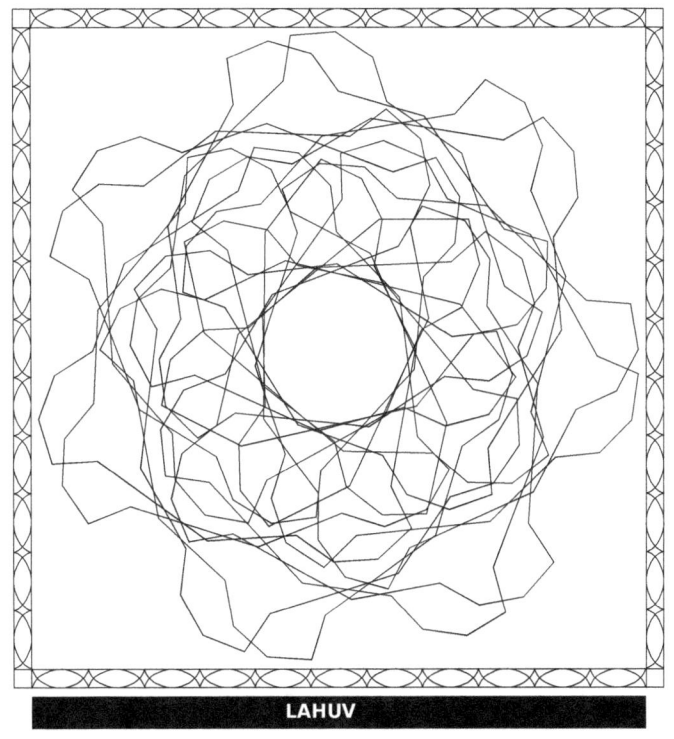

LAHUV

I feel awed by the mystery of being both so finite and yet so infinite, so much and so little, so conscious and yet, so coincidental.

Warren Farrell

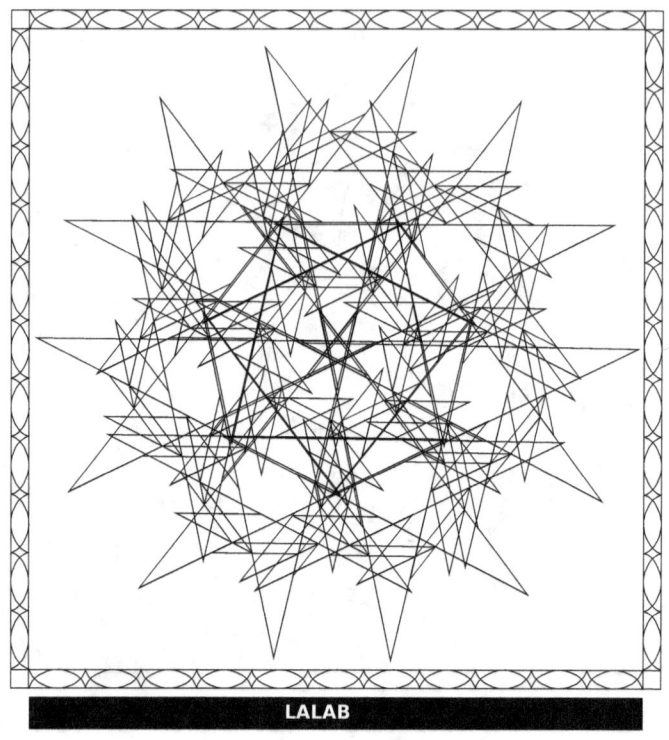

LALAB

Make your ego porous. Will is of little importance, complaining is nothing, fame is nothing. Openness, patience, receptivity, solitude is everything.
Rainer Maria Rilke

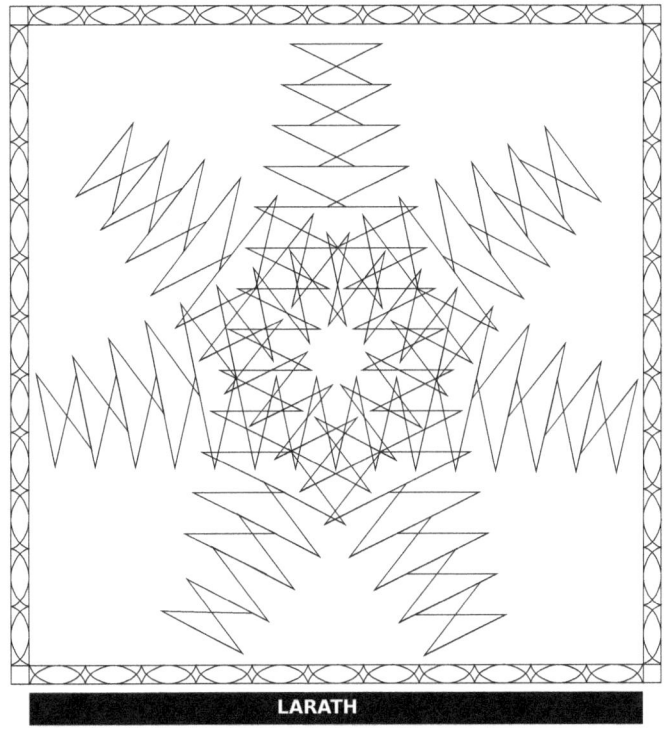

LARATH

In its pure and simple form religion is not often encountered today. It is almost as rare, indeed, as pure democracy or pure reason.

H. L. Mencken

141

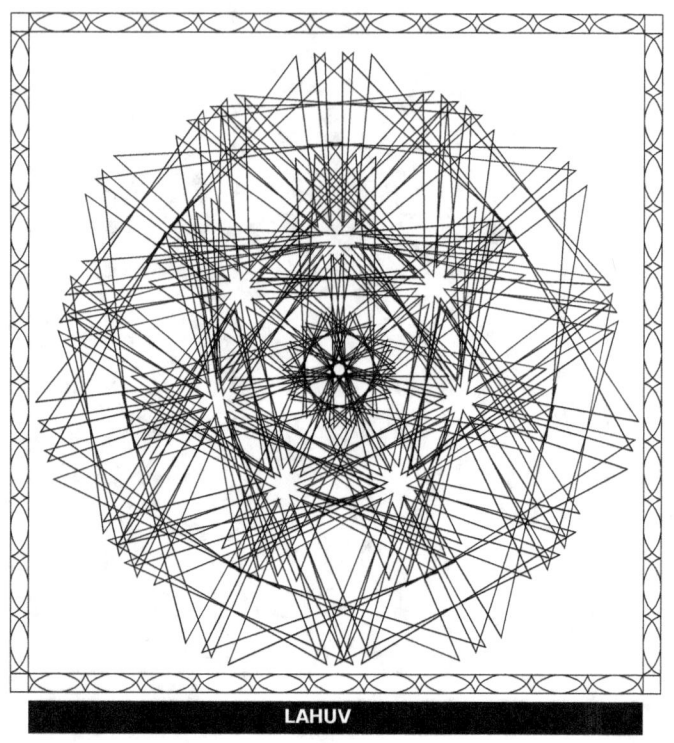

LAHUV

Represent your figures in such action as may be fitted to express what purpose is in the mind of each; otherwise your art will not be admirable.

Leonardo da Vinci

142

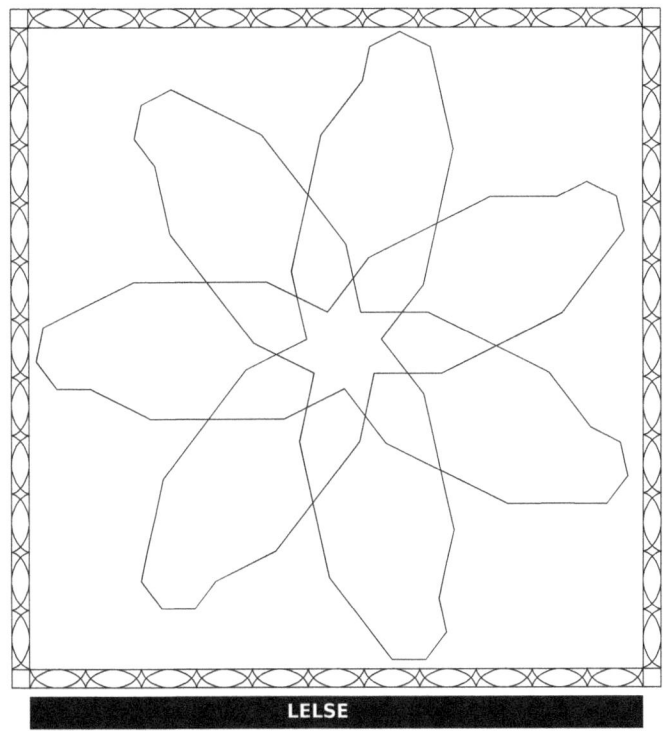

LELSE

Science intensifies religious truth by cleansing it of ignorance and superstition.
Charles Lindbergh

143

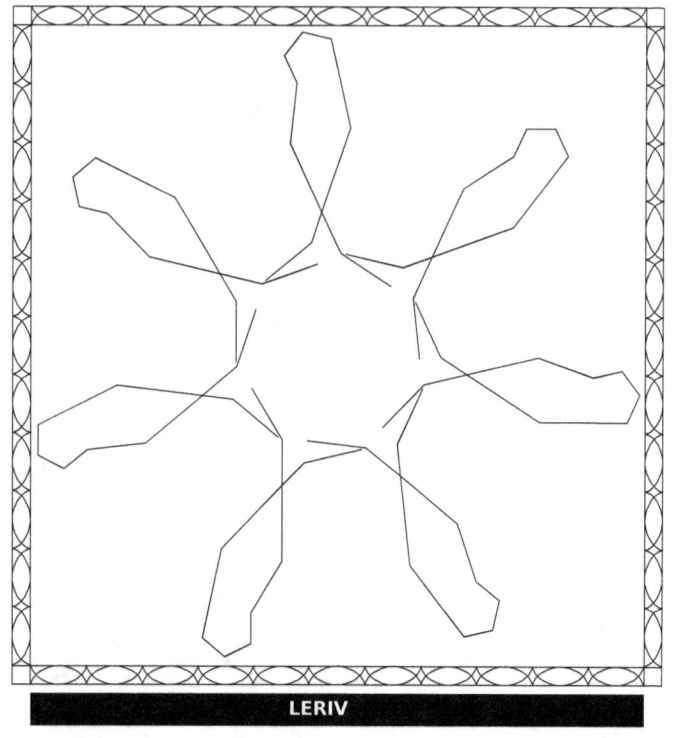

LERIV

All the things an artist must be: poet, explorer of nature, philosopher!
Paul Klee

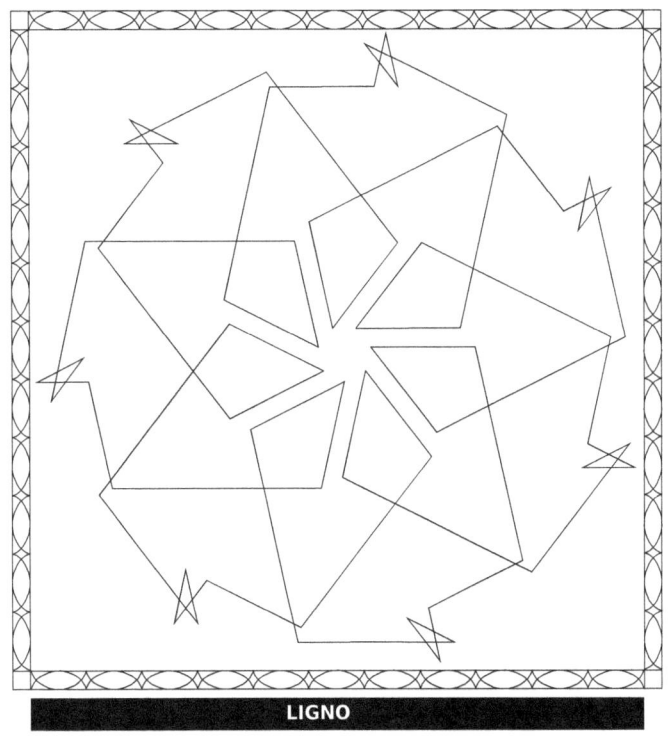

LIGNO

Inspiration is never genuine if it is known as inspiration at the time. True inspiration always steals on a person; its importance not being fully recognised for some time.
Samuel Butler

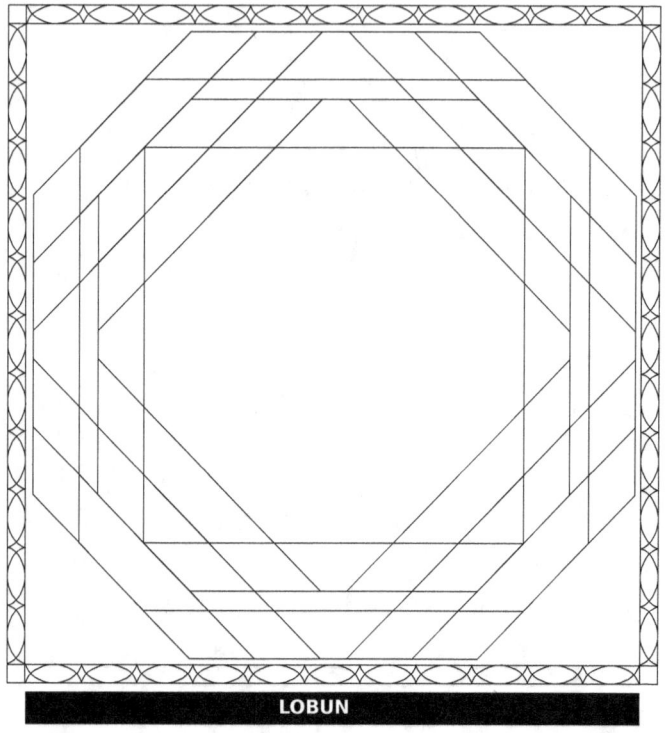

LOBUN

Fight the tendency to become complacent and do one kind
of music - that is the death of a musician.
Georg Solti

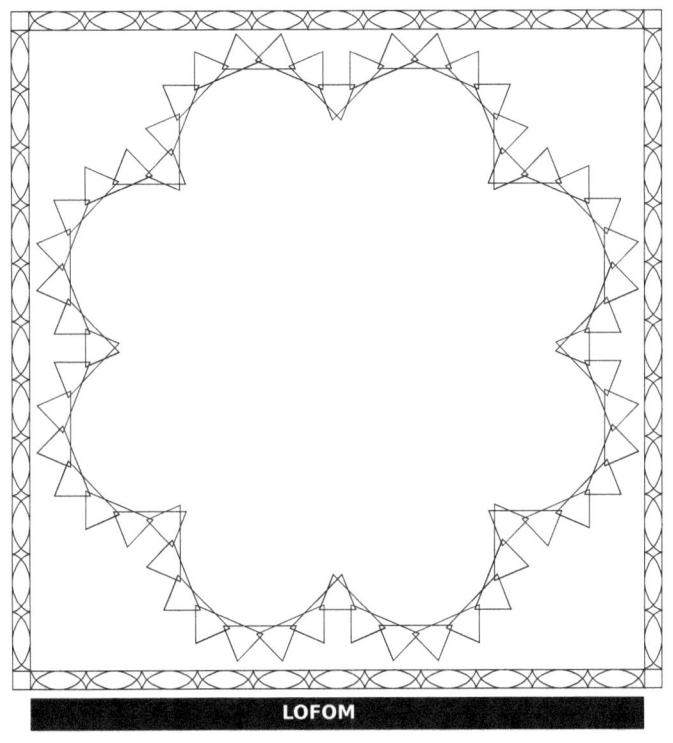

LOFOM

When the mind grasps the universe, the senses retreat.
Subhash Kak

147

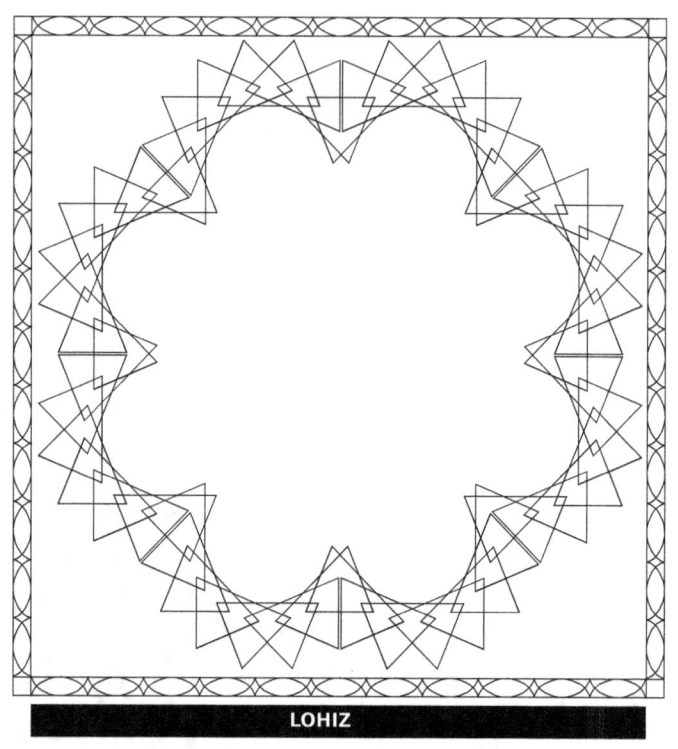

LOHIZ

Veganism has given me a higher level of awareness and spirituality.
Dexter Scott King

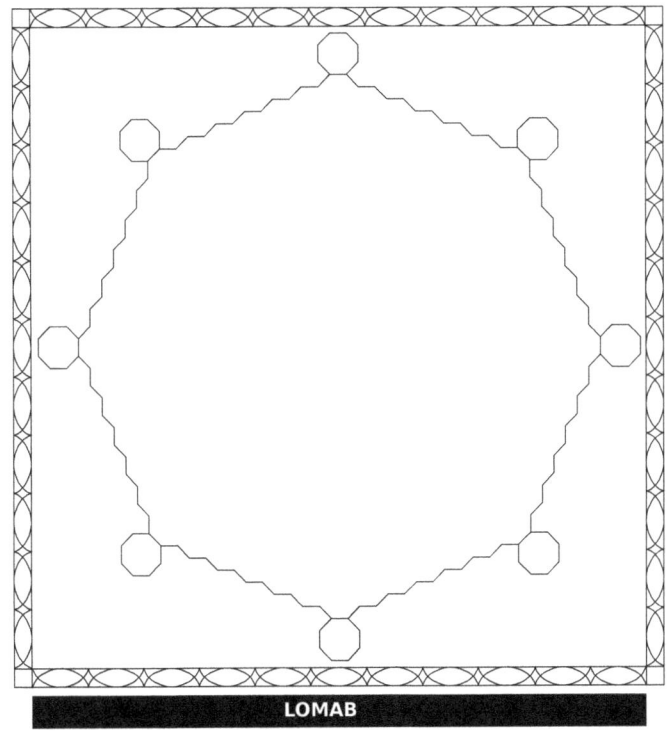

LOMAB

Fantasy is a higher form of art, indeed the most nearly pure form, and so (when achieved) the most potent.
J. R. R. Tolkien

149

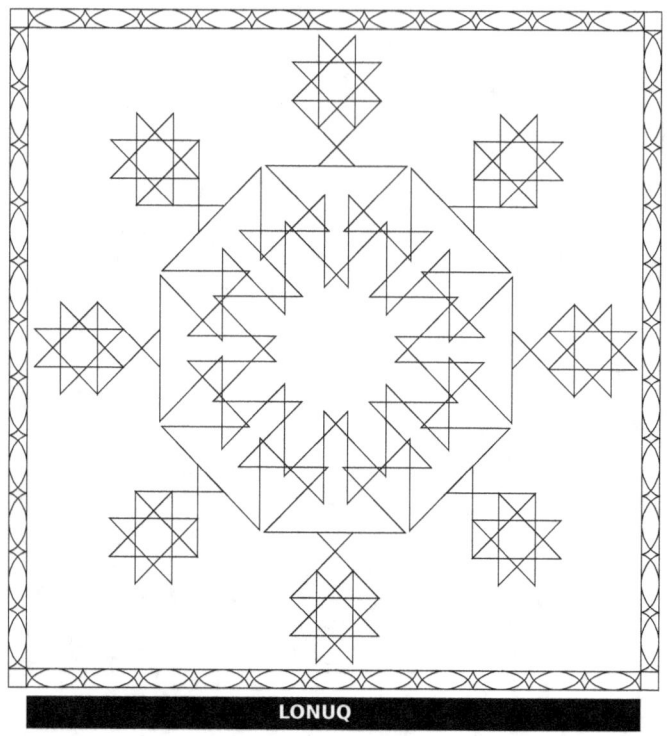

LONUQ

The abundance of our definitive words about God shows that we don't view him as a great mystery anymore, but as a sterile calculation without ambiguity or obscurity.
Skye Jethani

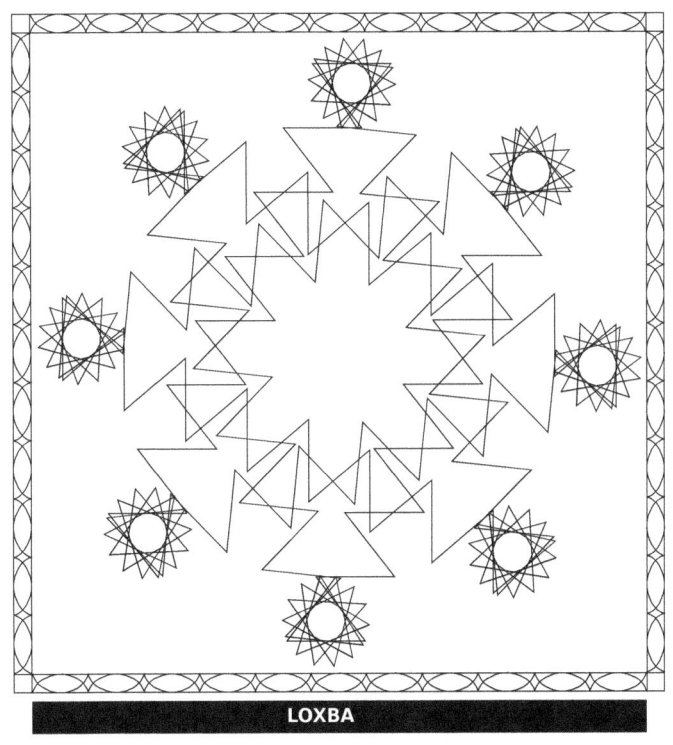

LOXBA

Let your mind alone, and see what happens.
Virgil Thomson

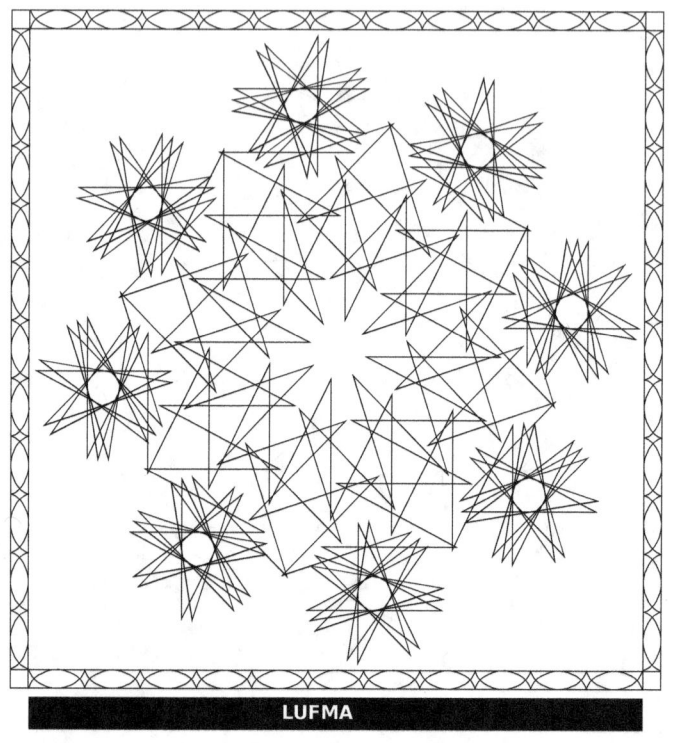

LUFMA

Can wealth give happiness? look round and see; What gay
distress! what splendid misery! Whatever fortunes lavishly
can pour, The mind annihilates, and calls for more.
Edward Young

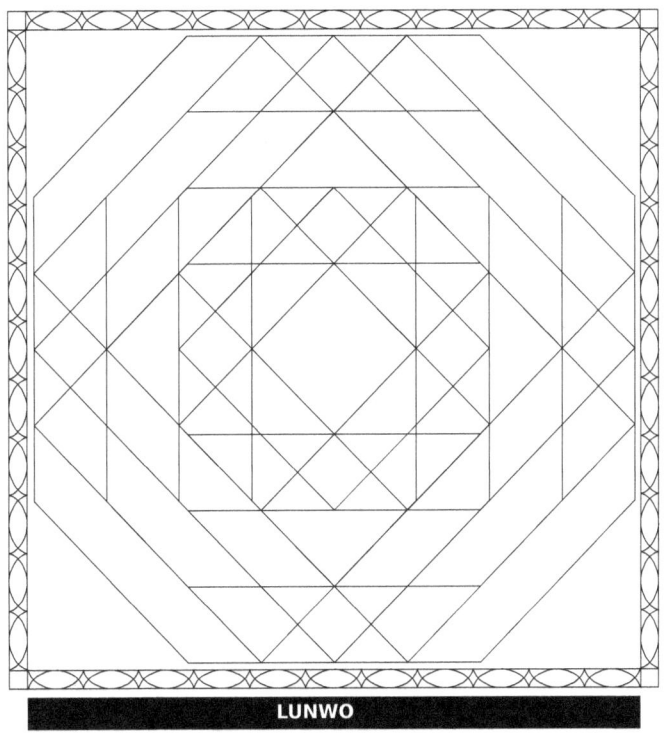

LUNWO

The earth has music for those who listen.
Reginald Vincent Holmes

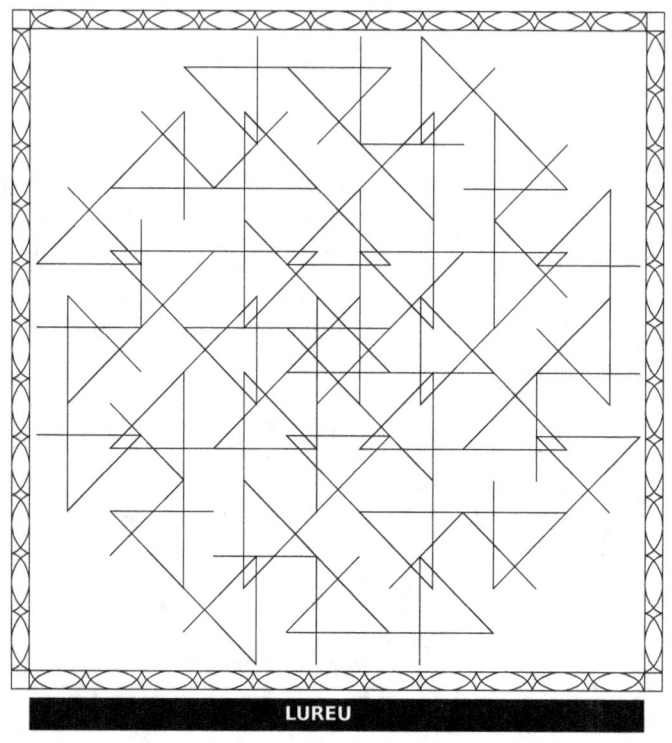

LUREU

I think there is a profound and enduring beauty in simplicity. In clarity. In efficiency. True simplicity is derived from
so much more than just the absence of clutter.
Jonathan Ive

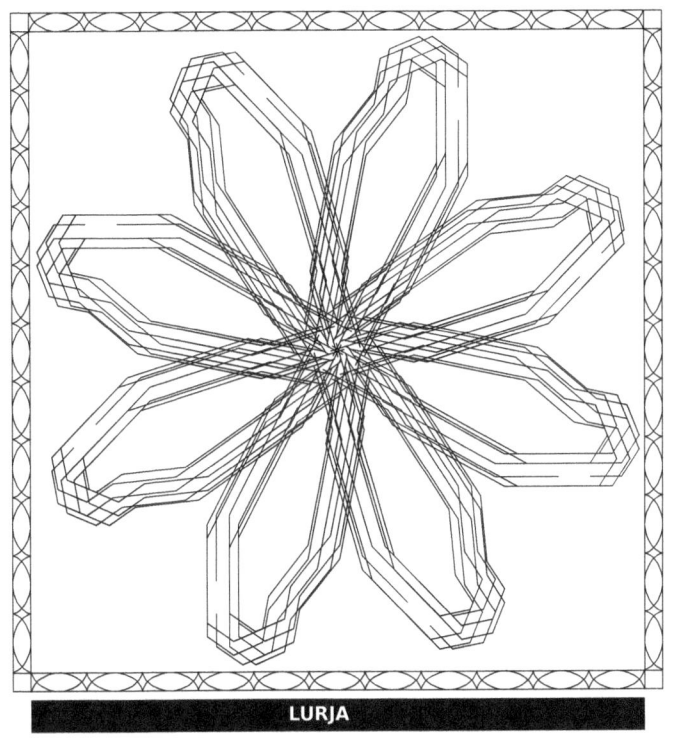

LURJA

When you suffer, think not on how you can escape suffering, but concentrate your efforts on what kind of inner moral and spiritual perfection this suffering requires.
Leo Tolstoy

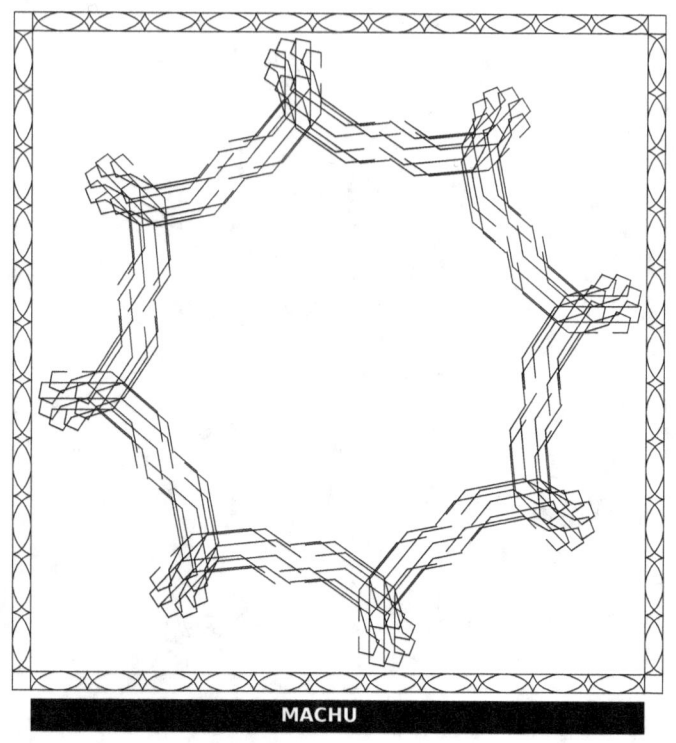

MACHU

Charms strike the sight, but merit wins the soul.
Alexander Pope

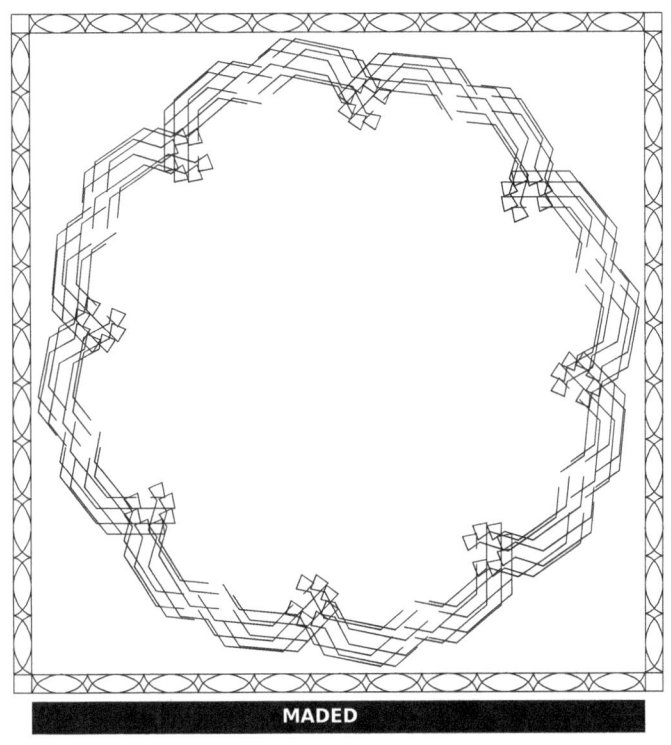

MADED

Dreams do not foretell the future. They reveal states of mind in which the future may be implicit.
Robertson Davies

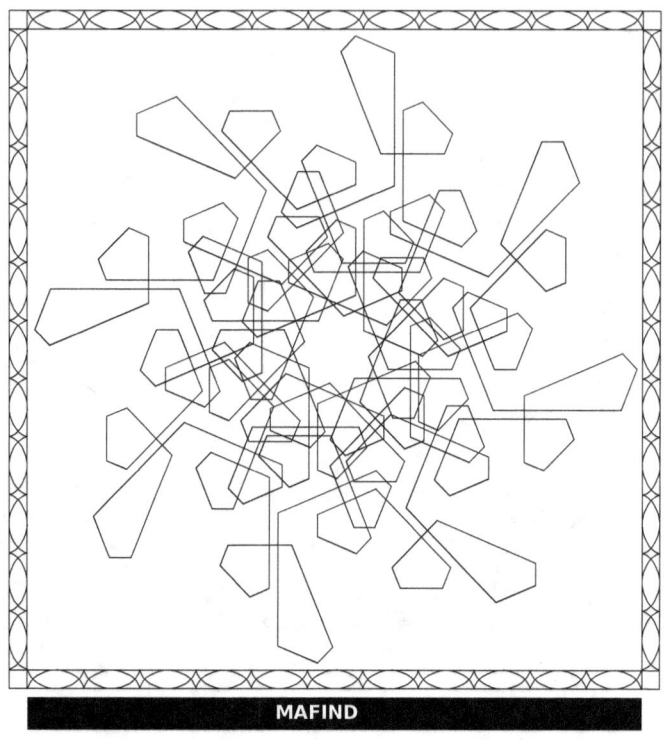

MAFIND

Seek goodness and be goodness. Seek beauty and be beauty.
Seek love and be love.
Bryant McGill

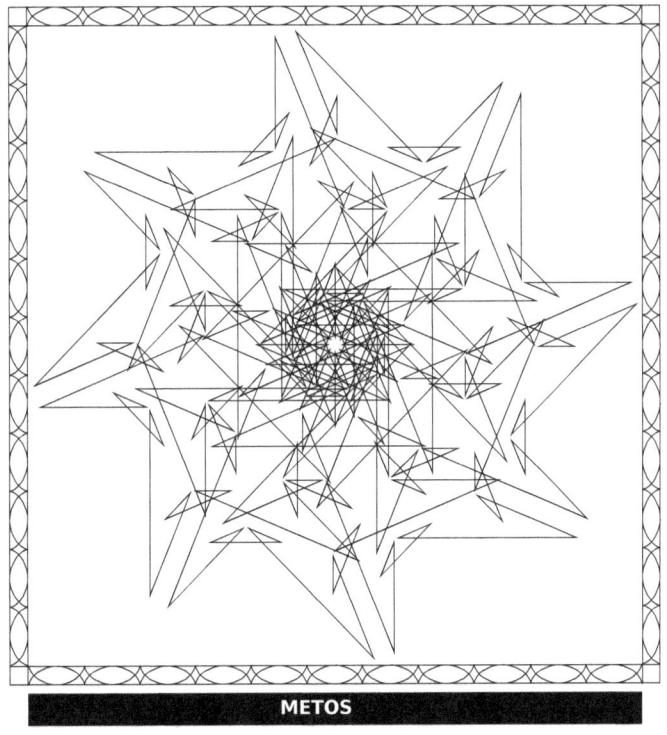

METOS

You know, there are two good things in life, freedom of
thought and freedom of action.
W. Somerset Maugham

159

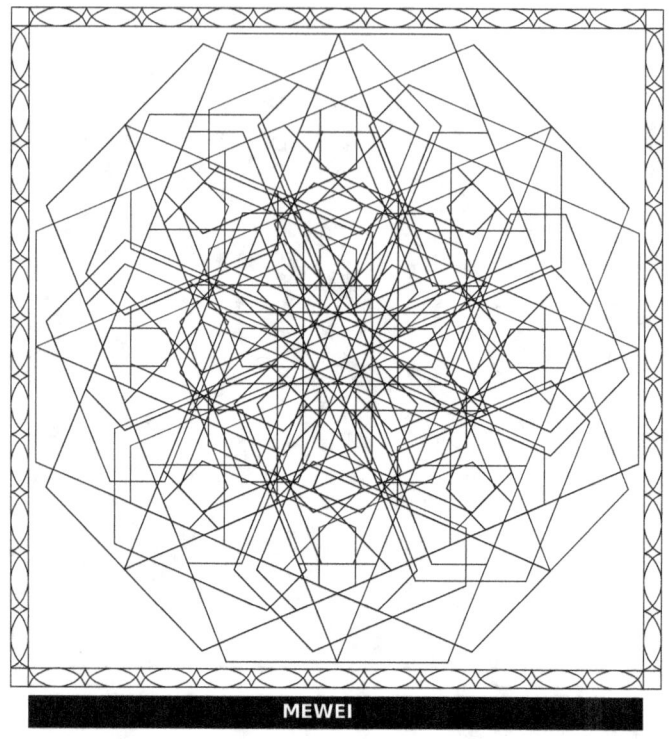

MEWEI

The form most contradictory to human life that can appear among the human species is the self-satisfied man.
Jos Ortega y Gasset

160

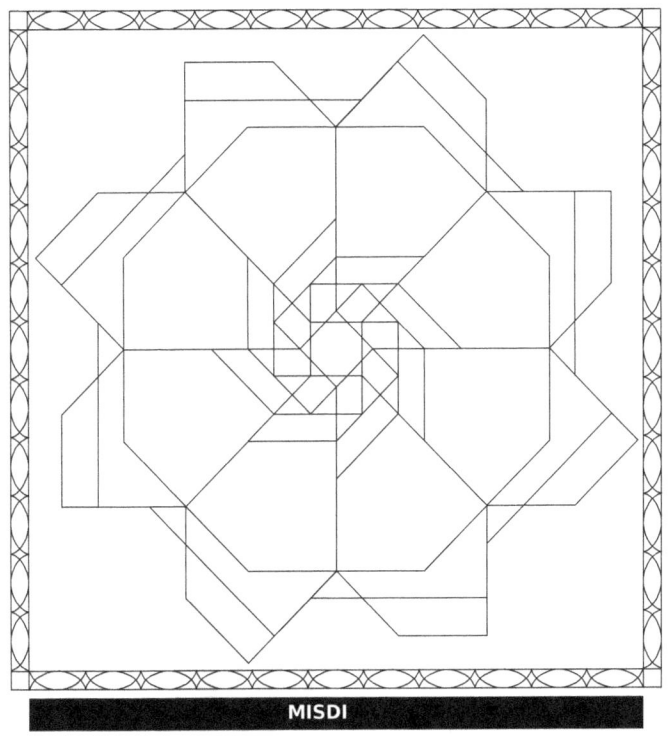

MISDI

Believe in no triumph which is won by the deadening of human faculty or the dwarfing of human life. Strive for truth and love, not for victory.
John Lancaster Spalding

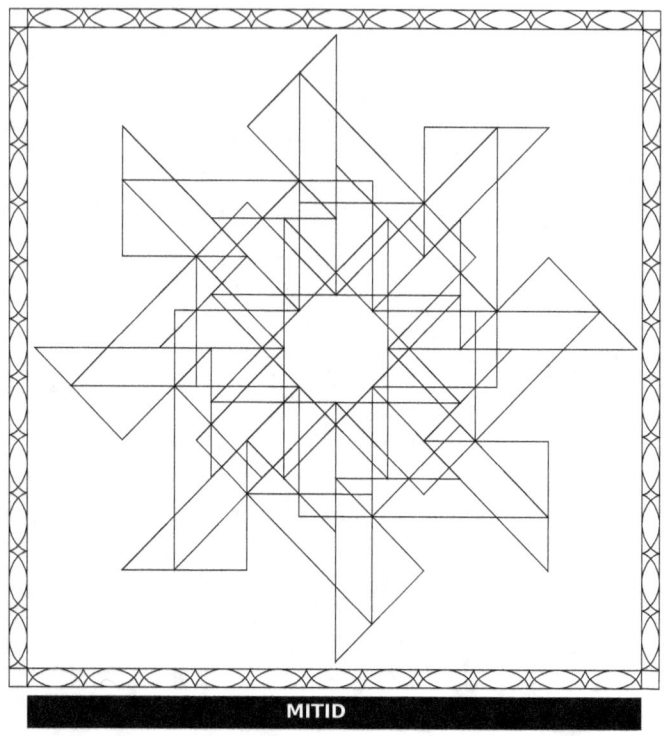

MITID

The awareness of imagery is part of living ... a life which
derives its power from within itself will focus on the perception ... of images.
Oskar Kokoschka

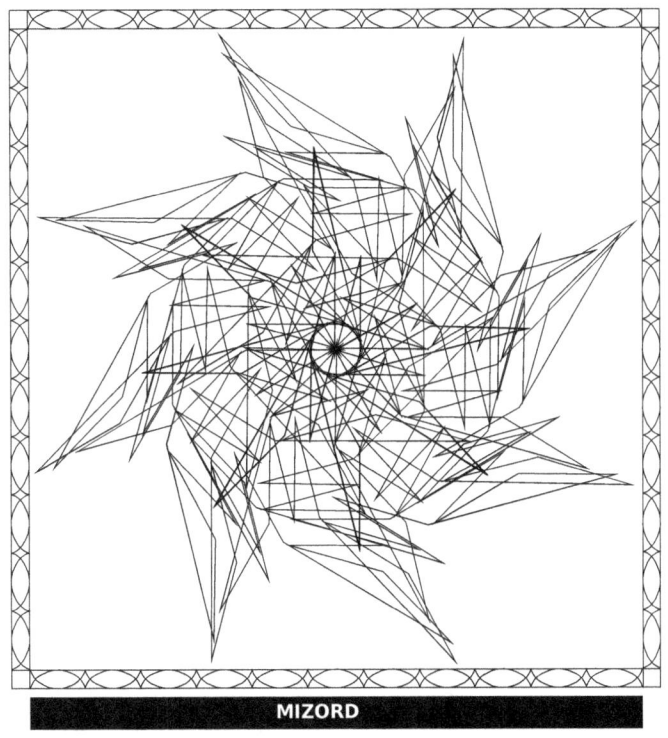

MIZORD

The human species, according to the best theory I can form of it, is composed of two distinct races, the men who borrow and the men who lend.
Charles Lamb

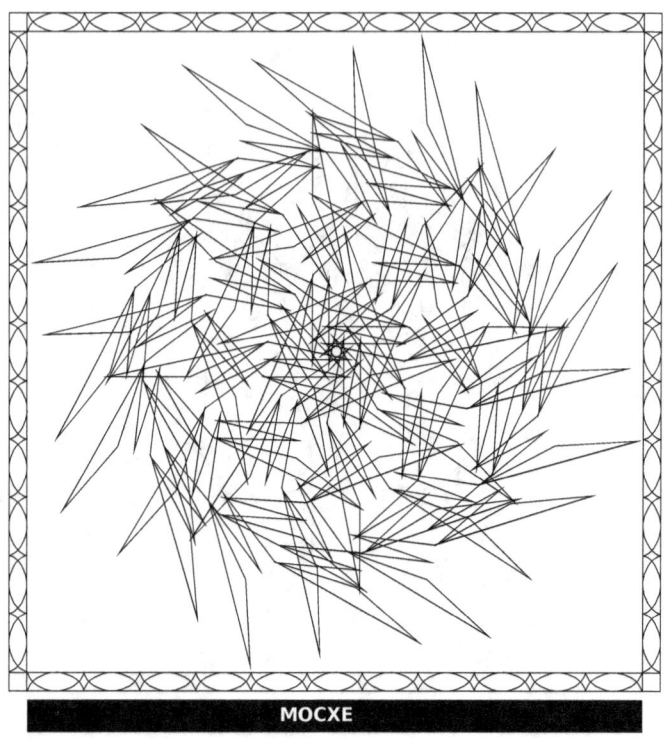

MOCXE

I always want to design a frame that's open to everyone. I don't see art as a secret code.
Ai Weiwei

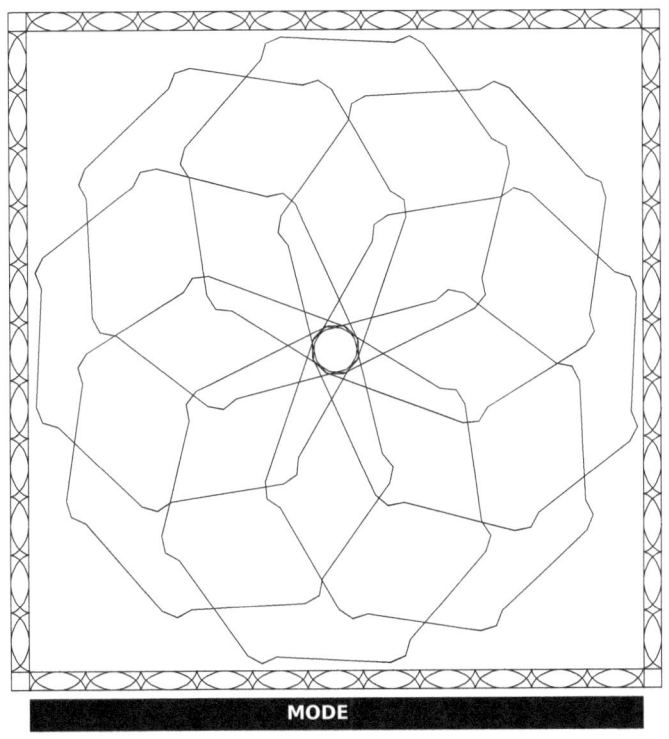

MODE

Nothing has such power to broaden the mind as the ability to investigate systematically and truly all that comes under thy observation in life.
Marcus Aurelius

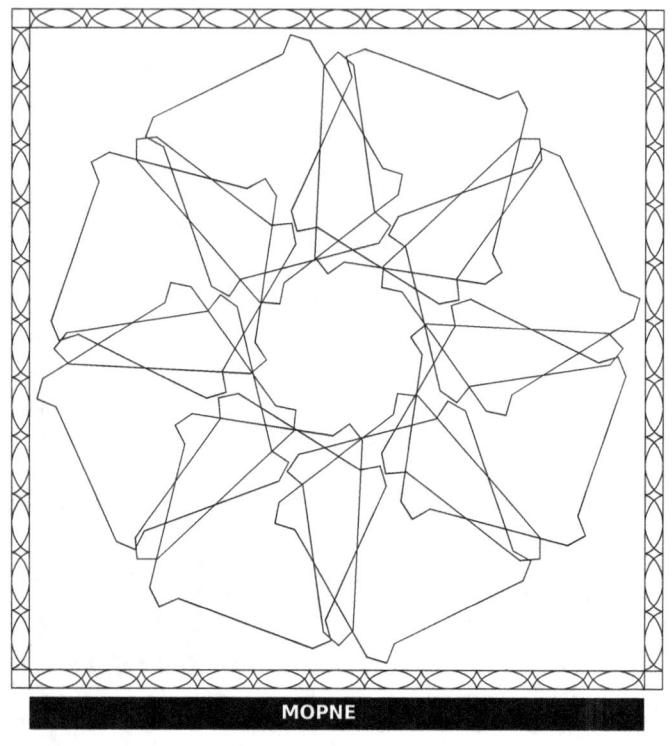

MOPNE

So long as the human spirit thrives on this planet, music in some living form will accompany and sustain it.
Aaron Copland

166

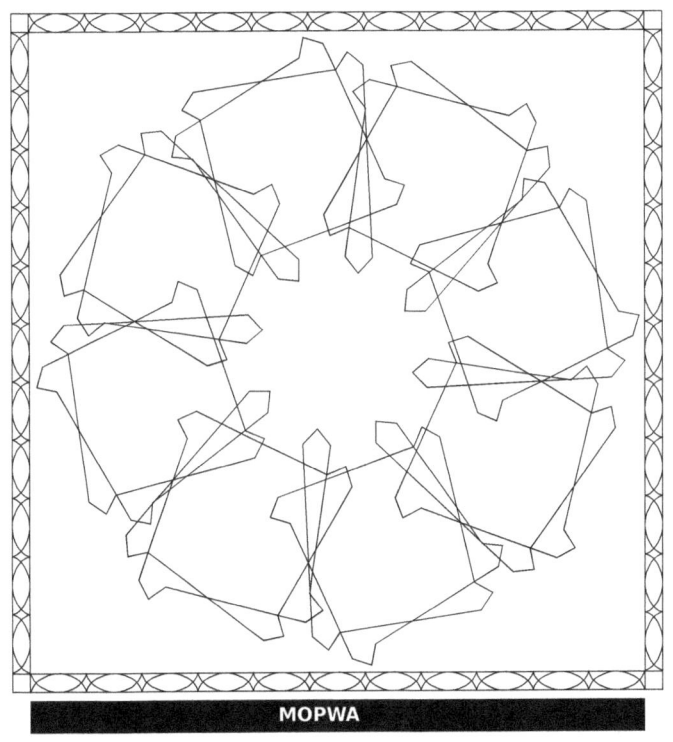

MOPWA

I read the newspapers avidly. It is my one form of continuous fiction.

Aneurin Bevan

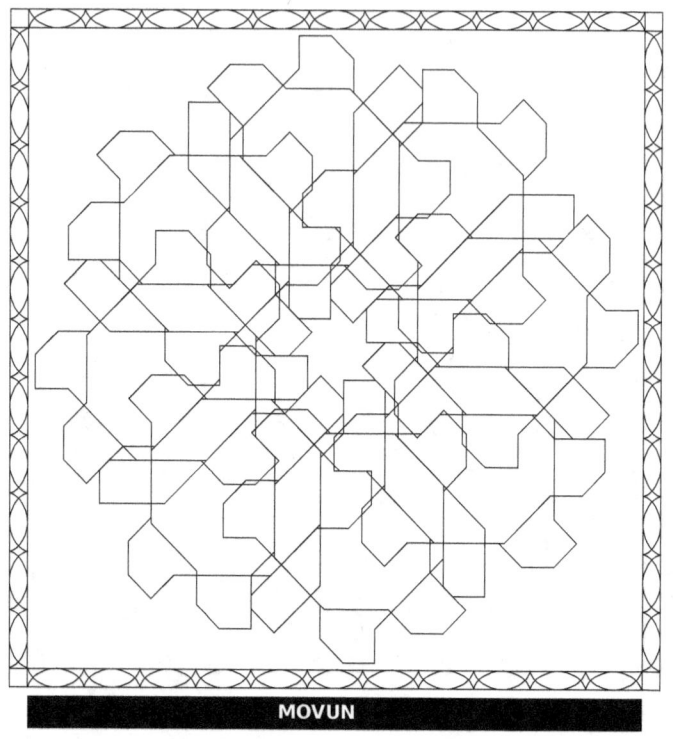

MOVUN

Don't put the key to your happiness in someone else's pocket.

Chinmayananda Saraswati

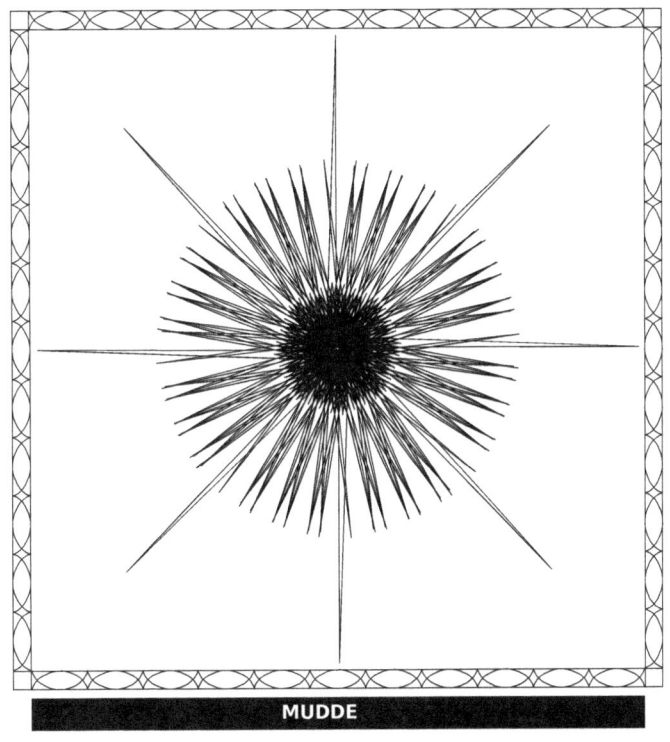

MUDDE

Free yourself from the complexities of your life! A life of simplicity and happiness awaits you.
Steve Maraboli

169

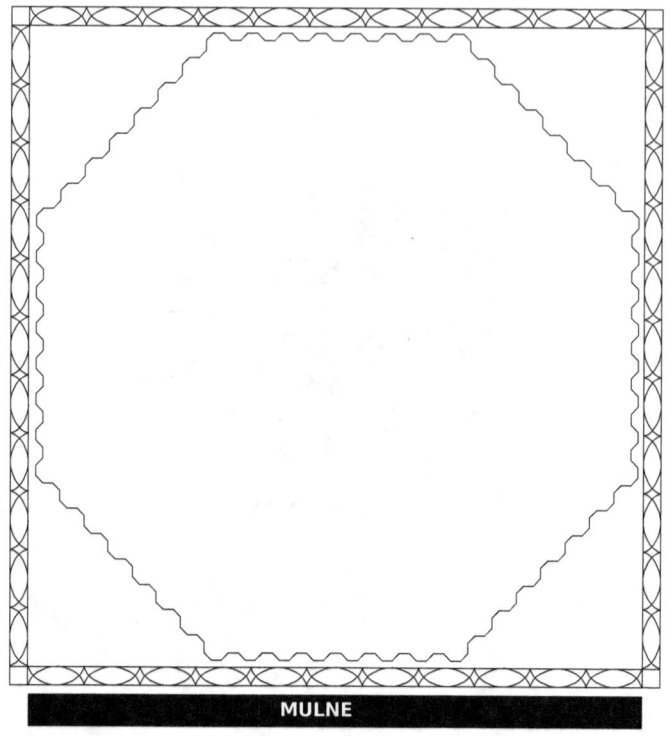

MULNE

Get yourself out of whatever cage you find yourself in.
John Cage

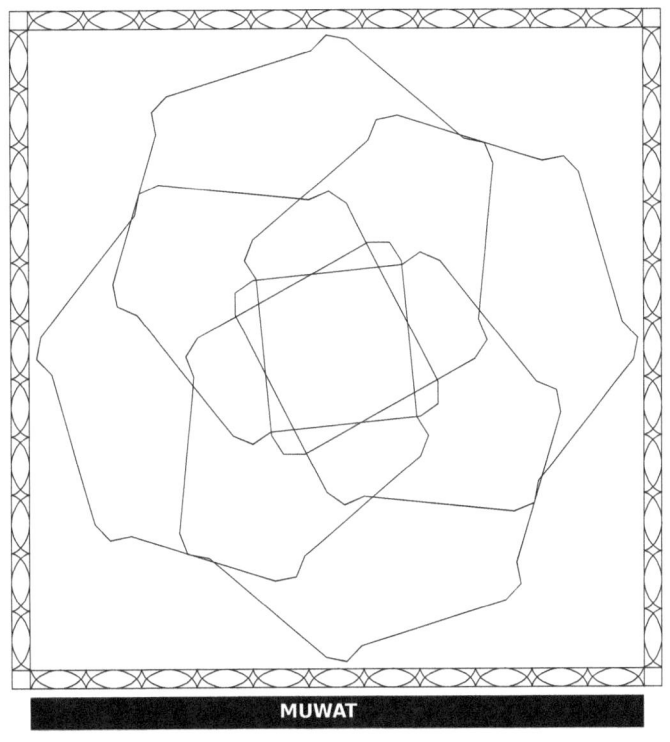

MUWAT

Beauty is one in the universe, and, whatever form it assumes, it always arouses a religious feeling in the hearts of mankind.

Anne Louise Germaine de Stal

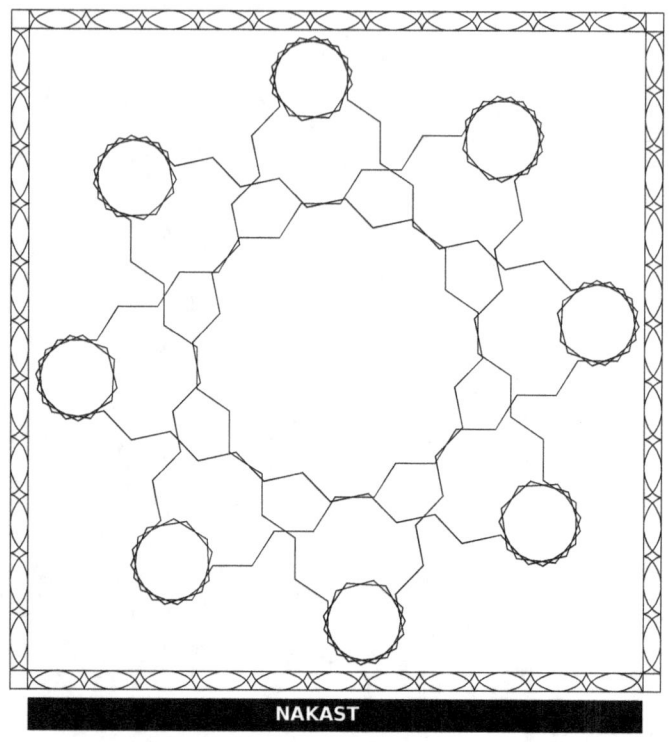

NAKAST

I can't understand why people are frightened of new ideas.
I'm frightened of the old ones.
John Cage

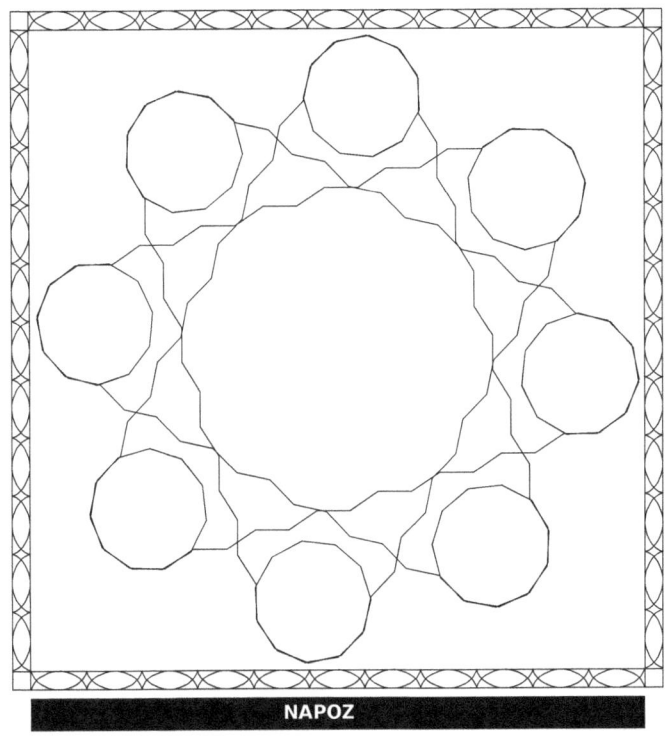

NAPOZ

Life - a culmination of the past, an awareness of the present, an indication of a future beyond knowledge, the quality that gives a touch of divinity to matter.
Charles Lindbergh

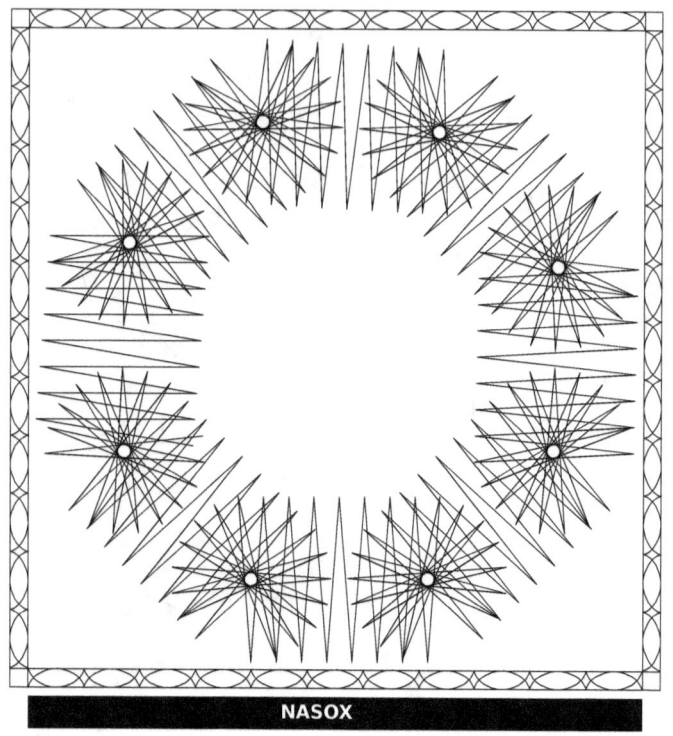

NASOX

Surely it is more interesting to argue about what the truth is, than about what some particular thinker, however great, did or did not think.

David Deutsch

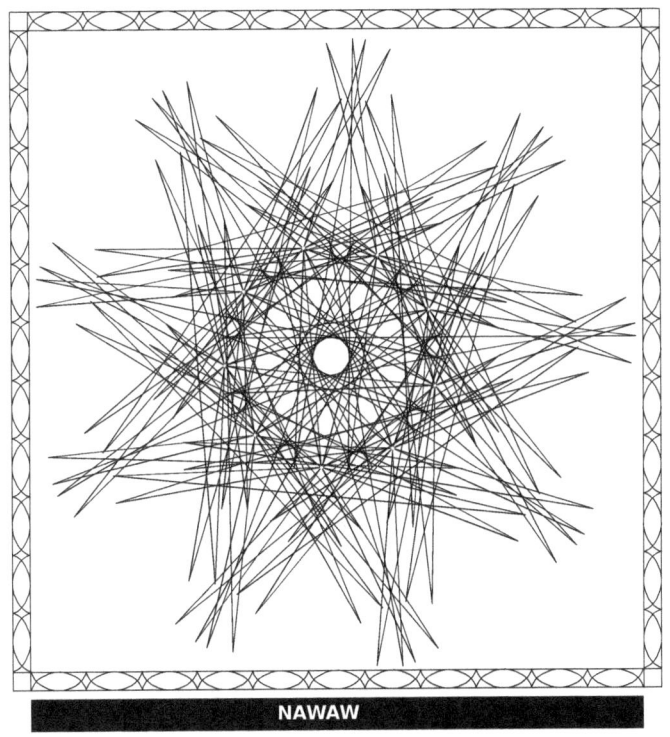

NAWAW

Anger is the most useless emotion; destructive to the mind
and hurtful of the heart.
Stephen King

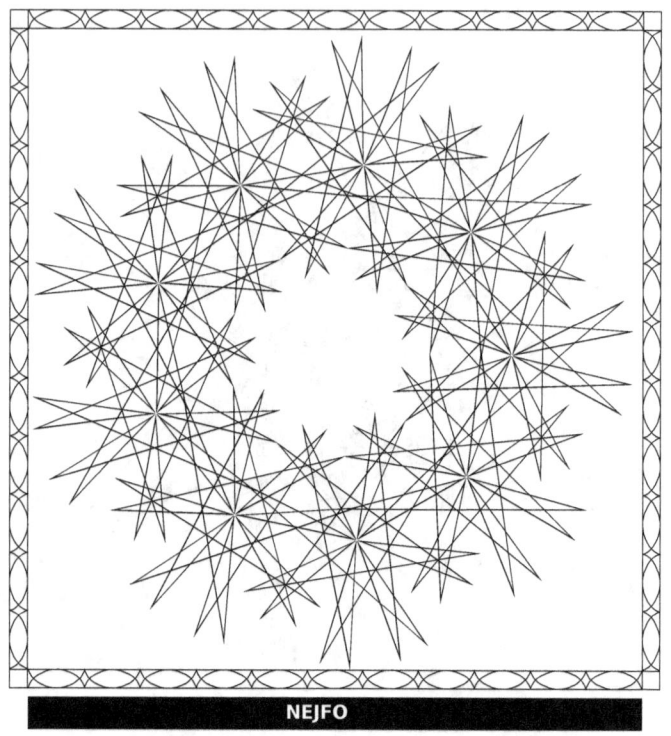

NEJFO

The search for truth is more precious than its possession.
Albert Einstein

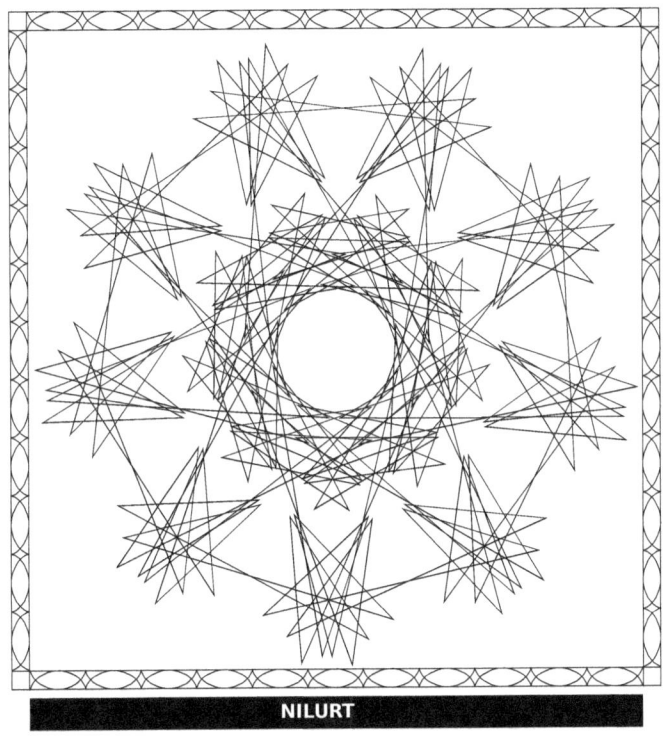

NILURT

They who know the truth are not equal to those who love it, and they who love it are not equal to those who delight in it.

Confucius

177

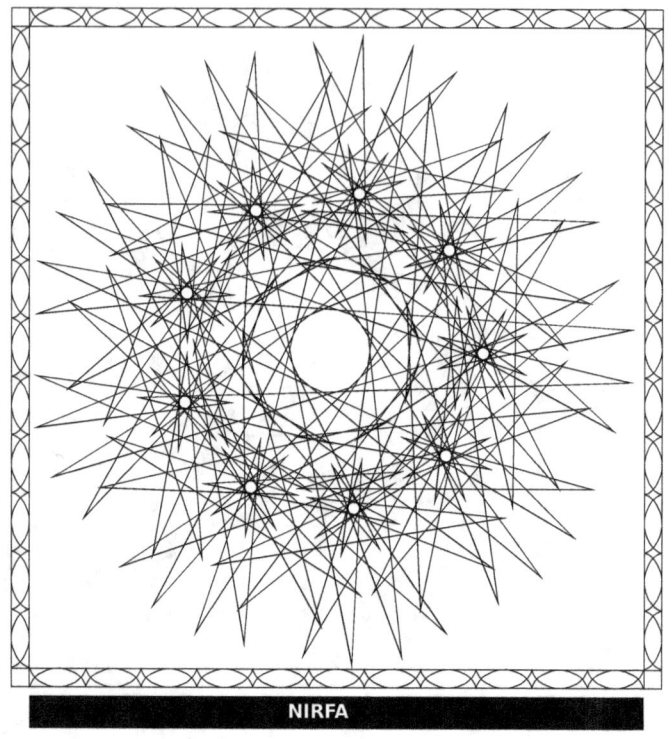

NIRFA

If art reflects life, it does so with special mirrors.
Bertolt Brecht

178

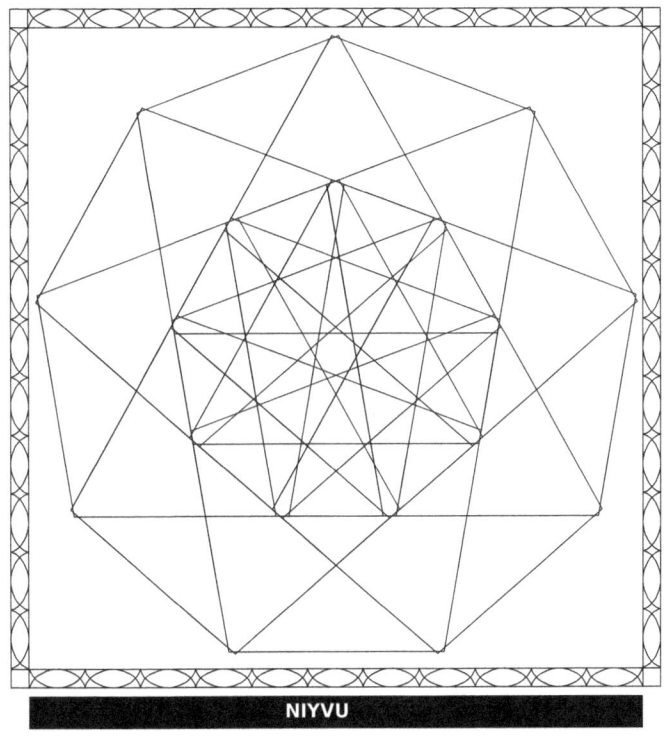

NIYVU

Now happiness consists in activity: such is the constitution of our nature: it is a running stream, and not a stagnant pool.

John Mason Good

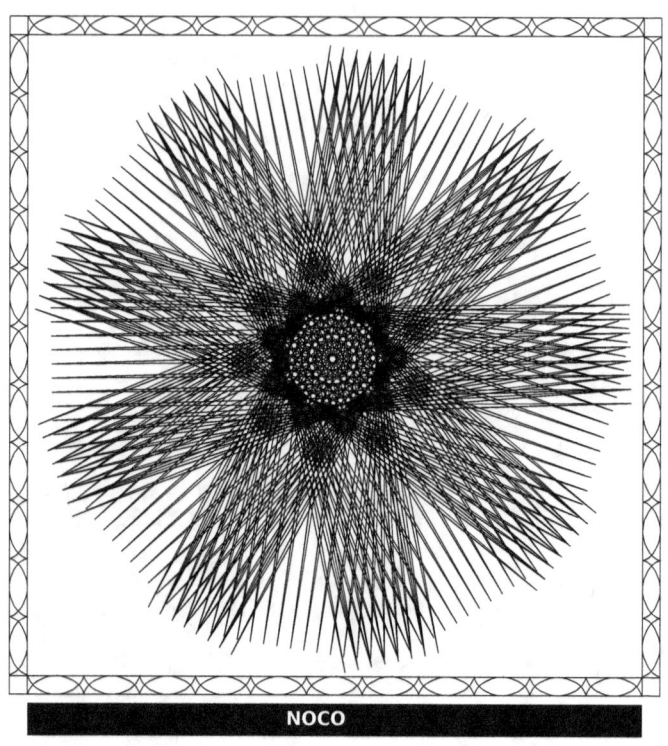

NOCO

Common sense is nothing more than a deposit of prejudices laid down by the mind before you reach eighteen.
Albert Einstein

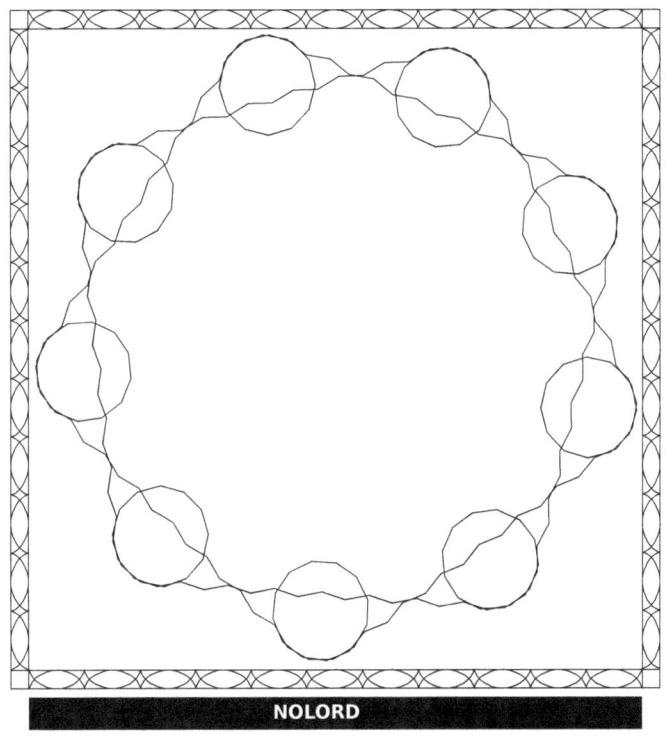

NOLORD

I don't know whether I believe in God or not. I think, really, I'm some kind of a Buddhist. But the essential thing is to put oneself in a frame of mind which is close to that of prayer.
Henri Matisse

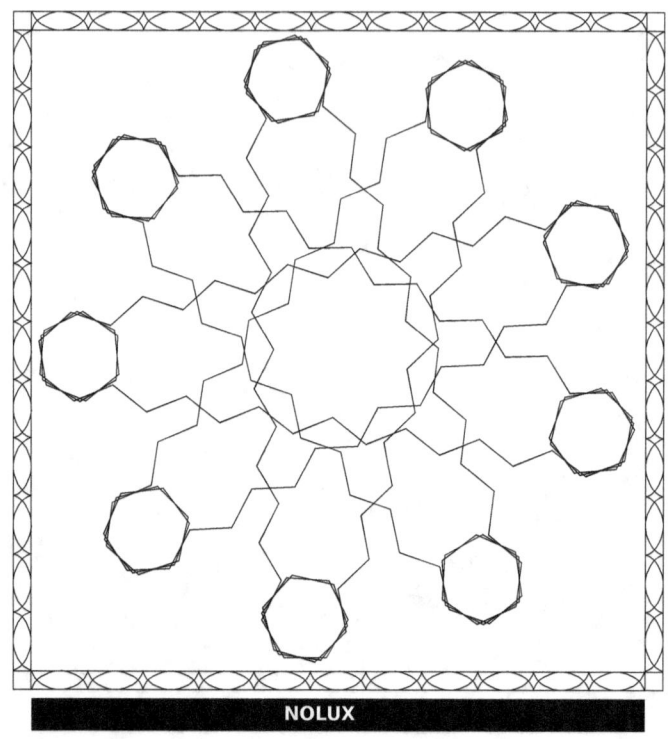

NOLUX

Let pride go afore, shame will follow after.
George Chapman

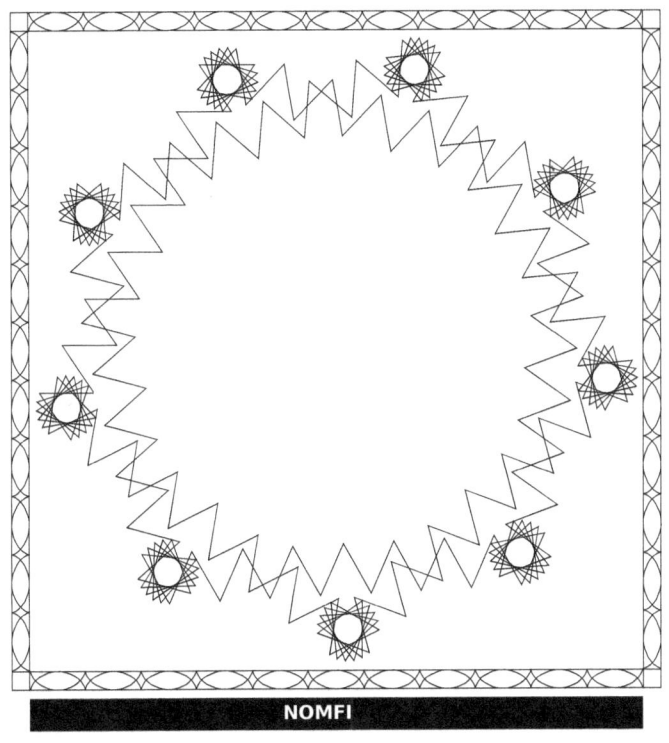

NOMFI

The truth is the kindest thing we can give folks in the end.
Harriet Beecher Stowe

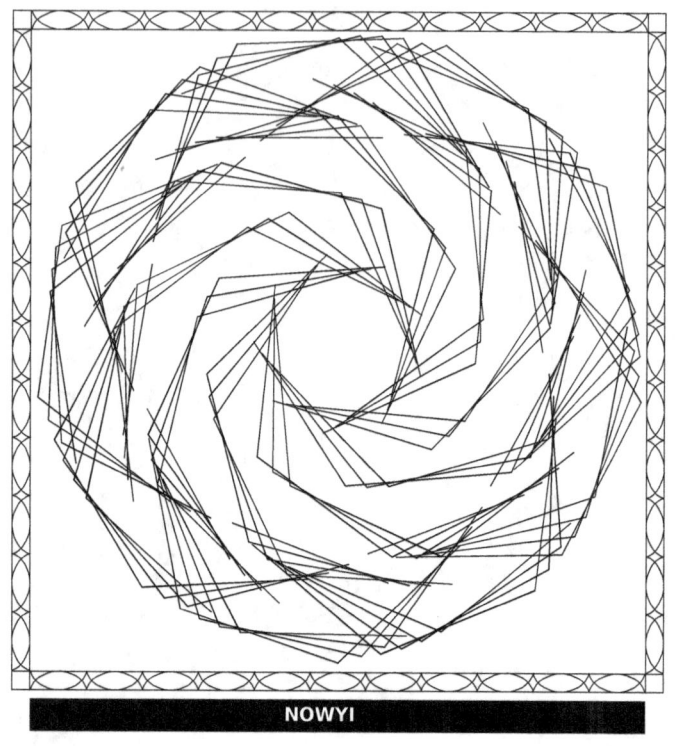

NOWYI

All great art has madness, and quite a lot of bad art has it, too.
William Saroyan

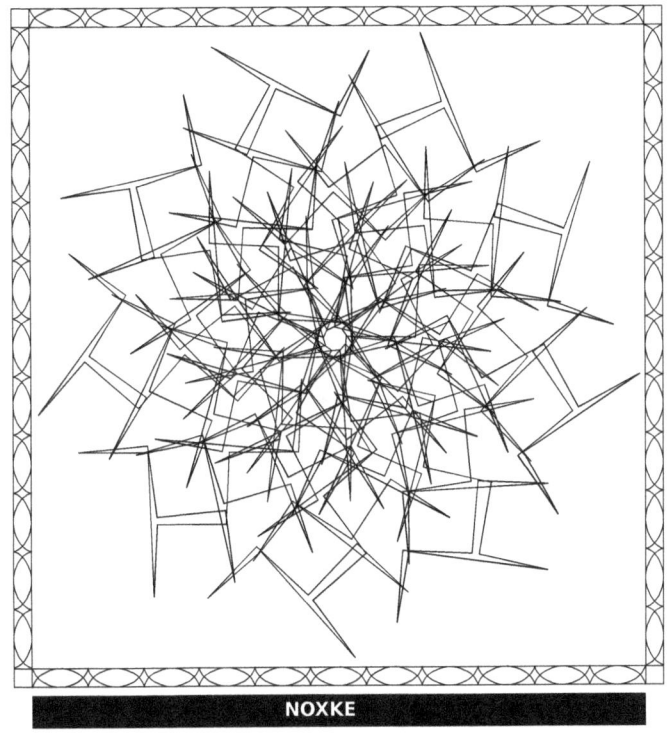

NOXKE

God only pours out his light into the mind after having subdued the rebellion of the will by an altogether heavenly gentleness which charms and wins it.
Blaise Pascal

185

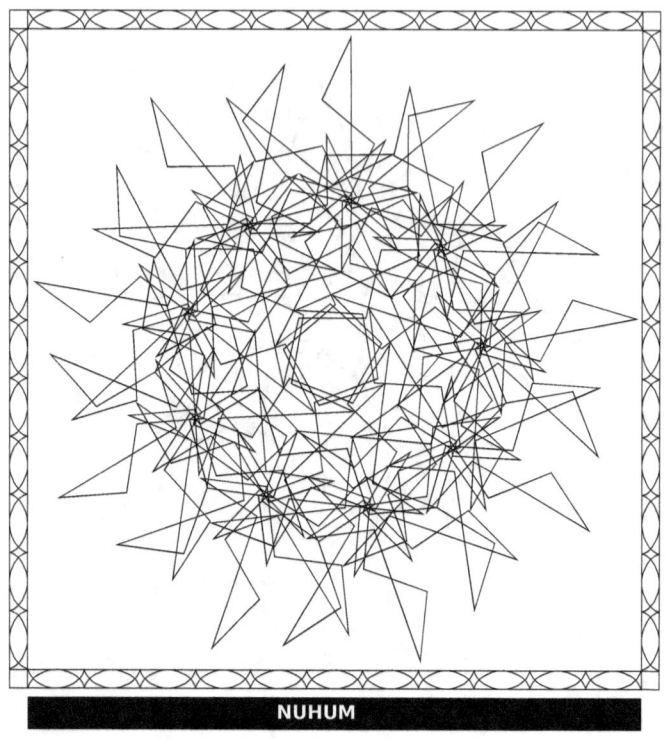

NUHUM

A weak mind is like a microscope, which magnifies trifling things but cannot receive great ones.
G. K. Chesterton

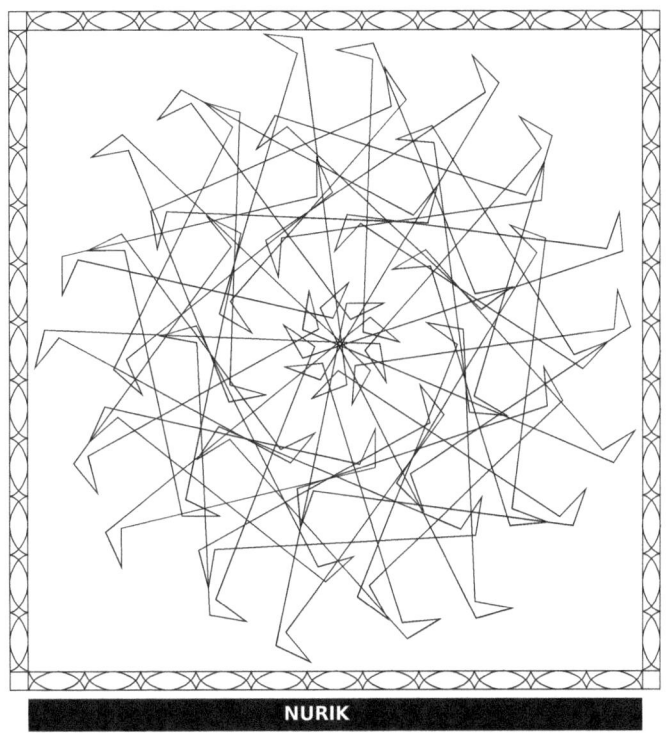

NURIK

The highest form of grace is silence.
Chinmayananda Saraswati

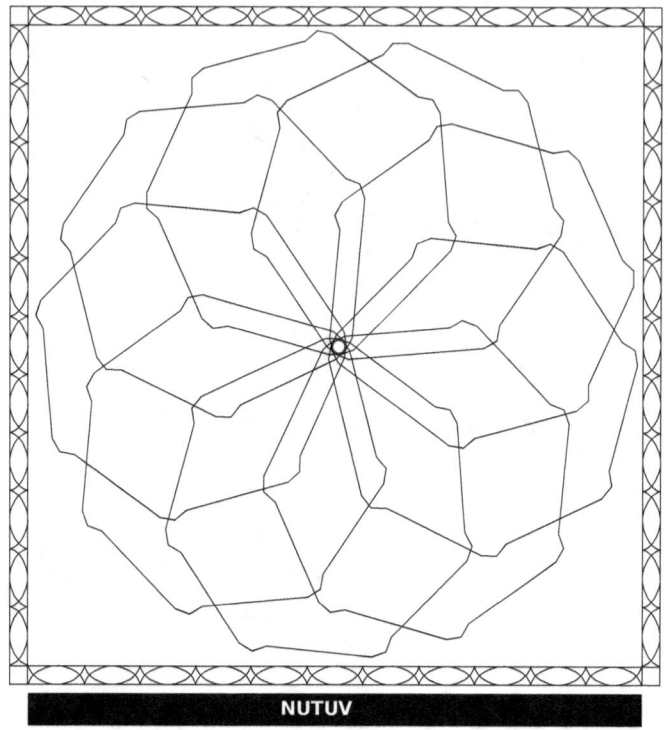

NUTUV

An artist can't produce great art unless he has a philoso-
phy. He can't say something unless he has something to
say.

L. S. Lowry

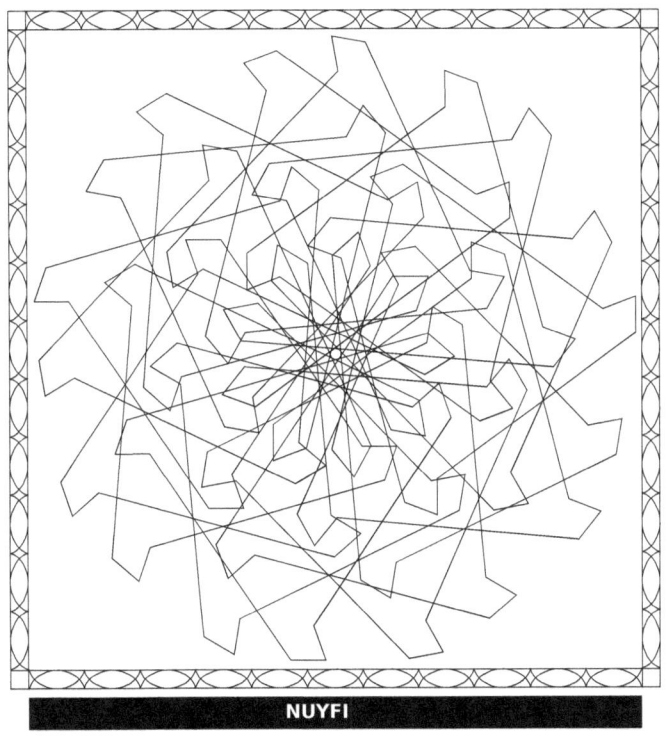

NUYFI

The greatest happiness you can have is knowing that you do not necessarily require happiness.

William Saroyan

189

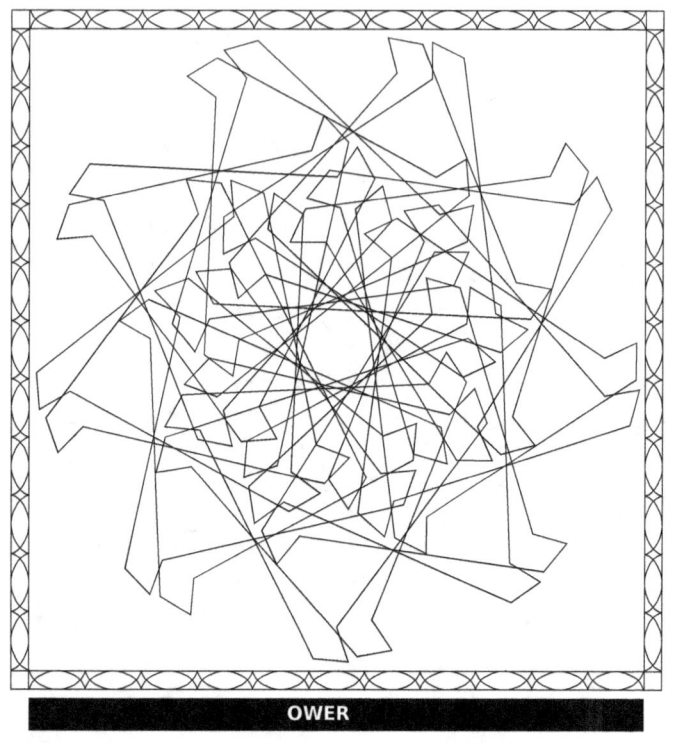

OWER

In happiness and suffering, in joy and grief, we should regard all creatures as we regard our own self.
Mahavira

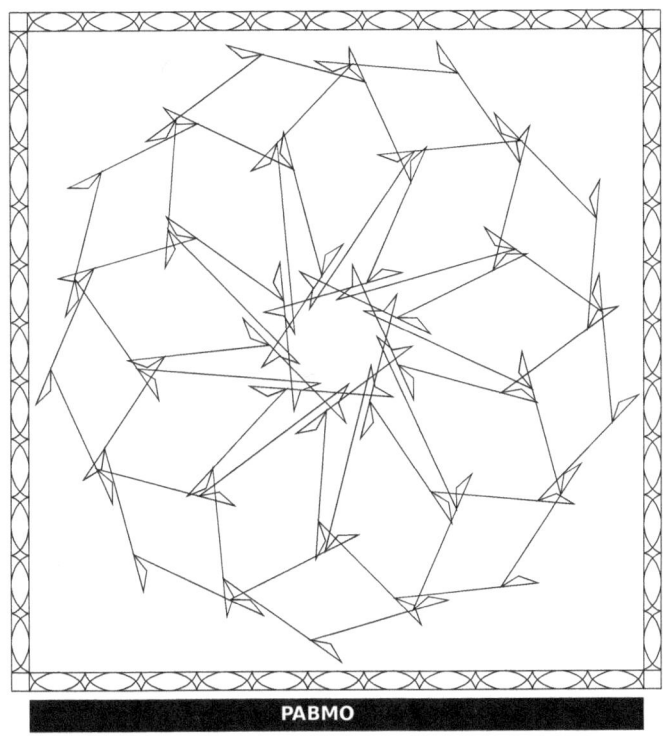

PABMO

Just because Beethoven doesn't sound like currently pop-
ular art doesn't mean his music is worthless.
John Varley

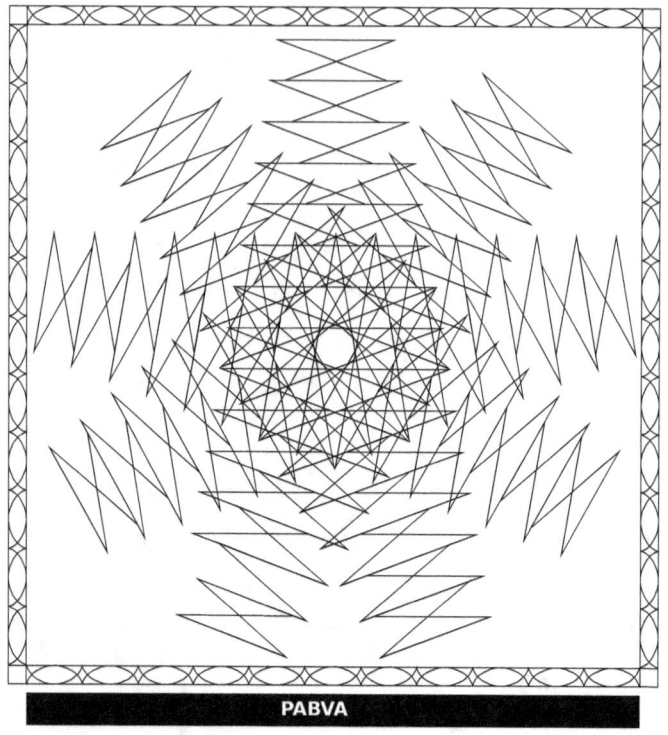

PABVA

The academic mind reflects infinity, and is full of light by the simple process of being shallow and standing still.
G. K. Chesterton

192

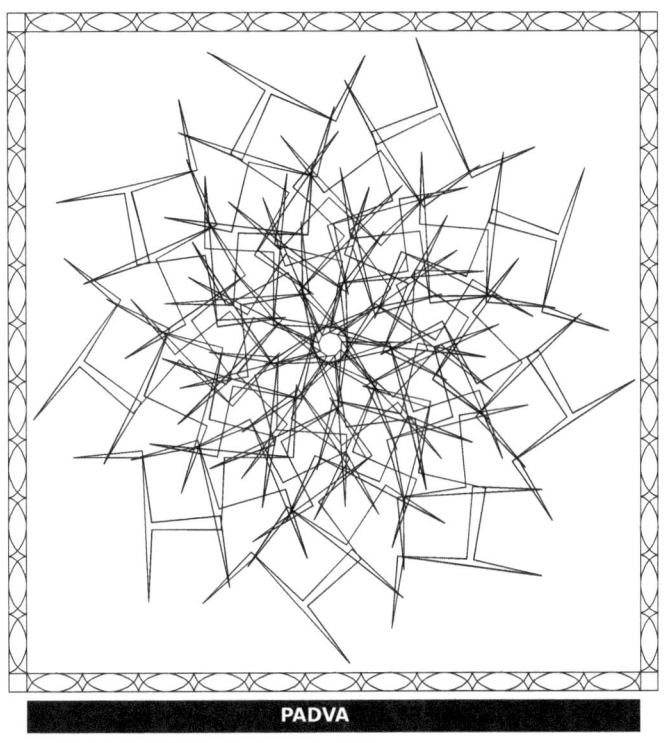

PADVA

The awareness of the relationship between the self and the
world is precisely what breaks down in anxiety.
Rollo May

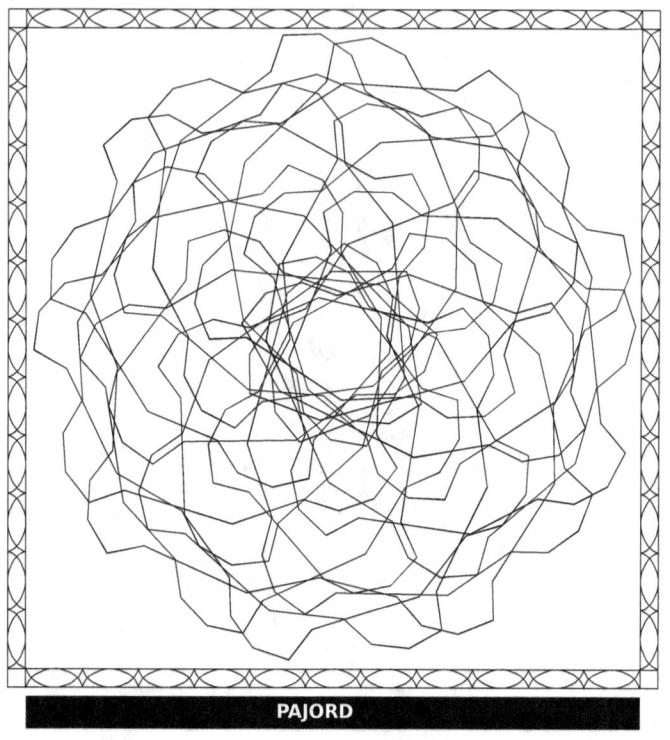

PAJORD

He that sympathizes in all the happiness of others, perhaps himself enjoys the safest happiness.

Charles Caleb Colton

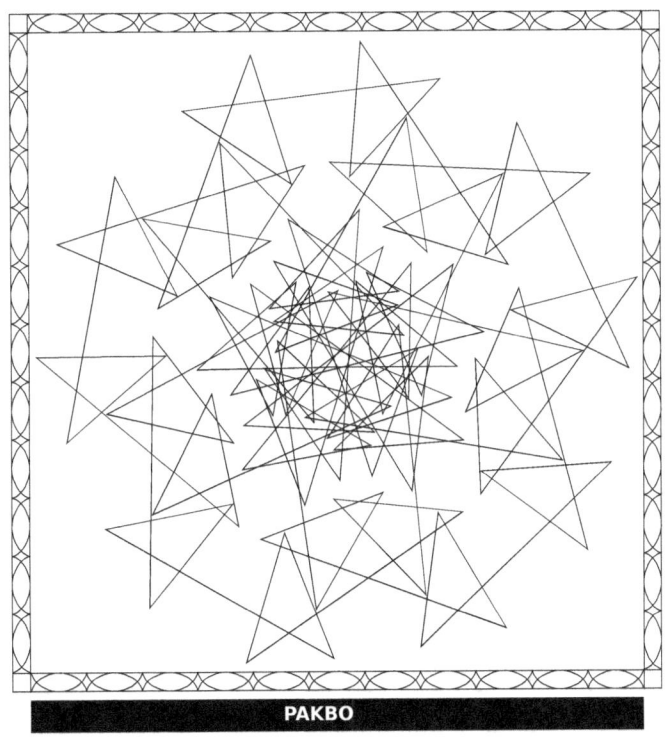

PAKBO

We state with a unified voice that religions through which Almighty God sought to bring happiness to mankind should not be turned into instruments to cause misery,
Abdullah of Saudi Arabia

195

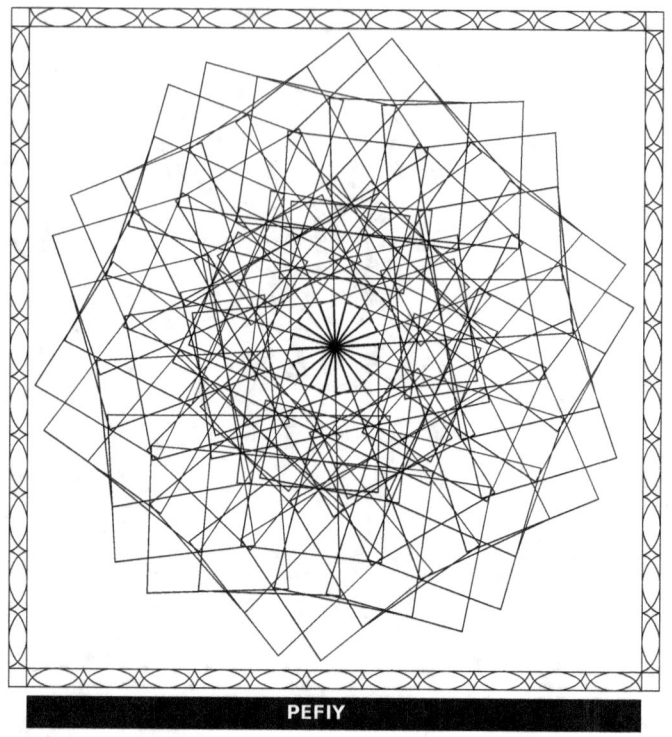

PEFIY

Philosophers and aestheticians may offer elegant and profound definitions of art and beauty, but for the painter they are all summed up in this phrase: To create a harmony.
Gino Severini

196

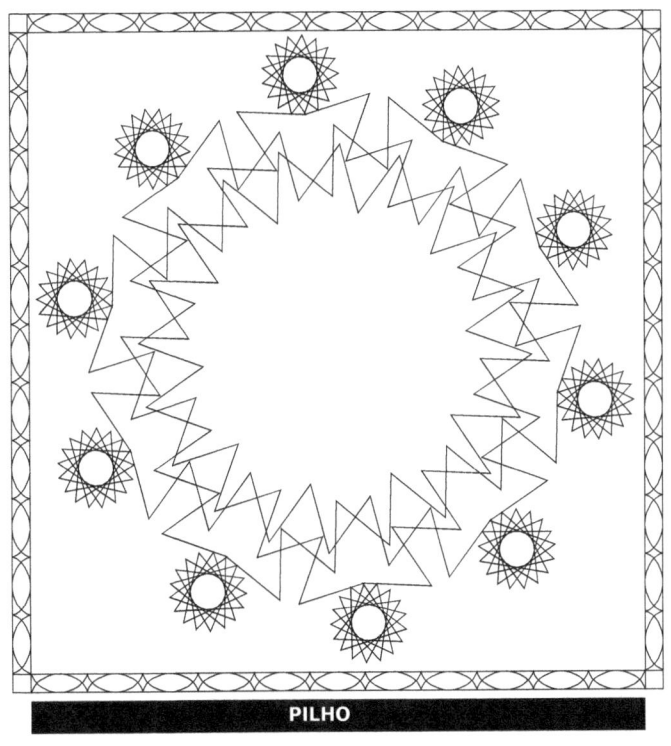

PILHO

> Trifles make perfection, and perfection is no trifle.
>
> *Michelangelo*

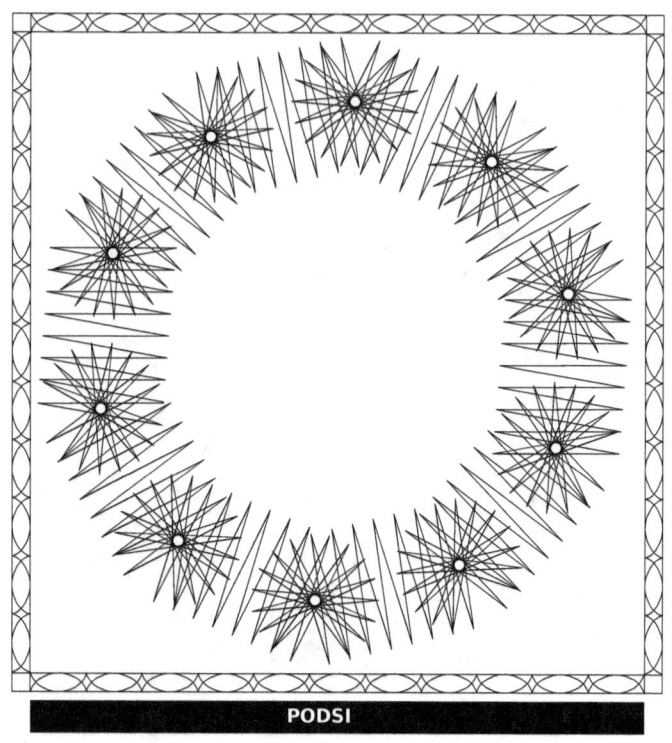

PODSI

Vision is the art of seeing things invisible.
Jonathan Swift

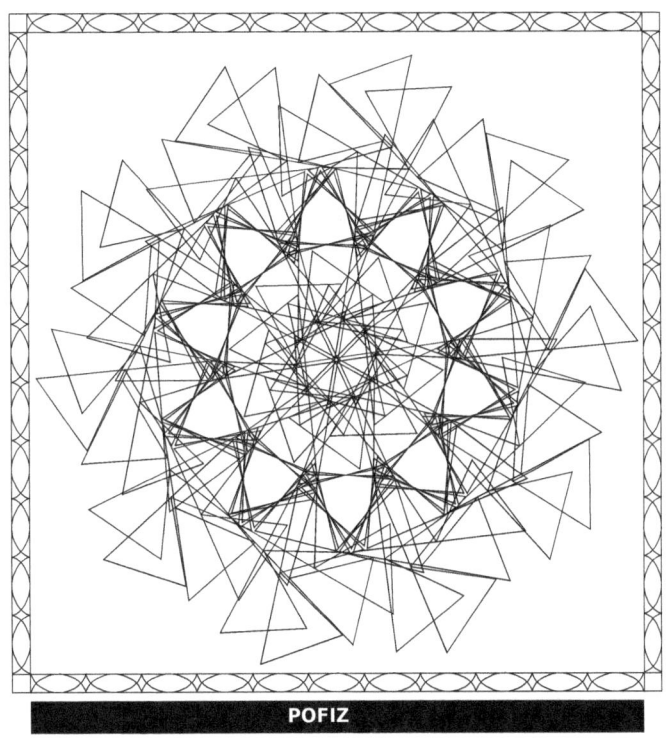

POFIZ

For intellectuals, everyone's mind is closed but their own.
Anthony Daniels

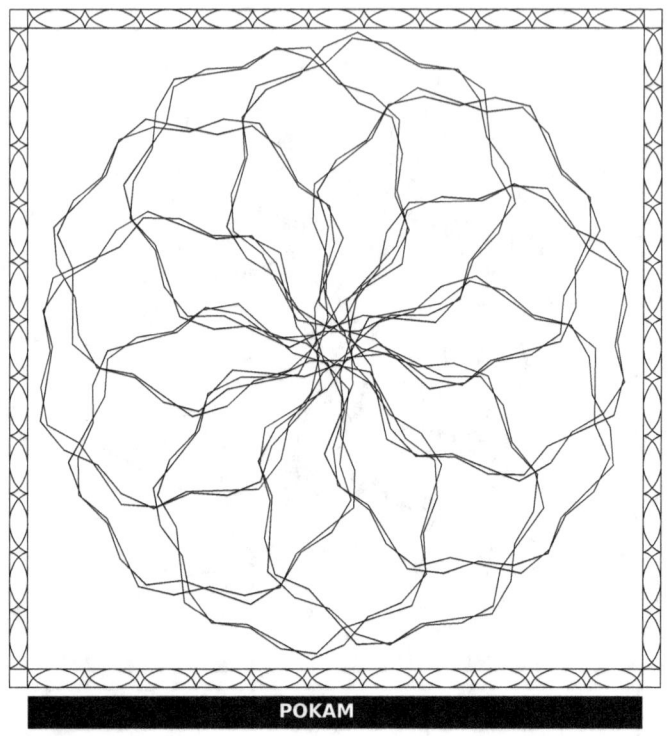

POKAM

The reason why the music is important is because it's an art form - an ancient art form - that takes in the mythology of our people.
Wynton Marsalis

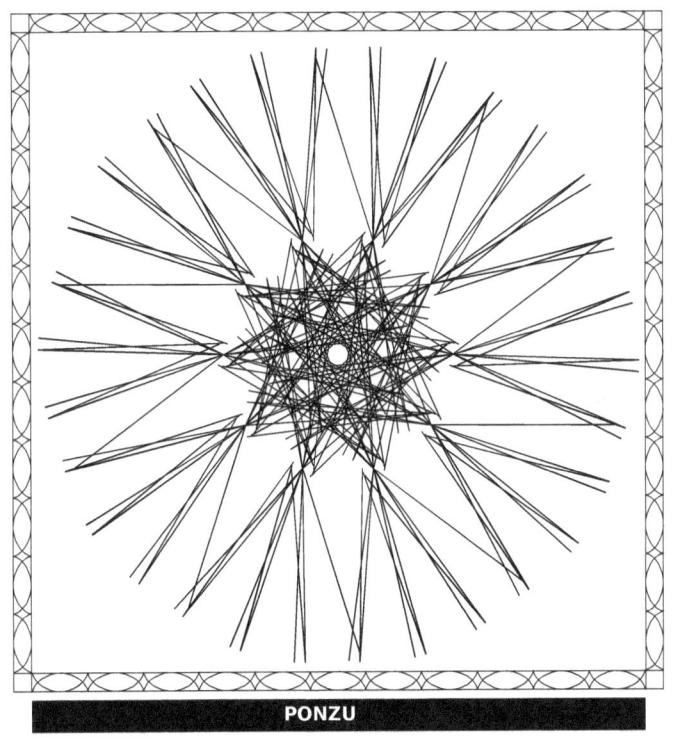

PONZU

The devil is not abroad at night in the form of a cat or a wolf or any other animal. He lives eternally in the hearts of men.

Craig Ferguson

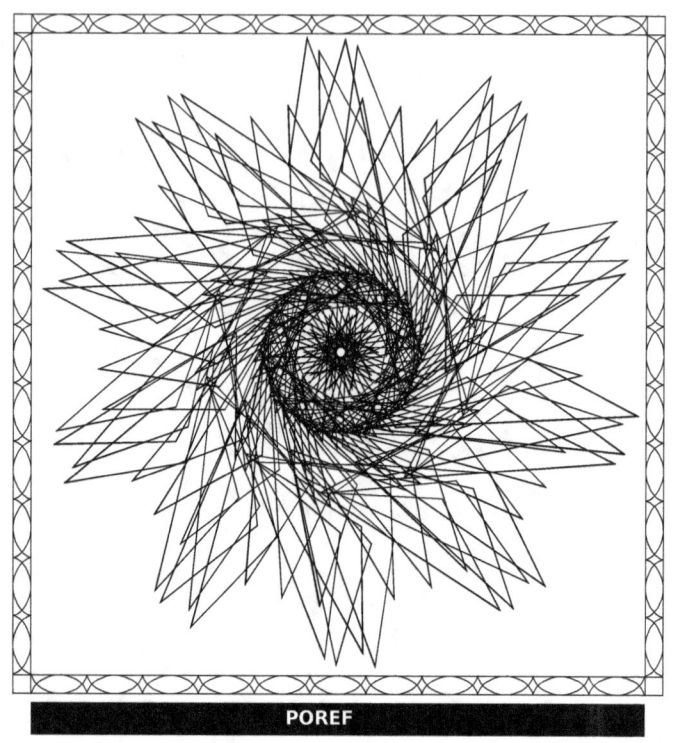

POREF

The truth isn't always beauty, but the hunger for it is.
Nadine Gordimer

202

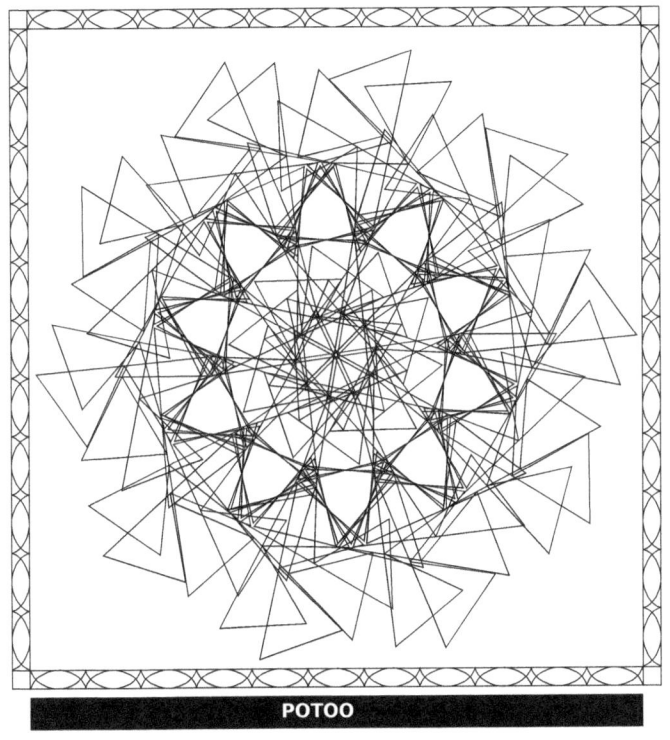

POTOO

Accept the truth from whatever source it comes.
Maimonides

203

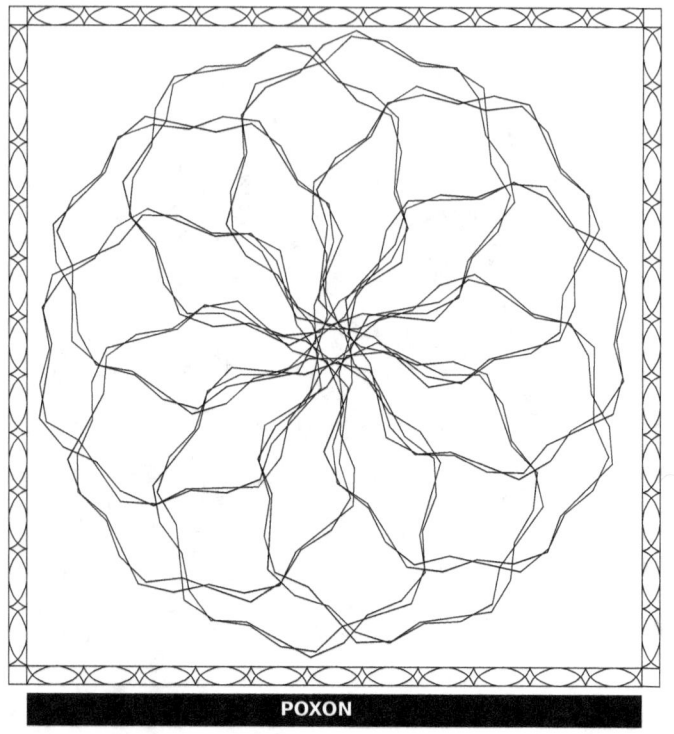

POXON

I would rather have a mind opened by wonder than one closed by belief.
Gerry Spence

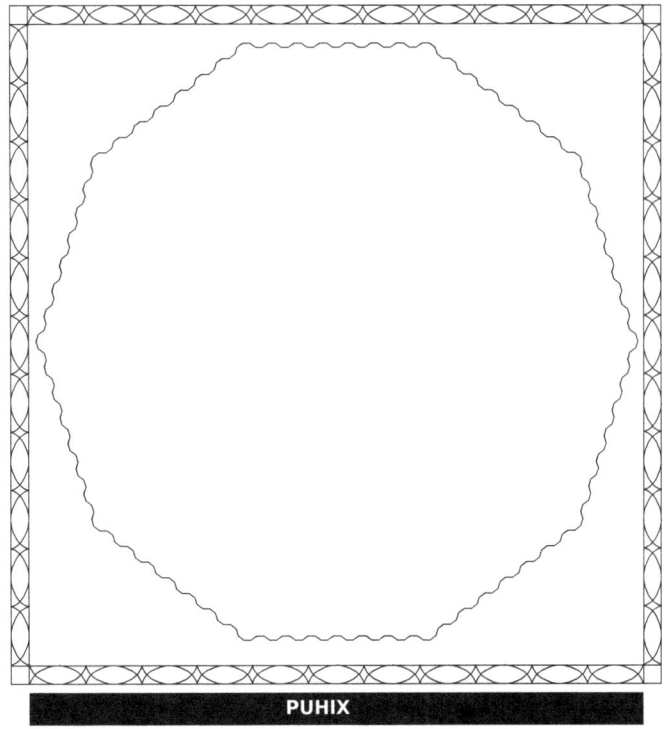

PUHIX

The direction of the mind is more important than its progress.
Joseph Joubert

205

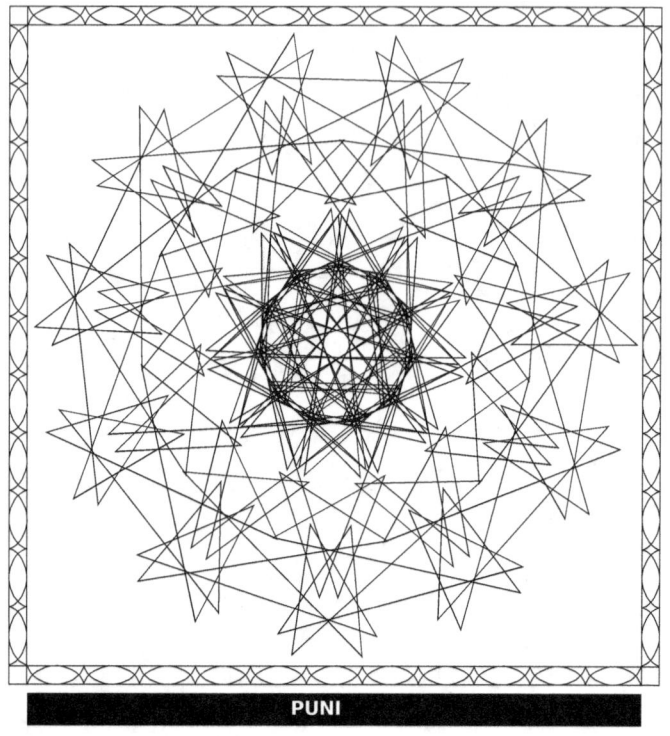

PUNI

The tragedy of human history is decreasing happiness in the midst of increasing comforts.
Chinmayananda Saraswati

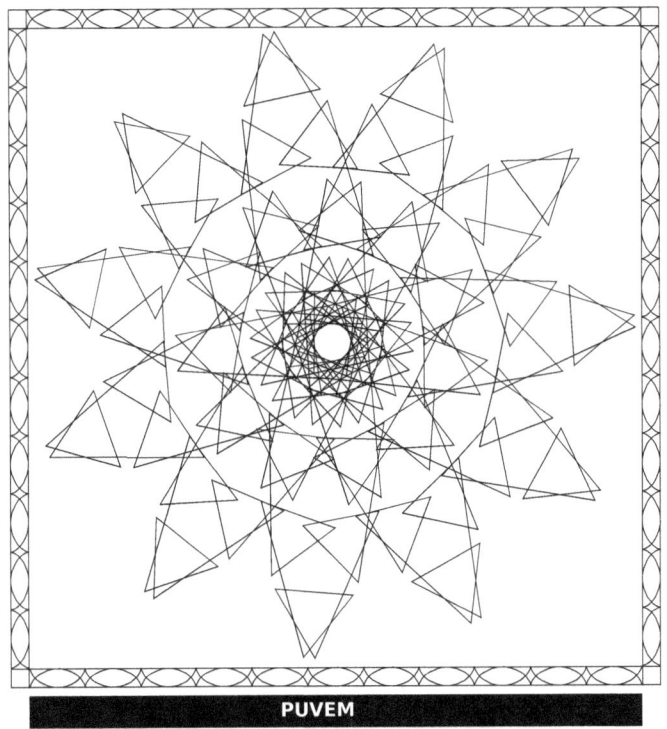

PUVEM

It is not the possession of truth, but the success which attends the seeking after it, that enriches the seeker and brings happiness to him.

Max Planck

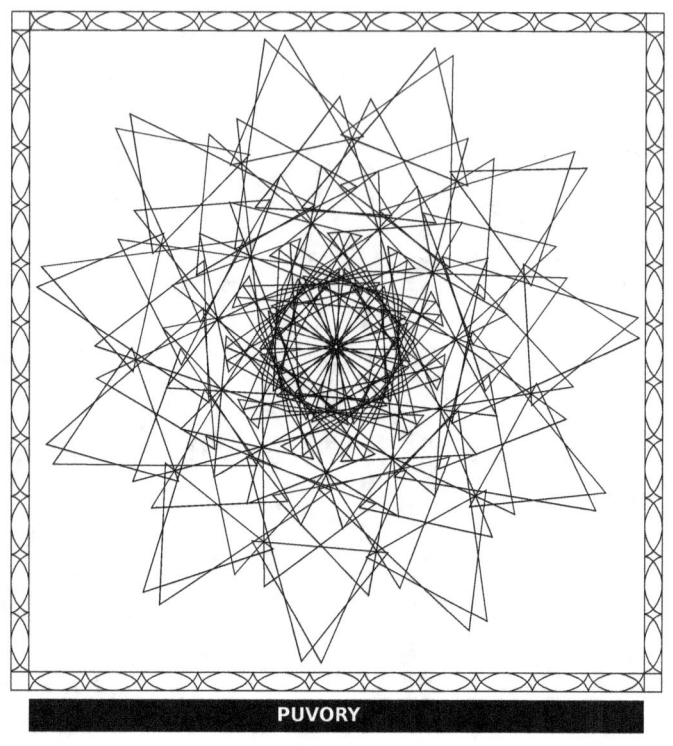

PUVORY

The happiness of a man in this life does not consist in the absence but in the mastery of his passions.
Alfred, Lord Tennyson

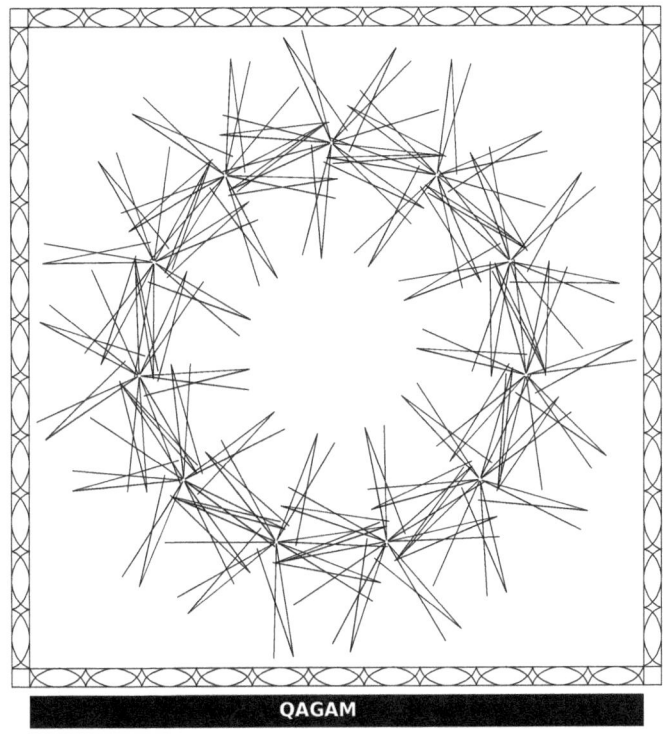

QAGAM

All truth passes through three stages. First, it is ridiculed. Second, it is violently opposed. Third, it is accepted as being self-evident.

Arthur Schopenhauer

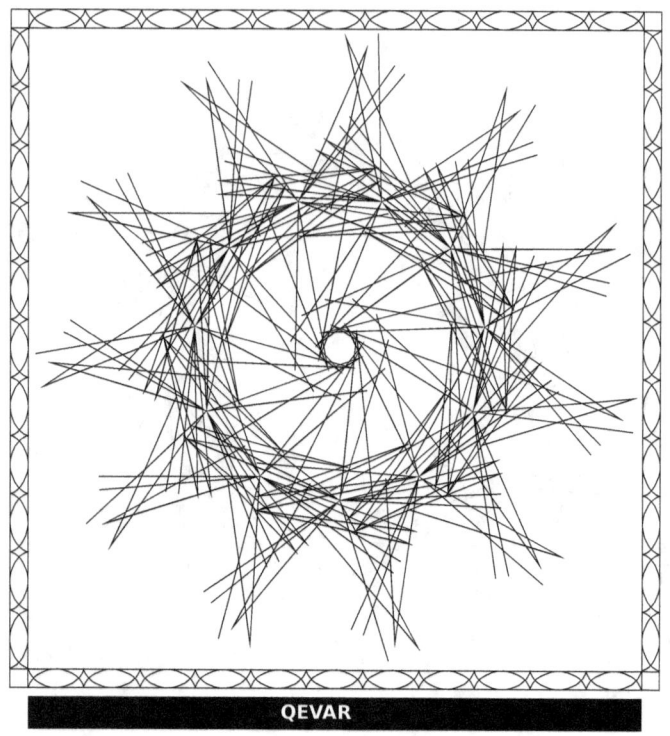

QEVAR

Only through apprehending, by means of present-day creations, how art is created, can the creations of other periods be genuinely appreciated.

Harold Rosenberg

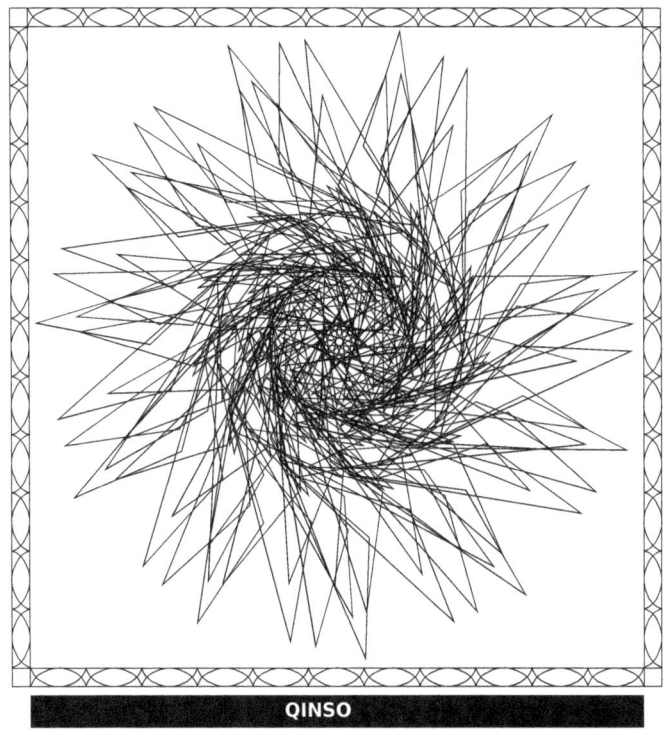

QINSO

The task of the artist at any time is uncompromisingly simple to discover what has not yet been done, and to do it.

Craig Raine

211

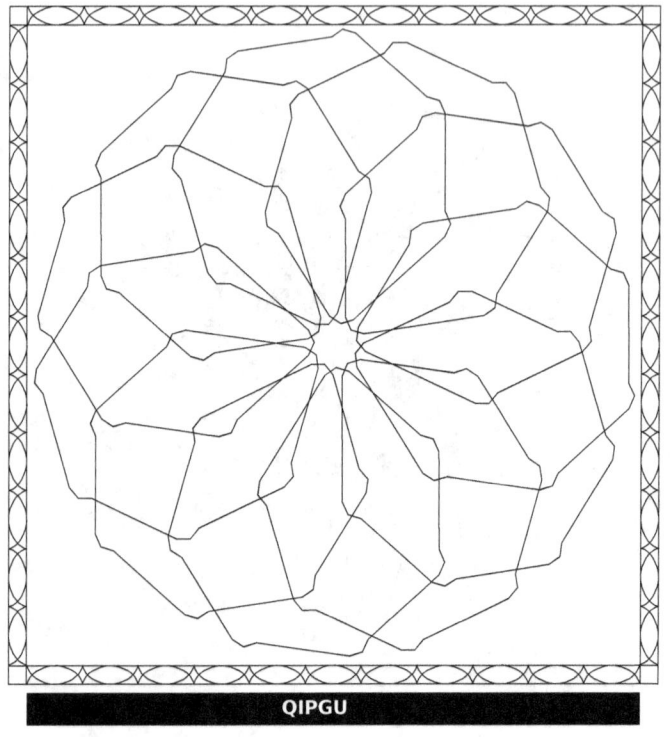

QIPGU

The truth of art keeps science from becoming inhuman, and the truth of science keeps art from becoming ridiculous.
Raymond Chandler

212

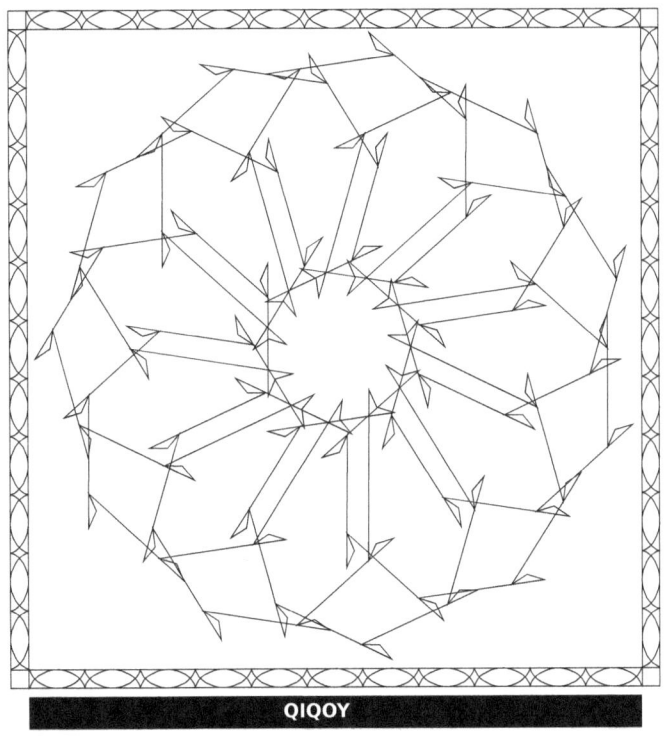

QIQOY

Every person has only one purpose: to find perfection in goodness. Therefore, only that knowledge is necessary which leads to this.

Leo Tolstoy

213

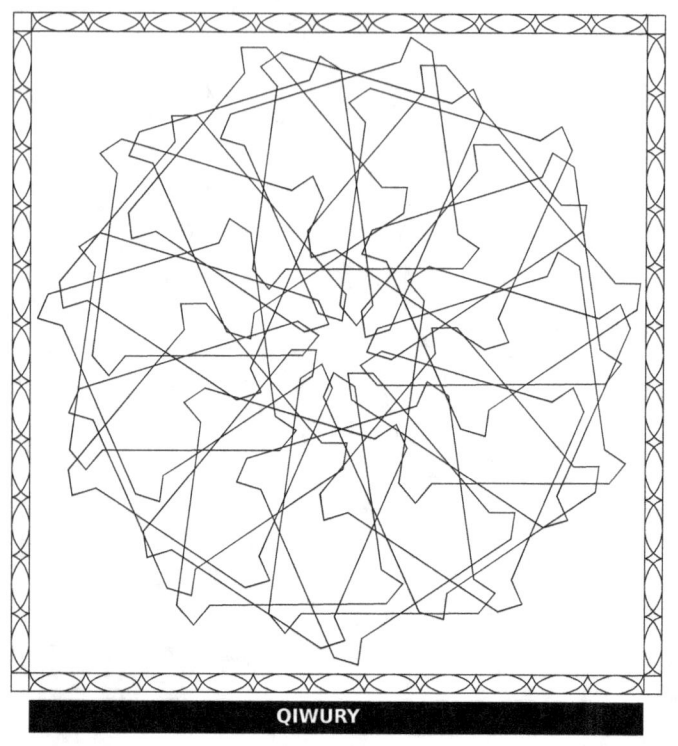

QIWURY

Military power wins battles, but spiritual power wins wars.
George Marshall

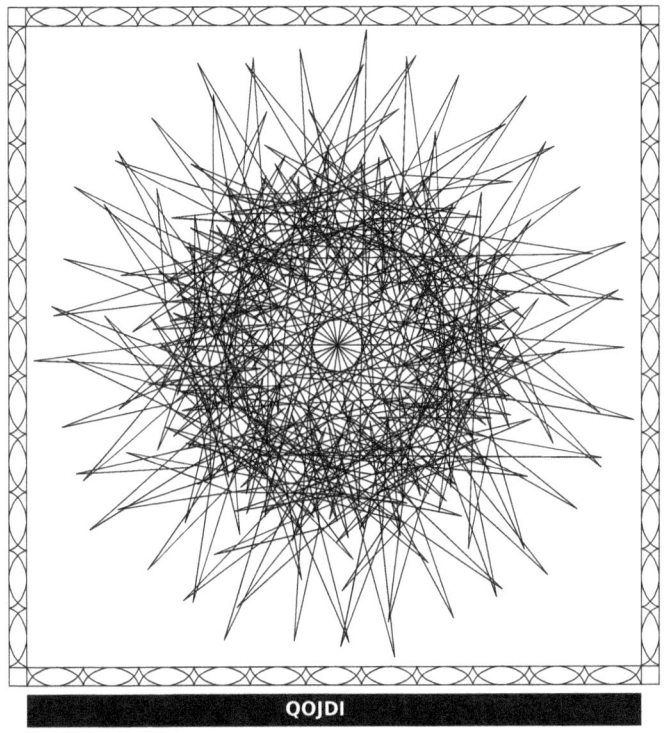

QOJDI

People who like to display complicated technique in their verse are more given to pride themselves on their work than are those who write for their own solace.
Halldor Laxness

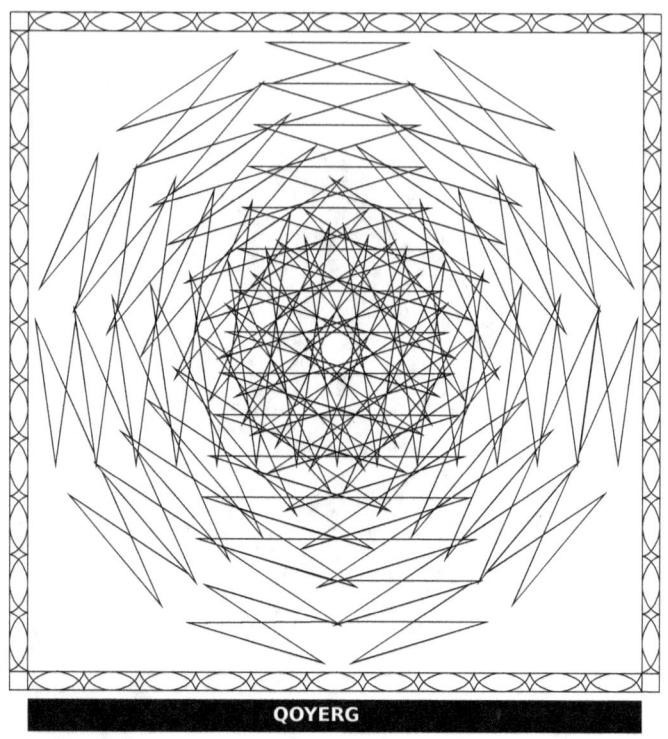

QOYERG

We are afraid of having and showing a small mind and we are not afraid of having and showing a small heart.
Joseph Joubert

216

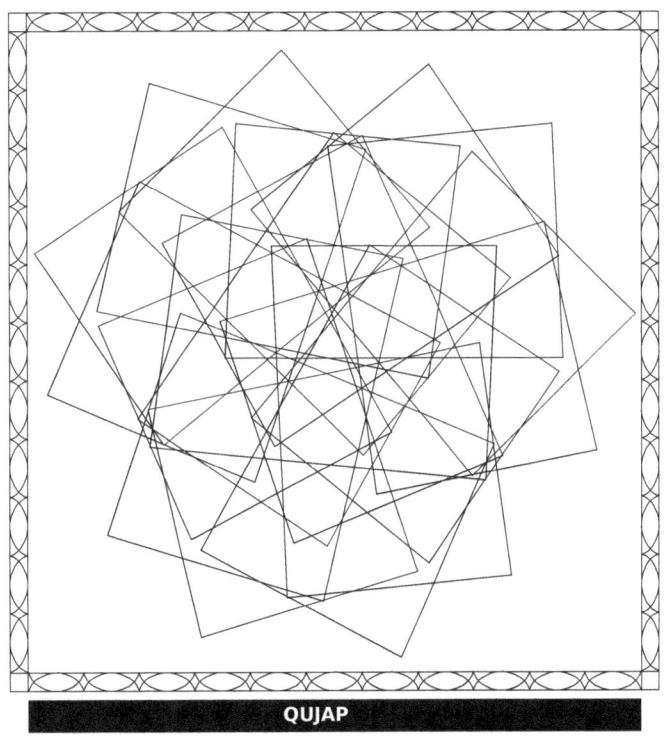

QUJAP

To listen, to learn, your mind has to be still. Have you ever observed that you can have only one thought in your mind at a time?

Barry Long

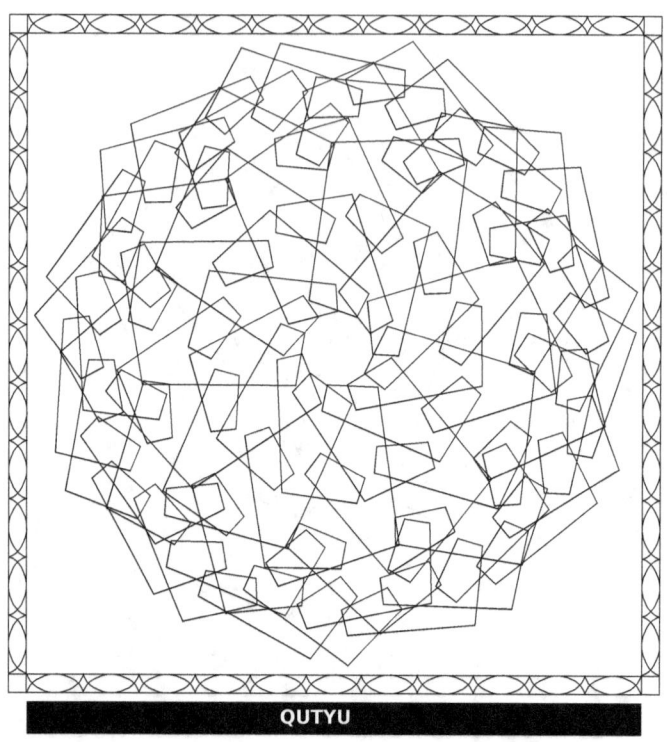

QUTYU

He who sees his life as a process of spiritual perfection does not fear external events.
Leo Tolstoy

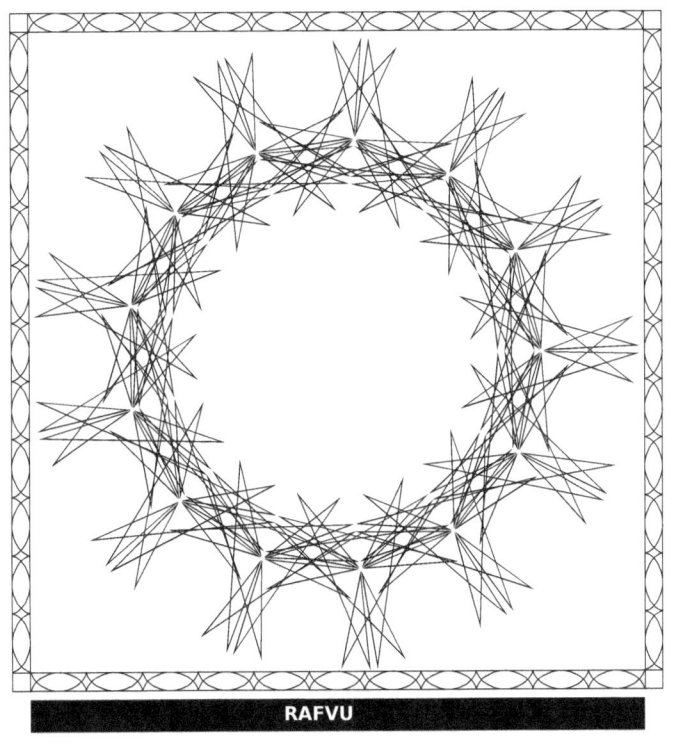

RAFVU

Don't run behind success, run behind perfection and success will come behind you.

English proverb

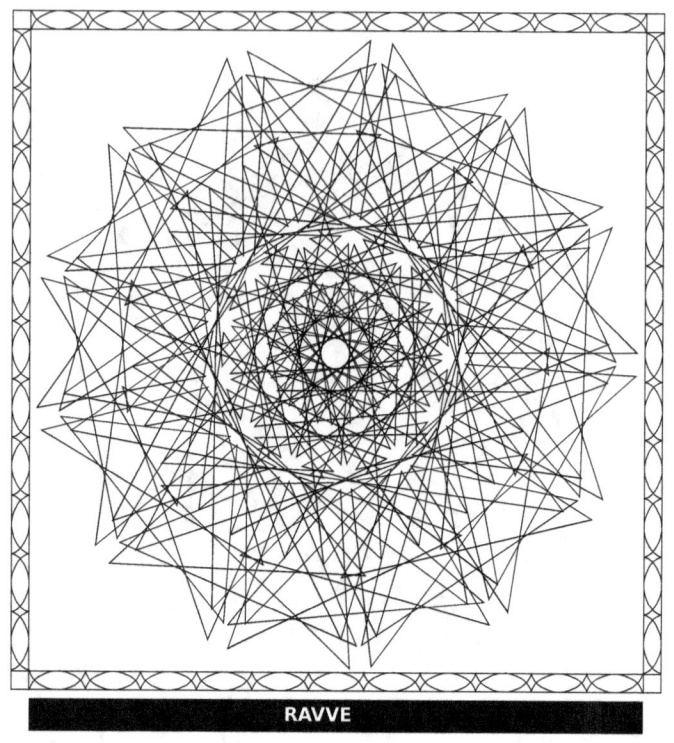

RAVVE

Poetry is the art of substantiating shadows, and of lending existence to nothing.
Edmund Burke

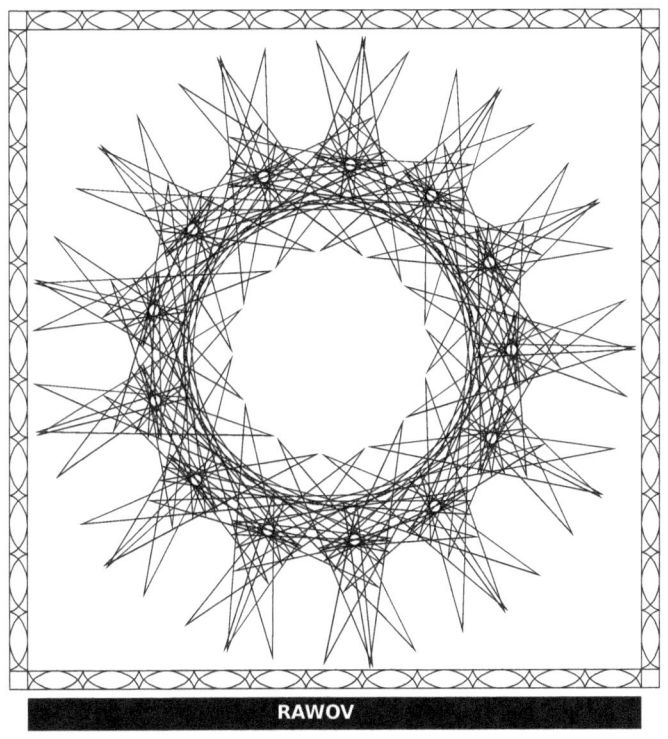

RAWOV

Happiest are the people who give most happiness to others.
Denis Diderot

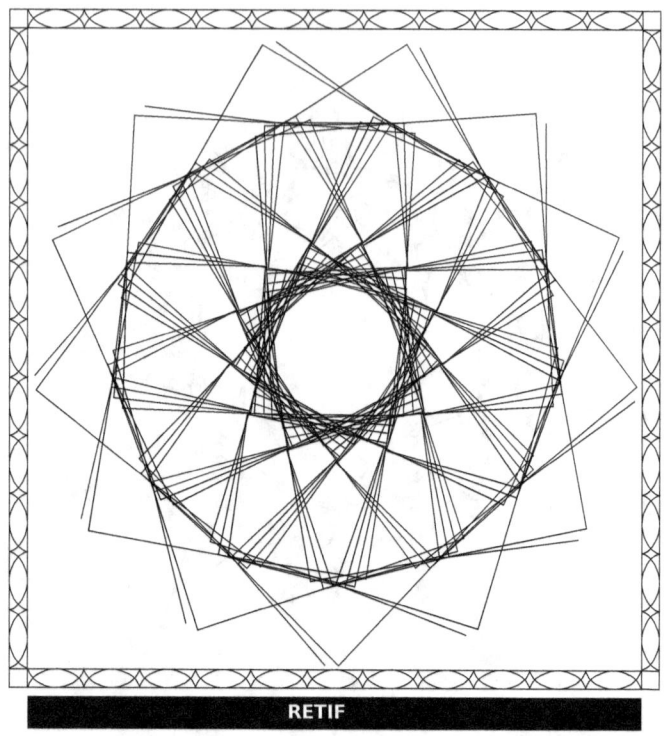

RETIF

Age imprints more wrinkles in the mind than it does on the face.
Michel de Montaigne

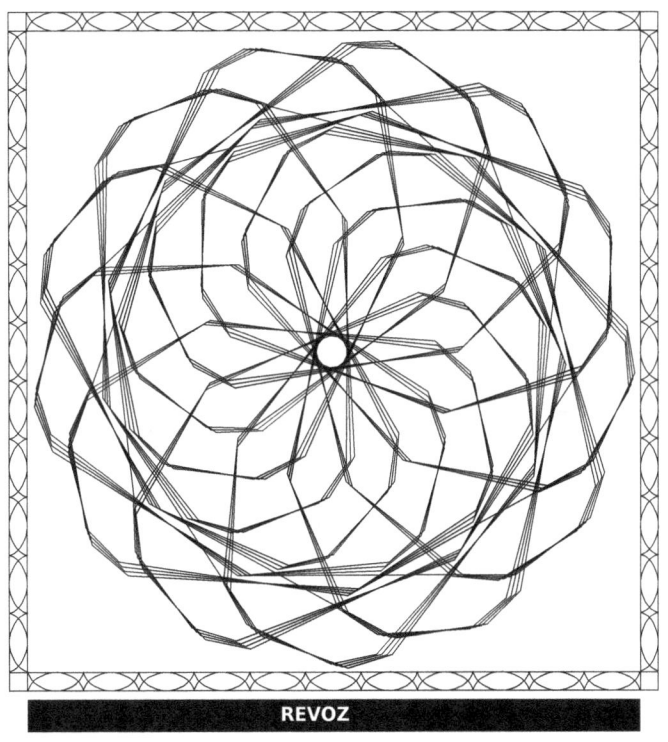

REVOZ

It is through beauty that we arrive at freedom.
Friedrich Schiller

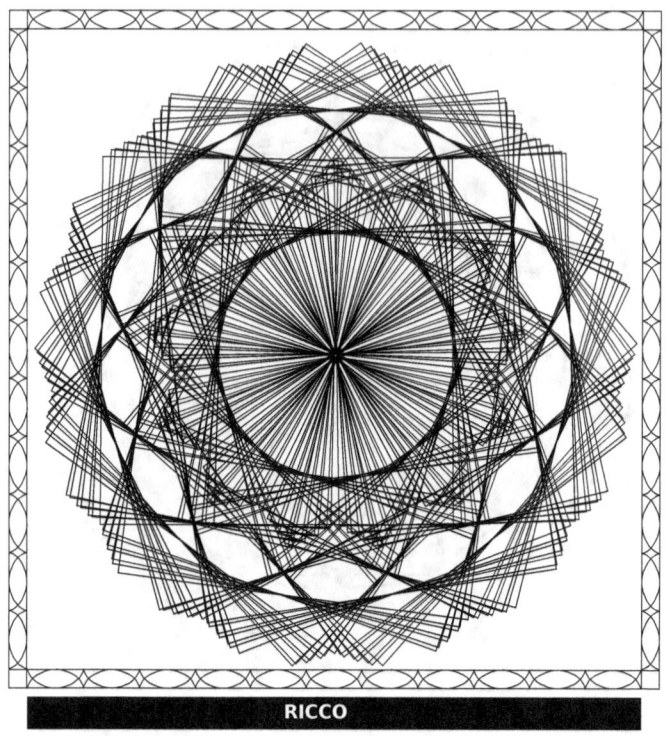

RICCO

In many cases a dull proof can be supplemented by a geo-
metric analogue so simple and beautiful that the truth of
a theorem is almost seen at a glance.
Martin Gardner

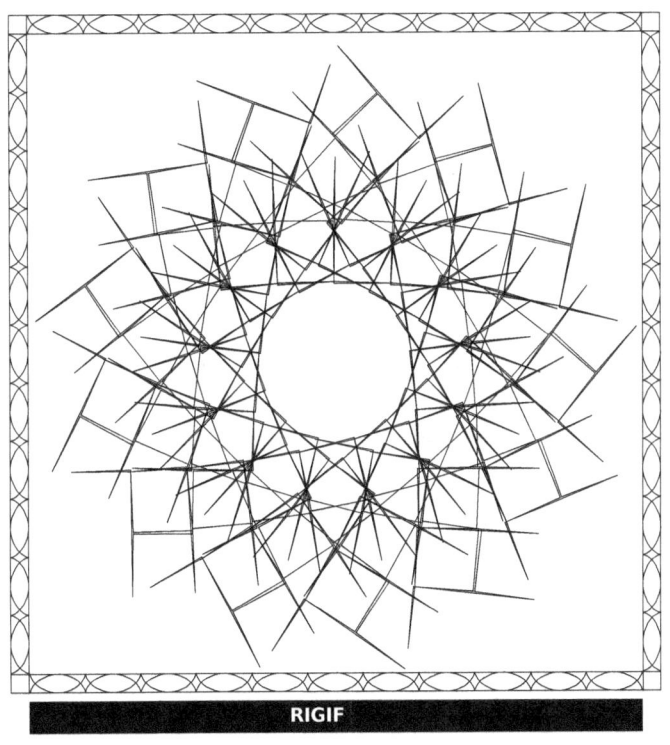

RIGIF

Oh why do we not say the important things, it would be so easy, and we are damned because we do not.
Bertolt Brecht

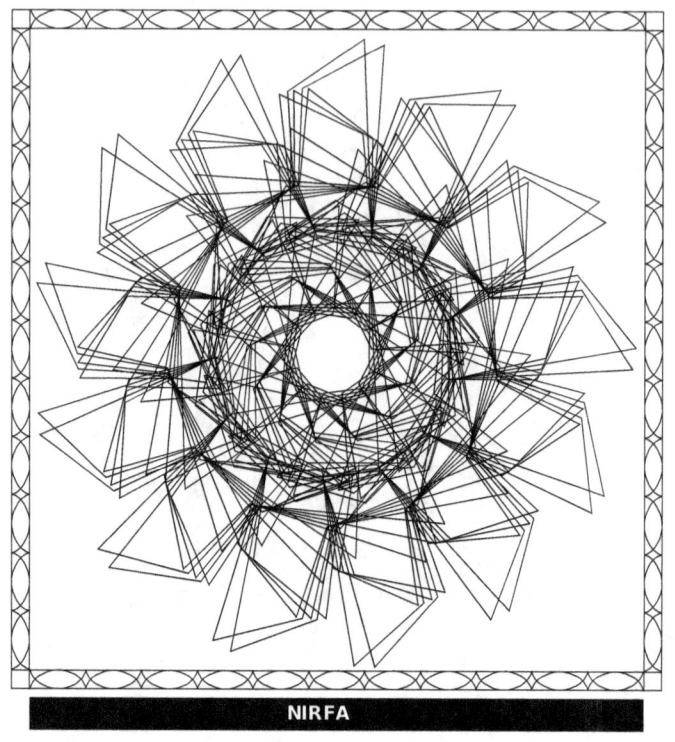

NIRFA

The search for happiness is one of the chief sources of un-
happiness.
Eric Hoffer

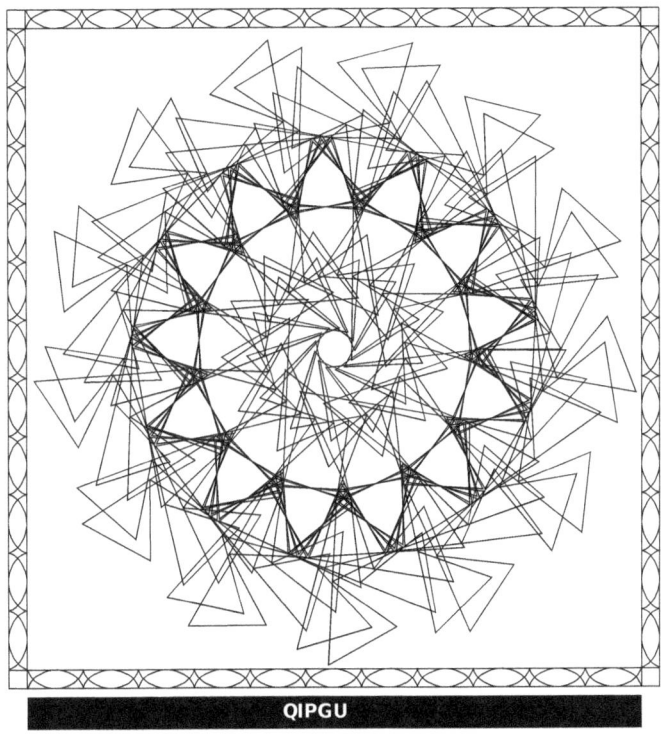

QIPGU

I love the pride whose measure is its own eminence and not
the insignificance of someone else.
Franz Grillparzer

227

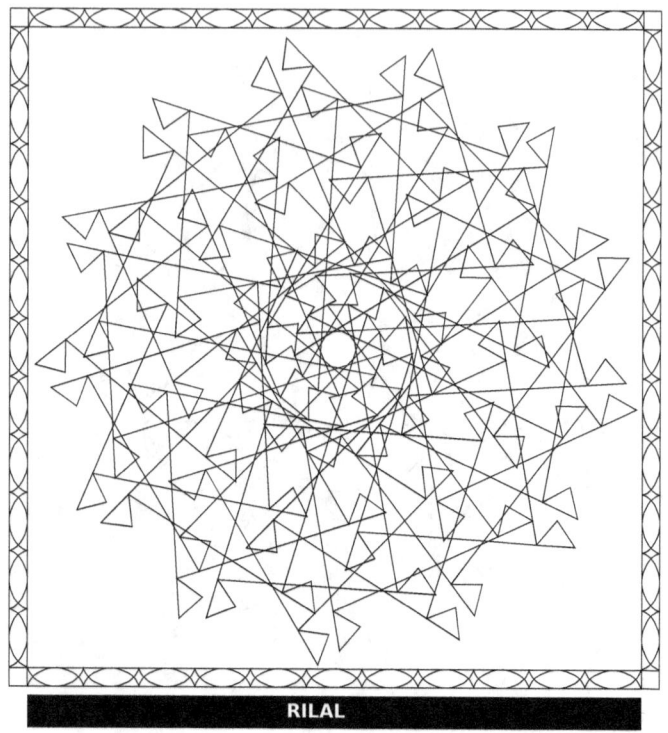

RILAL

Your mind is like this water my friend, when it is agitated it becomes difficult to see. But if you allow it to settle, the answer becomes clear.

Kung Fu Panda

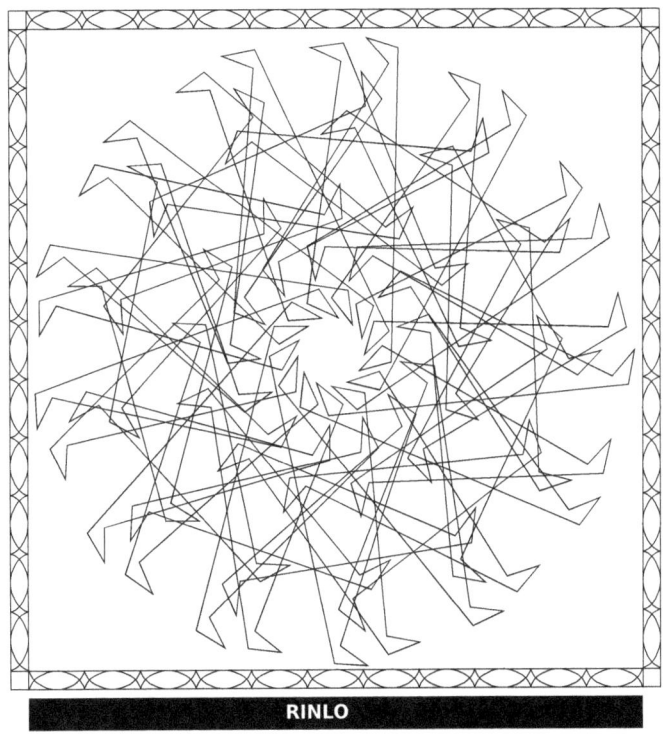

RINLO

Music and silence ... combine strongly because music is done with silence, and silence is full of music.
Marcel Marceau

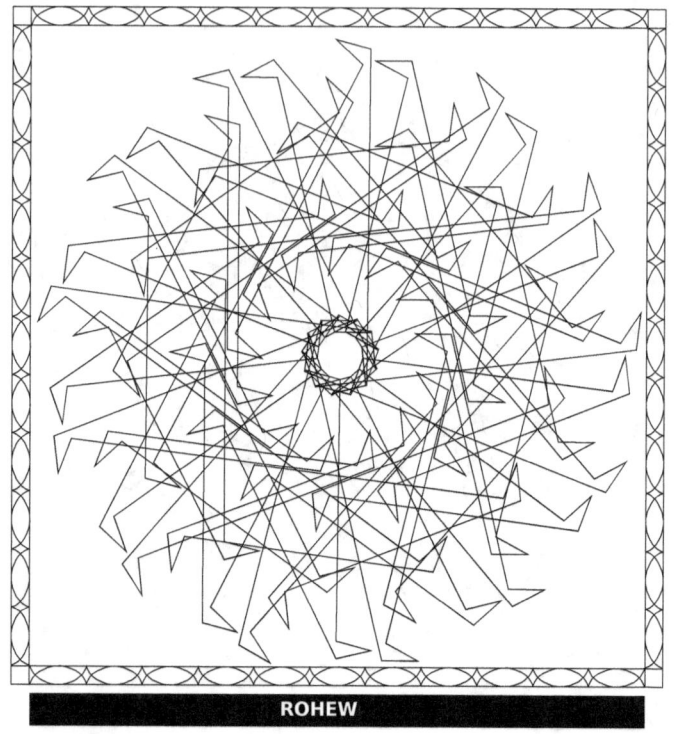

ROHEW

We rise in glory as we sink in pride.
Edward Young

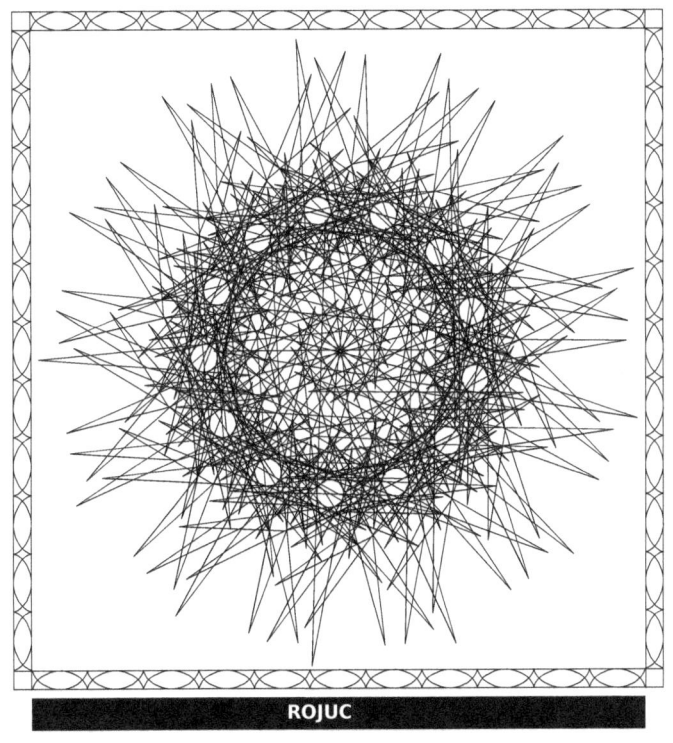

ROJUC

Practise meditation, and by and by your mind will be so calm and fixed that you will find it hard to keep away from meditation.

Sarada Devi

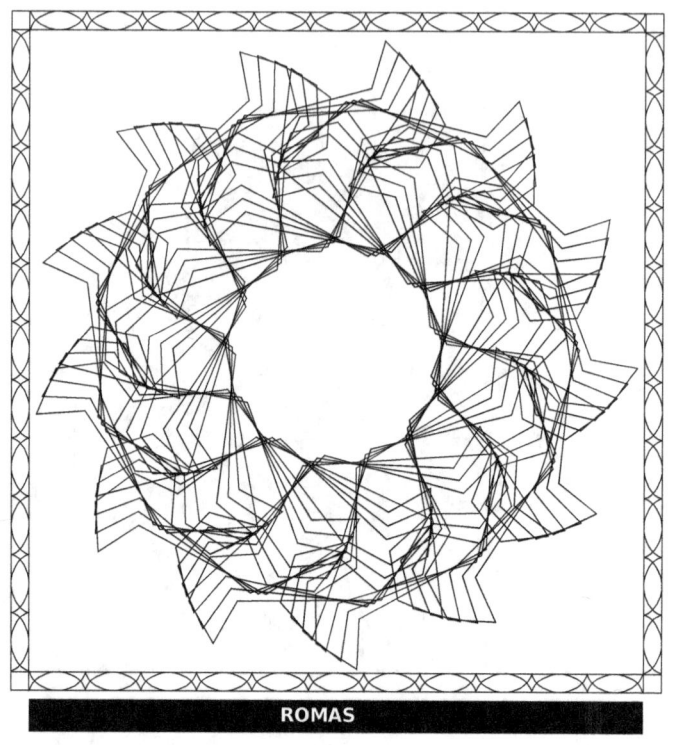

ROMAS

Emerson said that music helps people to find the greatness in their souls. The same can be said about any form of art.
Leo Tolstoy

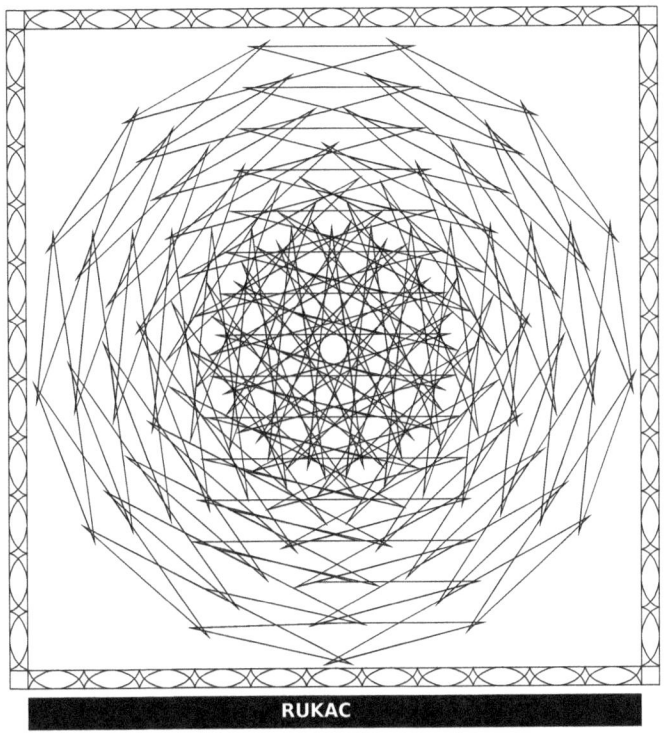

RUKAC

Any highly evolved form is beautiful.
Kevin Kelly

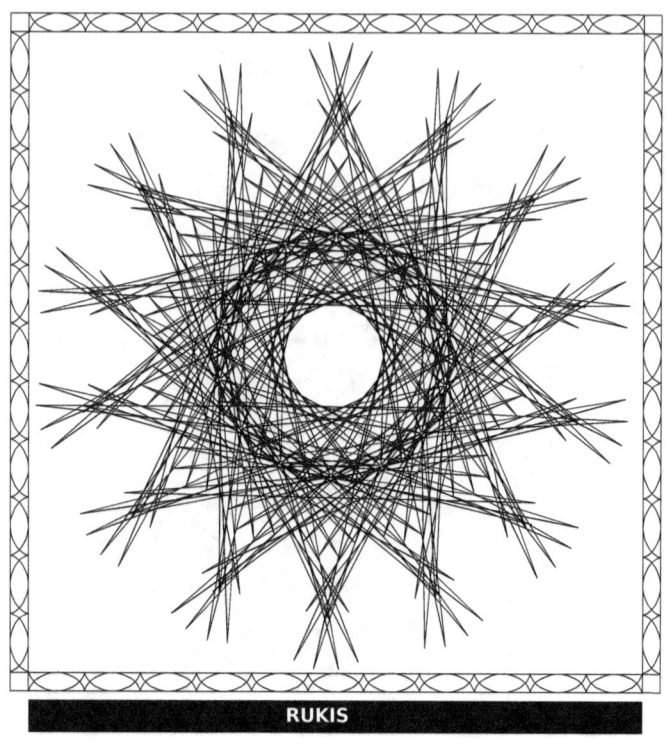

RUKIS

Art does not imitate, but interpret. It searches out the idea lying dormant in the symbol, in order to present the symbol to men in such form as to enable them to penetrate through it to the idea. Were it otherwise, what would be the use or value of art?

Giuseppe Mazzini

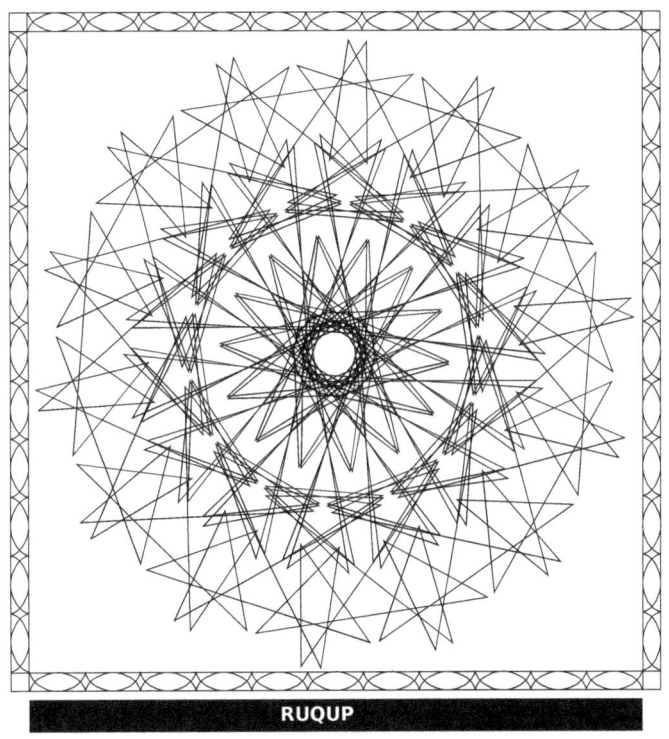

RUQUP

The course of Nature is the art of God.
Edward Young

235

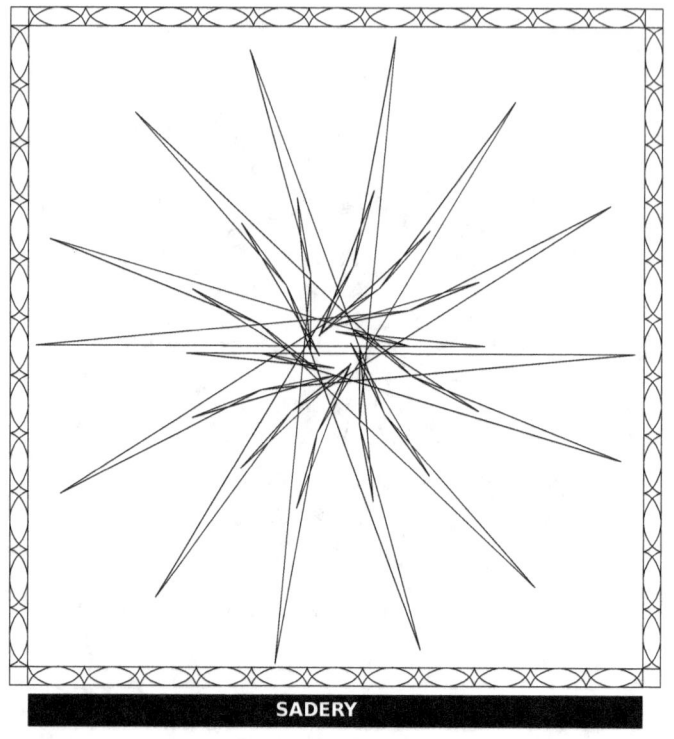

SADERY

A man's mind stretched to a new idea never goes back to its original dimensions.
Oliver Wendell Holmes, Jr.

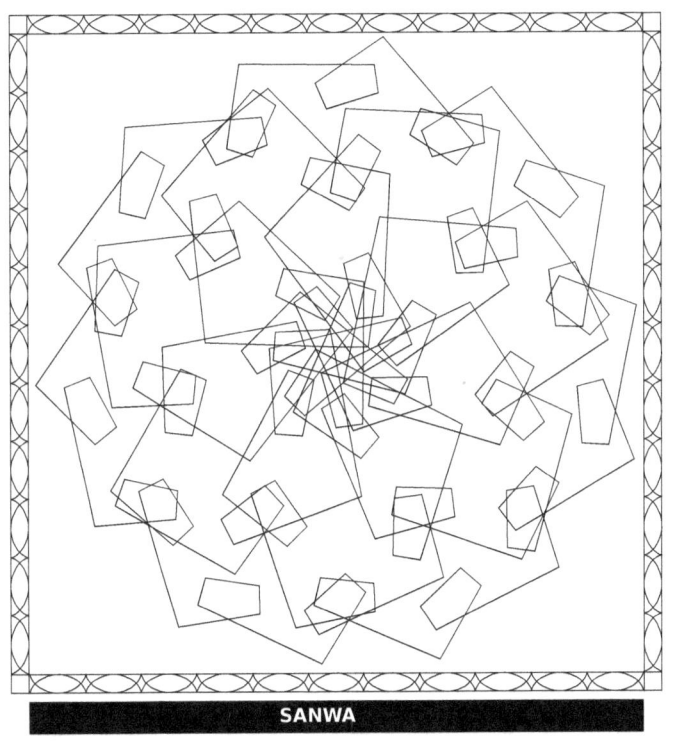

SANWA

All we who write put me in mind of sailors hastily making rafts upon doomed ships.

Edward Plunkett, 18th Baron of Dunsany

237

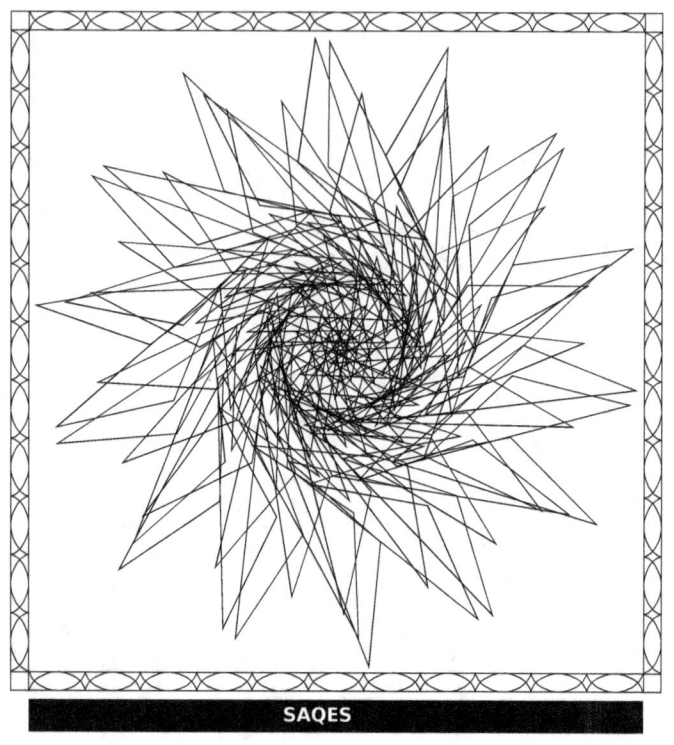

SAQES

The mind of man is like a clock that is always running down, and requires to be as constantly wound up.
William Hazlitt

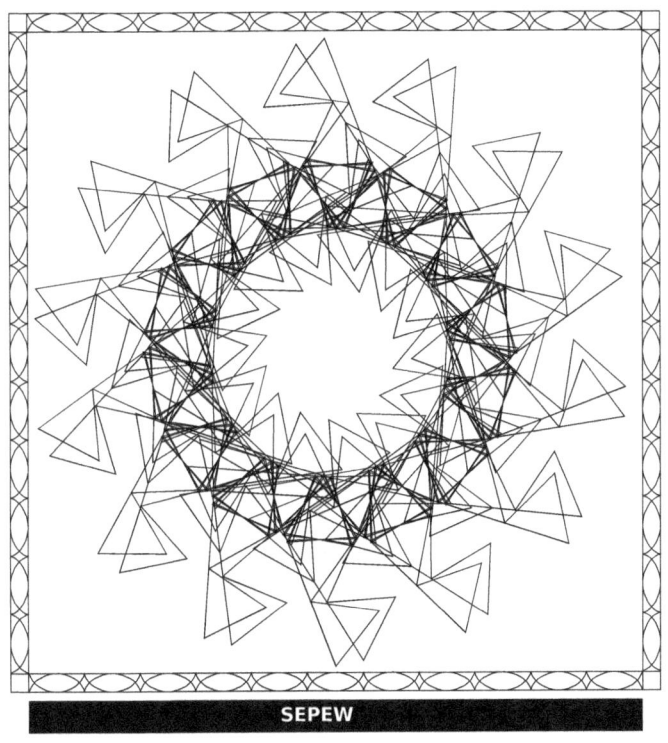

SEPEW

If God be God and man a creature made in image of the divine intelligence, his noblest function is the search for truth.

Morris West

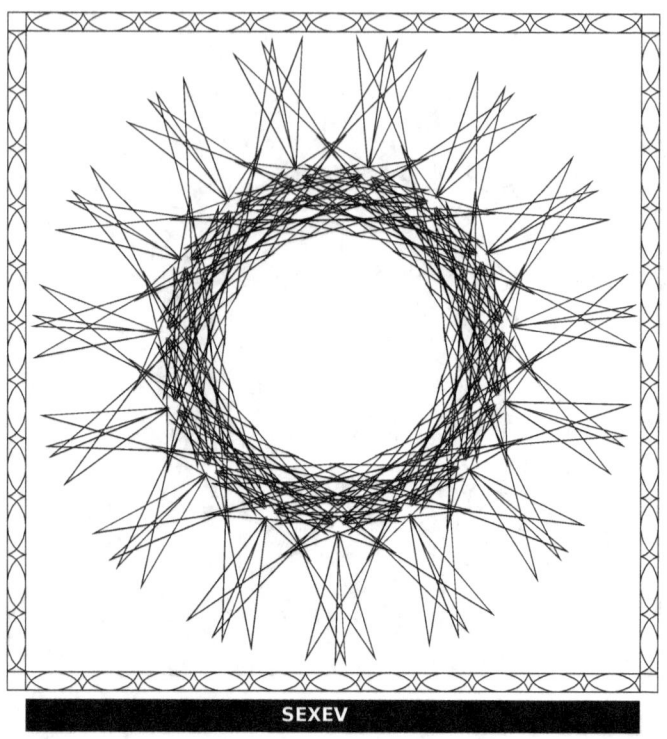

SEXEV

I may not know much, but I do know the difference between
chicken shit and chicken salad.
Lyndon B. Johnson

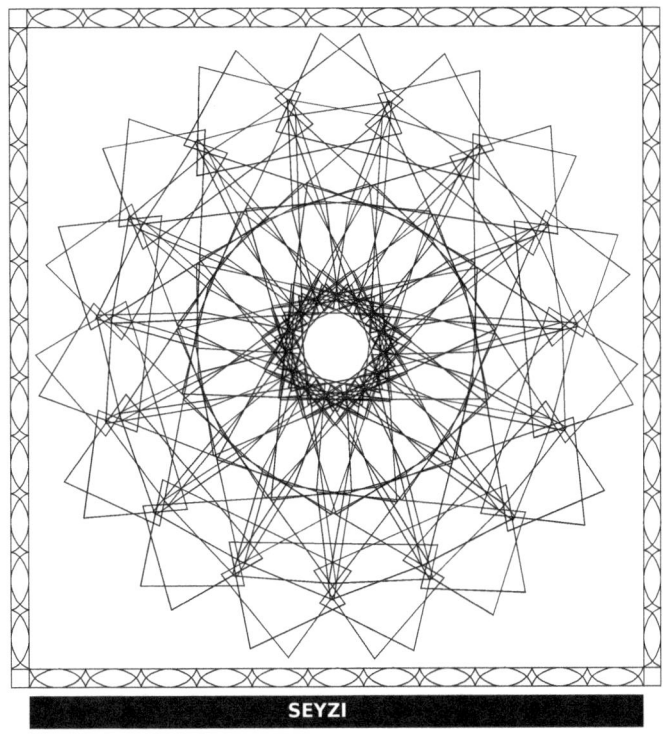

SEYZI

There is no mystery whatever - only inability to perceive
the obvious.
Wei Wu Wei

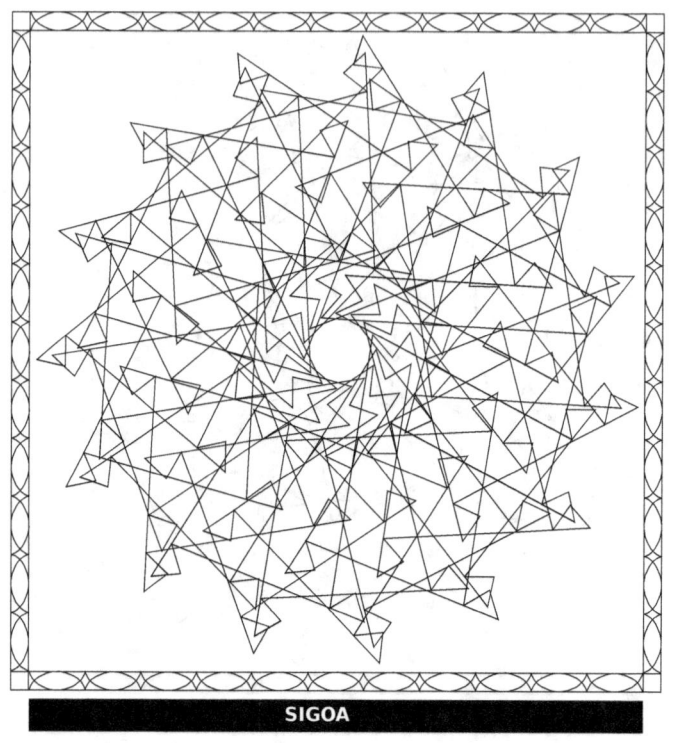

SIGOA

Men are disturbed, not by things, but by the principles and notions which they form concerning things.
Epictetus

242

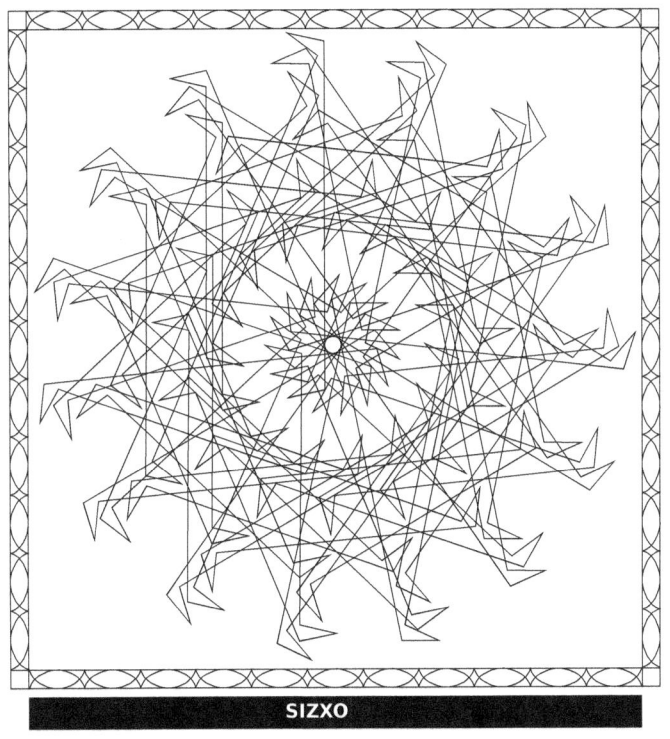

SIZXO

Nothing that was worthy in the past departs; no truth or goodness realized by man ever dies, or can die.
Thomas Carlyle

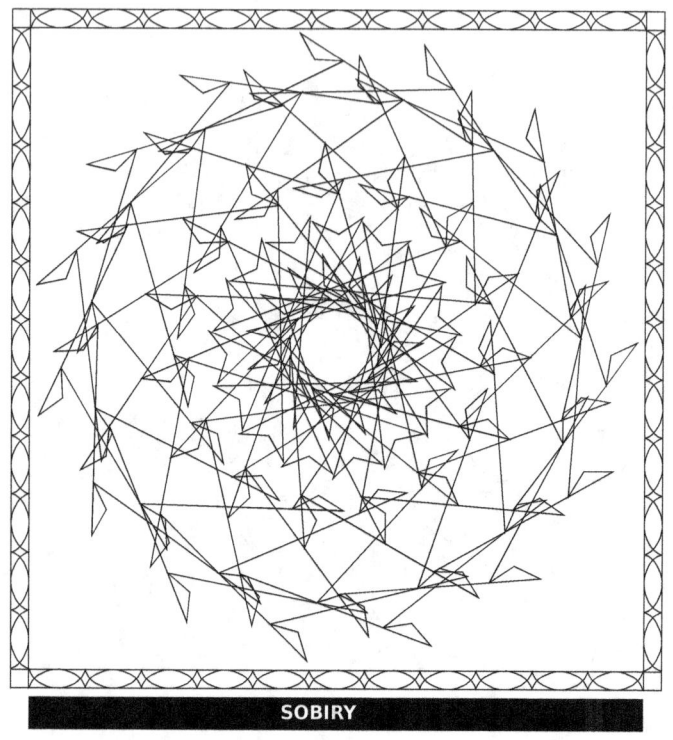

SOBIRY

The essential thing is to spring forth, to express the bolt of lightning one senses upon contact with a thing. The function of the artist is not to translate an observation but to express the shock of the object on his nature; the shock, with the original reaction.

Henri Matisse

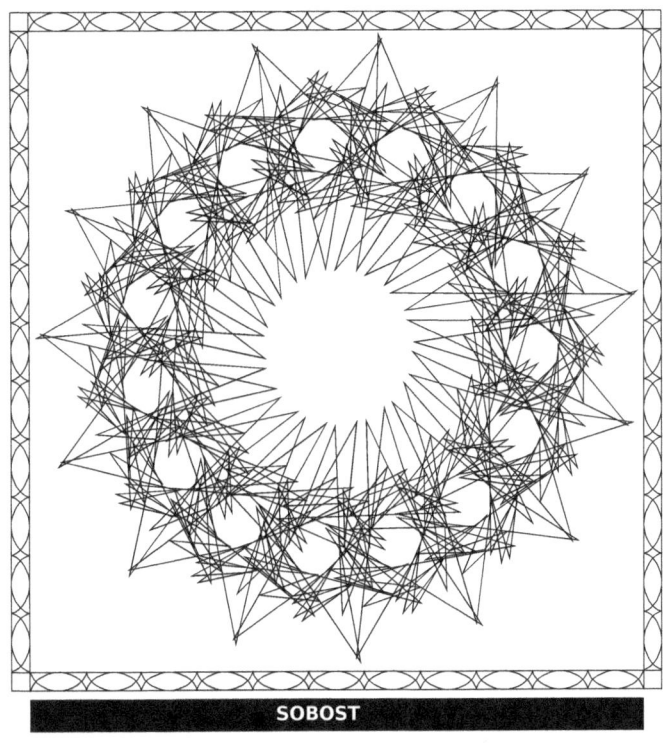

SOBOST

There is always an unconscious collaboration among artists, the artist who imagines himself a Robinson Crusoe is either a primitive or a fool.
William Baziotes

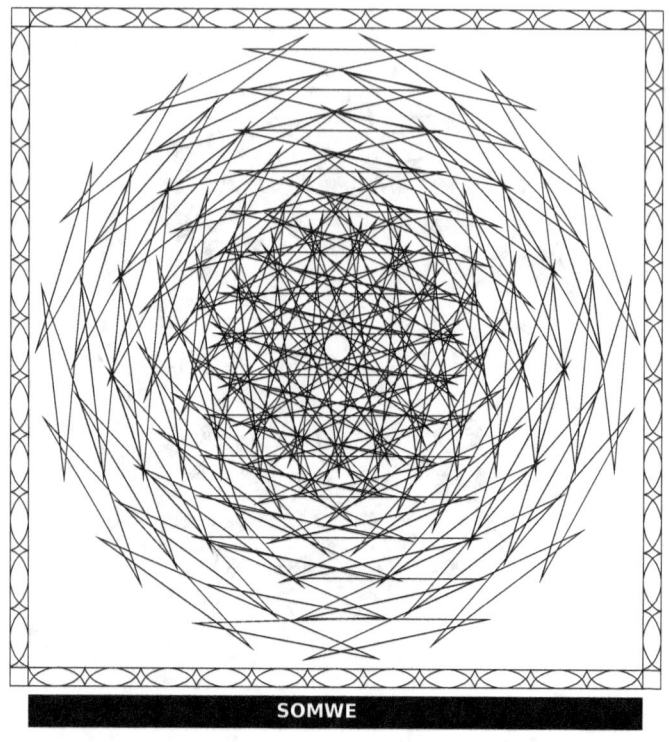

SOMWE

To understand the heart and mind of a person, look not at what he has already achieved, but what he aspires to.
Khalil Gibran

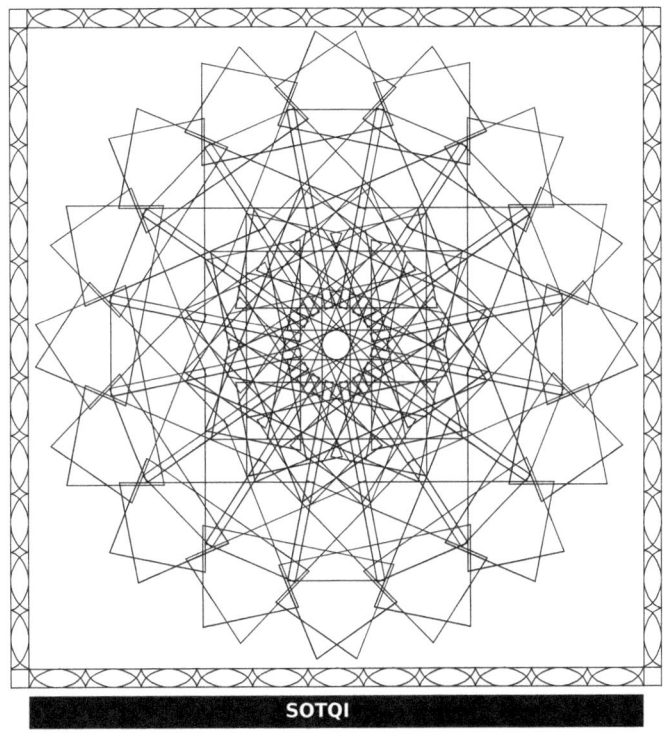

SOTQI

The jaws of power are always open to devour, and her arm is always stretched out, if possible, to destroy the freedom of thinking, speaking, and writing.
John Adams

247

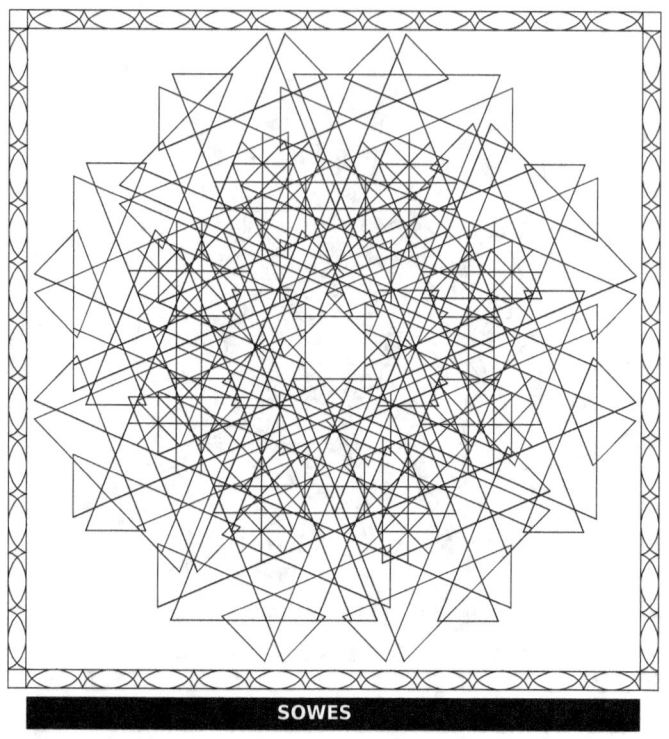

SOWES

It is your mind that creates this world.
Gautama Buddha

248

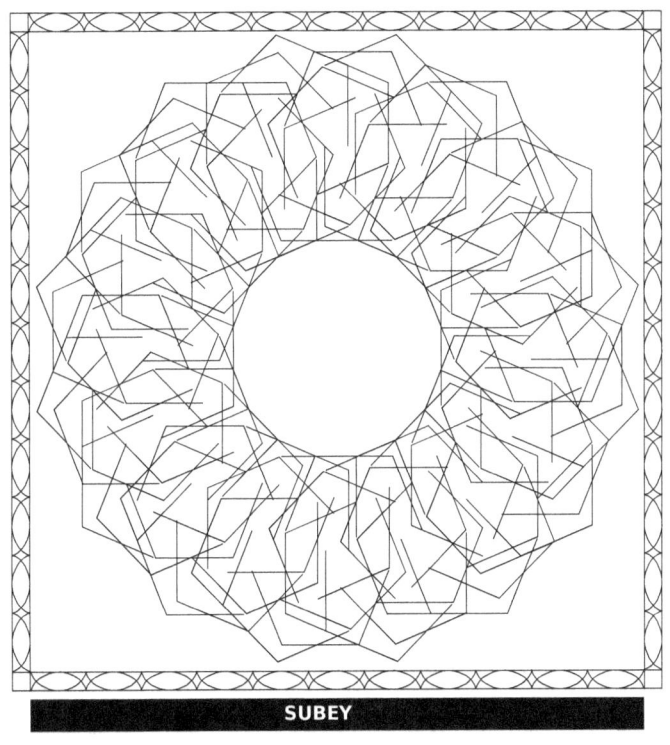

SUBEY

To avoid all evil, to cultivate good, and to cleanse one's mind - this is the teaching of the Buddhas.

Dhammapada

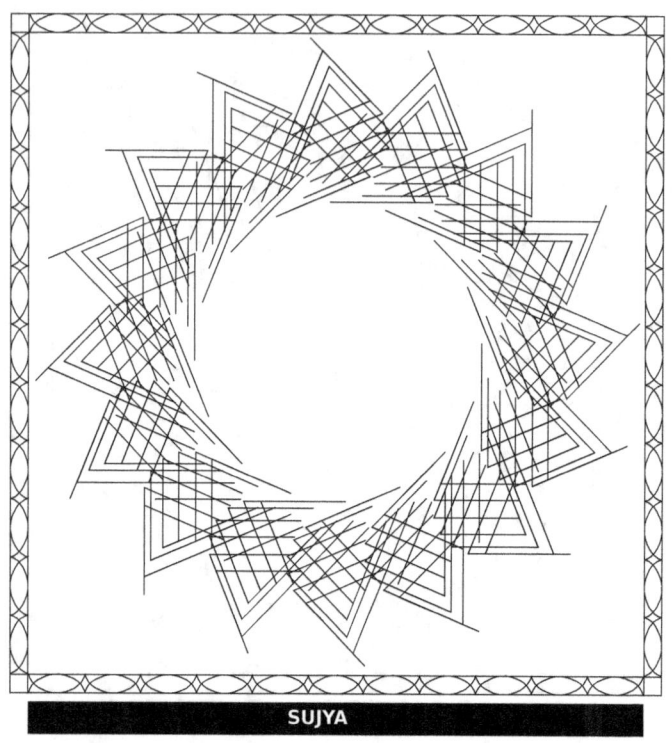

SUJYA

The most important thing in life is the path to perfection, and what kind of perfection can exist if a person is proud and satisfied with himself?
Leo Tolstoy

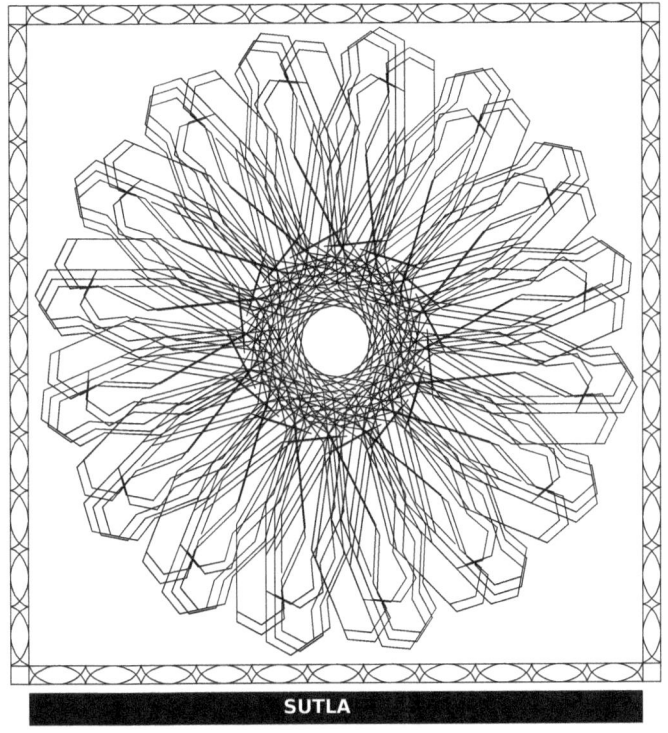

SUTLA

One of the major activities of art consists in sharpening the
edge of platitudes to make them enter the soul as realities.
Northrop Frye

251

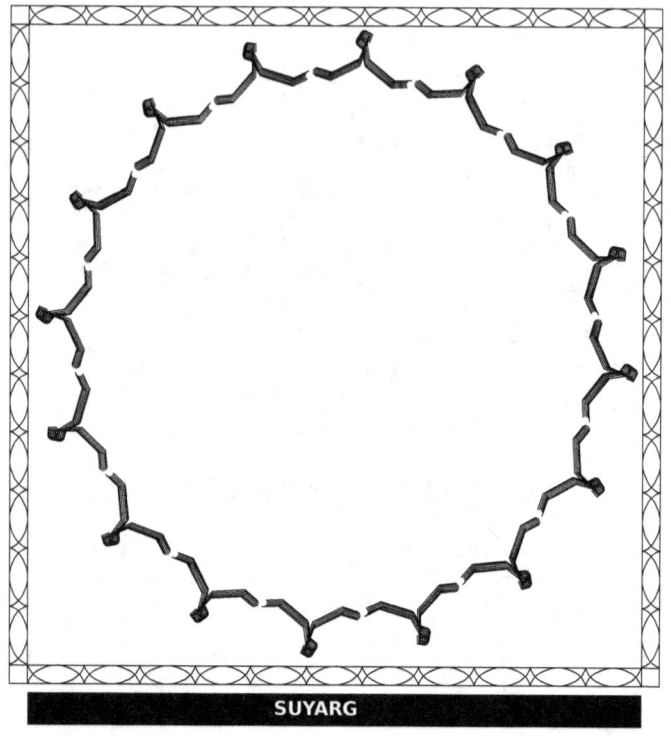

SUYARG

An intellectual is someone whose mind watches itself.
Albert Camus

TAMIK

I love to see two truths at the same time. Every good comparison gives the mind this advantage.
Joseph Joubert

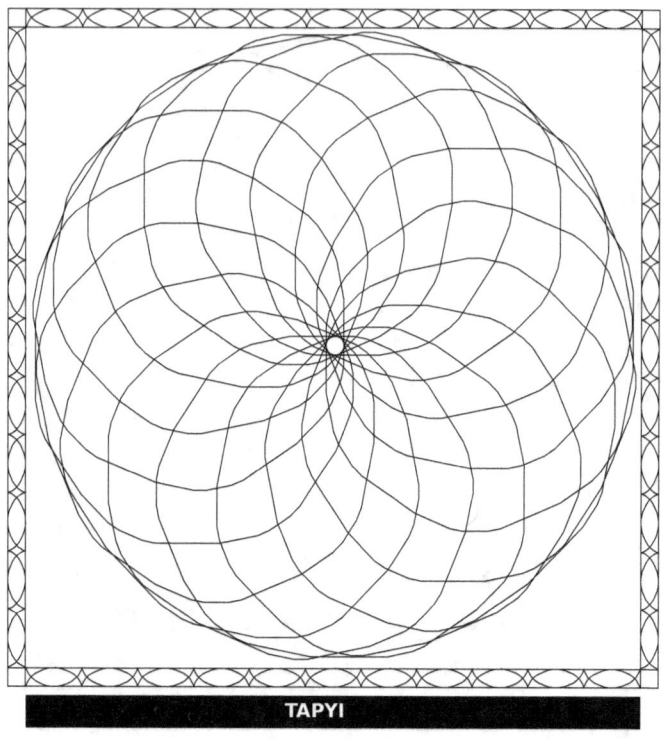

TAPYI

Consciousness spreads out its web, in the form of time, over reality.
Hermann Weyl

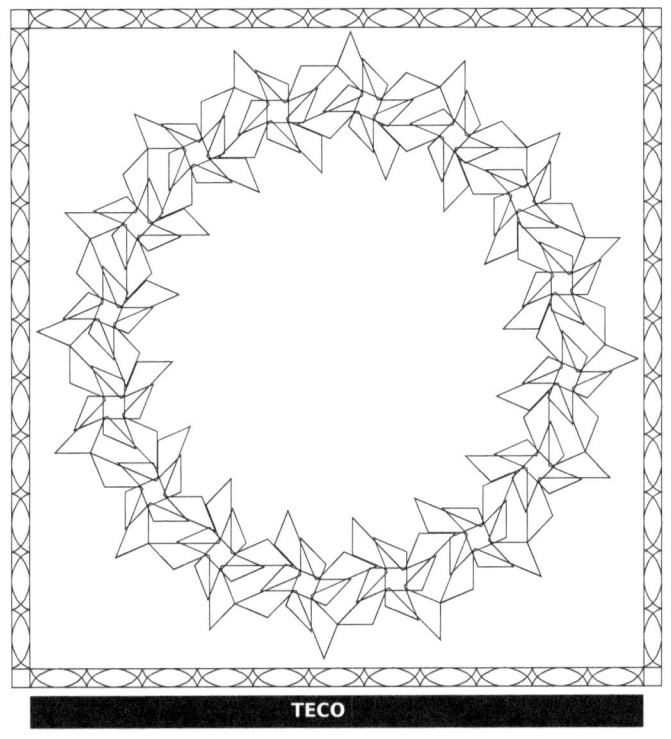

TECO

The mind is not a vessel to be filled, but a fire to be kindled.
Plutarch

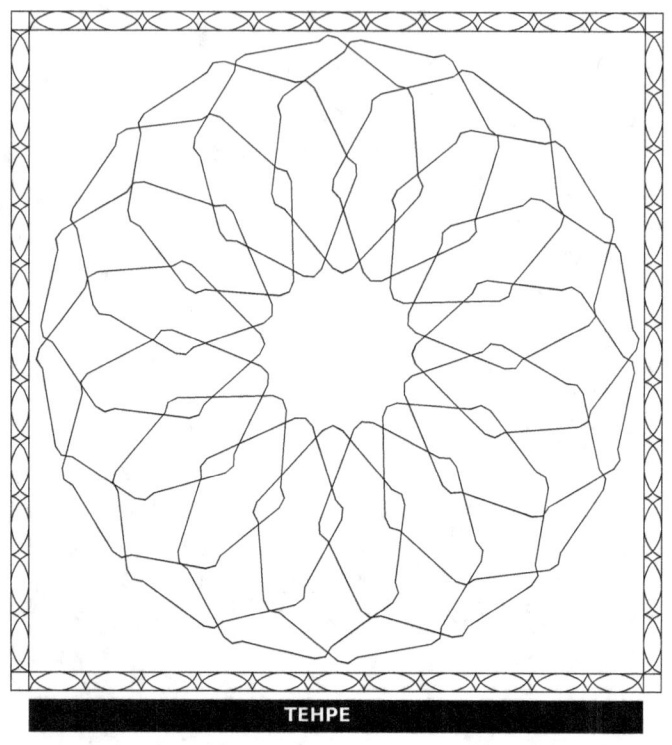

TEHPE

There is no truth which cannot be given in fifty words; the
truth is always concise.

Barry Malzberg

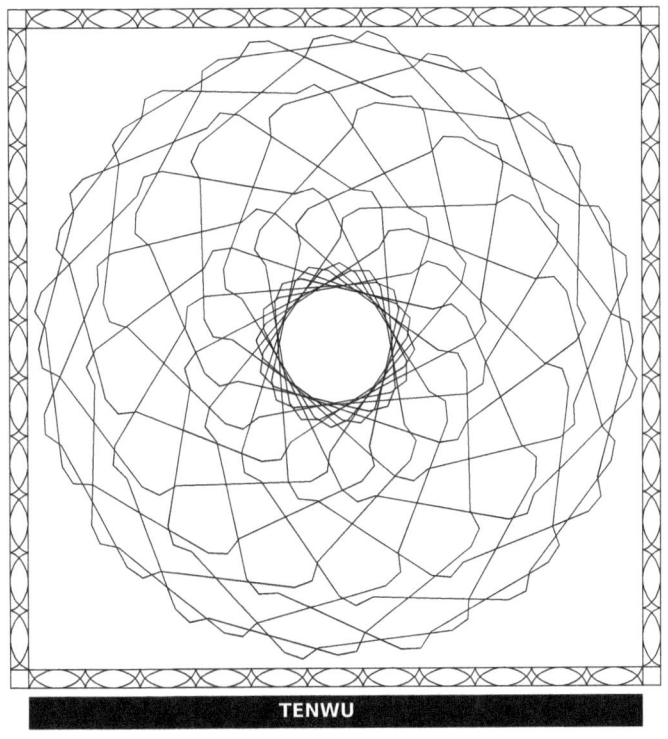

TENWU

All great art contains at its center contemplation, a dynamic contemplation.
Susan Sontag

257

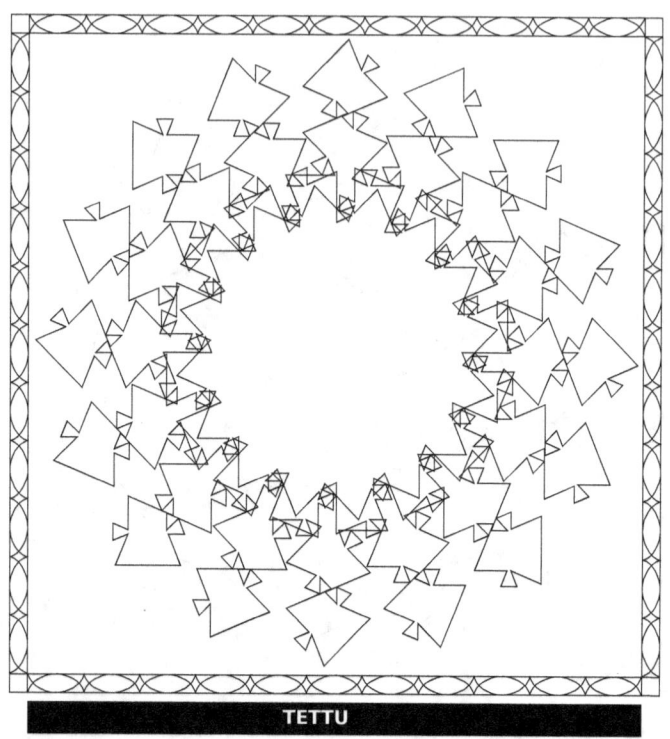

TETTU

The essence of the independent mind lies not in what it thinks, but in how it thinks.
Christopher Hitchens

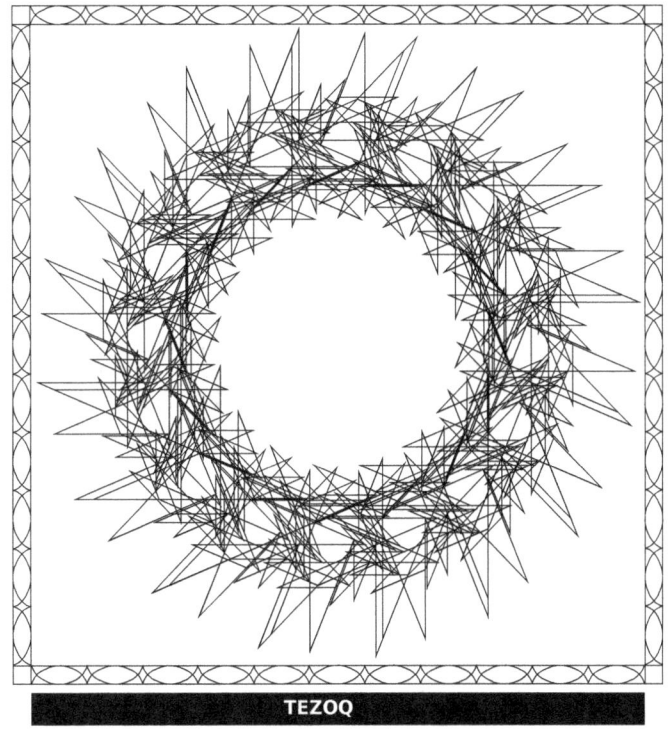

TEZOQ

The artist must be in his work as God is in creation, invisible and all-powerful; one must sense him everywhere but never see him.
Gustave Flaubert

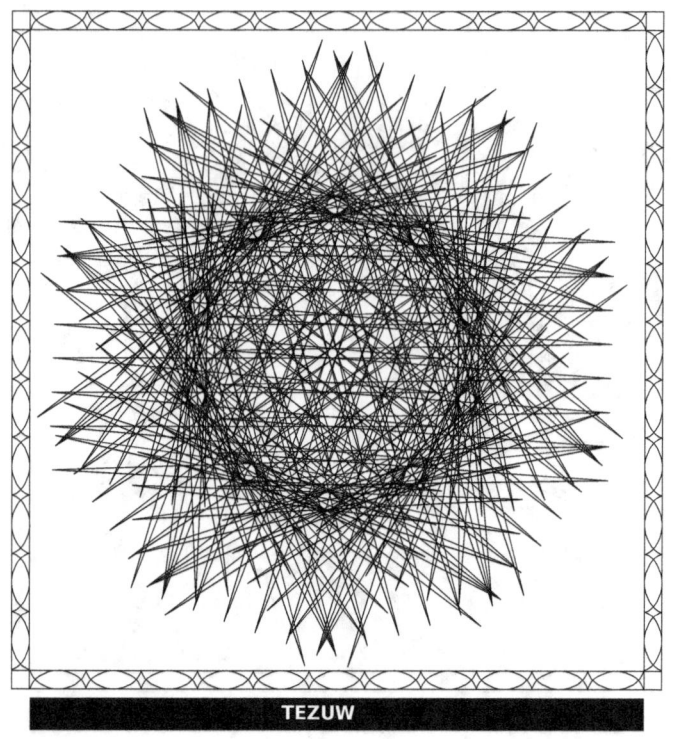

TEZUW

Each work of art generate its own rules.
Robert Pinsky

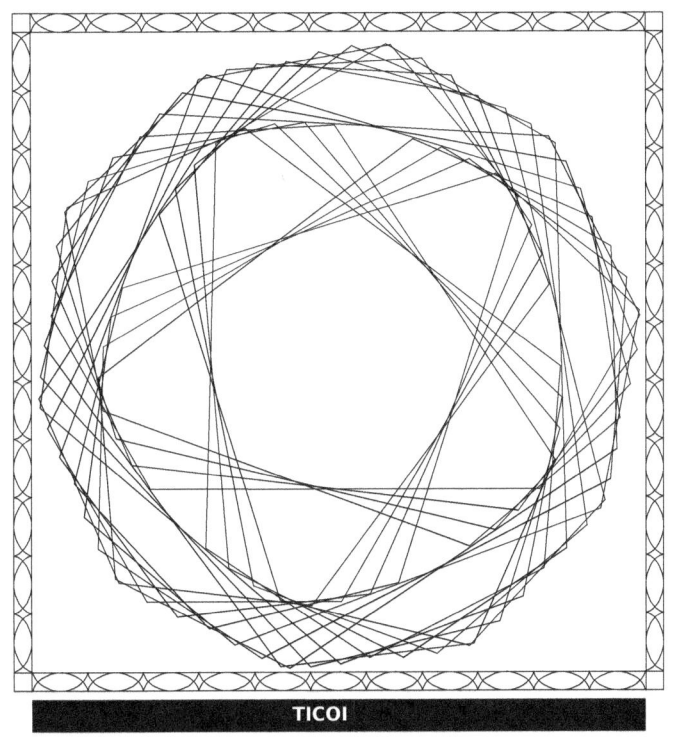

TICOI

Upon the whole, a contented mind is the greatest blessing a man can enjoy in this world.
Joseph Addison

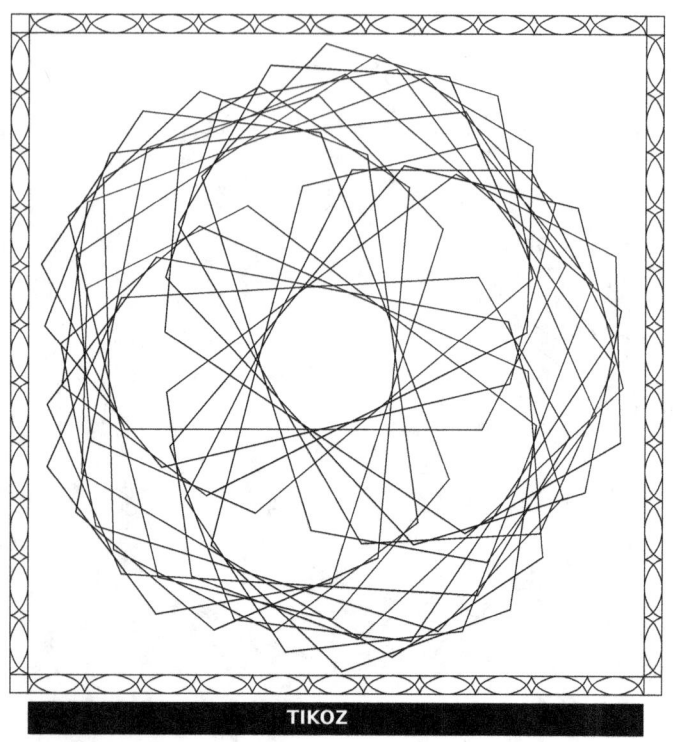

TIKOZ

The artist must imitate that which is within the thing, that which is active through form and figure, and discourses to us by symbols.
Samuel Taylor Coleridge

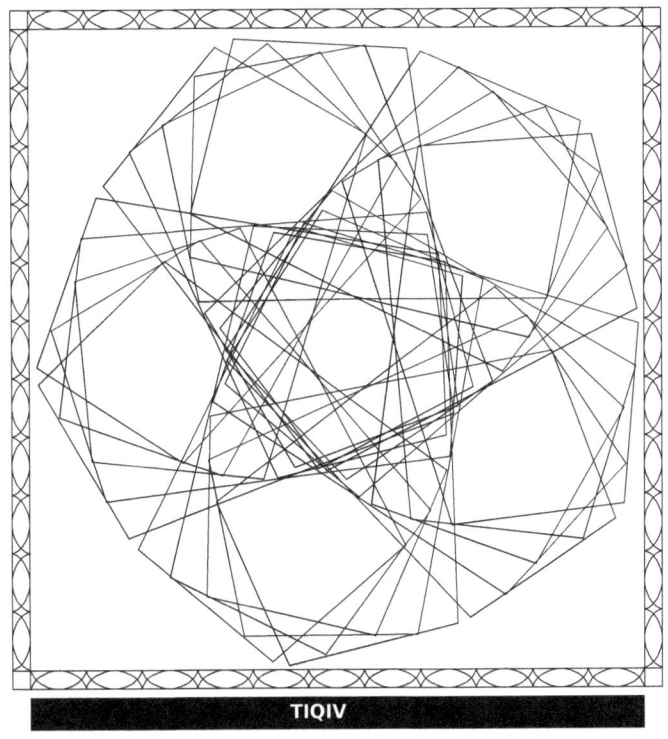

TIQIV

The foolish man seeks happiness in the distance; The wise grows it under his feet.
James Oppenheim

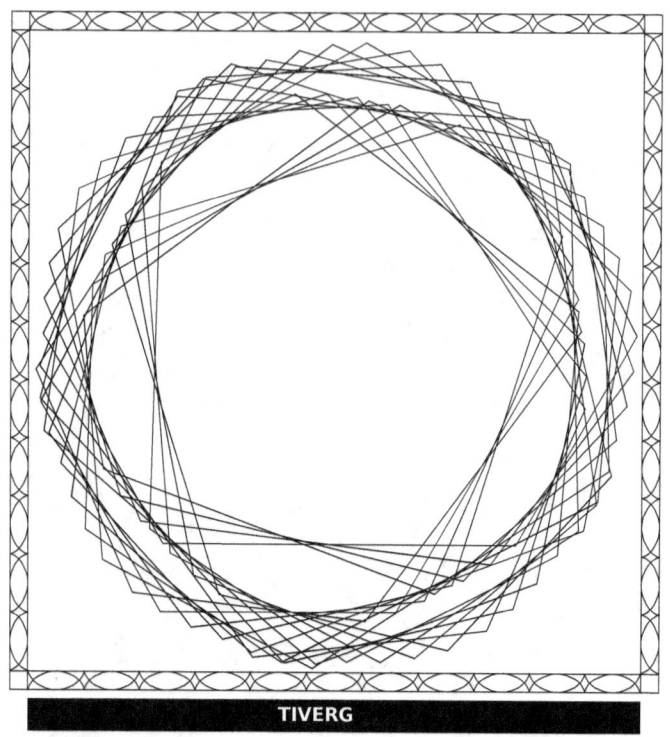

TIVERG

The primary purpose of a liberal education is to make one's mind a pleasant place in which to spend one's time.
Thomas Henry Huxley

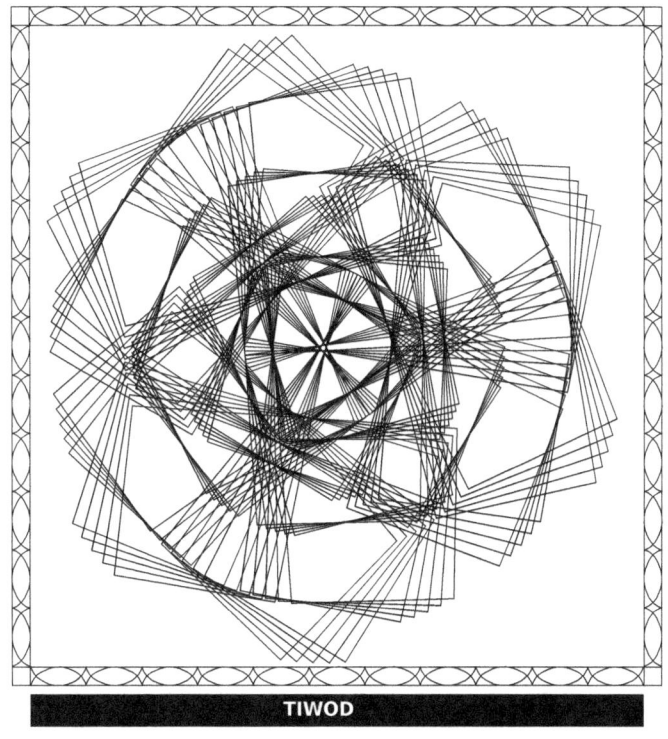

TIWOD

Symbols are to the mind what tools are to the hand - an
extended application of its powers.

Dion Fortune

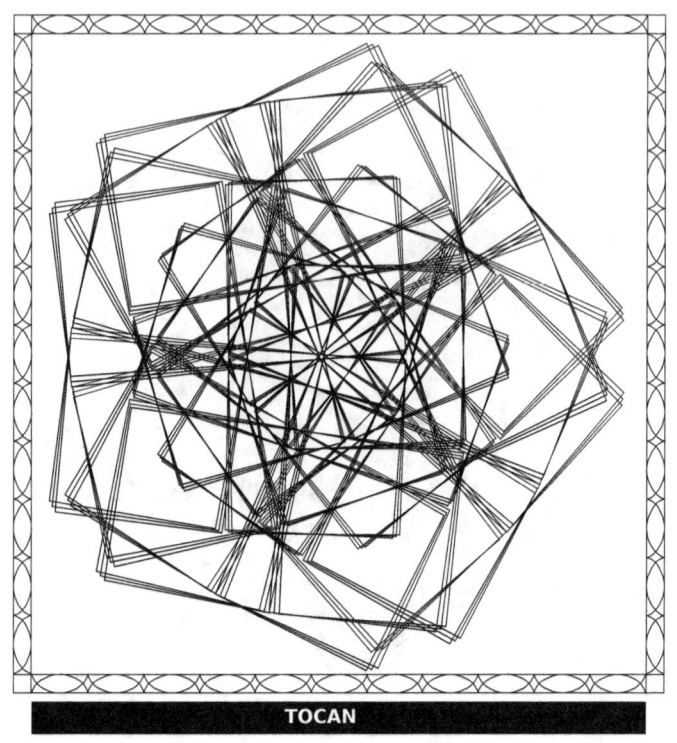

TOCAN

The greater perfection a soul aspires after, the more dependent it is upon Divine Grace.
Brother Lawrence

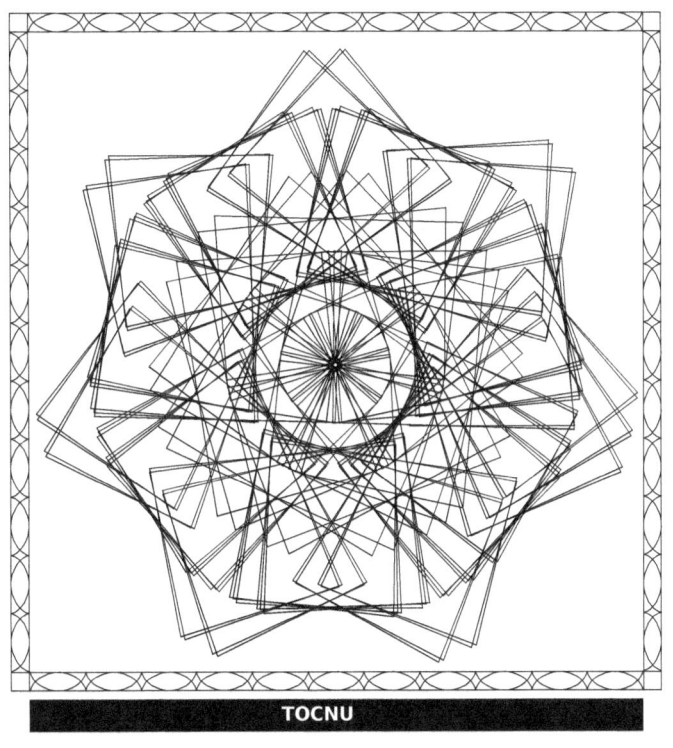

TOCNU

Happiness will never come if it's a goal in itself; happiness is a by-product of a commitment to worthy causes.
Norman Vincent Peale

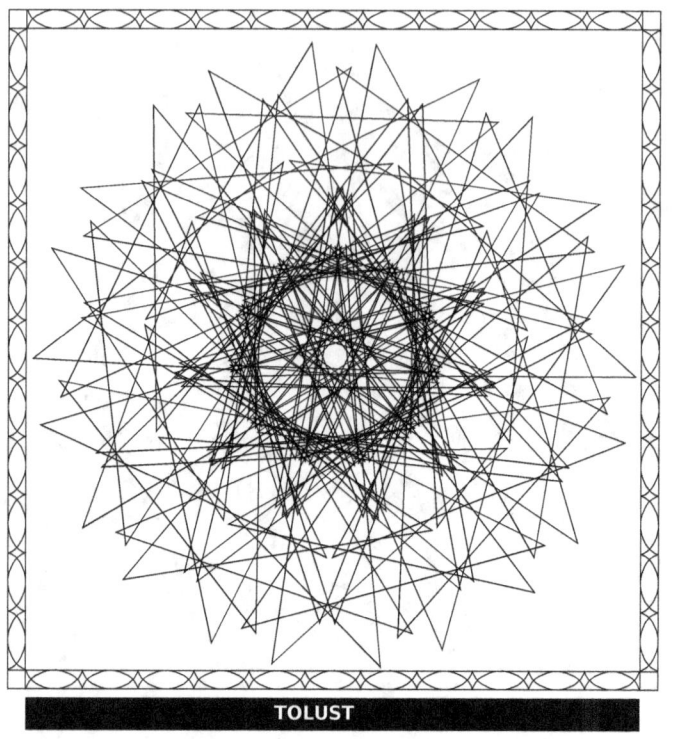

TOLUST

Each individual bears within himself an ideal man, and to bring him forth in perfect form is his divinely imposed life-work.

John Lancaster Spalding

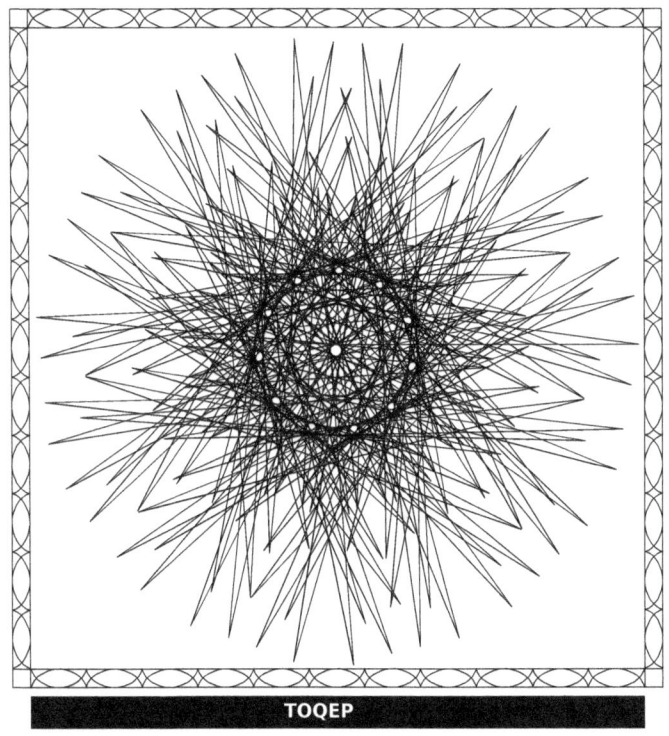

TOQEP

If in other sciences we should arrive at certainty without doubt and truth without error, it behooves us to place the foundations of knowledge in mathematics.

Roger Bacon

269

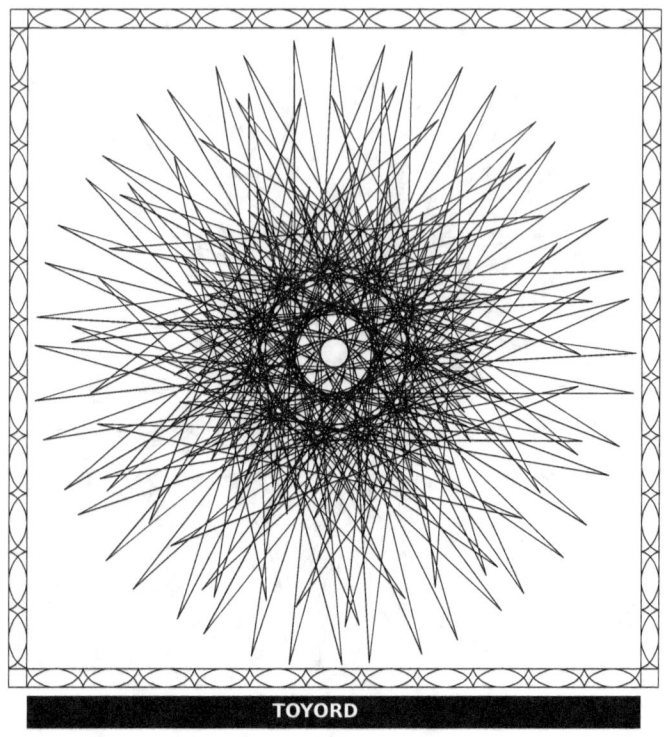

TOYORD

I climbed on the back of a giant albatross, Which flew through a crack in the cloud, To a place where happiness reigned all year round, Where music played ever so loudly.
Traffic, Hole in My Shoe, Dave Mason

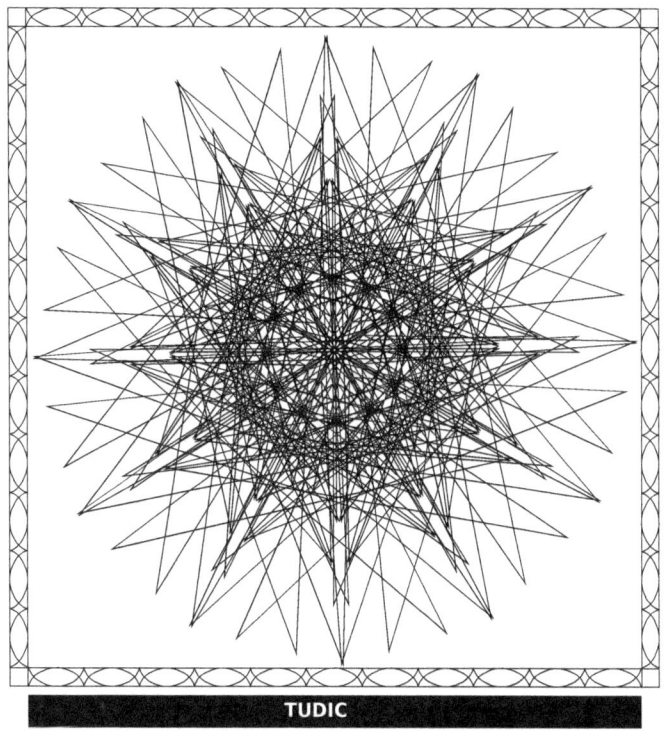

TUDIC

So somebody has talent? So what? Dime a dozen. And
we're overpopulated. Actually we have more food than we
have people and more art. We've gotten to the point of
burning food. When will we begin to burn our art?
John Cage

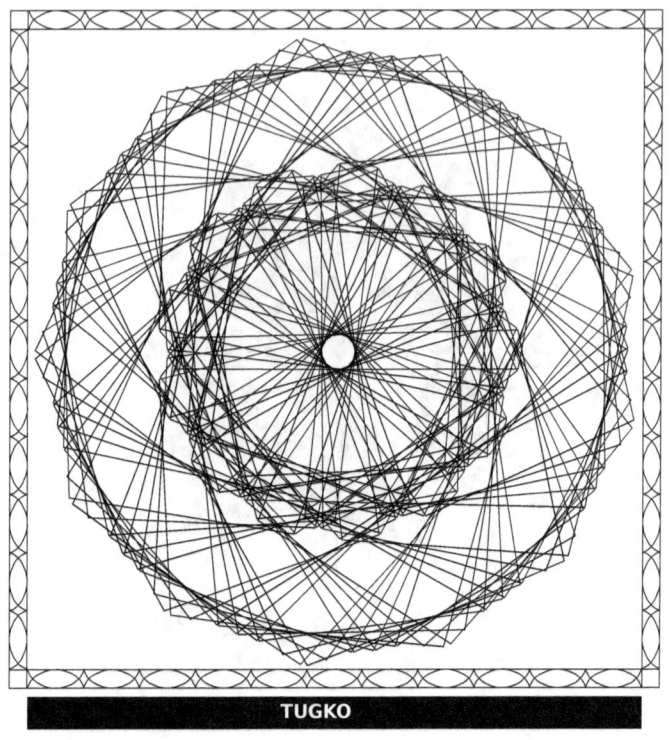

TUGKO

The art of doing mathematics consists in finding that special case which contains all the germs of generality.
David Hilbert

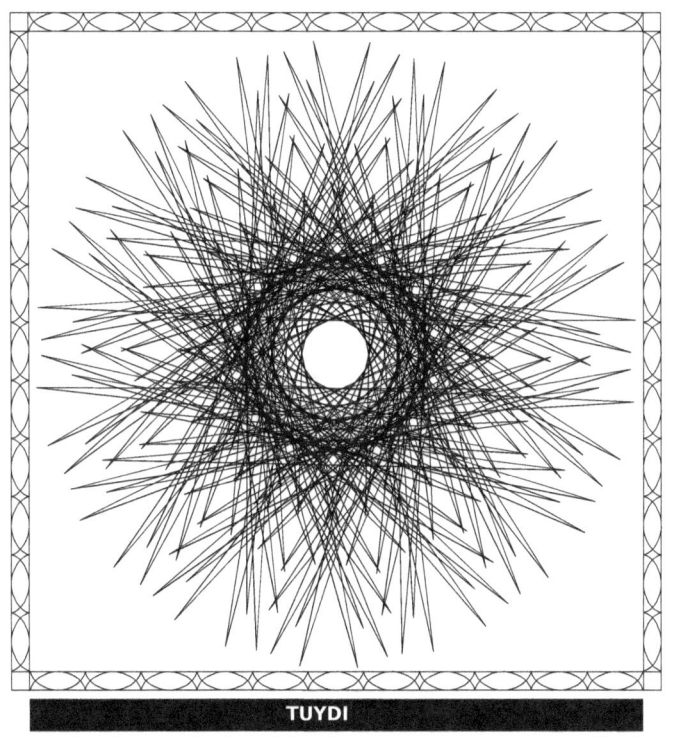

TUYDI

We should understand that our problems do not exist outside of ourself, but are part of our mind that experiences unpleasant feelings.
Kelsang Gyatso

273

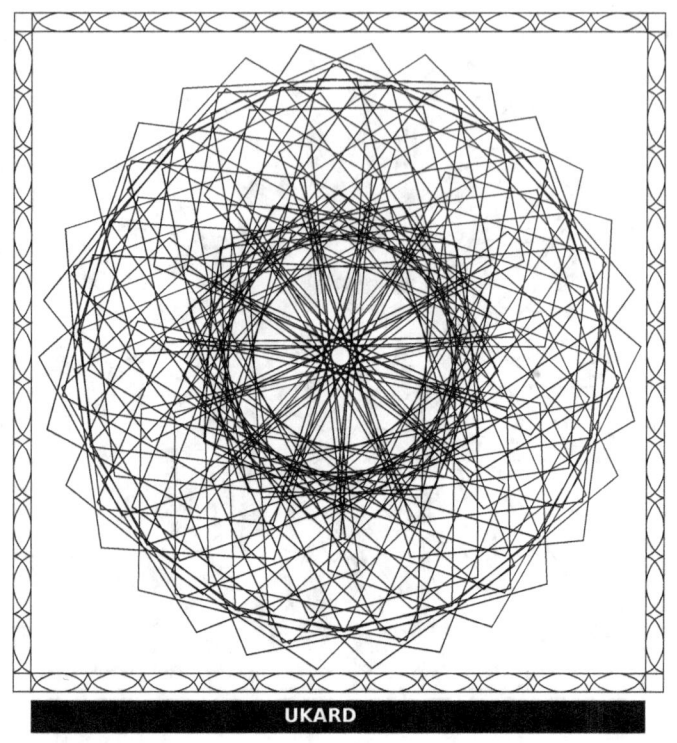

UKARD

Whoever said money can't buy happiness wasn't spending it helping people who needed it.
Keshia Chante

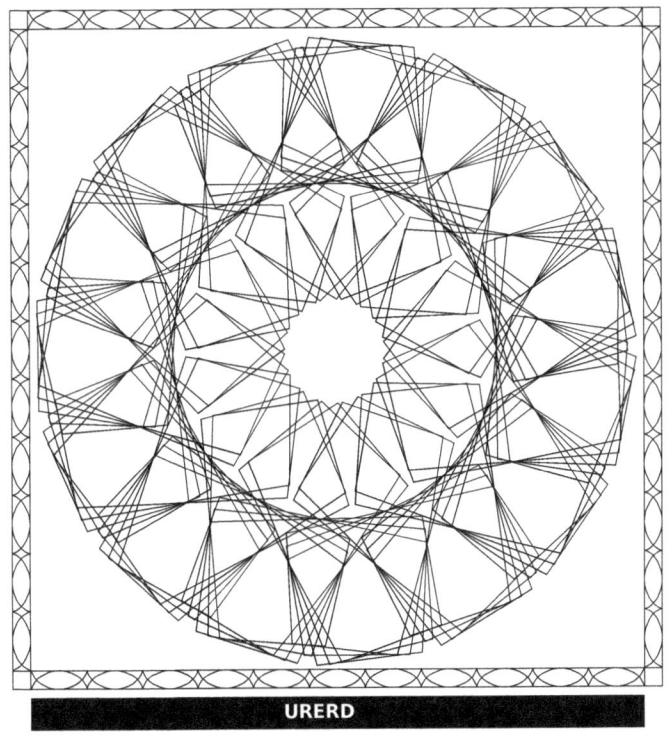

URERD

One truth discovered is immortal, and entitles its author
to be so: for, like a new substance in nature, it cannot be
destroyed.
William Hazlitt

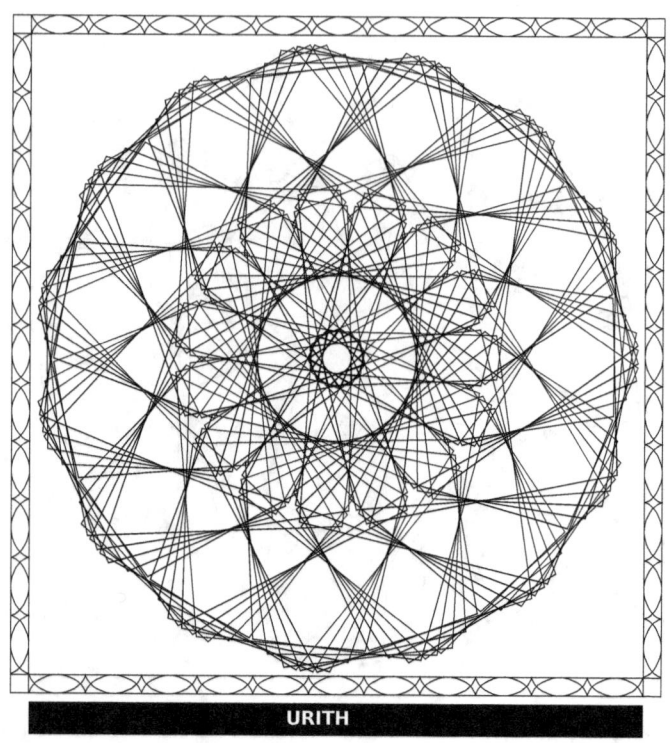

URITH

Artists use lies to tell the truth, while politicians use them to cover the truth up.

V for Vendetta (film)

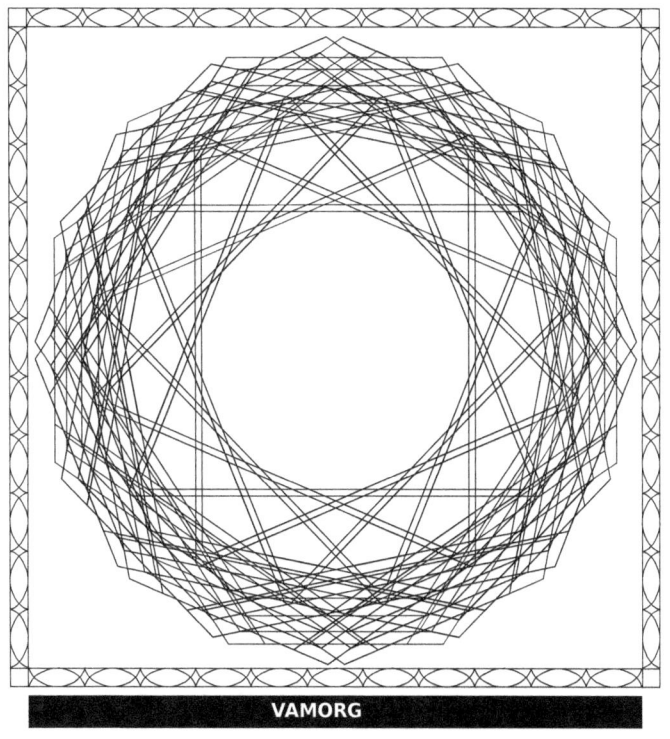

VAMORG

If you think about it, the inside of your own mind is the only thing you can be sure of.
Thomas Nagel

277

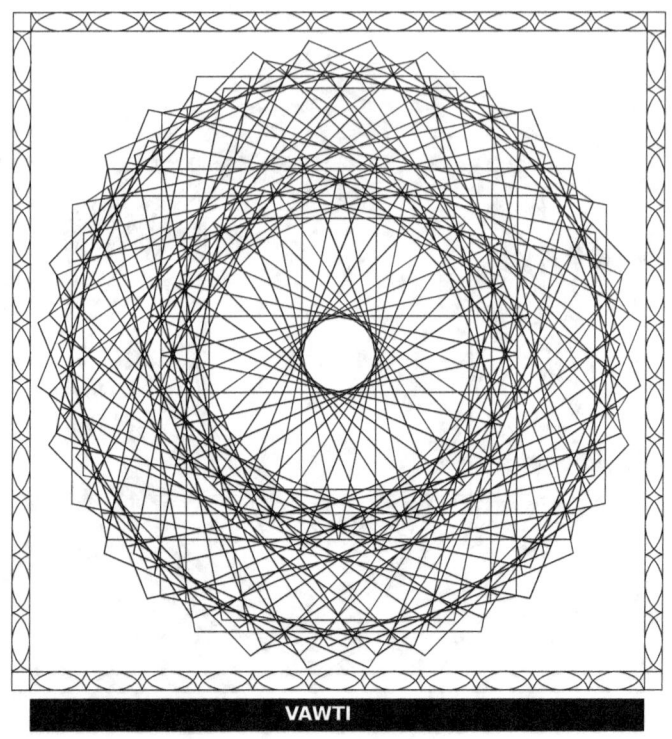

VAWTI

Nurture your mind with great thoughts. To believe in the
heroic makes heroes.
Benjamin Disraeli

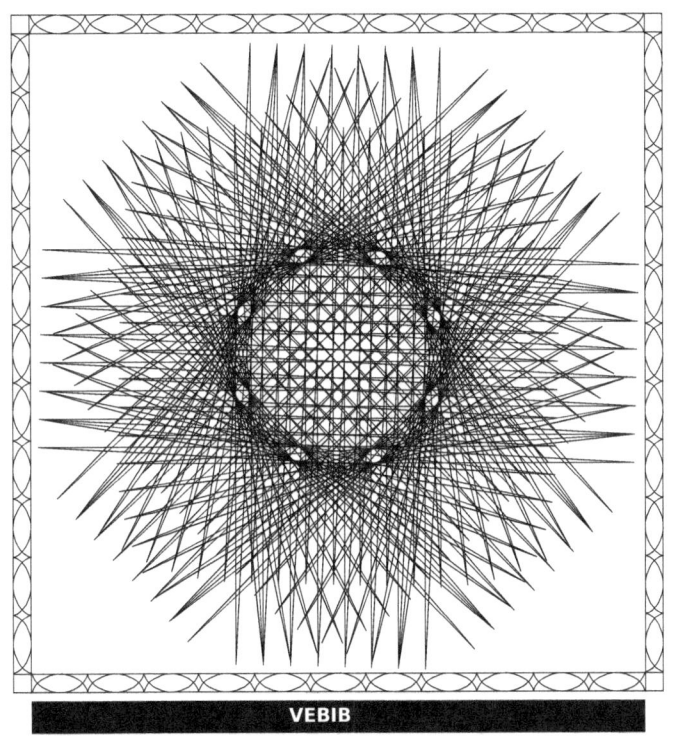

VEBIB

Karma is the natural law of cause and effect whereby positive actions produce happiness and negative actions produce suffering.

Tashi Tsering

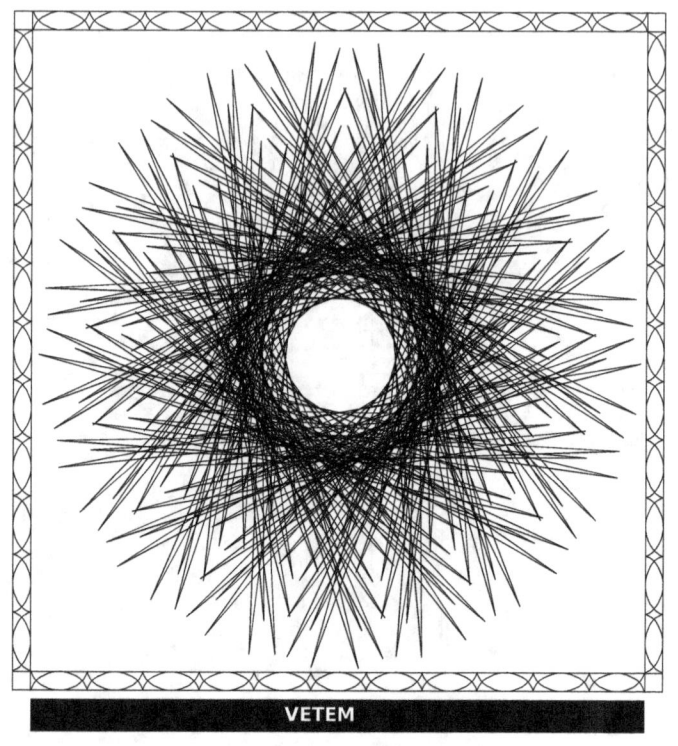

VETEM

Your mind is all you truly have.
Sam Harris

280

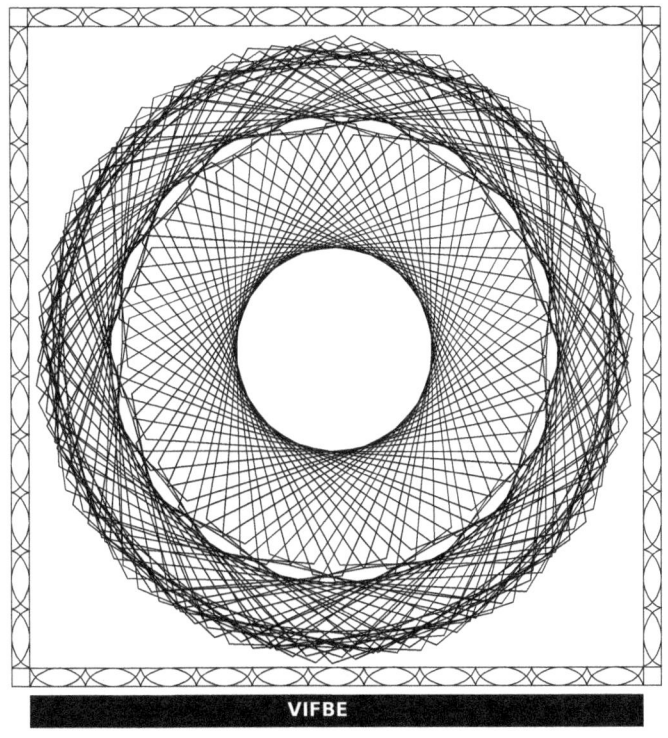

VIFBE

No form remains permanently in a substance; a constant change takes place, one form is taken off and another is put on.
Maimonides

281

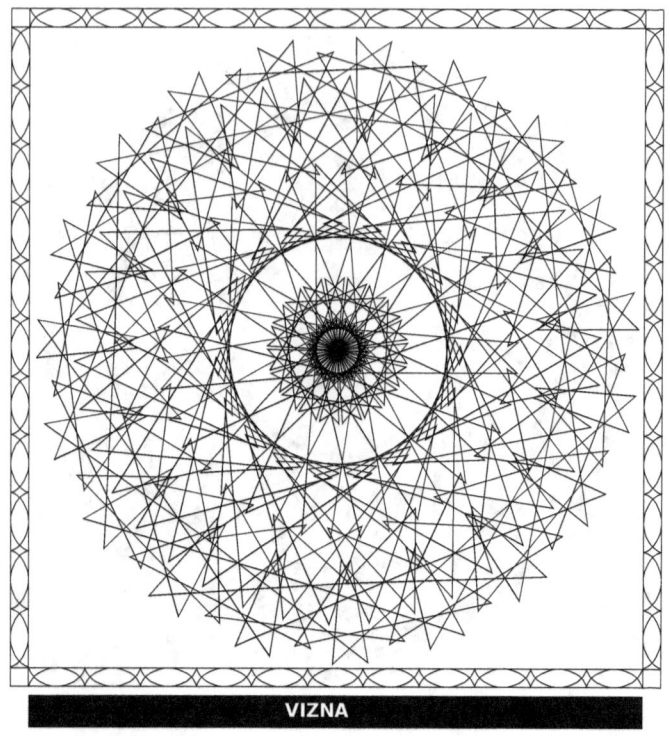

VIZNA

Aesthetic value is often the by-product of the artist striving
to do something else.
Evelyn Waugh

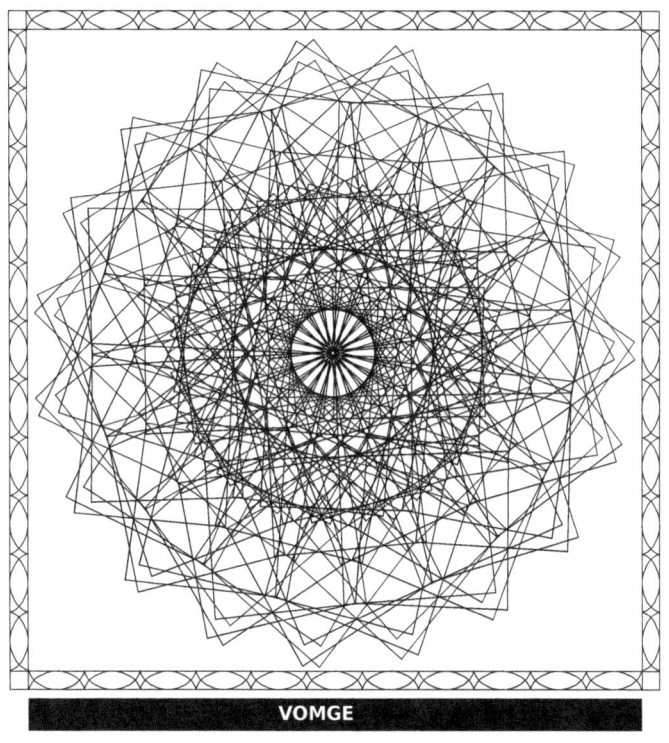

VOMGE

Attachment to status, power, wealth or comforts gives rise to ego. It is ego that separates man from God.

Sirshree

283

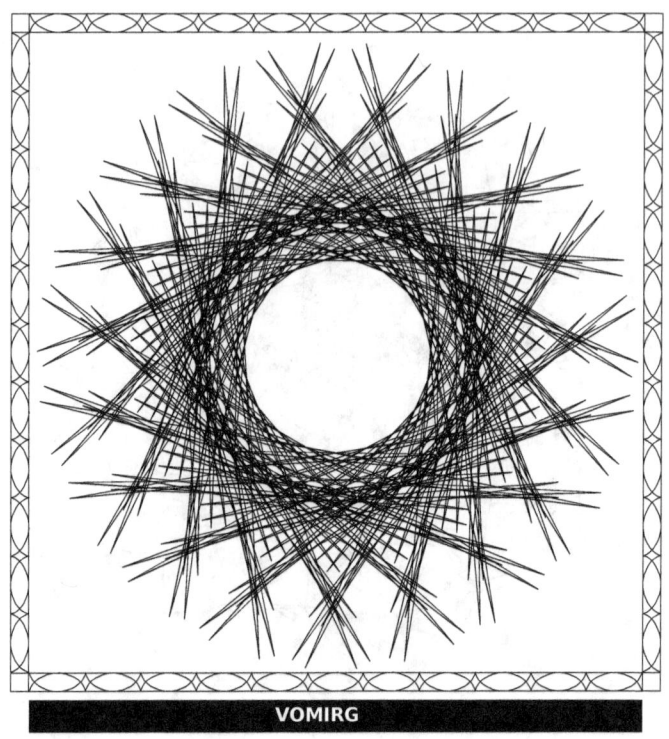

VOMIRG

You go to truth by way of poetry and I go to poetry by way of truth.
Joseph Joubert

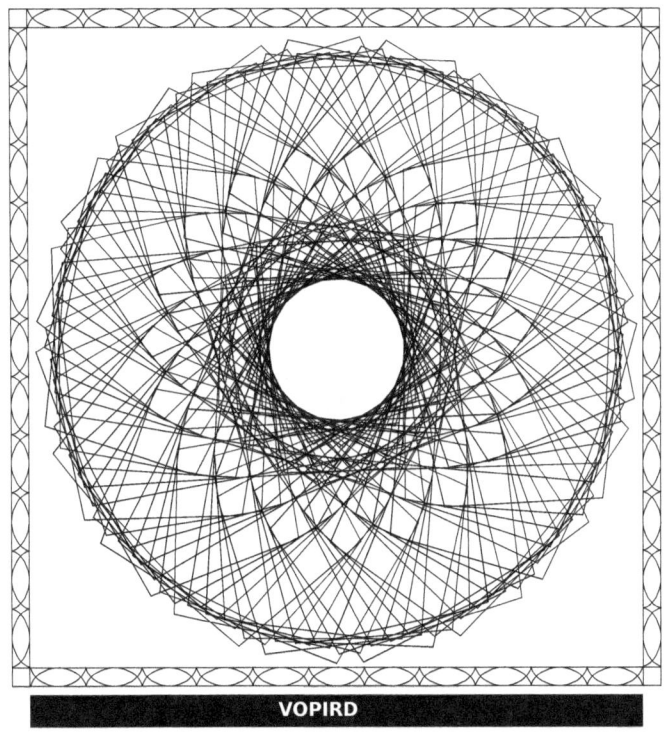

VOPIRD

Men of genius are scarce, but men of genius who use their genius for the benefit of the world are scarcer.

Josh Billings

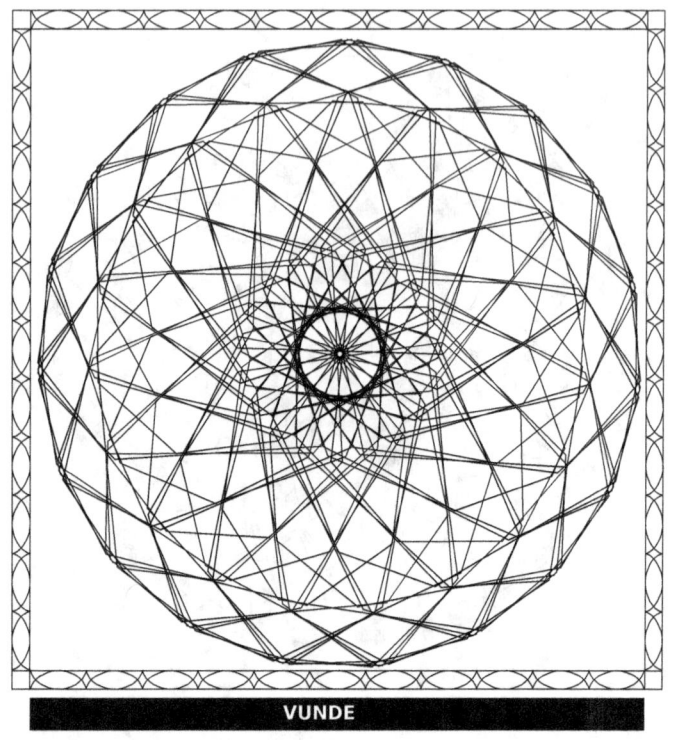

VUNDE

I think art certainly is the vehicle for us to develop any new ideas, to be creative, to extend our imagination, to change the current conditions.
Ai Weiwei

286

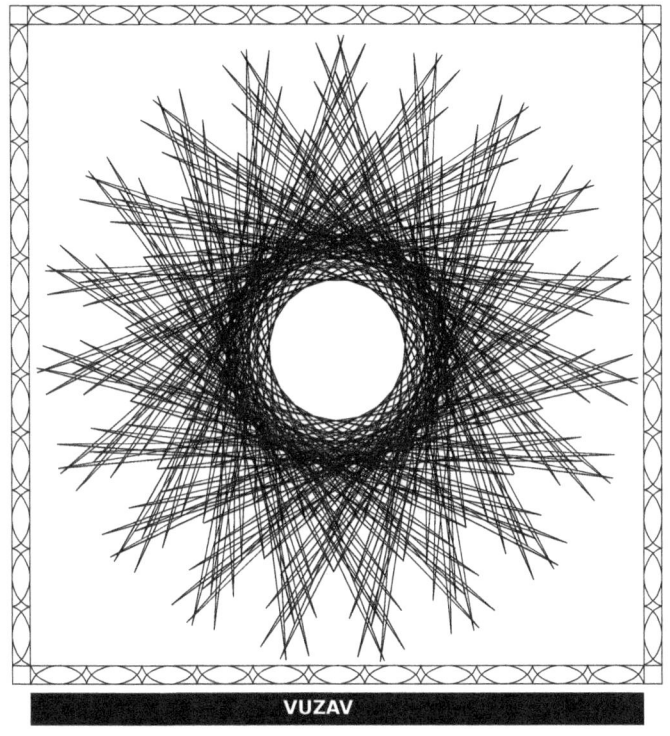

VUZAV

Every now and then a man's mind is stretched by a new idea or sensation, and never shrinks back to its former dimensions.

Oliver Wendell Holmes, Sr.

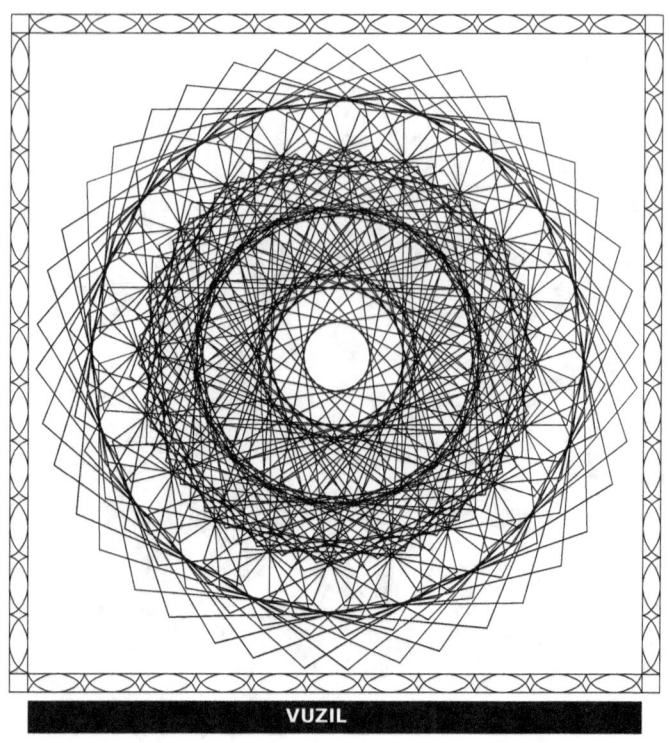

VUZIL

By ignorance is pride increased; They most assume who know the least.
John Gay

288

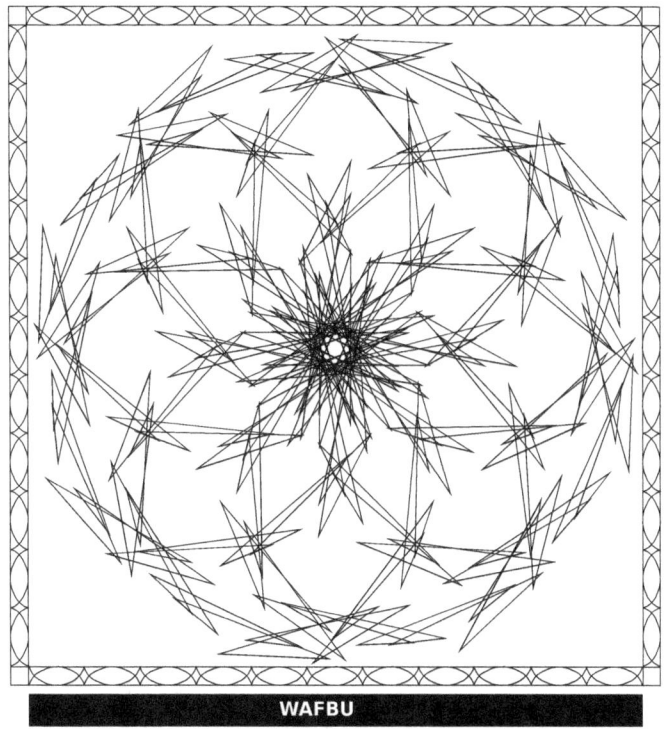

WAFBU

Where the writer produces that combination of perfect technique, human interest, and thruth, and can add to it that supreme touch, the perfection of art has been attained.
Ernest Dimnet

289

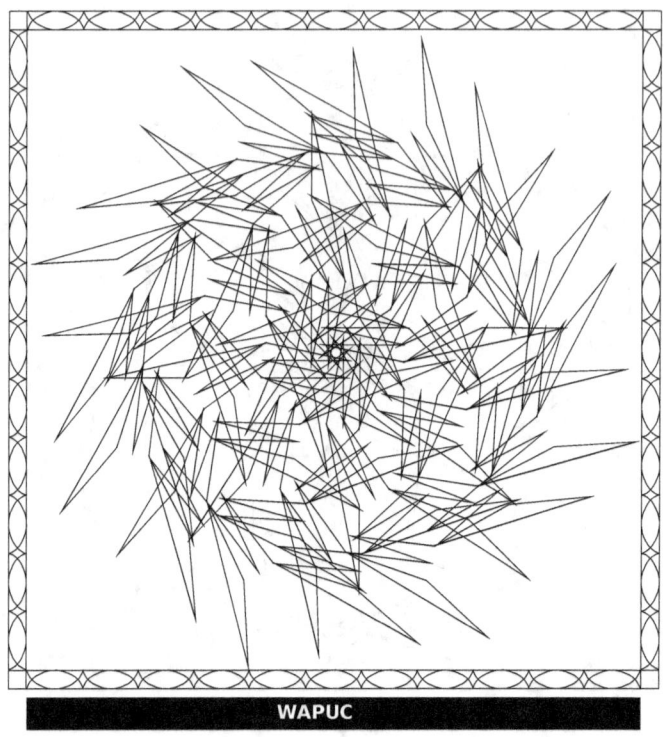

WAPUC

All that the conscious ego can do is to formulate wishes, which are then carried out by forces which it controls very little and understands not at all.
Aldous Huxley

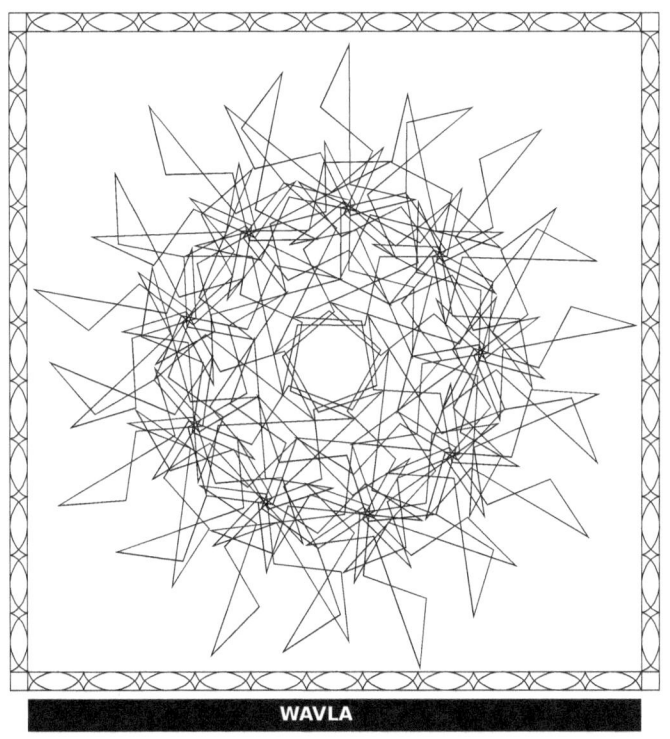

WAVLA

The most elementary form of rebellion, paradoxically, expresses an aspiration for order.
Albert Camus

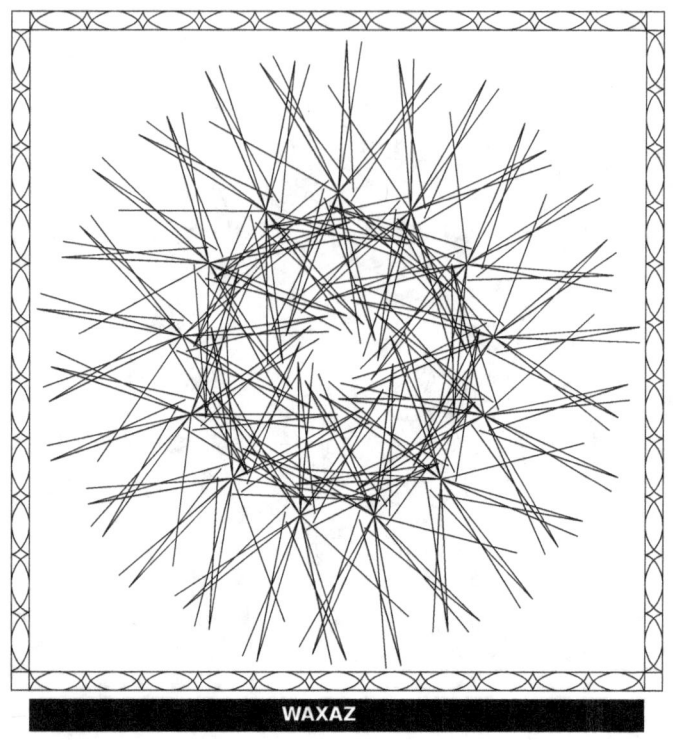

WAXAZ

The only way to maintain a moderate sum of happiness in this life, is not to worry about the future or regret the past too much.
Mel Gibson

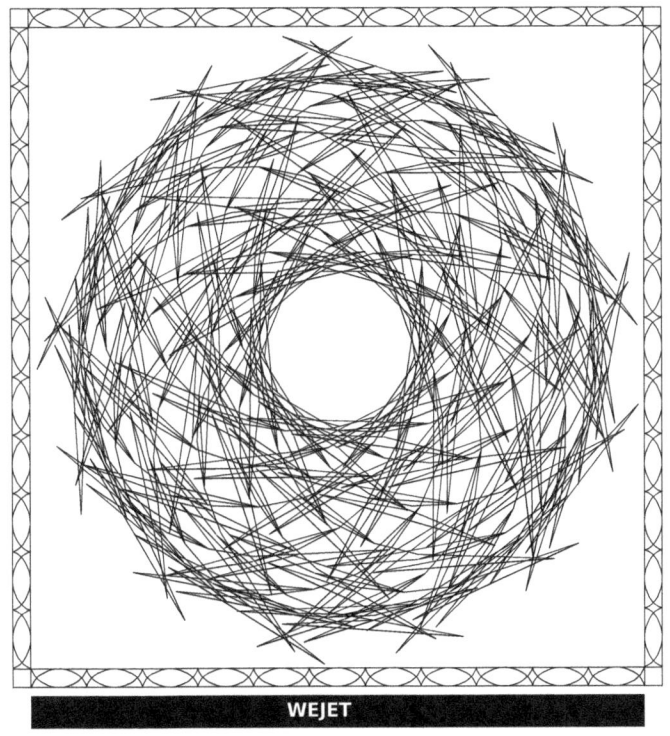

WEJET

Through all God's works there runs a beautiful harmony. The remotest truth in his universe is linked to that which lies nearest the throne.

Edwin Hubbell Chapin

293

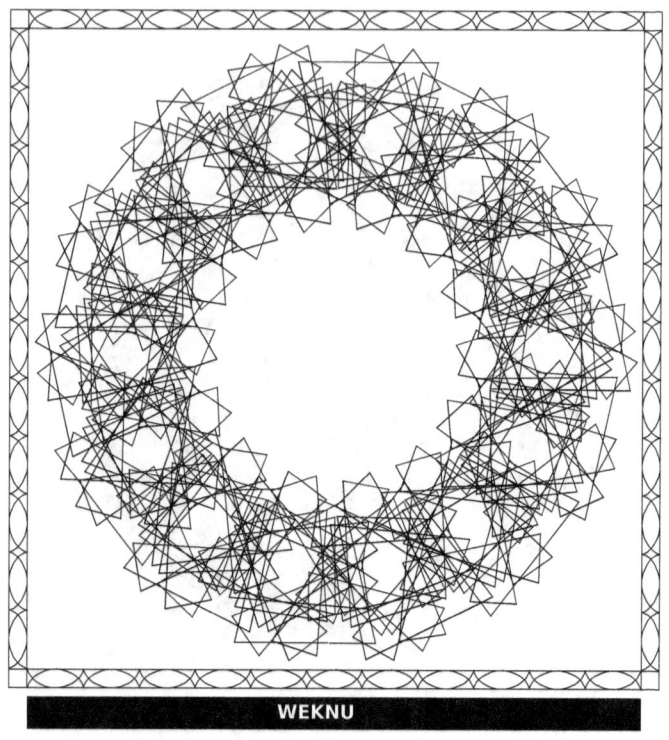

WEKNU

The human mind cannot be absolutely destroyed with the body, but something of it remains which is eternal ... We feel and know by experience that we are eternal.
Baruch Spinoza

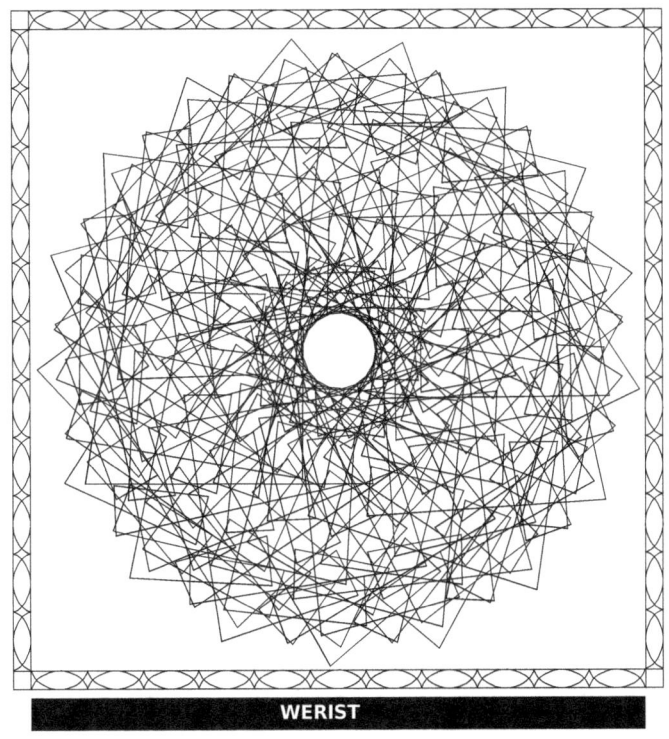

WERIST

God is what mind becomes when it has passed beyond the
scale of our comprehension.
Freeman Dyson

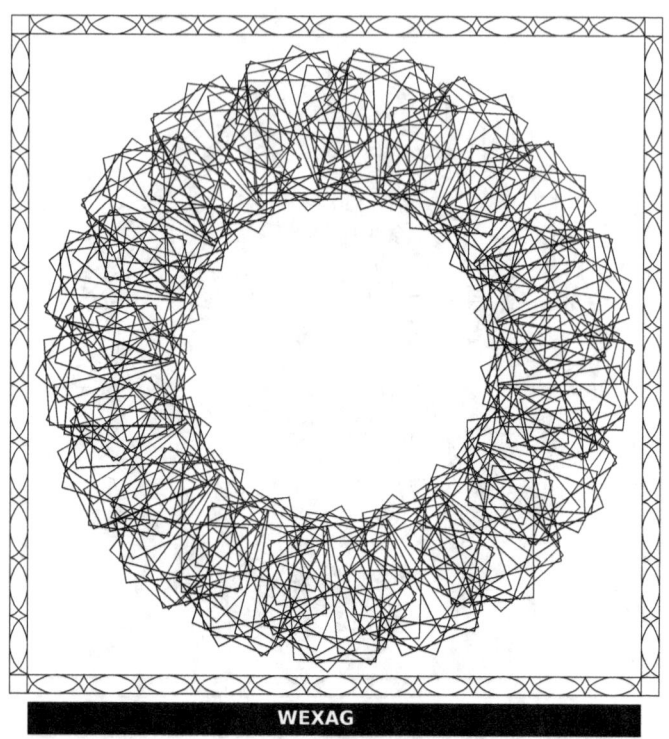

WEXAG

He who fights with monsters should look to it that he himself does not become a monster. And when you gaze long into an abyss the abyss also gazes into you.
Friedrich Nietzsche

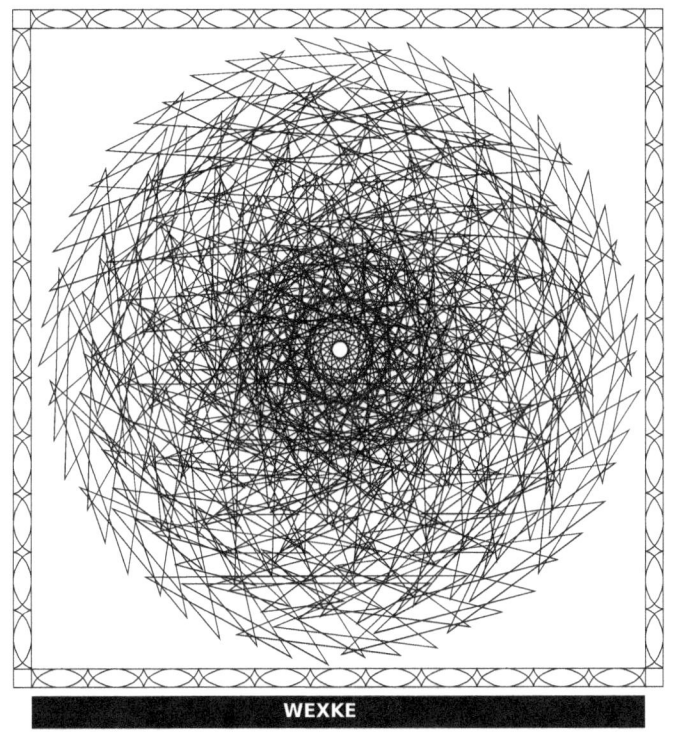

WEXKE

That is the true perfection of man to find out his imperfections.
Augustine of Hippo

297

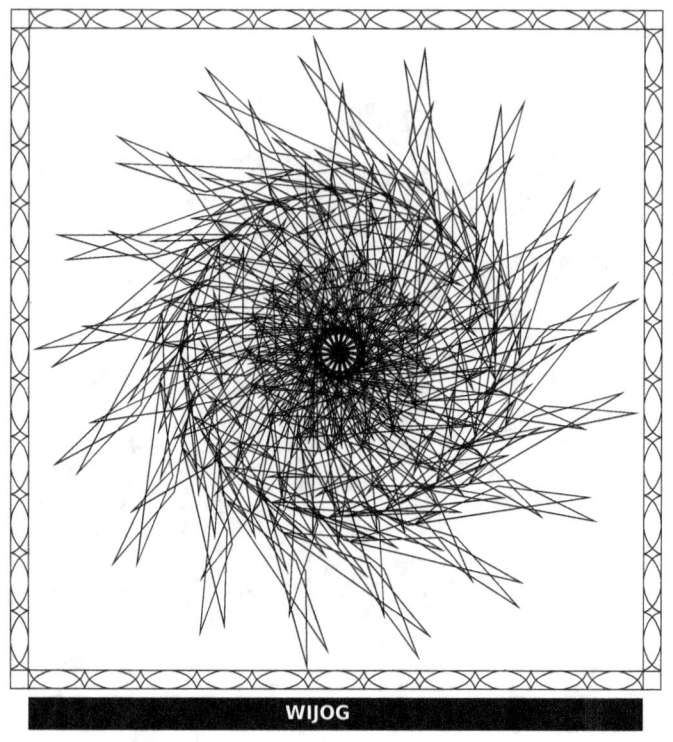

WIJOG

Those who have achieved all their aims probably set them too low.

Herbert von Karajan

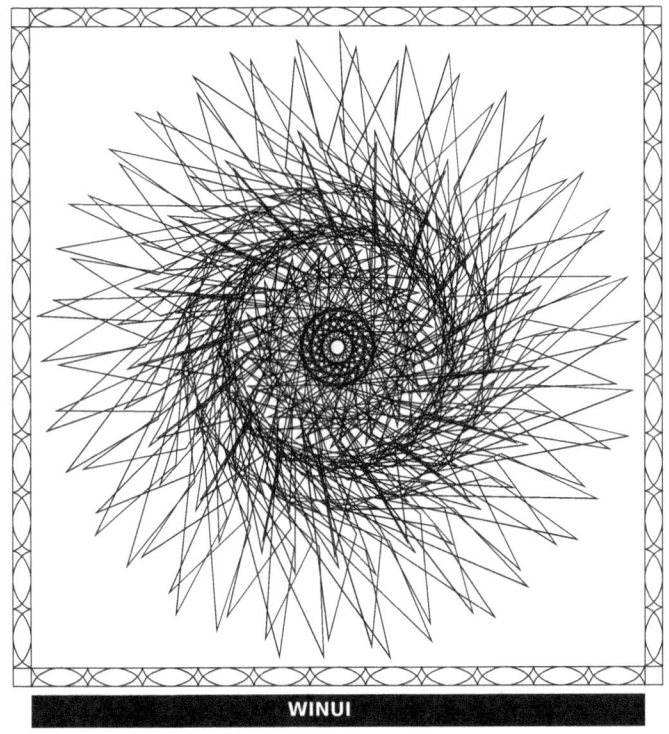

WINUI

It is necessary to abandon yourself completely, and let the music do as it will with you. All people come to music to seek oblivion.

Claude Debussy

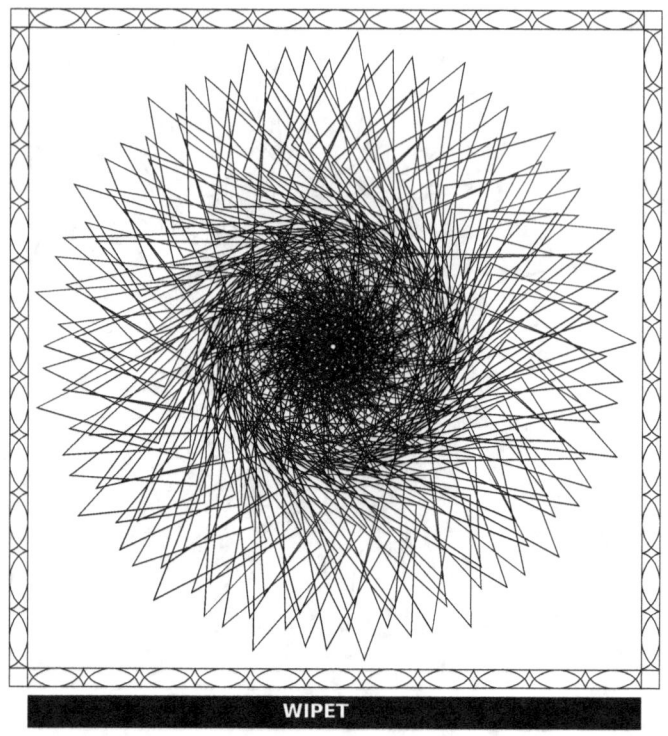

WIPET

Many are willing to suffer for their art. Few are willing to learn to draw.
Simon Munnery

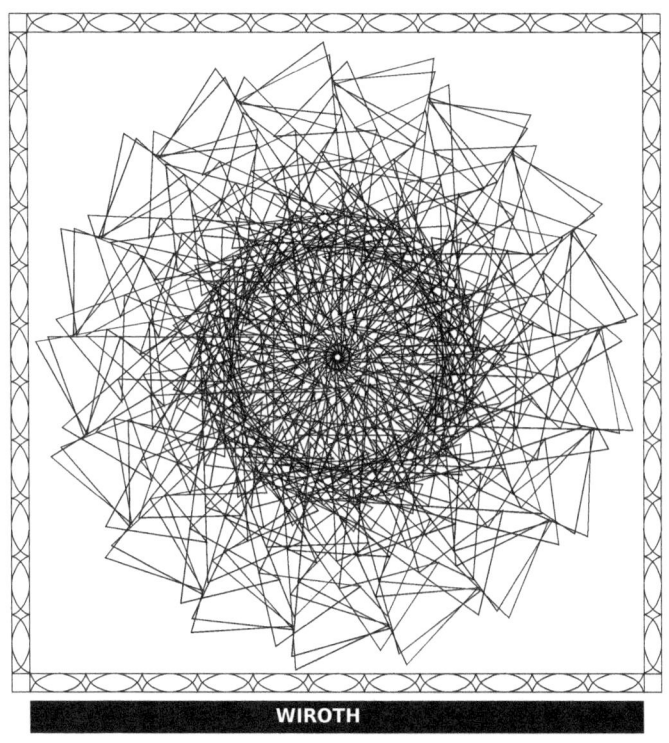

WIROTH

To be without music was, for the ancient Greeks, to be already dead ... Ancient Greece was a culture of song.
Thomas Cahill

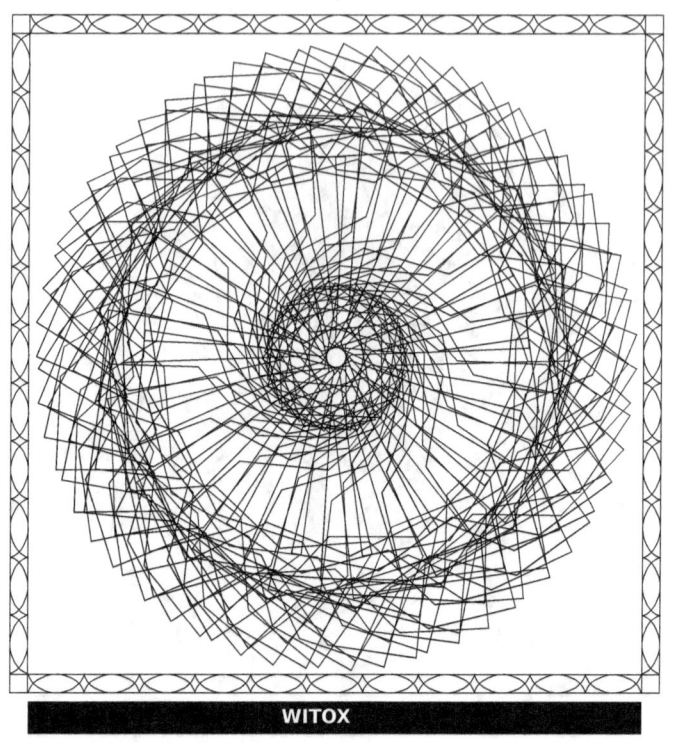

WITOX

Good painting is not produced by any unintelligent following of inspiration or temperament.
Patrick Swift

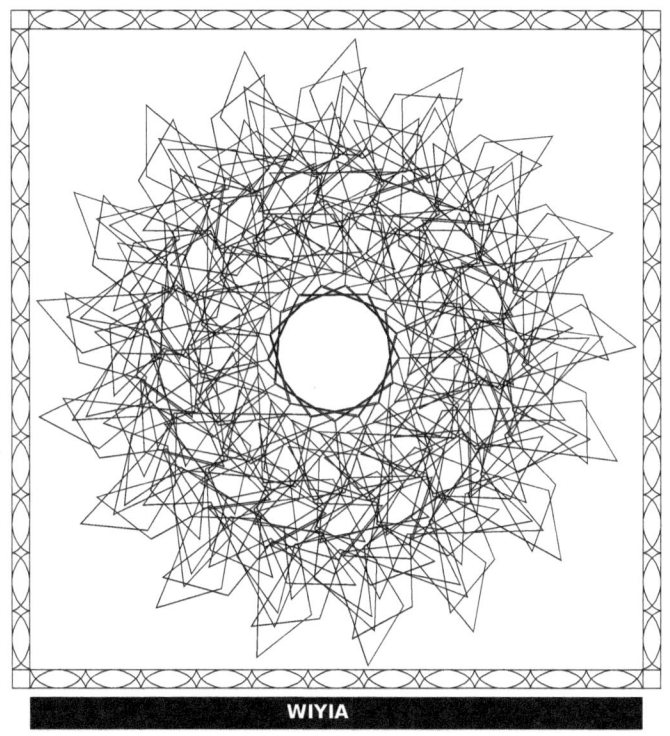

WIYIA

An intellectual is a man who says a simple thing in a difficult way; an artist is a man who says a difficult thing in a simple way.

Charles Bukowski

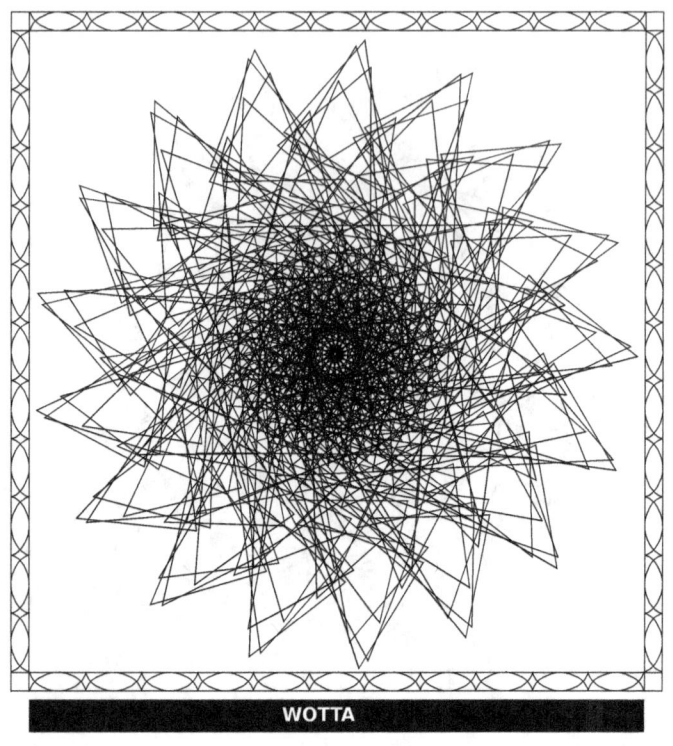

WOTTA

The mind is but the subtle part of the body. You must retain great strength in your mind and words.
Swami Vivekananda

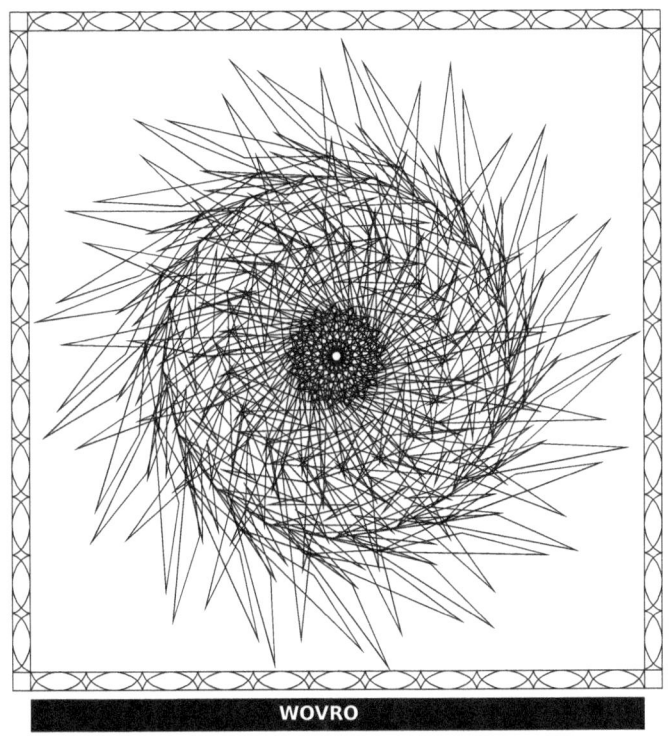

WOVRO

Writing is a socially acceptable form of schizophrenia.
E. L. Doctorow

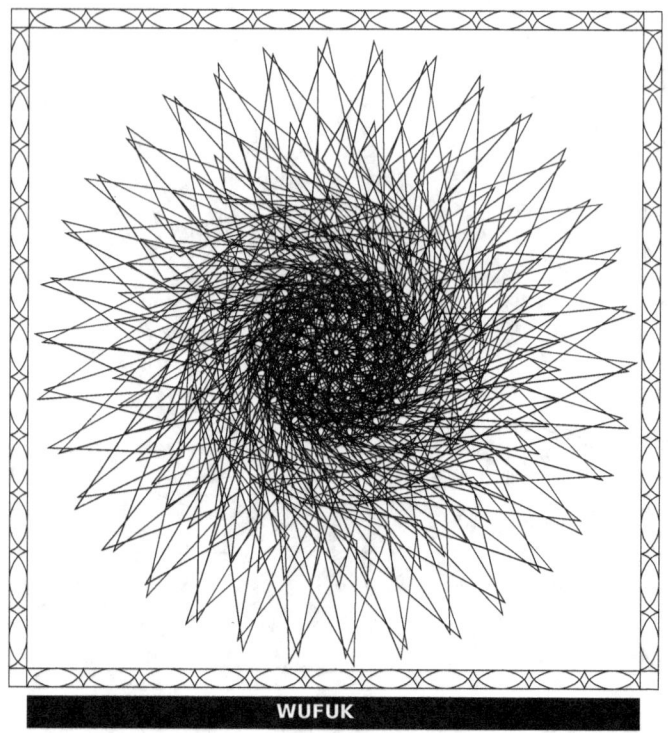

WUFUK

Naps are essential to my process. Not dreams, but that state adjacent to sleep, the mind on waking.
William Gibson

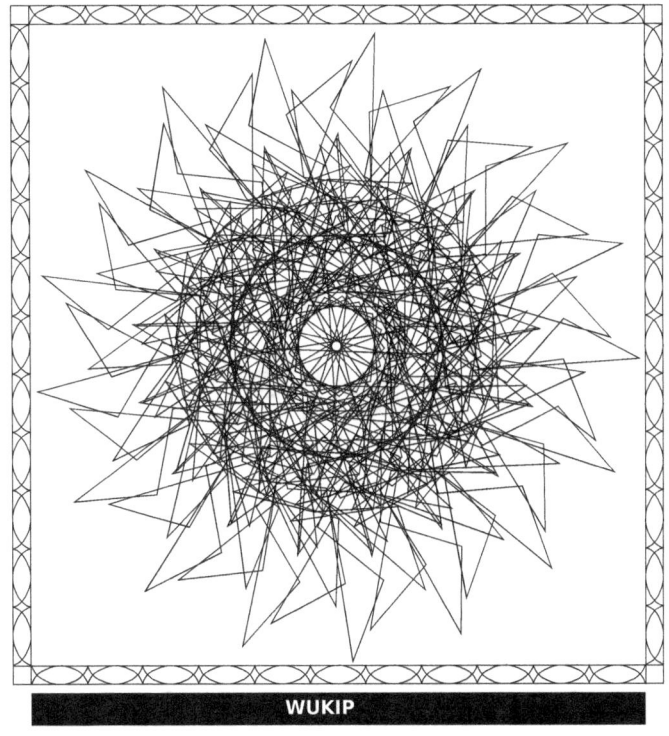

WUKIP

You measure democracy by the freedom it gives its dissidents, not the freedom it gives its assimilated conformists.
Abbie Hoffman

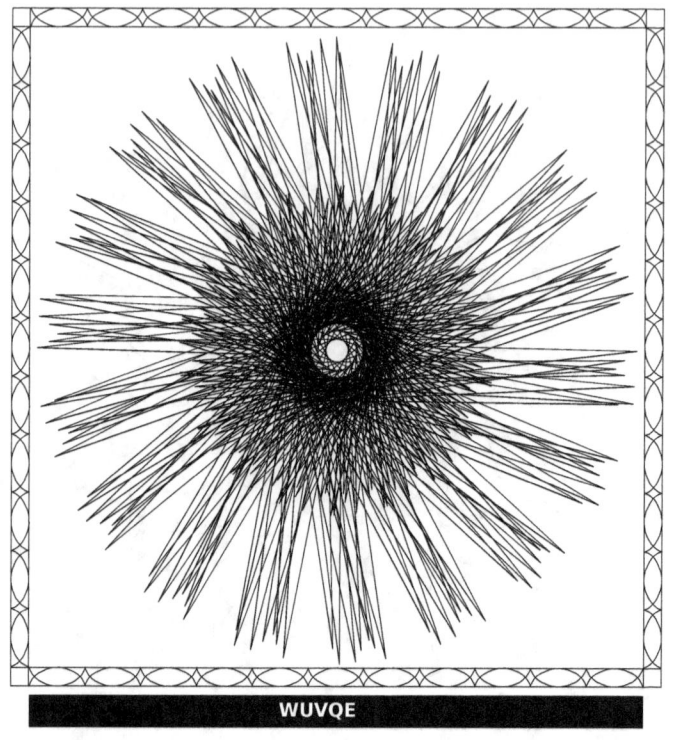

WUVQE

No man is great enough or wise enough for any of us to surrender our destiny to. The only way in which anyone can lead us is to restore to us the belief in our own guidance.
Henry Miller

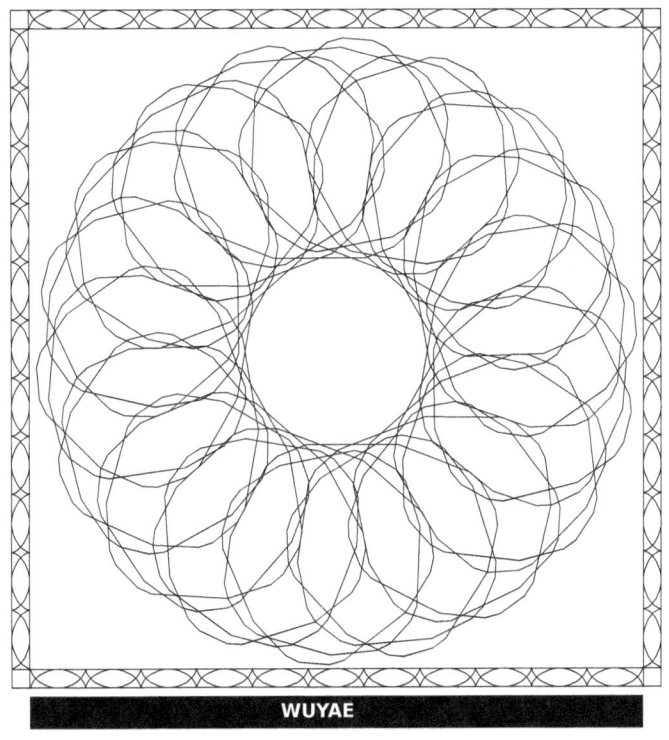

WUYAE

Religion and art spring from the same root and are close kin. Economics and art are strangers.
Nathaniel Hawthorne

309

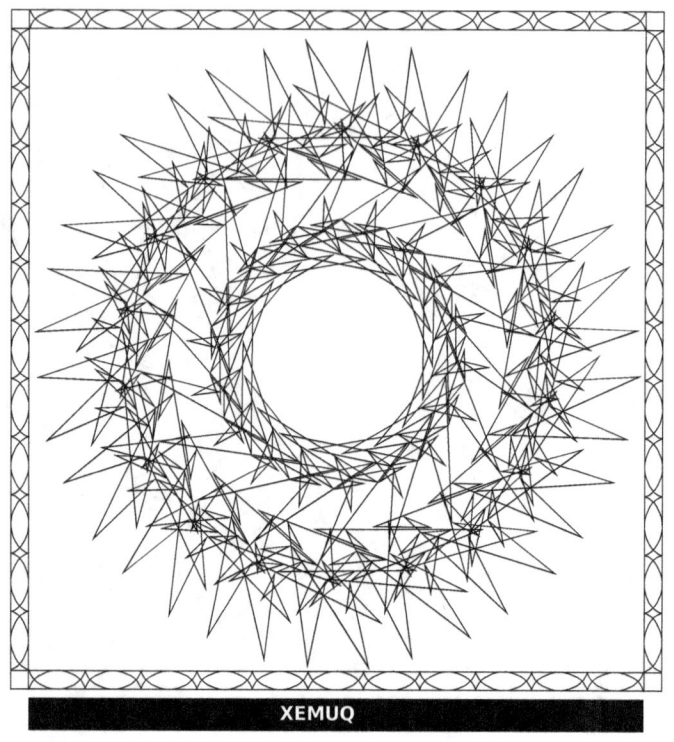

XEMUQ

If you tend to text and skim the surface of the Internet, you indirectly shape your mind to only deal with superficial matters.

Piero Scaruffi

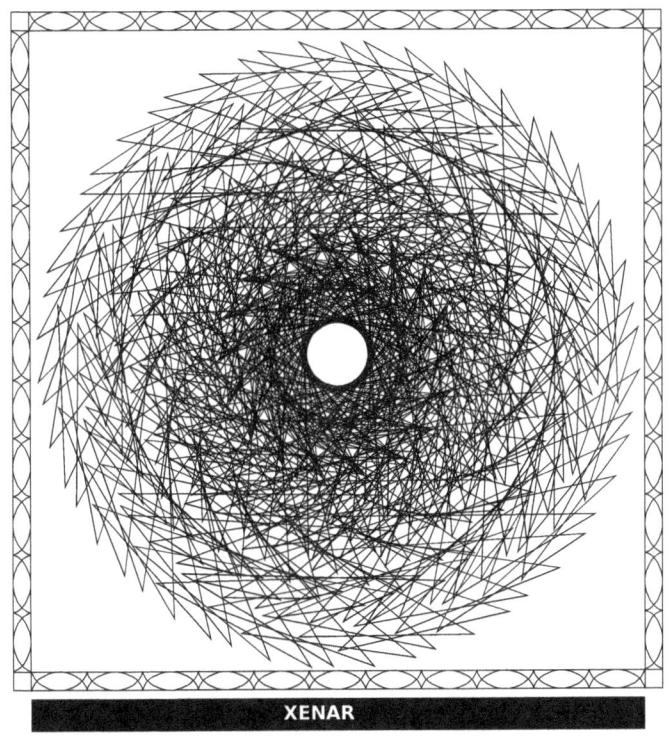

XENAR

Pictures must be miraculous.
Mark Rothko

311

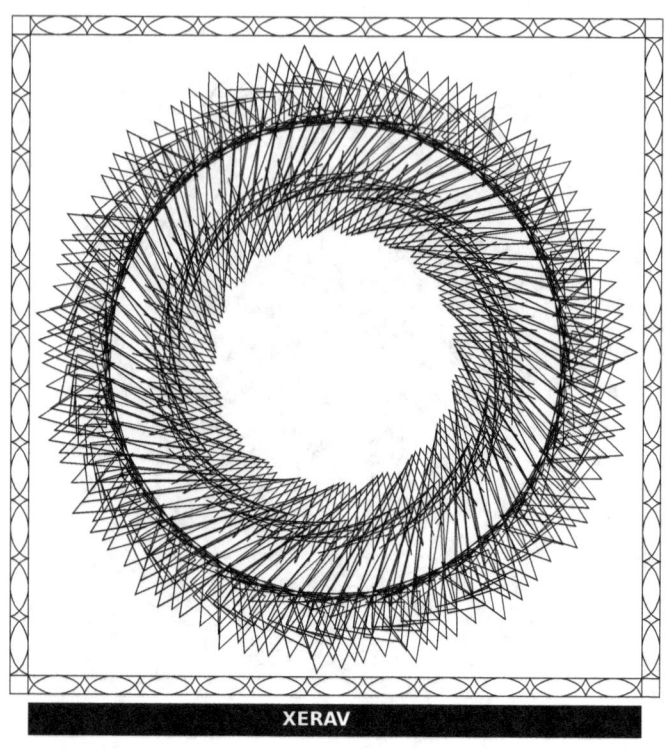

XERAV

Happiness and suffering are states of mind and so their main causes are not to be found outside the mind.
Kelsang Gyatso

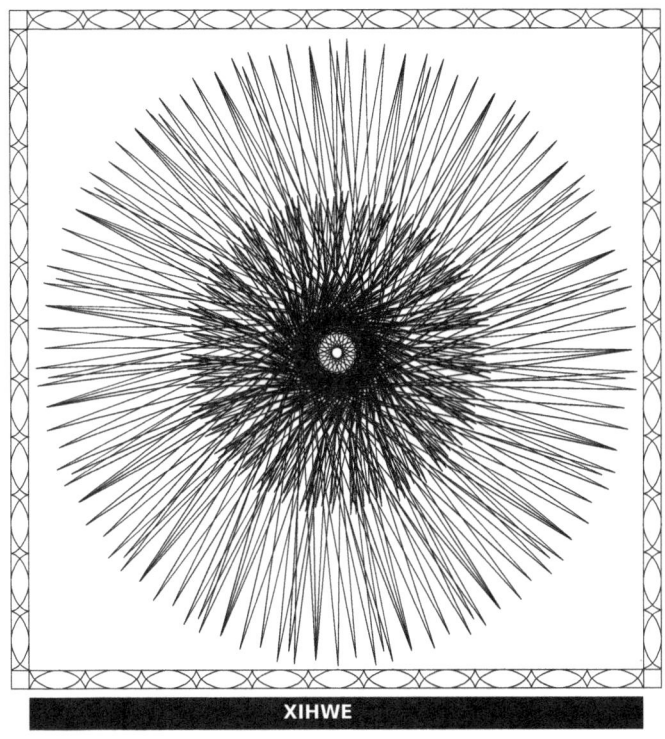

XIHWE

The powers of the mind are like the rays of the sun when they are concentrated they illumine.
Swami Vivekananda

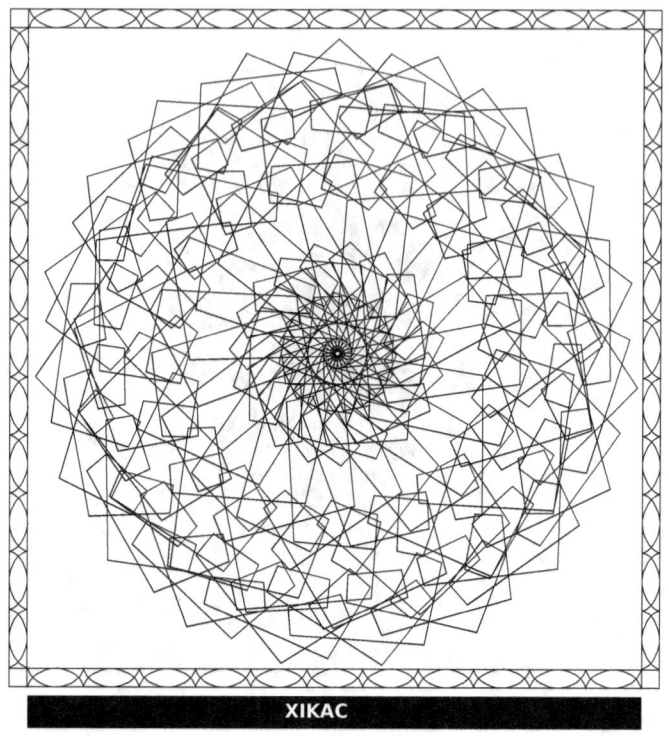

XIKAC

Some of the greatest poetry is revealing to the reader the beauty in something that was so simple you had taken it for granted.
Neil deGrasse Tyson

314

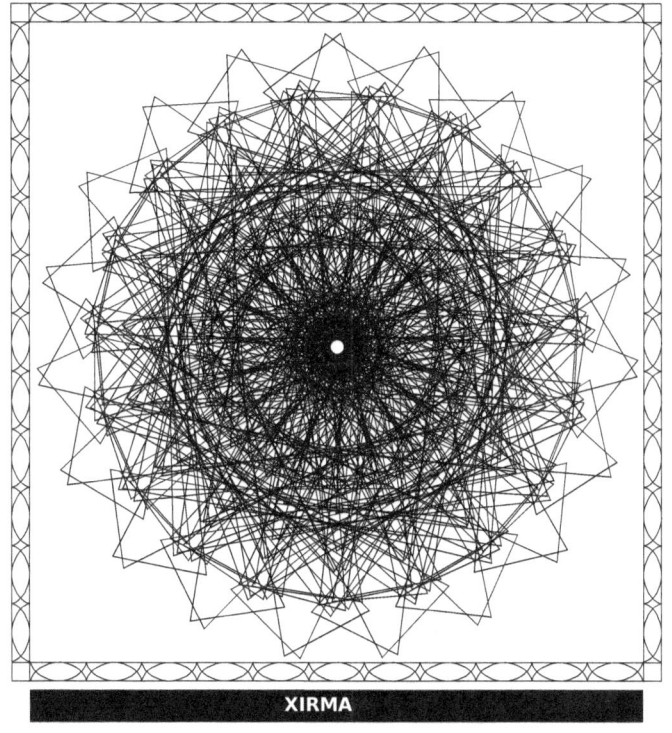

XIRMA

Each person designs his own life, freedom gives him the power to carry out his own designs, and power gives the freedom to interfere with the designs of others.
Eric Berne

315

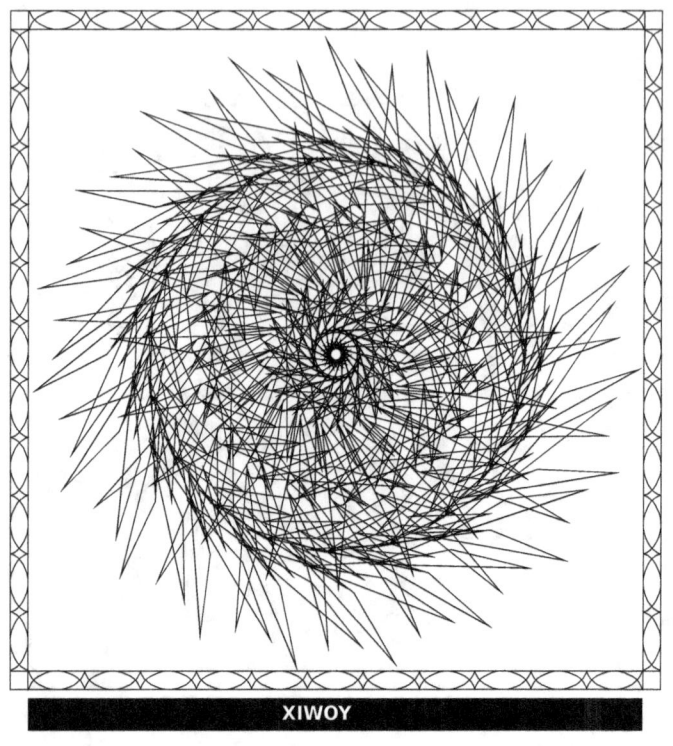

XIWOY

In art there are tears that do often lie too deep for thoughts.
Louis Kronenberger

316

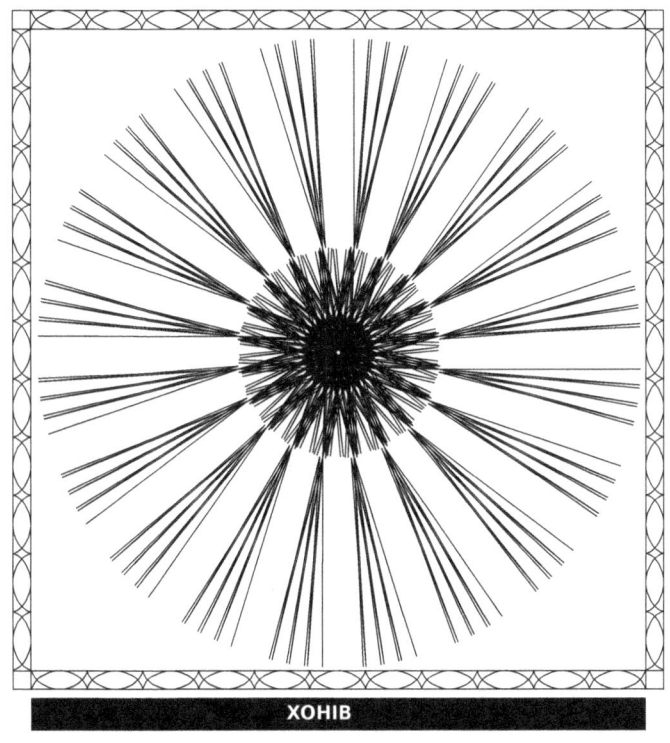

XOHIB

Art can only be truly art by presenting an adequate outward symbol of some fact in the interior life.
Margaret Fuller

317

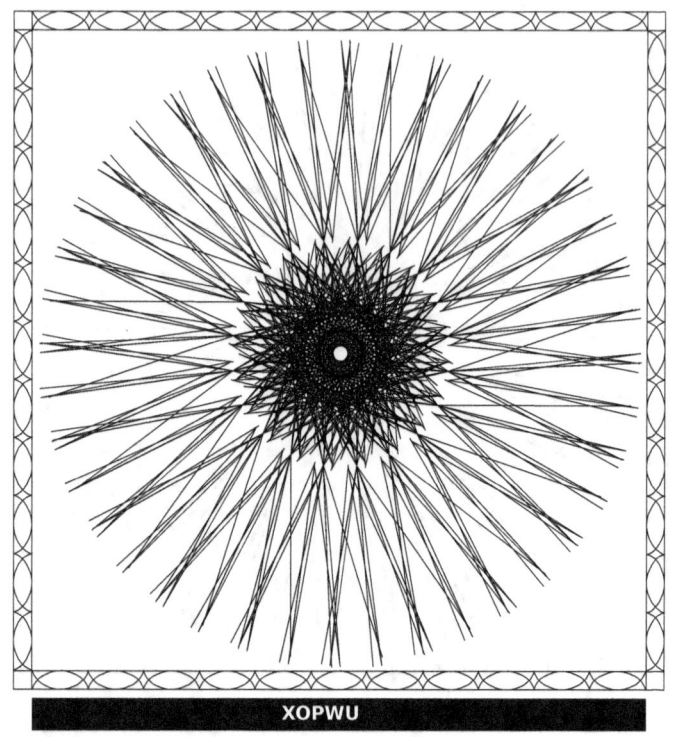

XOPWU

In art, truth is a means to an end; in science, it is the only end.
William Whewell

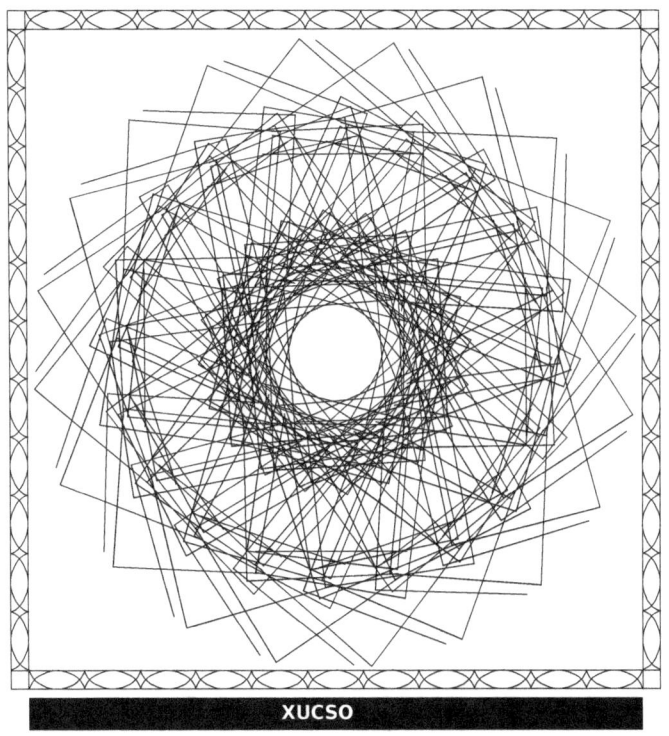

XUCSO

Far from making peace, wars invariably serve as classrooms and laboratories where men and techniques and states of mind are prepared for the next war.
Wendell Berry

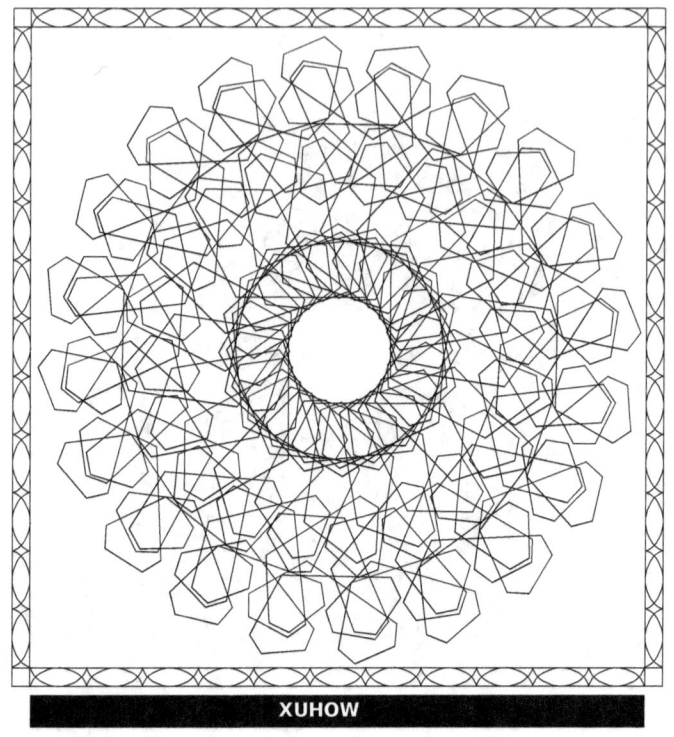

XUHOW

Real freedom lies in wildness, not in civilization.
Charles Lindbergh

320

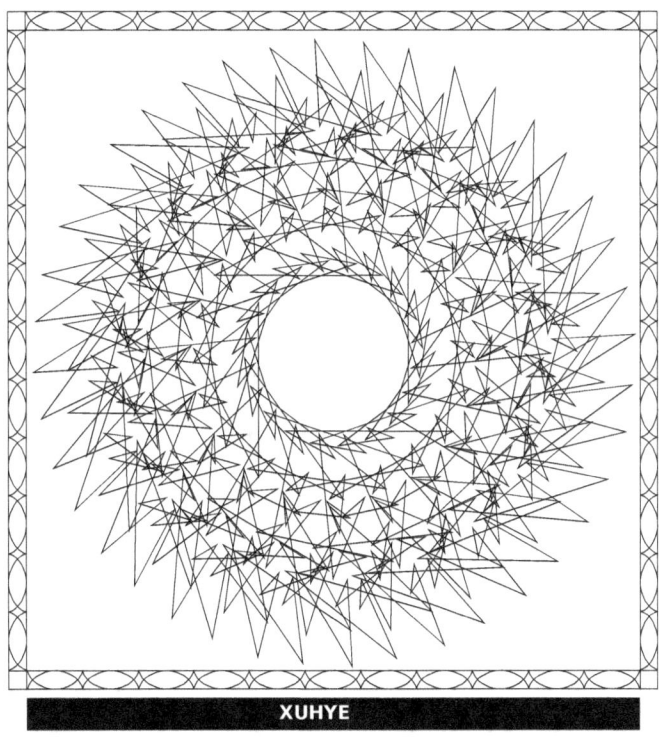

XUHYE

In shallow men the fish of little thoughts cause much commotion. In oceanic minds the whales of inspiration make hardly a ruffle.

Yukteswar Giri

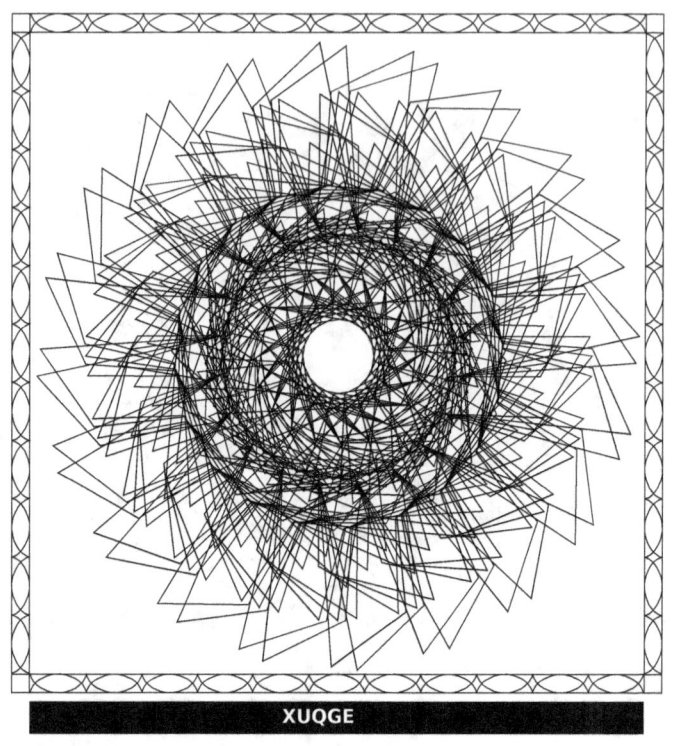

XUQGE

Meditation is a state of mind in which the operation and exercise of will is not.
Jiddu Krishnamurti

322

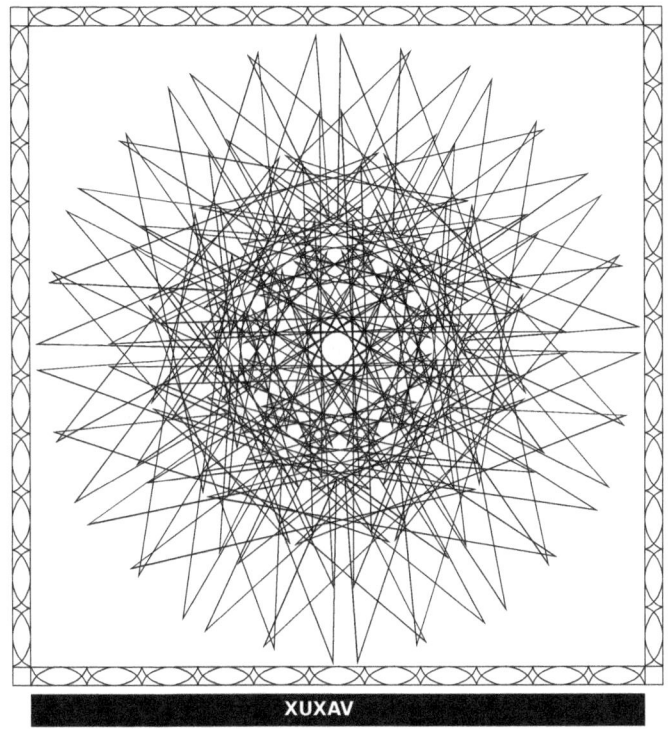

XUXAV

Man ... thinks continually without knowing it. The thinking that rises to consciousness is only the smallest part of this - the most superficial and worst part.
Friedrich Nietzsche

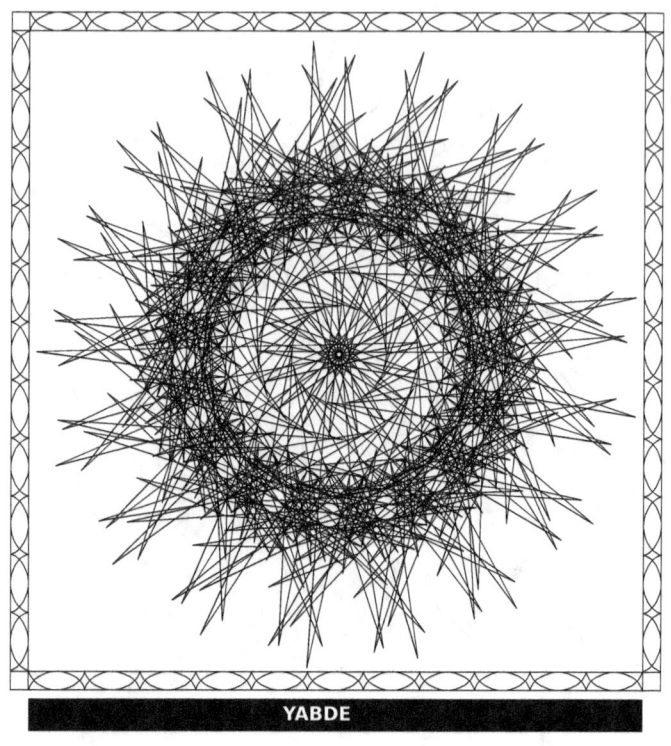

YABDE

We've known about the transcendent power of solitude for centuries; it's only recently that we've forgotten it.
Susan Cain

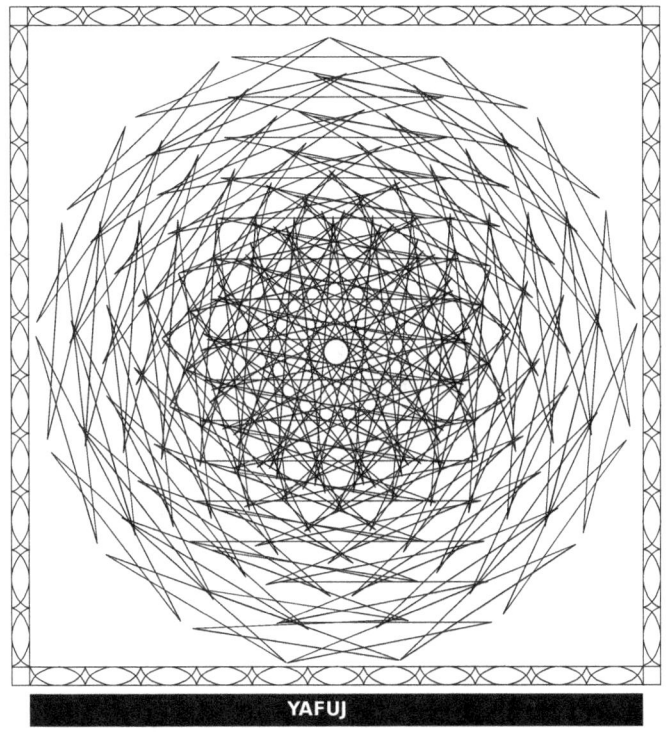

YAFUJ

The true, strong, and sound mind is the mind that can embrace equally great things and small.
Samuel Johnson

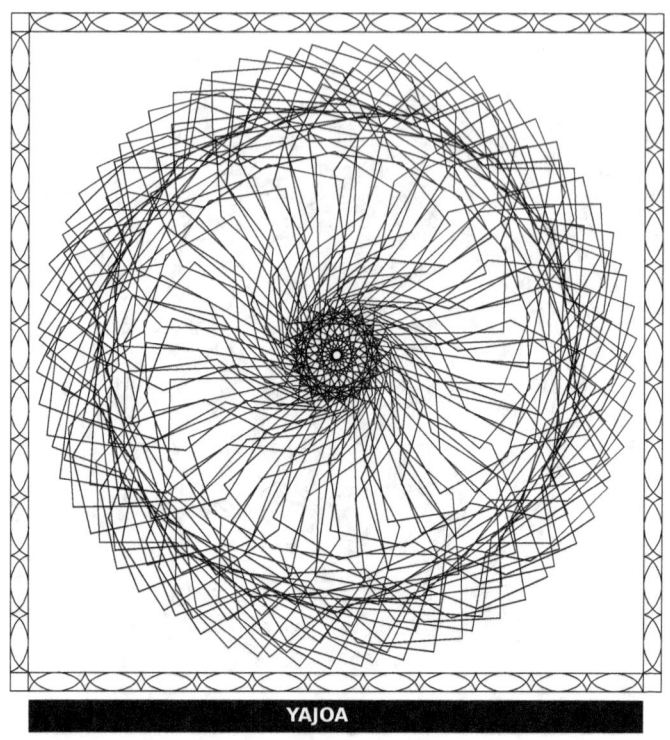

YAJOA

Don't follow any advice, no matter how good, until you feel as deeply in your spirit as you think in your mind that the counsel is wise.
Joan Rivers

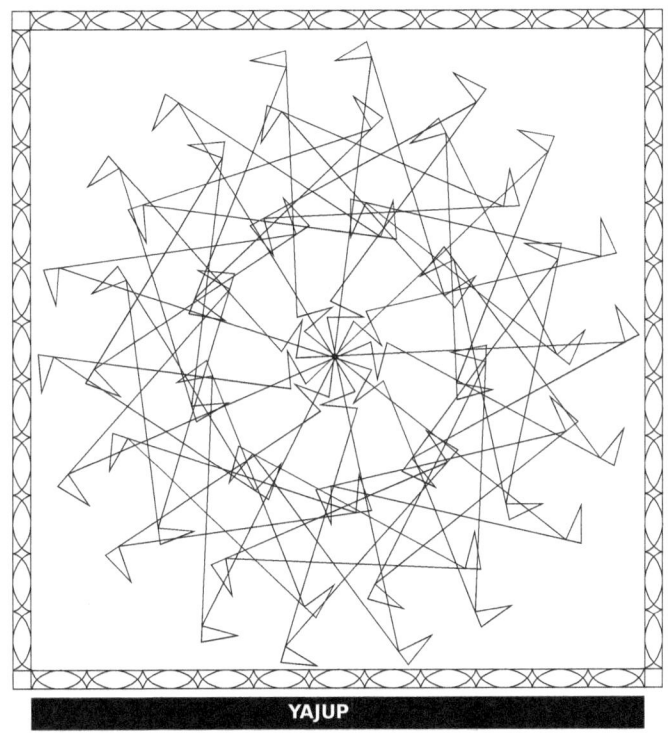

YAJUP

Misquotation is, in fact, the pride and privilege of the learned. A widely-read man never quotes accurately, for the rather obvious reason that he has read too widely.
Hesketh Pearson

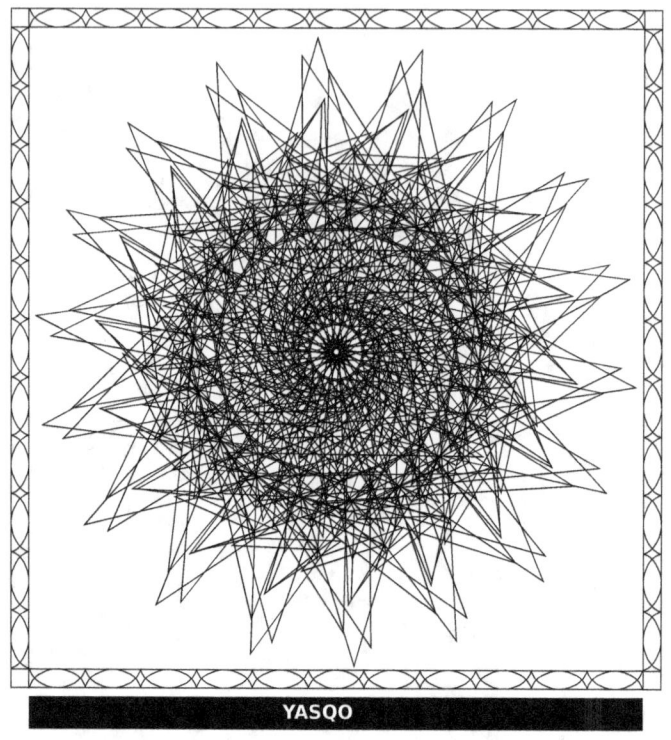

YASQO

The great sixteenth century divorce between art and science came with accelerated calculators.
Marshall McLuhan

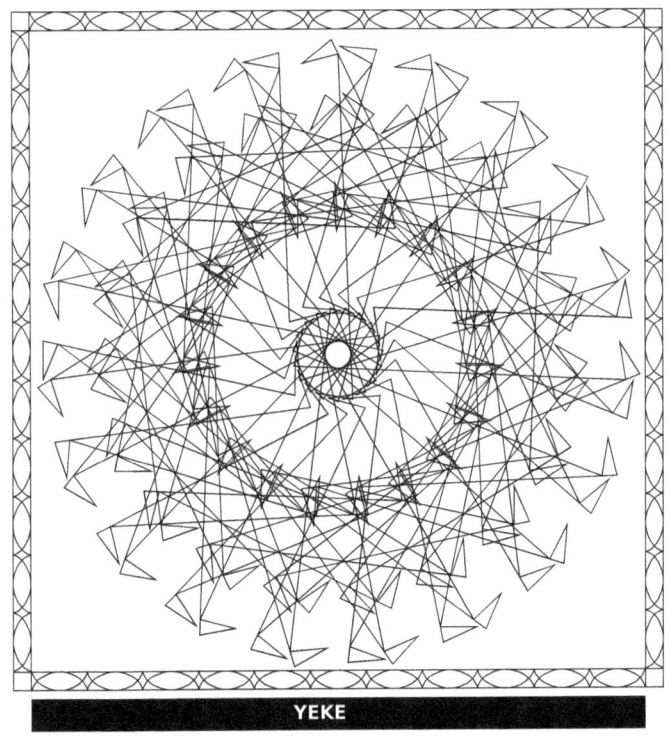

YEKE

Medieval and ancient sensibility now dominates our time as acoustic and multisensory awareness displaces the merely visual.

Marshall McLuhan

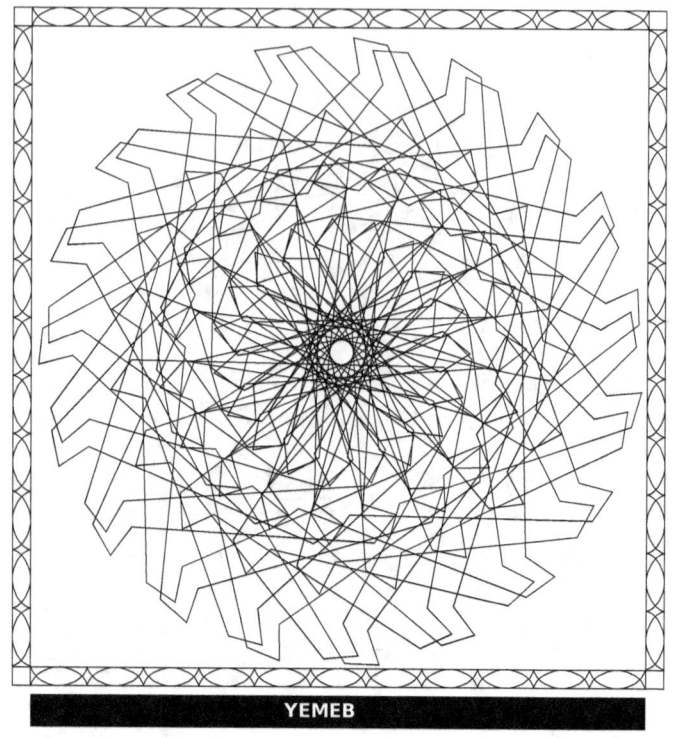

YEMEB

Good music is very close to primitive language.
Denis Diderot

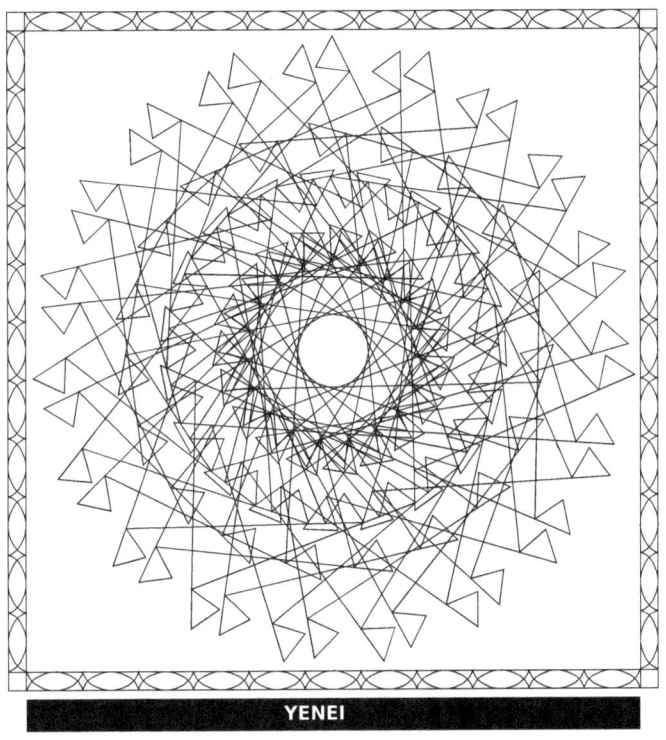

YENEI

Believe in all the good things you keep inside; There is no freedom in life without freedom of mind.
Jeremy Enigk

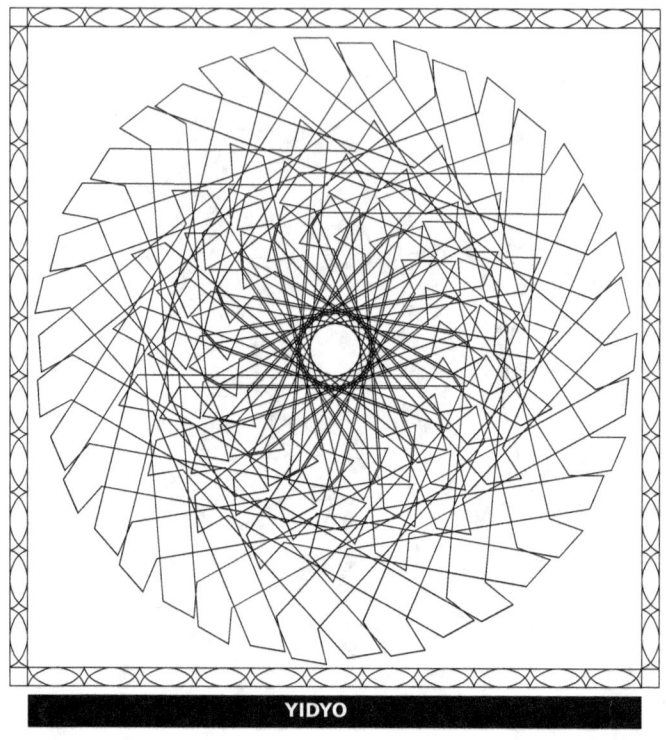

YIDYO

Art's purpose is to sober and quiet the mind so that it is
in accord with what happens.
John Cage

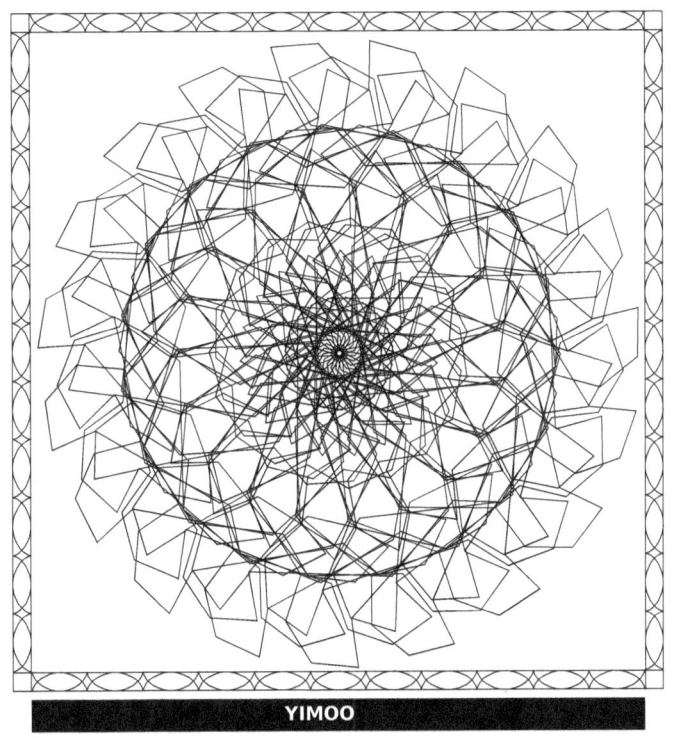

YIMOO

It is man's own fault, it is from want of use, if his mind grows torpid in old age.
Samuel Johnson

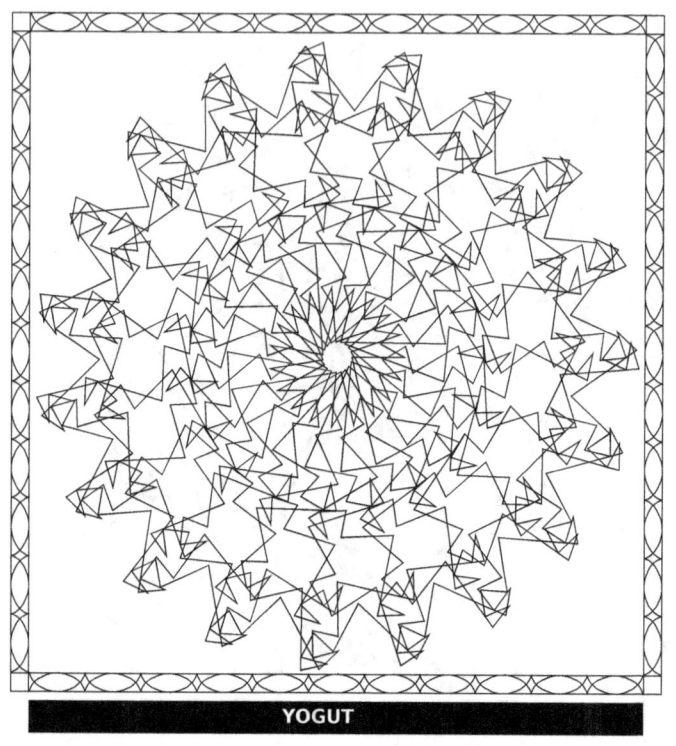

YOGUT

I think it's a responsibility for any artist to protect freedom of expression and to use any way to extend this power.
Ai Weiwei

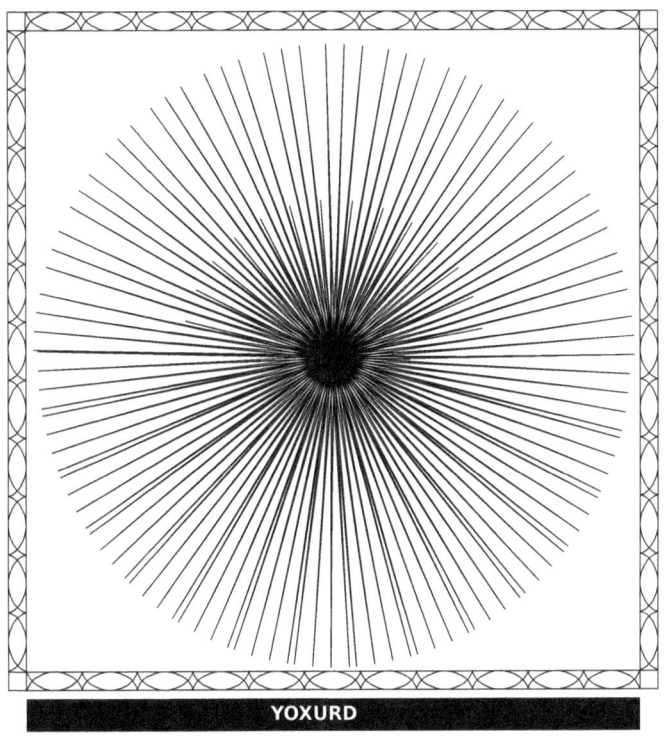

YOXURD

The pendulum of the mind alternates between sense and nonsense, not between right and wrong.
Carl Jung

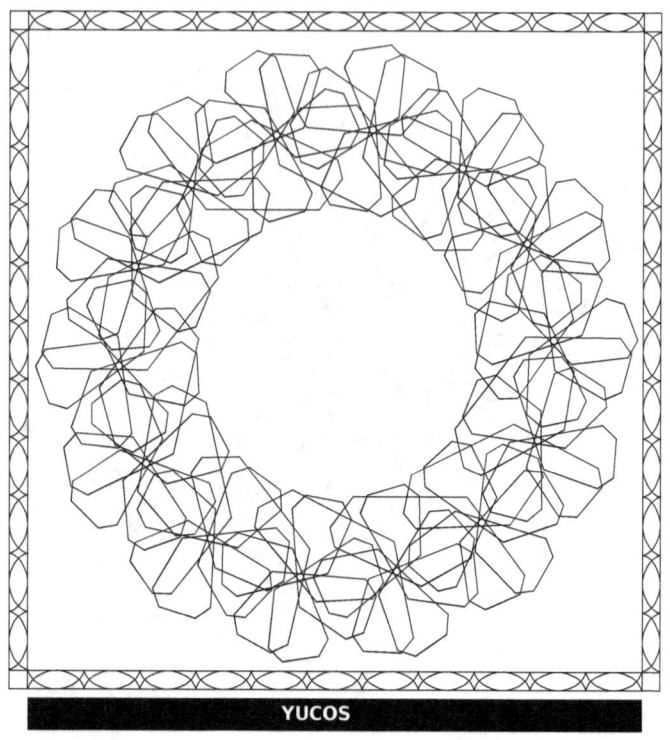

YUCOS

Don't mind anything anyone tells you about anyone else.
Judge everyone and everything for yourself.
Henry James

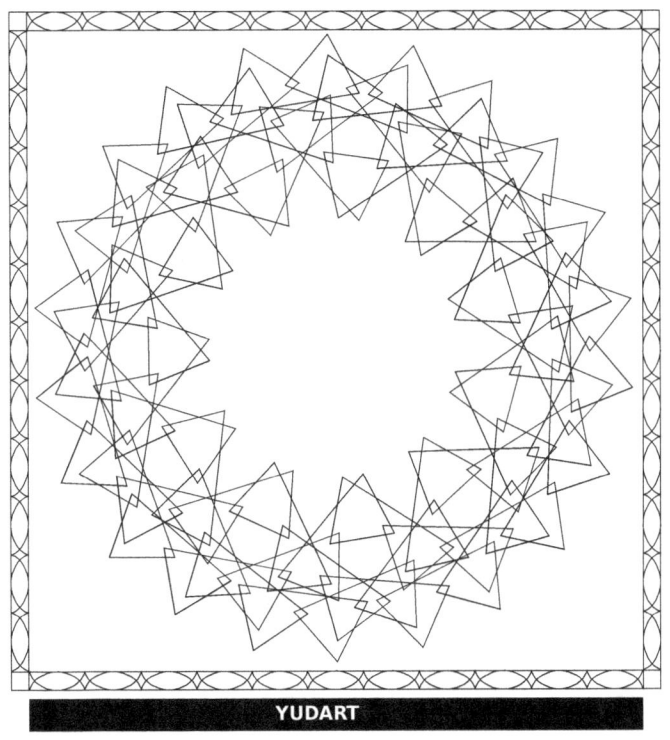

YUDART

An honest curator will admit that judgement is fallible, especially for art made yesterday.
Nicholas Serota

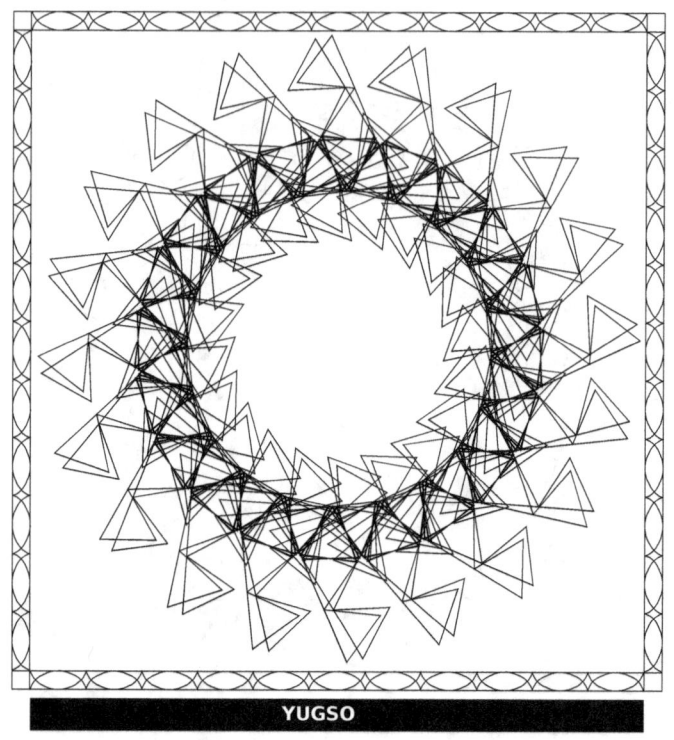

YUGSO

An artist cannot speak about his art any more than a plant
can discuss horticulture.
Jean Cocteau

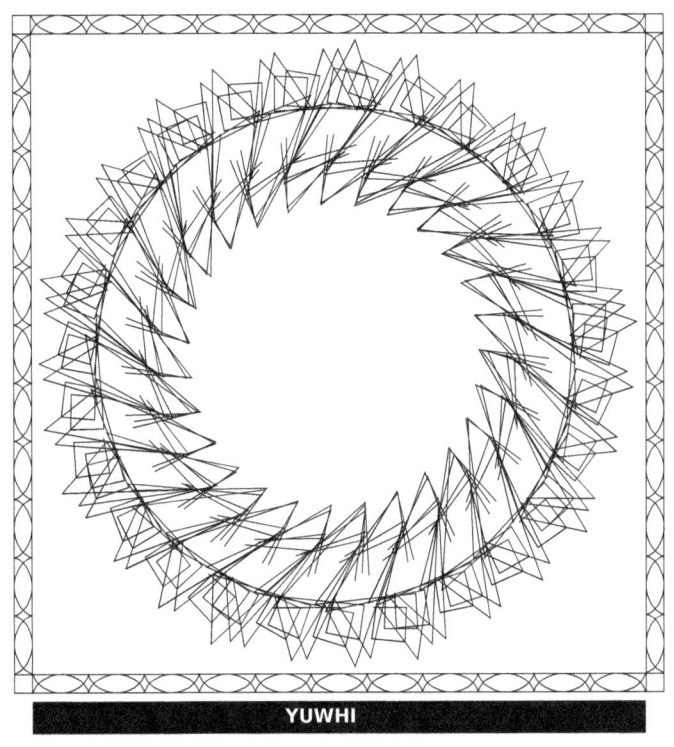

YUWHI

What pride to discover that nothing belongs to you - what
a revelation.
Emil Cioran

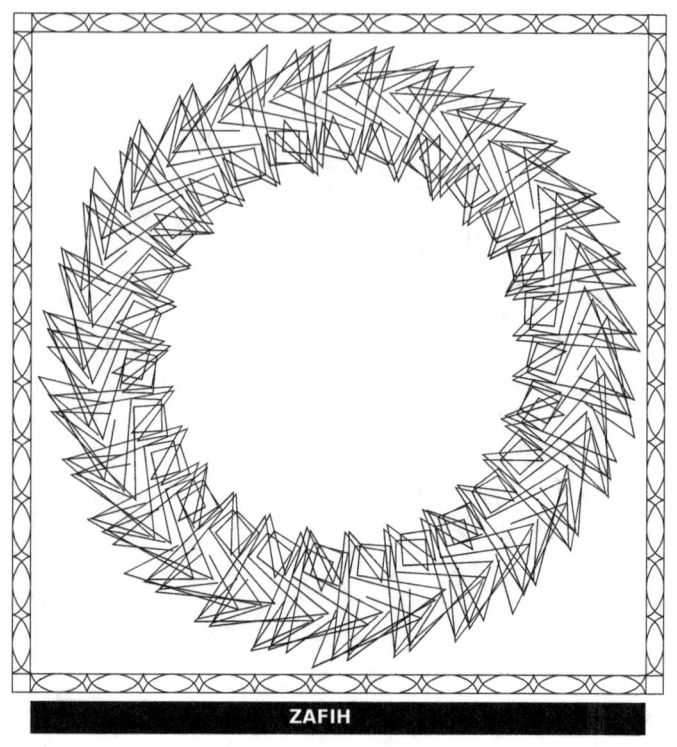

ZAFIH

Humility has its origin in an awareness of unworthiness, and sometimes too in a dazzled awareness of saintliness.
Sidonie-Gabrielle Colette

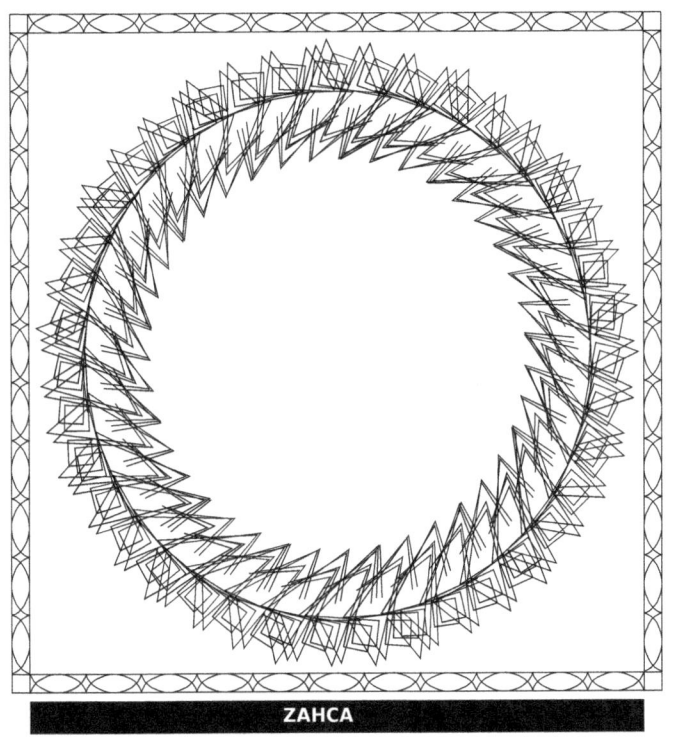

ZAHCA

Nothing in education is so astonishing as the amount of ignorance it accumulates in the form of inert facts.
Henry Adams

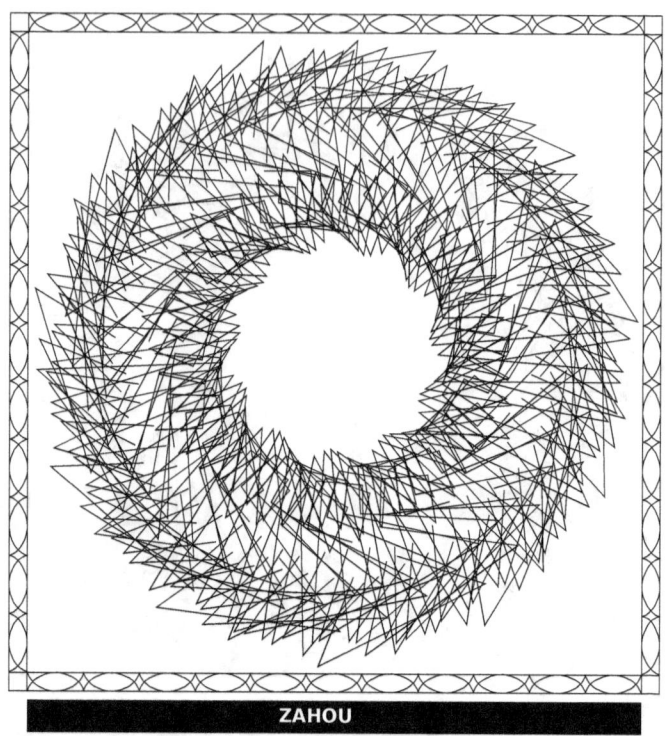

ZAHOU

The mind was a marvellous instrument, thought Shimrod; when left to wander untended, it often arrived at curious destinations.

Jack Vance

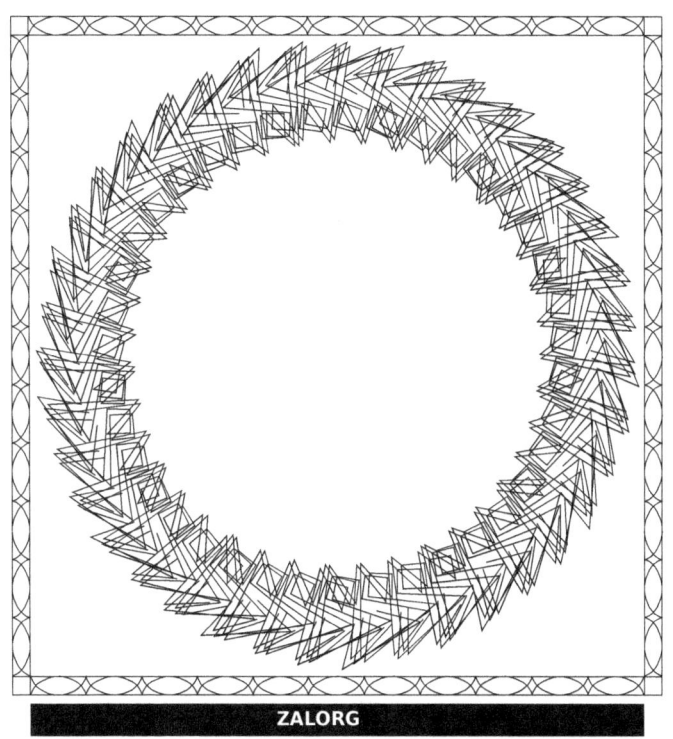

ZALORG

The most dangerous diminutions of freedom come from those who are convinced of their moral rectitude.
Daniel Hannan

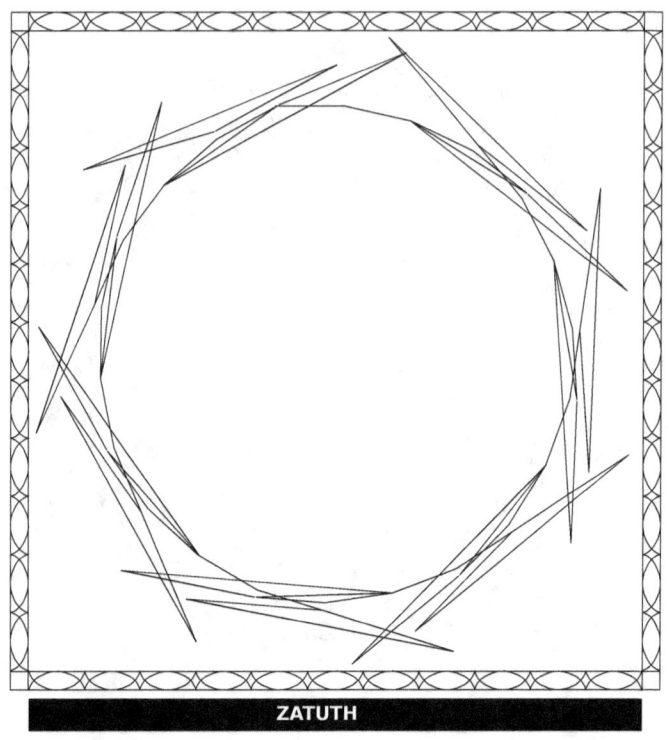

ZATUTH

A day without laughter is a day wasted.
Charlie Chaplin

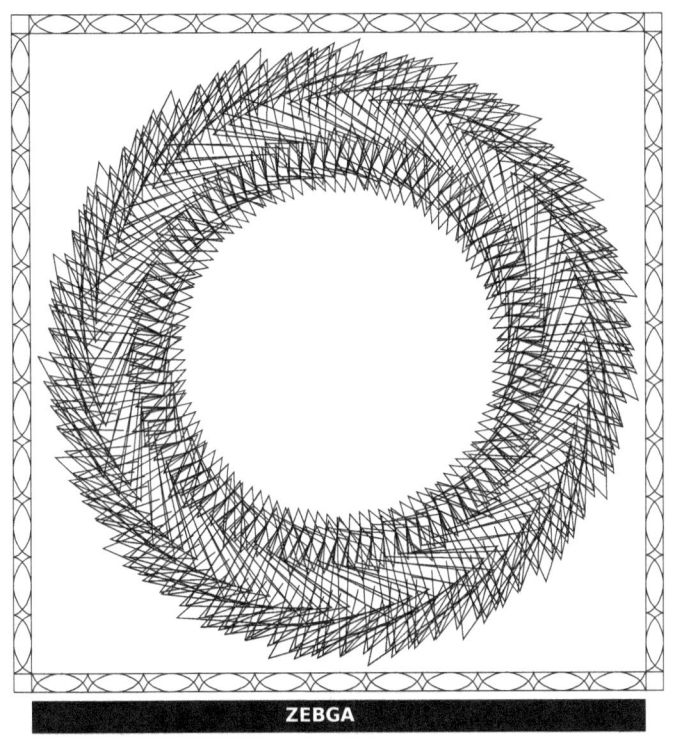

ZEBGA

The mathematical forms of order which the mind of a physicist manipulates coincides miraculously with experimental measurements.

Marie-Louise von Franz

345

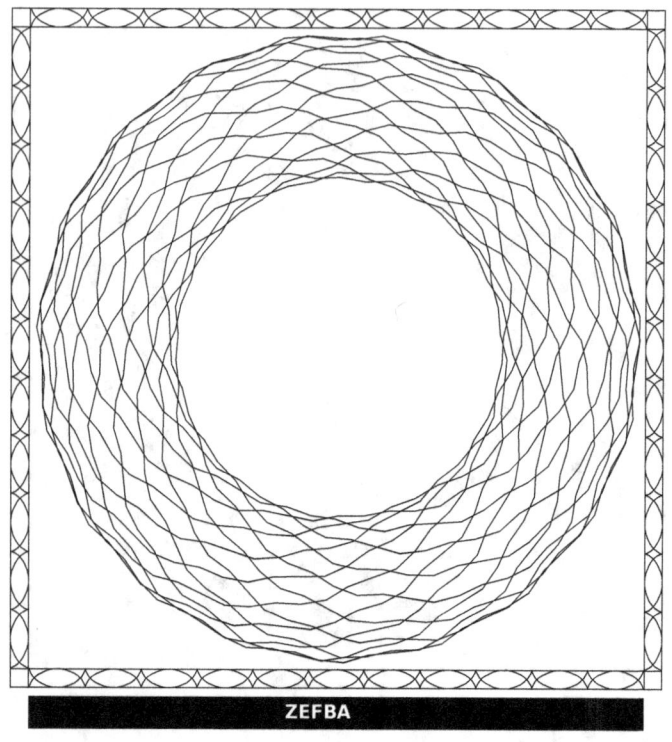

ZEFBA

Truth, like a woman, must be wooed and won - and this only through the purity of mind and the heart's deep love.
David Zindell

346

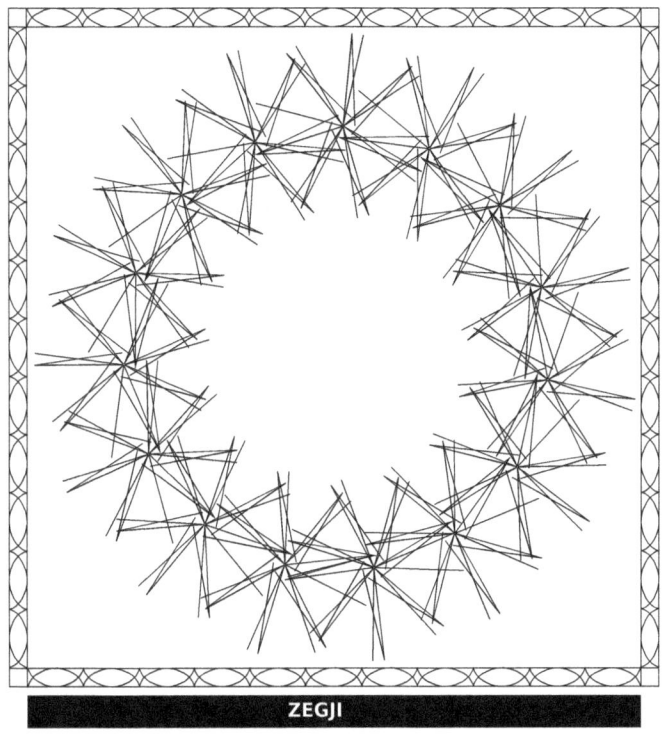

ZEGJI

My limited experience of such things told me that you get closest to the truth by not giving it advance warning that you're coming after it.
Michael Marshall Smith

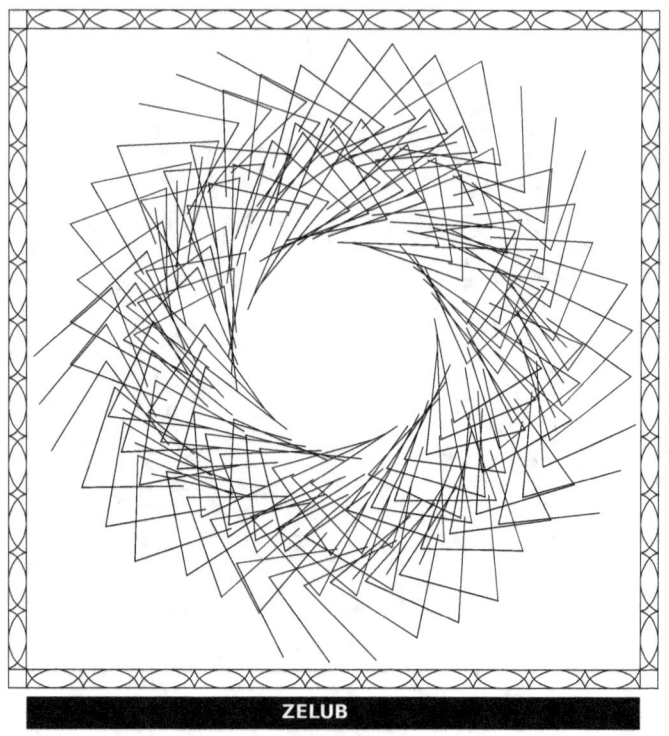

ZELUB

Our business in living is to become fluent with the life we are living, and art can help this.
John Cage

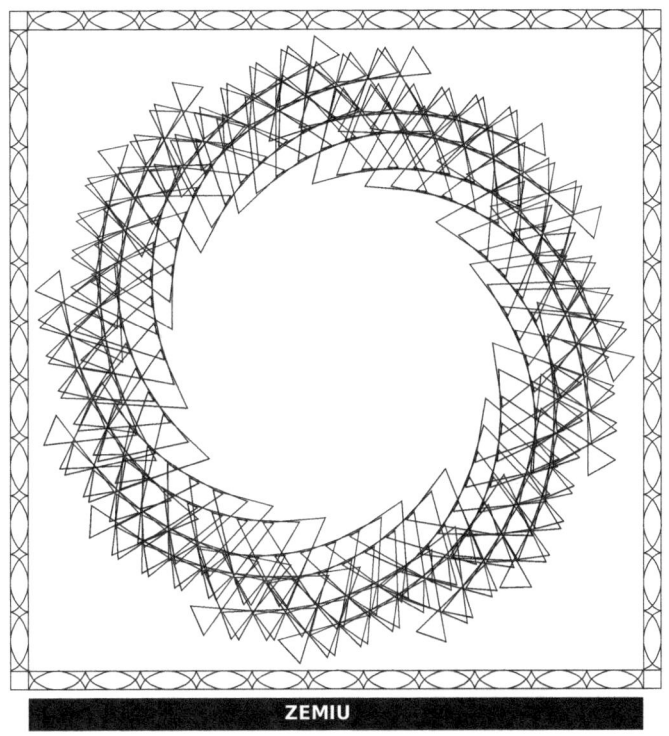

ZEMIU

The goods of this world, Phillip, are soon lost. Fire, storm, thieves, and war are ever with us, but what is stored in the mind is ours forever.
Louis L'Amour

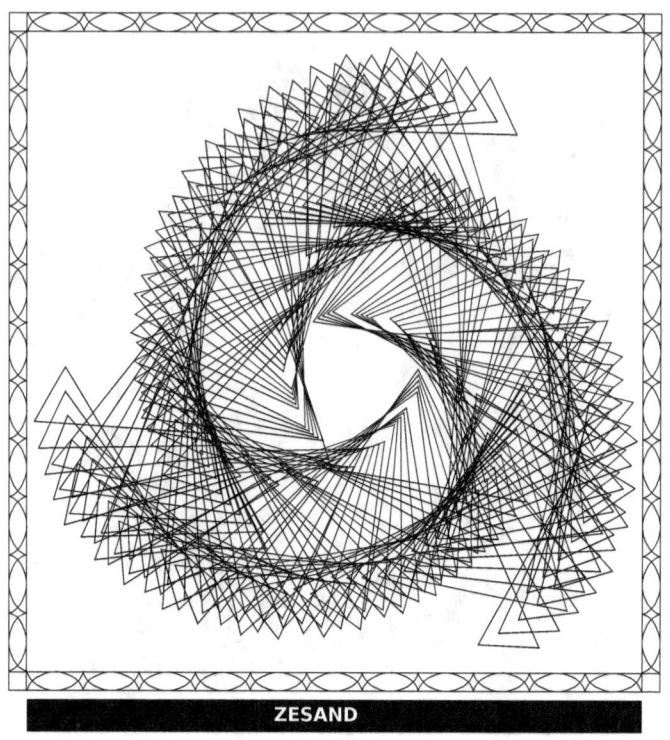

ZESAND

The grace and beauty of life will be clean gone when we all become useful men.
Anthony Trollope

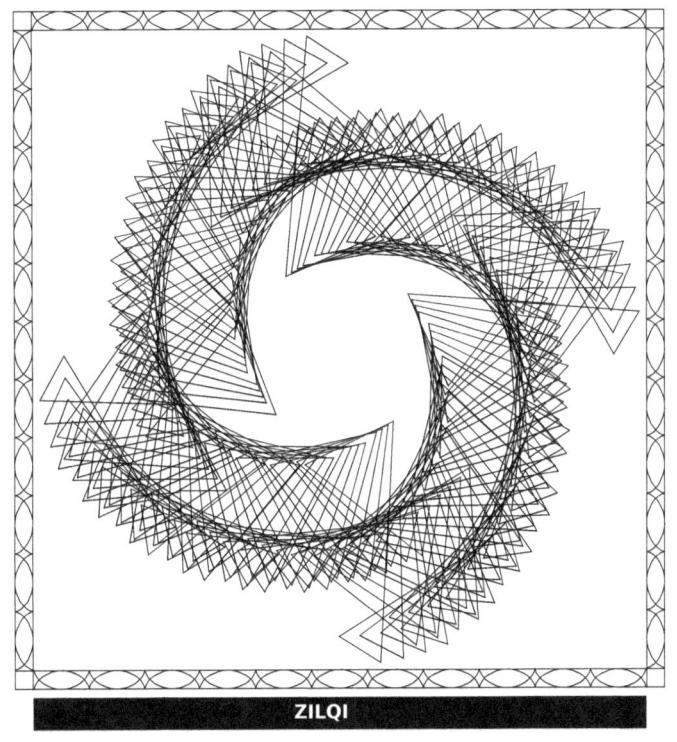

ZILQI

Poetry comes fine-spun from a mind at peace.
Ovid

351

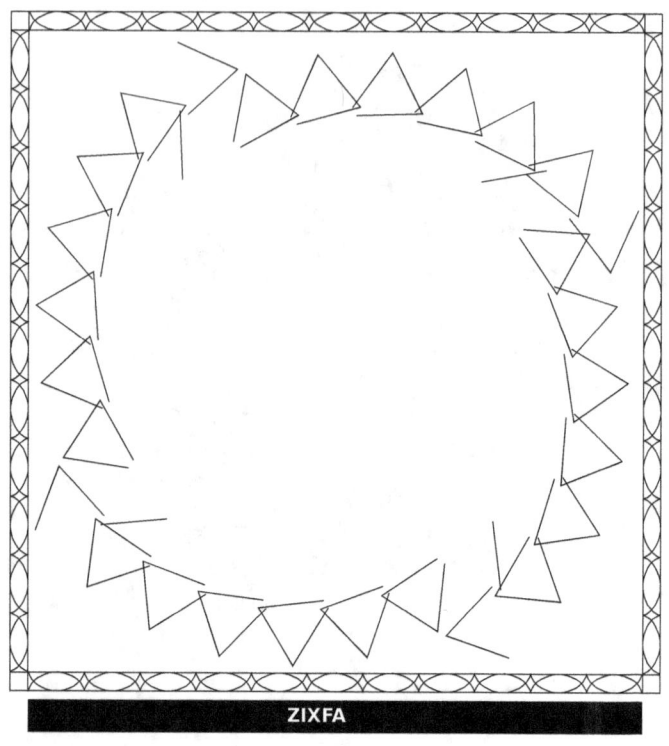

ZIXFA

You'll only find the truth by looking with your own eyes and walking with your own feet.
Tales of the Abyss, Namco Tales Studio

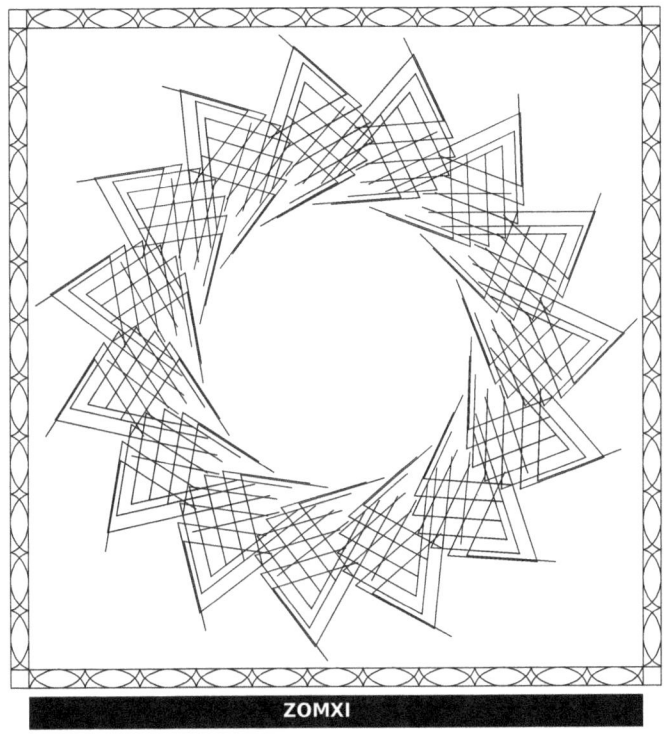

ZOMXI

And now I understand something so frightening, and wonderful - how the mind clings to the road it knows, rushing through crossroads, sticking like lint to the familiar.
Mary Oliver

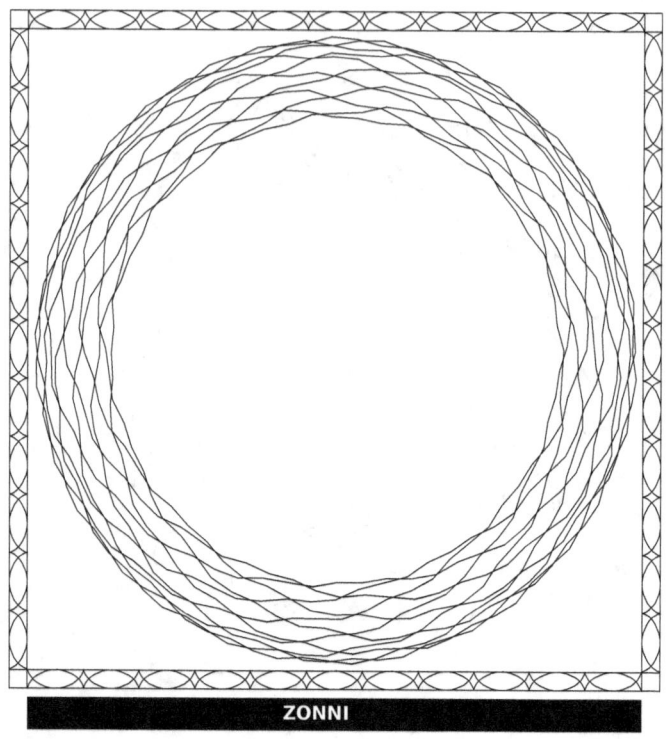

ZONNI

It is not irritating to be where one is. It is only irritating
to think one would like to be somewhere else.
John Cage

354

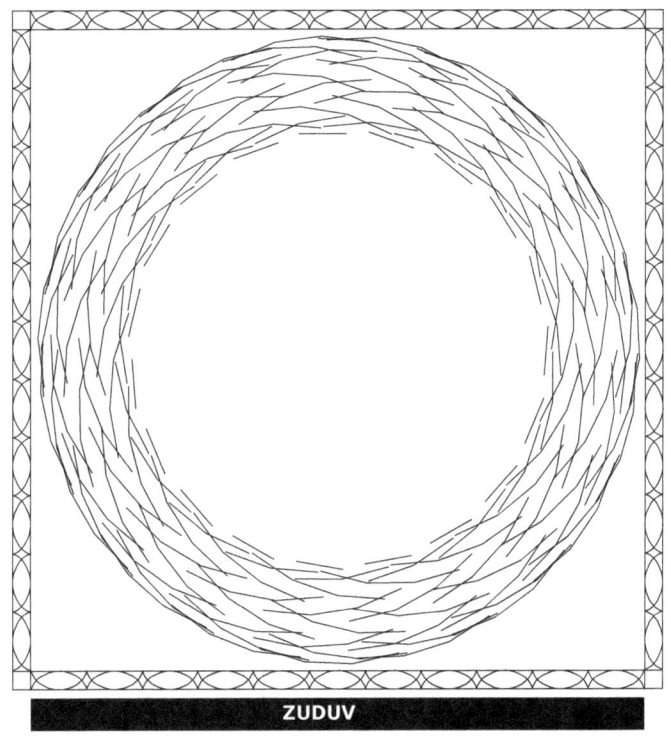

ZUDUV

A modern philosopher who has never once suspected himself of being a charlatan must be such a shallow mind that his work is probably not worth reading.
Leszek Kolakowski

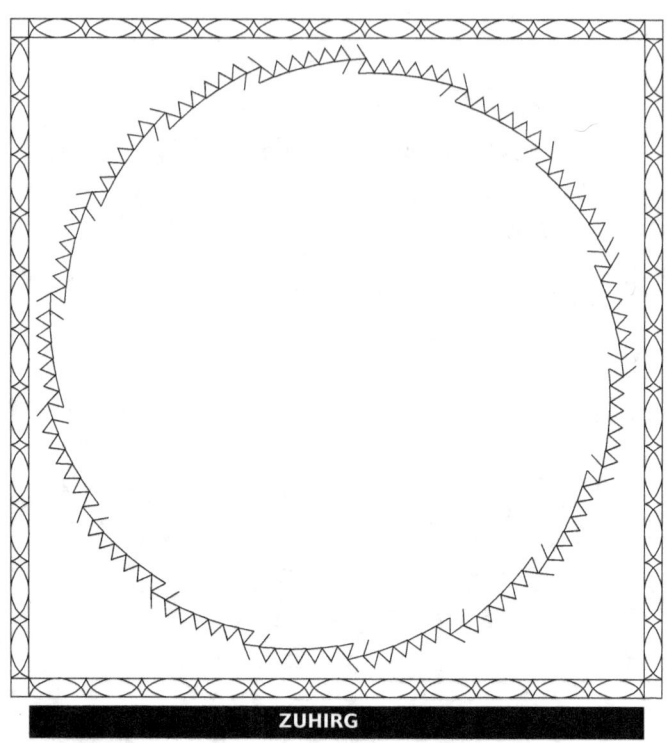

ZUHIRG

The artist has no concern as to what the picture means.
His attitude is absolute objectivity.
Stuart Davis

356

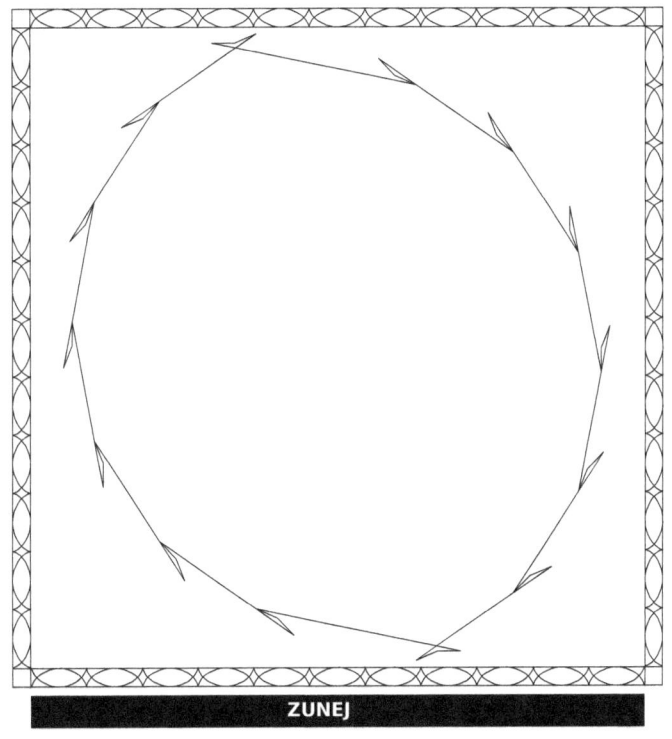

ZUNEJ

A defeat borne with pride is also a victory.
Marie von Ebner-Eschenbach

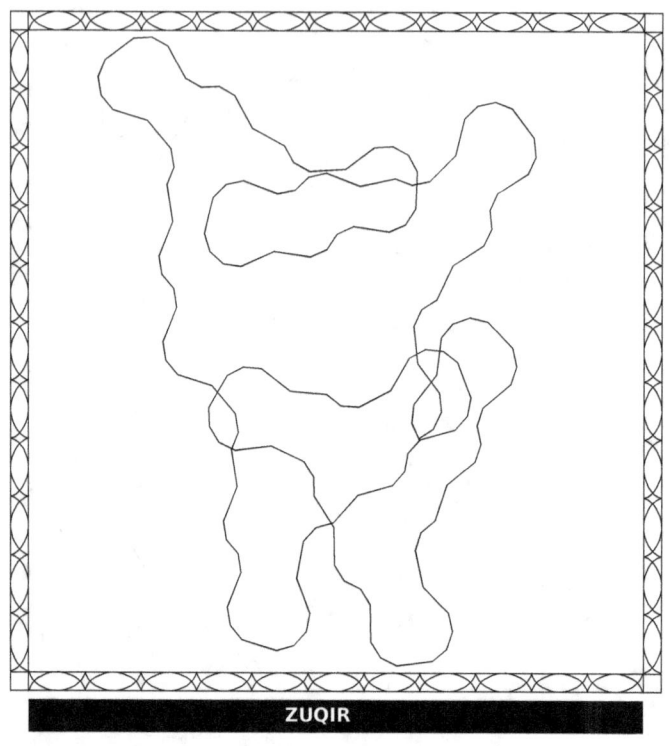

ZUQIR

There is no such thing as a dumb poet or a handless painter.
The essence of an artist is that he should be articulate.
Algernon Charles Swinburne

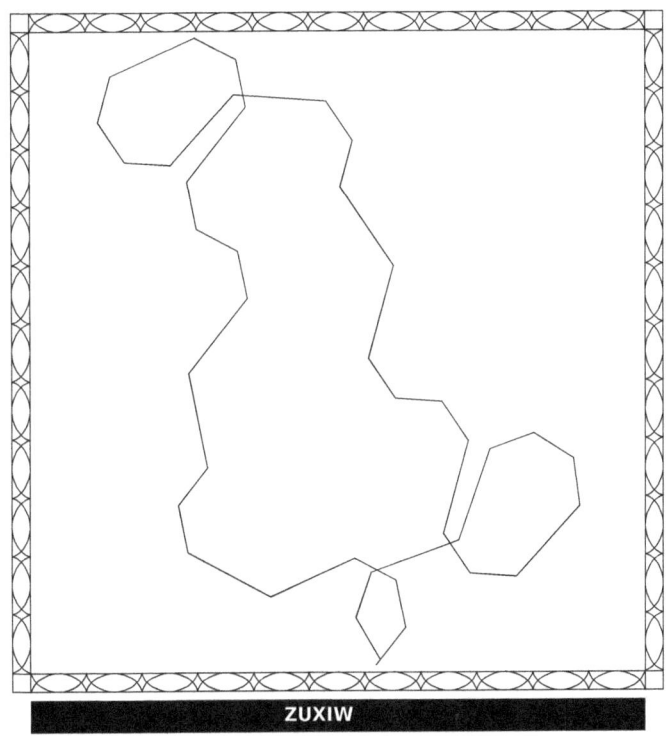

ZUXIW

Understanding the law of karma is known as the light of the world because through this understanding we can take responsibility for our destinies and be truly more guided to greater fulfillment in our lives.

Jon Kabat-Zinn

359

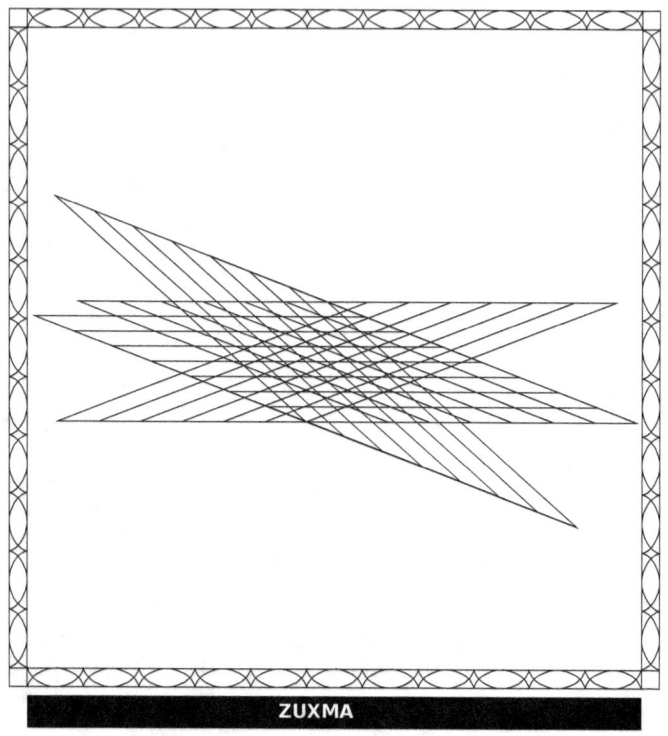

ZUXMA

Both the physicist and the mystic want to communicate their knowledge, and when they do so with words their statements are paradoxical and full of logical contradictions.

Fritjof Capra

APPENDIX A: WHAT IS PI?

Pi is a number equal to the ratio of a circle's circumference to its diameter. The symbol mathematicians use to represent pi is π. If c represents the length of a circle's circumference and d its diameter, then

$$\pi = \frac{c}{d}$$

This equation holds for all circles no matter how small or large. It is a universal property of circles.

The numerical value of π, in the base 10 number system, is

$$\pi = 3.14159265358979323846264338327950288\ldots$$

where the dots at the end of the number indicate that the digits go on forever without repeating, which is another way of saying that π is an irrational number. An irrational number is one that cannot be written as the ratio of two integers. The irrationality of π is not obvious and it was not proven to be so until 1761 by the Swiss mathematician Johann Heinrich Lambert.

What this means is that it is impossible to find a unit of measure where both the circumference and diameter of a circle are integers. But we can find rational

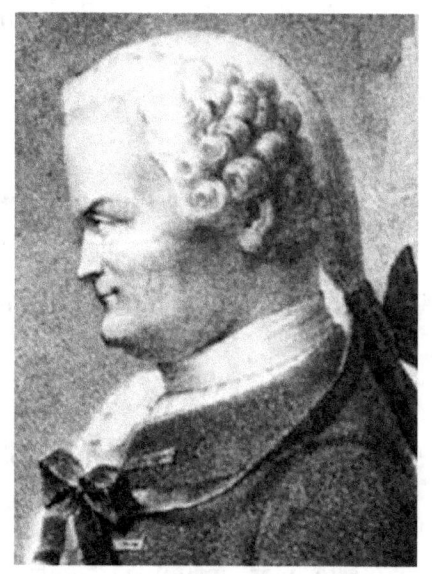

Figure 1: Johann Heinrich Lambert (1728-1777).
Photo credit: wikipedia.org

approximations. The simplest approximation is just 3. To get better approximations, we need to create two sets of numbers a_n and b_n, $n = 0, 1, 2 \ldots$ as follows. First set a_0 equal to the integer part of π, $a_0 = 3$ and let $b_0 = 1/(\pi - 3) = 7.062513305931052$. So far we have

$$\pi = a_0 + \frac{1}{b_0} = 3 + \frac{1}{7.062513305931052}$$

Now, repeat the process with the number $b_0 = 7.062513305931052$. Set a_1 equal to the integer part of b_0, $a_1 = 7$ and let $b_1 = 1/(b_0 - 7) = 15.9965944066841$. Now we have

$$\pi = a_0 + \cfrac{1}{a_1 + \cfrac{1}{b_1}}$$

Next, repeat the process with b_1 and so on. At each step set a_n equal to the integer part of b_{n-1} and set $b_n = 1/(b_{n-1} - a_n)$. The set of numbers a_n, $n = 0, 1, 2 \ldots$ is called the continued fraction expansion of π. The name comes from the fact that π can be written as follows:

$$\pi = a_0 + \cfrac{1}{a_1 + \cfrac{1}{a_2 + \cfrac{1}{a_3 + \cdots}}}$$

with the fraction continuing forever. The first 24 a_n values are

$[3, 7, 15, 1, 292, 1, 1, 1, 2, 1, 3, 1, 14, 2, 1, 1, 2, 2, 2, 2, 1, 84, 2, 1, \ldots]$.

To get a rational approximation for π, all you have to do is truncate the continued fraction at some point and evaluate the result. These rational approximations are also called continued fraction convergents. The following table shows the first few convergents.

364

π	3.14159265358979323844...
$\frac{3}{1}$	3.0
$\frac{22}{7}$	3.14285714285714285714
$\frac{333}{106}$	3.14150943396226415094
$\frac{355}{113}$	3.14159292035398230088
$\frac{103993}{33102}$	3.14159265301190260407
$\frac{104348}{33215}$	3.14159265392142104470
$\frac{208341}{66317}$	3.14159265346743670552

The rational approximations (continued fraction convergents) to π are used to generate the images in this book. The ratios are used as the slope of a line plotted on a Cartesian plane. Starting at the origin, whenever the line crosses a horizontal grid line, mark it with a 1, and when it crosses a vertical grid line, mark it with a 0. In this way, each ratio defines a binary sequence. The sequence is then converted into drawing instructions. This is how each of the images in this book was created. For more information on this process, see our book *Pattern Generation for Computational Art*.

APPENDIX B: IMAGE GENERATION

Below is a list of commands for generating each image in this book. An explanation of their meaning can be found in our book *Pattern Generation for Computational Art*.

ANDROQ chseq 22 7 58 | katrans t0.kat | turtledraw 0.0 155.457 f02m01.svg

APOJ chseq 22 7 58 | katrans t0.kat | turtledraw 0.0 171.826 f02m02.svg

ATHEU chseq 22 7 58 | katrans t0a.kat | turtledraw 0.0 171.826 f02m03.svg

BAFYI chseq 22 7 58 | katrans t0a.kat | turtledraw 0.0 139.087 f02m04.svg

BANAU chseq 22 7 58 | katrans t1.kat | turtledraw 0.0 99.3384 f02m05.svg

BANDO chseq 22 7 86 | katrans t2.kat | turtledraw 0.0 175.0 f02m06.svg

BAQNO chseq 22 7 116 | katrans t0.kat | turtledraw 0.0 139.087 f02m07.svg

BAQOV chseq 22 7 116 | katrans t1.kat | turtledraw 0.0 151.0 f02m08.svg

BAROT chseq 22 7 116 | katrans t3.kat | turtledraw 0.0 84.0 f02m09.svg

BAROU chseq 22 7 116 | katrans t3.kat | turtledraw 0.0 156.0 f02m10.svg

BEFET chseq 22 7 116 | katrans t3.kat | turtledraw 0.0 108.0 f02m11.svg

BEJXI chseq 22 7 58 | katrans t7.kat | turtledraw 0.0 90.0000 f02m12.svg

BELU chseq 22 7 58 | katrans t7.kat | turtledraw 0.0 79.4092 f02m13.svg

BEPOST chseq 22 7 58 | katrans t9.kat | turtledraw 0.0 99.9976 f02m14.svg

BERBO chseq 22 7 58 | katrans t0.kat | turtledraw 0.0 106.37 f02m15.svg

BETIG chseq 22 7 522 | katrans t4.kat | turtledraw 0.0 174.0010 f02m16.svg

BIRJO chseq 22 7 58 | katrans t11.kat | turtledraw 0.0 33.7500 f02m17.svg

BITYE chseq 22 7 58 | katrans t11.kat | turtledraw 0.0 78.7500 f02m18.svg

BOLMI chseq 22 7 58 | katrans t11.kat | turtledraw 0.0 101.2500 f02m19.svg

BUNCU chseq 22 7 58 | katrans t12.kat | turtledraw 0.0 86.0889 f02m20.svg

BUNEQ chseq 22 7 58 | katrans t12.kat | turtledraw 0.0 101.7330 f02m21.svg

BURAR chseq 22 7 58 | katrans t12.kat | turtledraw 0.0 54.7778 f02m22.svg

CABGE chseq 22 7 116 | katrans t12.kat | turtledraw 0.0 133.0440 f02m23.svg

CACCU chseq 333 106 438 | katrans t1.kat | turtledraw 0.0 49.0 f02m24.svg

CAGUE chseq 333 106 439 | katrans t1.kat | turtledraw 0.0 98.4595 f02m25.svg

CALCE chseq 355 113 468 | katrans t0.kat | turtledraw 0.0 171.9140 f02m26.svg

CEGURG chseq 355 113 468 | katrans t0a.kat | turtledraw 0.0 106.1940 f02m27.svg

CELAS chseq 355 113 468 | katrans t1.kat | turtledraw 0.0 150.1390 f02m28.svg

CESSO chseq 22 7 87 | katrans t0.kat | turtledraw 0.0 158.181 f03m01.svg

CIGI chseq 22 7 87 | katrans t0.kat | turtledraw 0.0 141.812 f03m02.svg

CIGIJ chseq 22 7 87 | katrans t0a.kat | turtledraw 0.0 152.732 f03m03.svg

CIJYE chseq 22 7 145 | katrans t2.kat | turtledraw 0.0 156.797 f03m04.svg

CIKUK chseq 22 7 174 | katrans t2.kat | turtledraw 0.0 176.0 f03m05.svg

CIPON chseq 22 7 174 | katrans t2.kat | turtledraw 0.0 88.0 f03m06.svg

CITLE chseq 22 7 174 | katrans t2.kat | turtledraw 0.0 160.0 f03m07.svg

COVED chseq 22 7 174 | katrans t3.kat | turtledraw 0.0 152.0 f03m08.svg

COYIO chseq 22 7 174 | katrans t3.kat | turtledraw 0.0 80.0 f03m09.svg

CUDDE chseq 22 7 87 | katrans t7.kat | turtledraw 0.0 123.5300 f03m10.svg

CUKYA chseq 22 7 87 | katrans t7.kat | turtledraw 0.0 112.9390 f03m11.svg

CUQAB chseq 22 7 87 | katrans t7.kat | turtledraw 0.0 102.3490 f03m12.svg

CURAB chseq 22 7 87 | katrans t7.kat | turtledraw 0.0 134.1210 f03m13.svg

CUSHU chseq 22 7 87 | katrans t9.kat | turtledraw 0.0 97.7783 f03m14.svg

CUVPA chseq 22 7 87 | katrans t11.kat | turtledraw 0.0 105.0070 f03m15.svg

DAQAX chseq 22 7 87 | katrans t12.kat | turtledraw 0.0 104.3480 f03m16.svg

DERARY chseq 22 7 87 | katrans t12.kat | turtledraw 0.0 67.8296 f03m17.svg

DEWAST chseq 22 7 87 | katrans t12.kat | turtledraw 0.0 57.3926 f03m18.svg

DEYET chseq 355 113 468 | katrans t12.kat | turtledraw 0.0 177.5390 f03m19.svg

DIDLI chseq 333 106 85 | katrans t13.kat | turtledraw 0.0 120.0 f03m20.svg

DIHJI chseq 22 7 87 | katrans t0.kat | turtledraw 0.0 120.0 f03m21.svg

DIJOP chseq 22 7 116 | katrans t0a.kat | turtledraw 0.0 120.0 f03m22.svg

DILUX chseq 22 7 87 | katrans t12.kat | turtledraw 0.0 120.0 f03m23.svg

DIPOV chseq 22 7 116 | katrans t0.kat | turtledraw 0.0 159.543 f04m01.svg

DIROS chseq 22 7 116 | katrans t0a.kat | turtledraw 0.0 135.0 f04m02.svg

DISOTH chseq 22 7 232 | katrans t2.kat | turtledraw 0.0 174.0 f04m03.svg

DOBZE chseq 22 7 232 | katrans t3.kat | turtledraw 0.0 150.0 f04m04.svg

DOSEM chseq 22 7 58 | katrans t6.kat | turtledraw 0.0 112.5000 f04m05.svg

DOXCO chseq 22 7 116 | katrans t7.kat | turtledraw 0.0 124.4090 f04m06.svg

DOZI chseq 22 7 116 | katrans t9.kat | turtledraw 0.0 76.6626 f04m07.svg

DURCO chseq 22 7 348 | katrans t4.kat | turtledraw 0.0 45.0000 f04m08.svg

DUSAT chseq 22 7 580 | katrans t7.kat | turtledraw 0.0 45.0000 f04m09.svg

DUTO chseq 22 7 580 | katrans t7.kat | turtledraw 0.0 135.0000 f04m10.svg

DUXOV chseq 22 7 580 | katrans t8.kat | turtledraw 0.0 135.0000 f04m11.svg

ESAF chseq 22 7 580 | katrans t9.kat | turtledraw 0.0 90.0000 f04m12.svg

EXIM chseq 22 7 116 | katrans t11.kat | turtledraw 0.0 50.6250 f04m13.svg

FATORY chseq 22 7 116 | katrans t11.kat | turtledraw 0.0 61.8750 f04m14.svg

FENGI chseq 22 7 116 | katrans t11.kat | turtledraw 0.0 84.3750 f04m15.svg

FEXOI chseq 22 7 116 | katrans t12.kat | turtledraw 0.0 50.8667 f04m16.svg

FIXART chseq 22 7 116 | katrans t12.kat | turtledraw 0.0 176.0890 f04m17.svg

FIYIX chseq 22 7 580 | katrans t11.kat | turtledraw 0.0 39.3750 f04m18.svg

FODWU chseq 22 7 580 | katrans t12.kat | turtledraw 0.0 90.0000 f04m19.svg

FOXNI chseq 355 113 468 | katrans t0.kat | turtledraw 0.0 90.0220 f04m20.svg

FUBLE chseq 22 7 116 | katrans t0.kat | turtledraw 0.0 118.639 f04m21.svg

FUHEJ chseq 22 7 116 | katrans t0a.kat | turtledraw 0.0 118.639 f04m22.svg

FULIE chseq 22 7 145 | katrans t0.kat | turtledraw 0.0 176.726 f05m01.svg

FUWAN chseq 22 7 145 | katrans t0.kat | turtledraw 0.0 173.452 f05m02.svg

FUYOR chseq 22 7 145 | katrans t0.kat | turtledraw 0.0 121.091 f05m03.svg

GAGAN chseq 22 7 145 | katrans t0a.kat | turtledraw 0.0 121.091 f05m04.svg

GAXERD chseq 22 7 290 | katrans t2.kat | turtledraw 0.0 177.605 f05m05.svg

GIWAJ chseq 22 7 290 | katrans t2.kat | turtledraw 0.0 158.401 f05m06.svg

GOFUL chseq 22 7 290 | katrans t2.kat | turtledraw 0.0 105.6 f05m07.svg

GOGAST chseq 22 7 290 | katrans t2.kat | turtledraw 0.0 148.8 f05m08.svg

GOYFA chseq 22 7 290 | katrans t2.kat | turtledraw 0.0 172.793 f05m09.svg

GUCEI chseq 22 7 290 | katrans t3.kat | turtledraw 0.0 62.4023 f05m10.svg

GUCJE chseq 22 7 145 | katrans t7.kat | turtledraw 0.0 101.6460 f05m11.svg

GUDUST chseq 22 7 145 | katrans t9.kat | turtledraw 0.0 29.3335 f05m12.svg

GURER chseq 22 7 435 | katrans t4.kat | turtledraw 0.0 170.3980 f05m13.svg

GURMO chseq 22 7 435 | katrans t4.kat | turtledraw 0.0 31.2012 f05m14.svg

HECVU chseq 22 7 580 | katrans t8.kat | turtledraw 0.0 90.8569 f05m15.svg

HEHIF chseq 22 7 580 | katrans t8.kat | turtledraw 0.0 89.1431 f05m16.svg

HEJVU chseq 22 7 145 | katrans t10.kat | turtledraw 0.0 58.6670 f05m17.svg

HEKOM chseq 22 7 145 | katrans t10.kat | turtledraw 0.0 88.0005 f05m18.svg

HEQVI chseq 22 7 145 | katrans t11.kat | turtledraw 0.0 49.5044 f05m19.svg

HEYQO chseq 22 7 145 | katrans t11.kat | turtledraw 0.0 76.5088 f05m20.svg

HIFAM chseq 22 7 145 | katrans t11.kat | turtledraw 0.0 103.4910 f05m21.svg

HIKQI chseq 22 7 145 | katrans t11.kat | turtledraw 0.0 130.4960 f05m22.svg

HIPSE chseq 22 7 145 | katrans t11.kat | turtledraw 0.0 152.9960 f05m23.svg

HOYIC chseq 22 7 145 | katrans t11.kat | turtledraw 0.0 72.0044 f05m24.svg

HUFUE chseq 22 7 145 | katrans t11.kat | turtledraw 0.0 54.0088 f05m25.svg

HUJOY chseq 22 7 145 | katrans t15.kat | turtledraw 0.0 144.5360 f05m26.svg

HUMID chseq 333 106 439 | katrans t4.kat | turtledraw 0.0 89.0332 f05m27.svg

ILIG chseq 22 7 24 | katrans t0.kat | turtledraw 0.0 140.0 f06m01.svg

IVIG chseq 22 7 348 | katrans t2.kat | turtledraw 0.0 172.0 f06m02.svg

JAGYI chseq 22 7 24 | katrans t9.kat | turtledraw 0.0 165.0000 f06m03.svg

JAJAZ chseq 22 7 174 | katrans t7.kat | turtledraw 0.0 118.2350 f06m04.svg

JAVHO chseq 22 7 522 | katrans t4.kat | turtledraw 0.0 178.0000 f06m05.svg

JAWSI chseq 22 7 522 | katrans t4.kat | turtledraw 0.0 170.0020 f06m06.svg

JEBET chseq 22 7 174 | katrans t12.kat | turtledraw 0.0 75.6519 f06m07.svg

JEKAX chseq 22 7 175 | katrans t13.kat | turtledraw 0.0 60.0 f06m08.svg

JEKHI chseq 22 7 24 | katrans t8.kat | turtledraw 0.0 110.0 f06m09.svg

JERIC chseq 22 7 28 | katrans t0.kat | turtledraw 0.0 172.0 f07m01.svg

JEWUTH chseq 22 7 203 | katrans t0.kat | turtledraw 0.0 168.311 f07m02.svg

JIJEL chseq 22 7 203 | katrans t0.kat | turtledraw 0.0 95.8447 f07m03.svg

JIJIST chseq 22 7 203 | katrans t0a.kat | turtledraw 0.0 95.8447 f07m04.svg

JIMEP chseq 22 7 406 | katrans t2.kat | turtledraw 0.0 178.286 f07m05.svg

JIQFA chseq 22 7 406 | katrans t2.kat | turtledraw 0.0 174.858 f07m06.svg

JOBUP chseq 22 7 406 | katrans t2.kat | turtledraw 0.0 89.1431 f07m07.svg

JONEZ chseq 22 7 406 | katrans t2.kat | turtledraw 0.0 171.431 f07m08.svg

JUDOB chseq 22 7 406 | katrans t3.kat | turtledraw 0.0 85.7153 f07m09.svg

JUQOE chseq 22 7 406 | katrans t3.kat | turtledraw 0.0 157.72 f07m10.svg

JUVUJ chseq 22 7 406 | katrans t3.kat | turtledraw 0.0 161.147 f07m11.svg

JUZQU chseq 22 7 203 | katrans t6.kat | turtledraw 0.0 170.8150 f07m12.svg

KACWO chseq 22 7 203 | katrans t7.kat | turtledraw 0.0 104.3700 f07m13.svg

KAGURY chseq 22 7 203 | katrans t7.kat | turtledraw 0.0 142.1850 f07m14.svg

KAYURY chseq 22 7 203 | katrans t8.kat | turtledraw 0.0 153.0620 f07m15.svg

KEBAV chseq 22 7 203 | katrans t8.kat | turtledraw 0.0 126.1230 f07m16.svg

KEBIF chseq 22 7 203 | katrans t9.kat | turtledraw 0.0 60.9521 f07m17.svg

KEMU chseq 22 7 203 | katrans t9.kat | turtledraw 0.0 163.8060 f07m18.svg

KEPUND chseq 22 7 203 | katrans t9.kat | turtledraw 0.0 121.9040 f07m19.svg

KESNI chseq 22 7 203 | katrans t9.kat | turtledraw 0.0 140.9550 f07m20.svg

KEVUC chseq 22 7 203 | katrans t9.kat | turtledraw 0.0 24.7632 f07m21.svg

KICIH chseq 22 7 203 | katrans t11.kat | turtledraw 0.0 77.1460 f07m22.svg

KIHOZ chseq 22 7 203 | katrans t11.kat | turtledraw 0.0 80.3540 f07m23.svg

KIJLU chseq 22 7 203 | katrans t11.kat | turtledraw 0.0 54.6460 f07m24.svg

KIPLE chseq 22 7 203 | katrans t11.kat | turtledraw 0.0 51.4380 f07m25.svg

KOCURT chseq 22 7 203 | katrans t11.kat | turtledraw 0.0 57.8540 f07m26.svg

LAHUV chseq 22 7 203 | katrans t12.kat | turtledraw 0.0 38.0127 f07m27.svg

LALAB chseq 22 7 203 | katrans t12.kat | turtledraw 0.0 154.2920 f07m28.svg

LARATH chseq 22 7 203 | katrans t15.kat | turtledraw 0.0 154.4680 f07m29.svg

LAVUH chseq 355 113 468 | katrans t0a.kat | turtledraw 0.0 135.5490 f07m30.svg

LELSE chseq 22 7 29 | katrans t6.kat | turtledraw 0.0 25.715 f07m31.svg

LERIV chseq 22 7 29 | katrans t6.kat | turtledraw 0.0 32.143 f07m32.svg

LIGNO chseq 22 7 29 | katrans t6.kat | turtledraw 0.0 77.145 f07m33.svg

LOBUN chseq 22 7 116 | katrans t0.kat | turtledraw 0.0 45.0 f08m01.svg

LOFOM chseq 22 7 232 | katrans t0.kat | turtledraw 0.0 112.5 f08m02.svg

LOHIZ chseq 22 7 232 | katrans t0a.kat | turtledraw 0.0 112.5 f08m03.svg

LOMAB chseq 22 7 464 | katrans t2.kat | turtledraw 0.0 45.0 f08m04.svg

LONUQ chseq 22 7 464 | katrans t2.kat | turtledraw 0.0 135.0 f08m05.svg

LOXBA chseq 22 7 464 | katrans t3.kat | turtledraw 0.0 129.0 f08m06.svg

LUFMA chseq 22 7 464 | katrans t3.kat | turtledraw 0.0 153.0 f08m07.svg

LUNWO chseq 22 7 116 | katrans t8.kat | turtledraw 0.0 45.0000 f08m08.svg

LUREU chseq 22 7 232 | katrans t5.kat | turtledraw 0.0 135.0000 f08m09.svg

LURJA chseq 22 7 232 | katrans t6.kat | turtledraw 0.0 28.1250 f08m10.svg

MACHU chseq 22 7 232 | katrans t6.kat | turtledraw 0.0 39.3750 f08m11.svg

MADED chseq 22 7 232 | katrans t6.kat | turtledraw 0.0 50.6250 f08m12.svg

MAFIND chseq 22 7 232 | katrans t7.kat | turtledraw 0.0 67.5000 f08m13.svg

METOS chseq 22 7 232 | katrans t7.kat | turtledraw 0.0 157.5000 f08m14.svg

MEWEI chseq 22 7 232 | katrans t8.kat | turtledraw 0.0 67.5000 f08m15.svg

MISDI chseq 22 7 232 | katrans t9.kat | turtledraw 0.0 45.0000 f08m16.svg

MITID chseq 22 7 232 | katrans t9.kat | turtledraw 0.0 135.0000 f08m17.svg

MIZORD chseq 22 7 232 | katrans t9.kat | turtledraw 0.0 164.9930 f08m18.svg

MOCXE chseq 22 7 232 | katrans t10.kat | turtledraw 0.0 168.3330 f08m19.svg

MODE chseq 22 7 232 | katrans t11.kat | turtledraw 0.0 25.3125 f08m20.svg

MOPNE chseq 22 7 232 | katrans t11.kat | turtledraw 0.0 42.1875 f08m21.svg

MOPWA chseq 22 7 232 | katrans t11.kat | turtledraw 0.0 47.8125 f08m22.svg

MOVUN chseq 22 7 232 | katrans t12.kat | turtledraw 0.0 45.0000 f08m23.svg

MUDDE chseq 22 7 232 | katrans t12.kat | turtledraw 0.0 178.0440 f08m24.svg

MULNE chseq 22 7 233 | katrans t13.kat | turtledraw 0.0 45.0 f08m25.svg

MUWAT chseq 22 7 580 | katrans t11.kat | turtledraw 0.0 28.1250 f08m26.svg

NAKAST chseq 333 106 468 | katrans t3.kat | turtledraw 0.0 57.0 f08m27.svg

NAPOZ chseq 333 106 468 | katrans t3.kat | turtledraw 0.0 33.0 f08m28.svg

NASOX chseq 355 113 468 | katrans t3.kat | turtledraw 0.0 170.9470 f08m29.svg

NAWAW chseq 22 7 261 | katrans t0.kat | turtledraw 0.0 172.727 f09m01.svg

NEJFO chseq 22 7 261 | katrans t0.kat | turtledraw 0.0 165.454 f09m02.svg

NILURT chseq 22 7 261 | katrans t0.kat | turtledraw 0.0 150.908 f09m03.svg

NIRFA chseq 22 7 261 | katrans t0a.kat | turtledraw 0.0 165.454 f09m04.svg

NIYVU chseq 22 7 261 | katrans t0a.kat | turtledraw 0.0 80.0 f09m05.svg

NOCO chseq 22 7 522 | katrans t2.kat | turtledraw 0.0 178.66 f09m06.svg

NOLORD chseq 22 7 522 | katrans t2.kat | turtledraw 0.0 29.3335 f09m07.svg

NOLUX chseq 22 7 522 | katrans t2.kat | turtledraw 0.0 58.667 f09m08.svg

NOMFI chseq 22 7 522 | katrans t3.kat | turtledraw 0.0 125.332 f09m09.svg

NOWYI chseq 22 7 522 | katrans t5.kat | turtledraw 0.0 60.9521 f09m10.svg

NOXKE chseq 22 7 522 | katrans t9.kat | turtledraw 0.0 87.4072 f09m11.svg

NUHUM chseq 22 7 261 | katrans t10.kat | turtledraw 0.0 77.0361 f09m12.svg

NURIK chseq 22 7 261 | katrans t11.kat | turtledraw 0.0 77.4976 f09m13.svg

NUTUV chseq 22 7 261 | katrans t11.kat | turtledraw 0.0 25.0049 f09m14.svg

NUYFI chseq 22 7 261 | katrans t11.kat | turtledraw 0.0 54.9976 f09m15.svg

OWER chseq 22 7 261 | katrans t11.kat | turtledraw 0.0 57.5024 f09m16.svg

PABMO chseq 22 7 261 | katrans t11.kat | turtledraw 0.0 154.9950 f09m17.svg

PABVA chseq 22 7 261 | katrans t15.kat | turtledraw 0.0 160.0270 f09m18.svg

PADVA chseq 22 7 522 | katrans t10.kat | turtledraw 0.0 87.4072 f09m19.svg

PAJORD chseq 22 7 522 | katrans t12.kat | turtledraw 0.0 34.7827 f09m20.svg

PAKBO chseq 22 7 145 | katrans t0.kat | turtledraw 0.0 140.735 f10m01.svg

PEFIY chseq 22 7 290 | katrans t0.kat | turtledraw 0.0 93.2739 f10m02.svg

PILHO chseq 22 7 580 | katrans t2.kat | turtledraw 0.0 127.2 f10m03.svg

PODSI chseq 22 7 580 | katrans t3.kat | turtledraw 0.0 170.398 f10m04.svg

POFIZ chseq 22 7 290 | katrans t9.kat | turtledraw 0.0 121.3330 f10m05.svg

POKAM chseq 22 7 290 | katrans t9.kat | turtledraw 0.0 25.3345 f10m06.svg

PONZU chseq 22 7 580 | katrans t5.kat | turtledraw 0.0 176.5720 f10m07.svg

POREF chseq 22 7 580 | katrans t9.kat | turtledraw 0.0 150.6670 f10m08.svg

POTOO chseq 22 7 290 | katrans t10.kat | turtledraw 0.0 121.3330 f10m09.svg

POXON chseq 22 7 290 | katrans t10.kat | turtledraw 0.0 25.3345 f10m10.svg

PUHIX chseq 22 7 291 | katrans t13.kat | turtledraw 0.0 36.0 f10m11.svg

PUNI chseq 22 7 319 | katrans t0.kat | turtledraw 0.0 139.834 f11m01.svg

PUVEM chseq 22 7 319 | katrans t0.kat | turtledraw 0.0 124.958 f11m02.svg

PUVORY chseq 22 7 319 | katrans t0a.kat | turtledraw 0.0 124.958 f11m03.svg

QAGAM chseq 22 7 319 | katrans t5.kat | turtledraw 0.0 169.8710 f11m04.svg

QEVAR chseq 22 7 319 | katrans t5.kat | turtledraw 0.0 168.3110 f11m05.svg

QINSO chseq 22 7 319 | katrans t9.kat | turtledraw 0.0 153.9400 f11m06.svg

QIPGU chseq 22 7 319 | katrans t11.kat | turtledraw 0.0 24.5435 f11m07.svg

QIQOY chseq 22 7 319 | katrans t11.kat | turtledraw 0.0 155.4570 f11m08.svg

QIWURY chseq 22 7 319 | katrans t11.kat | turtledraw 0.0 49.0869 f11m09.svg

QOJDI chseq 22 7 319 | katrans t12.kat | turtledraw 0.0 170.7500 f11m10.svg

QOYERG chseq 22 7 319 | katrans t15.kat | turtledraw 0.0 163.5860 f11m11.svg

QUJAP chseq 22 7 87 | katrans t0a.kat | turtledraw 0.0 92.7246 f12m01.svg

QUTYU chseq 22 7 319 | katrans t7.kat | turtledraw 0.0 79.8926 f12m02.svg

RAFVU chseq 22 7 377 | katrans t0.kat | turtledraw 0.0 162.378 f13m01.svg

RAVVE chseq 22 7 377 | katrans t0a.kat | turtledraw 0.0 135.945 f13m02.svg

RAWOV chseq 22 7 377 | katrans t0a.kat | turtledraw 0.0 162.378 f13m03.svg

RETIF chseq 22 7 377 | katrans t5.kat | turtledraw 0.0 89.6704 f13m04.svg

REVOZ chseq 22 7 377 | katrans t7.kat | turtledraw 0.0 35.8374 f13m05.svg

RICCO chseq 22 7 377 | katrans t8.kat | turtledraw 0.0 90.3296 f13m06.svg

RIGIF chseq 22 7 377 | katrans t9.kat | turtledraw 0.0 89.2310 f13m07.svg

RIHEA chseq 22 7 377 | katrans t10.kat | turtledraw 0.0 60.5127 f13m08.svg

RIKOG chseq 22 7 377 | katrans t10.kat | turtledraw 0.0 121.0250 f13m09.svg

RILAL chseq 22 7 377 | katrans t11.kat | turtledraw 0.0 128.0790 f13m10.svg

RINLO chseq 22 7 377 | katrans t11.kat | turtledraw 0.0 74.4214 f13m11.svg

ROHEW chseq 22 7 377 | katrans t11.kat | turtledraw 0.0 76.1572 f13m12.svg

ROJUC chseq 22 7 377 | katrans t12.kat | turtledraw 0.0 170.9690 f13m13.svg

ROMAS chseq 22 7 377 | katrans t12.kat | turtledraw 0.0 58.9966 f13m14.svg

RUKAC chseq 22 7 377 | katrans t15.kat | turtledraw 0.0 166.0470 f13m15.svg

RUKIS chseq 22 7 406 | katrans t0.kat | turtledraw 0.0 174.155 f14m01.svg

RUQUP chseq 22 7 406 | katrans t0.kat | turtledraw 0.0 143.767 f14m02.svg

SADERY chseq 22 7 58 | katrans t7.kat | turtledraw 0.0 174.7050 f14m03.svg

SANWA chseq 22 7 203 | katrans t7.kat | turtledraw 0.0 81.6724 f14m04.svg

SAQES chseq 22 7 203 | katrans t9.kat | turtledraw 0.0 152.3800 f14m05.svg

SEPEW chseq 22 7 406 | katrans t10.kat | turtledraw 0.0 119.0480 f14m06.svg

SEXEV chseq 22 7 435 | katrans t0.kat | turtledraw 0.0 161.455 f15m01.svg

SEYZI chseq 22 7 435 | katrans t0.kat | turtledraw 0.0 102.546 f15m02.svg

SIGOA chseq 22 7 435 | katrans t11.kat | turtledraw 0.0 129.0010 f15m03.svg

SIZXO chseq 22 7 435 | katrans t11.kat | turtledraw 0.0 78.0029 f15m04.svg

SOBIRY chseq 22 7 435 | katrans t11.kat | turtledraw 0.0 151.5010 f15m05.svg

SOBOST chseq 22 7 435 | katrans t12.kat | turtledraw 0.0 155.4790 f15m06.svg

SOMWE chseq 22 7 435 | katrans t15.kat | turtledraw 0.0 167.8710 f15m07.svg

SOTQI chseq 22 7 464 | katrans t0.kat | turtledraw 0.0 101.25 f16m01.svg

SOWES chseq 22 7 232 | katrans t8.kat | turtledraw 0.0 112.5000 f16m02.svg

SUBEY chseq 22 7 464 | katrans t5.kat | turtledraw 0.0 67.5000 f16m03.svg

SUJYA chseq 22 7 464 | katrans t5.kat | turtledraw 0.0 112.5000 f16m04.svg

SUTLA chseq 22 7 464 | katrans t6.kat | turtledraw 0.0 30.9375 f16m05.svg

SUYARG chseq 22 7 464 | katrans t6.kat | turtledraw 0.0 42.1875 f16m06.svg

TAMIK chseq 22 7 464 | katrans t6.kat | turtledraw 0.0 47.8125 f16m07.svg

TAPYI chseq 22 7 464 | katrans t7.kat | turtledraw 0.0 11.2500 f16m08.svg

TECO chseq 22 7 464 | katrans t9.kat | turtledraw 0.0 67.5000 f16m09.svg

TEHPE chseq 22 7 464 | katrans t11.kat | turtledraw 0.0 23.9062 f16m10.svg

TENWU chseq 22 7 464 | katrans t11.kat | turtledraw 0.0 26.7188 f16m11.svg

TETTU chseq 22 7 464 | katrans t12.kat | turtledraw 0.0 112.5000 f16m12.svg

TEZOQ chseq 22 7 464 | katrans t12.kat | turtledraw 0.0 157.5000 f16m13.svg

TEZUW chseq 22 7 580 | katrans t3.kat | turtledraw 0.0 175.188 f17m01.svg

TICOI chseq 22 7 145 | katrans t0.kat | turtledraw 0.0 58.9087 f17m02.svg

TIKOZ chseq 22 7 145 | katrans t0.kat | turtledraw 0.0 62.1826 f17m03.svg

TIQIV chseq 22 7 145 | katrans t0.kat | turtledraw 0.0 78.5522 f17m04.svg

TIVERG chseq 22 7 145 | katrans t0a.kat | turtledraw 0.0 58.9087 f17m05.svg

TIWOD chseq 333 106 439 | katrans t0.kat | turtledraw 0.0 87.3193 f17m06.svg

TOCAN chseq 333 106 439 | katrans t0.kat | turtledraw 0.0 88.3740 f17m07.svg

TOCNU chseq 333 106 439 | katrans t0a.kat | turtledraw 0.0 95.8887 f17m08.svg

TOLUST chseq 22 7 319 | katrans t0a.kat | turtledraw 0.0 139.834 f17m09.svg

TOQEP chseq 22 7 319 | katrans t0a.kat | turtledraw 0.0 172.551 f17m10.svg

TOYORD chseq 22 7 319 | katrans t0a.kat | turtledraw 0.0 169.585 f17m11.svg

TUDIC chseq 22 7 348 | katrans t0a.kat | turtledraw 0.0 156.819 f17m12.svg

TUGKO chseq 22 7 377 | katrans t0a.kat | turtledraw 0.0 79.3 f17m13.svg

TUYDI chseq 22 7 406 | katrans t0a.kat | turtledraw 0.0 174.155 f17m14.svg

UKARD chseq 22 7 435 | katrans t0.kat | turtledraw 0.0 77.4536 f17m15.svg

URERD chseq 22 7 435 | katrans t0.kat | turtledraw 0.0 80.7275 f17m16.svg

URITH chseq 22 7 435 | katrans t0a.kat | turtledraw 0.0 80.7275 f17m17.svg

VAMORG chseq 22 7 464 | katrans t0.kat | turtledraw 0.0 56.25 f17m18.svg

VAWTI chseq 22 7 464 | katrans t0a.kat | turtledraw 0.0 78.75 f17m19.svg

VEBIB chseq 22 7 464 | katrans t3.kat | turtledraw 0.0 177.0 f17m20.svg

VETEM chseq 22 7 493 | katrans t0a.kat | turtledraw 0.0 175.188 f17m21.svg

VIFBE chseq 22 7 522 | katrans t0.kat | turtledraw 0.0 60.9082 f17m22.svg

VIZNA chseq 22 7 551 | katrans t0.kat | turtledraw 0.0 136.077 f17m23.svg

VOMGE chseq 22 7 551 | katrans t0.kat | turtledraw 0.0 92.1533 f17m24.svg

VOMIRG chseq 22 7 551 | katrans t0.kat | turtledraw 0.0 175.693 f17m25.svg

VOPIRD chseq 22 7 551 | katrans t0.kat | turtledraw 0.0 79.2334 f17m26.svg

VUNDE chseq 22 7 551 | katrans t0.kat | turtledraw 0.0 48.23 f17m27.svg

VUZAV chseq 22 7 551 | katrans t0a.kat | turtledraw 0.0 175.693 f17m28.svg

VUZIL chseq 22 7 580 | katrans t0.kat | turtledraw 0.0 72.8174 f17m29.svg

WAFBU chseq 22 7 232 | katrans t8.kat | turtledraw 0.0 161.7850 f17m30.svg

WAPUC chseq 22 7 232 | katrans t9.kat | turtledraw 0.0 168.3330 f17m31.svg

WAVLA chseq 22 7 261 | katrans t9.kat | turtledraw 0.0 77.0361 f17m32.svg

WAXAZ chseq 22 7 377 | katrans t5.kat | turtledraw 0.0 174.0670 f17m33.svg

WEJET chseq 22 7 377 | katrans t6.kat | turtledraw 0.0 174.0670 f17m34.svg

WEKNU chseq 22 7 406 | katrans t8.kat | turtledraw 0.0 103.4690 f17m35.svg

WERIST chseq 22 7 493 | katrans t7.kat | turtledraw 0.0 99.0308 f17m36.svg

WEXAG chseq 22 7 493 | katrans t8.kat | turtledraw 0.0 85.2100 f17m37.svg

WEXKE chseq 22 7 493 | katrans t8.kat | turtledraw 0.0 151.7650 f17m38.svg

WIJOG chseq 22 7 493 | katrans t9.kat | turtledraw 0.0 164.7070 f17m39.svg

WINUI chseq 22 7 493 | katrans t9.kat | turtledraw 0.0 156.8630 f17m40.svg

WIPET chseq 22 7 493 | katrans t9.kat | turtledraw 0.0 138.8230 f17m41.svg

WIROTH chseq 22 7 493 | katrans t9.kat | turtledraw 0.0 110.5880 f17m42.svg

WITOX chseq 22 7 493 | katrans t9.kat | turtledraw 0.0 46.2744 f17m43.svg

WIYIA chseq 22 7 493 | katrans t9.kat | turtledraw 0.0 64.3140 f17m44.svg

WOTTA chseq 22 7 493 | katrans t9.kat | turtledraw 0.0 128.6280 f17m45.svg

WOVRO chseq 22 7 493 | katrans t9.kat | turtledraw 0.0 167.0580 f17m46.svg

WUFUK chseq 22 7 493 | katrans t9.kat | turtledraw 0.0 149.0190 f17m47.svg

WUKIP chseq 22 7 493 | katrans t9.kat | turtledraw 0.0 74.5093 f17m48.svg

WUVQE chseq 22 7 522 | katrans t7.kat | turtledraw 0.0 172.3540 f17m49.svg

WUYAE chseq 22 7 522 | katrans t7.kat | turtledraw 0.0 20.5884 f17m50.svg

XEMUQ chseq 22 7 522 | katrans t7.kat | turtledraw 0.0 159.4120 f17m51.svg

XENAR chseq 22 7 522 | katrans t8.kat | turtledraw 0.0 150.9520 f17m52.svg

XERAV chseq 22 7 551 | katrans t6.kat | turtledraw 0.0 133.3080 f17m53.svg

XIHWE chseq 22 7 551 | katrans t7.kat | turtledraw 0.0 173.8700 f17m54.svg

XIKAC chseq 22 7 551 | katrans t7.kat | turtledraw 0.0 81.3647 f17m55.svg

XIRMA chseq 22 7 551 | katrans t8.kat | turtledraw 0.0 107.8200 f17m56.svg

XIWOY chseq 22 7 551 | katrans t9.kat | turtledraw 0.0 168.4200 f17m57.svg

XOHIB chseq 22 7 580 | katrans t5.kat | turtledraw 0.0 179.1430 f17m58.svg

XOPWU chseq 22 7 580 | katrans t5.kat | turtledraw 0.0 177.4290 f17m59.svg

XUCSO chseq 22 7 580 | katrans t5.kat | turtledraw 0.0 91.7139 f17m60.svg

XUHOW chseq 22 7 580 | katrans t7.kat | turtledraw 0.0 61.9409 f17m61.svg

XUHYE chseq 22 7 580 | katrans t7.kat | turtledraw 0.0 151.9410 f17m62.svg

XUQGE chseq 22 7 580 | katrans t9.kat | turtledraw 0.0 60.6665 f17m63.svg

XUXAV chseq 22 7 348 | katrans t0.kat | turtledraw 0.0 156.819 f17m64.svg

YABDE chseq 22 7 493 | katrans t12.kat | turtledraw 0.0 171.2550 f17m65.svg

YAFUJ chseq 22 7 493 | katrans t15.kat | turtledraw 0.0 169.2770 f17m66.svg

YAJOA chseq 22 7 522 | katrans t10.kat | turtledraw 0.0 43.7036 f17m67.svg

YAJUP chseq 22 7 522 | katrans t11.kat | turtledraw 0.0 102.5 f17m68.svg

YASQO chseq 22 7 522 | katrans t12.kat | turtledraw 0.0 145.2170 f17m69.svg

YEKE chseq 22 7 551 | katrans t11.kat | turtledraw 0.0 101.8430 f17m70.svg

YEMEB chseq 22 7 551 | katrans t11.kat | turtledraw 0.0 55.6567 f17m71.svg

YENEI chseq 22 7 551 | katrans t11.kat | turtledraw 0.0 124.3430 f17m72.svg

YIDYO chseq 22 7 551 | katrans t11.kat | turtledraw 0.0 56.8433 f17m73.svg

YIMOO chseq 22 7 551 | katrans t12.kat | turtledraw 0.0 51.8994 f17m74.svg

YOGUT chseq 22 7 551 | katrans t12.kat | turtledraw 0.0 103.7990 f17m75.svg

YOXURD chseq 333 106 439 | katrans t7.kat | turtledraw 0.0 179.6480 f17m76.svg

YUCOS chseq 22 7 406 | katrans t7.kat | turtledraw 0.0 52.1851 f18m01.svg

YUDART chseq 22 7 319 | katrans t0.kat | turtledraw 0.0 110.083 f18m02.svg

YUGSO chseq 22 7 580 | katrans t9.kat | turtledraw 0.0 119.3330 f18m03.svg

YUWHI chseq 22 7 261 | katrans t6.kat | turtledraw 0.0 133.5720 f18m04.svg

ZAFIH chseq 22 7 261 | katrans t6.kat | turtledraw 0.0 136.4280 f18m05.svg

ZAHCA chseq 22 7 377 | katrans t6.kat | turtledraw 0.0 134.0110 f18m06.svg

ZAHOU chseq 22 7 319 | katrans t6.kat | turtledraw 0.0 137.9220 f18m07.svg

ZALORG chseq 22 7 377 | katrans t6.kat | turtledraw 0.0 135.9890 f18m08.svg

ZATUTH chseq 22 7 29 | katrans t6.kat | turtledraw 0.0 173.8480 f18m09.svg

ZEBGA chseq 22 7 551 | katrans t6.kat | turtledraw 0.0 136.6920 f18m10.svg

ZEFBA chseq 22 7 551 | katrans t9.kat | turtledraw 0.0 11.2280 f18m11.svg

ZEGJI chseq 333 106 439 | katrans t5.kat | turtledraw 0.0 172.5730 f18m12.svg

ZELUB chseq 333 106 439 | katrans t5.kat | turtledraw 0.0 109.7970 f18m13.svg

ZEMIU chseq 333 106 439 | katrans t8.kat | turtledraw 0.0 118.8720 f18m14.svg

ZESAND chseq 333 106 439 | katrans t8.kat | turtledraw 0.0 117.1800 f18m15.svg

ZILQI chseq 355 113 468 | katrans t8.kat | turtledraw 0.0 117.8830 f18m16.svg

ZIXFA chseq 22 7 116 | katrans t5.kat | turtledraw 0.0 115.6 f18m17.svg

ZOMXI chseq 22 7 495 | katrans t5.kat | turtledraw 0.0 112.0 f18m18.svg

ZONNI chseq 22 7 435 | katrans t9.kat | turtledraw 0.0 9.7778 f18m19.svg

ZUDUV chseq 22 7 551 | katrans t5.kat | turtledraw 0.0 14.4360 f18m20.svg

ZUHIRG chseq 22 7 495 | katrans t5.kat | turtledraw 0.0 119.0 f18m21.svg

ZUNEJ chseq 22 7 58 | katrans t11.kat | turtledraw 0.0 168.7500 f18m22.svg

ZUQIR chseq 22 7 116 | katrans t4.kat | turtledraw 0.0 31.9702 f19m01.svg

ZUXIW chseq 22 7 29 | katrans t4.kat | turtledraw 0.0 50.86 f19m02.svg

ZUXMA chseq 22 7 57 | katrans t13.kat | turtledraw 0.0 159.609 f19m03.svg

FURTHER READING

- *Pi-Unleashed*, Arndt and Haenel, 2001

- *A History of Pi*, Petr Beckmann, 1971

- *Pi, a Source Book*, Berggren, Borwein and Borwein, 1997

- *The Joy of Pi*, David Blatner, 1999

- *The Number Pi*, Eymard and Lafon, 2004

- *Pattern Generation for Computational Art*, Hollos and Hollos, 2013

- *Pi: a Biography of the World's Most Mysterious Number*, Posamentier and Lehmann, 2004

- *Pi Wikipedia page*

ACKNOWLEDGMENTS

In ordinary life we hardly realize that we receive a great deal more than we give, and that it is only with gratitude that life becomes rich. It is very easy to overestimate the importance of our own achievements in comparison with what we owe to others.

Dietrich Bonhoeffer, letter to parents from prison, Sept. 13, 1943

We'd like to thank our parents, Istvan and Anna Hollos, for helping us in many ways.

We thank the makers and maintainers of all the software we've used in the production of this book, including: the Emacs text editor, the LaTex typesetting system, Inkscape, Mupdf & Evince document viewer, Maxima computer algebra system, gcc, Guile, awk, sed, bash shell, and the GNU/Linux operating system.

ABOUT THE AUTHORS

Stefan Hollos and **J. Richard Hollos** are physicists by training, and enjoy anything related to math, physics, and computing. They are the authors of

- Art of the Golden Ratio

- Information Theory: A Concise Introduction

- Recursive Digital Filters: A Concise Guide

- Creating Noise

- Creating Rhythms

- Pattern Generation for Computational Art

- Finite Automata and Regular Expressions: Problems and Solutions

- Probability Problems and Solutions

- Combinatorics Problems and Solutions

- The Coin Toss: Probabilities and Patterns

- Pairs Trading: A Bayesian Example

- Simple Trading Strategies That Work

- Bet Smart: The Kelly System for Gambling and Investing

- Signals from the Subatomic World: How to Build a Proton Precession Magnetometer

They are brothers and business partners at Exstrom Laboratories LLC in Longmont, Colorado. Their website is exstrom.com

THANK YOU

Thank you for buying this book.

Sign up for the Abrazol Publishing Newsletter and receive news on updates, new books, and special offers. Just go to

http://www.abrazol.com/

and enter your email address.

www.ingramcontent.com/pod-product-compliance
Lightning Source LLC
Chambersburg PA
CBHW071248220526
45468CB00001B/37